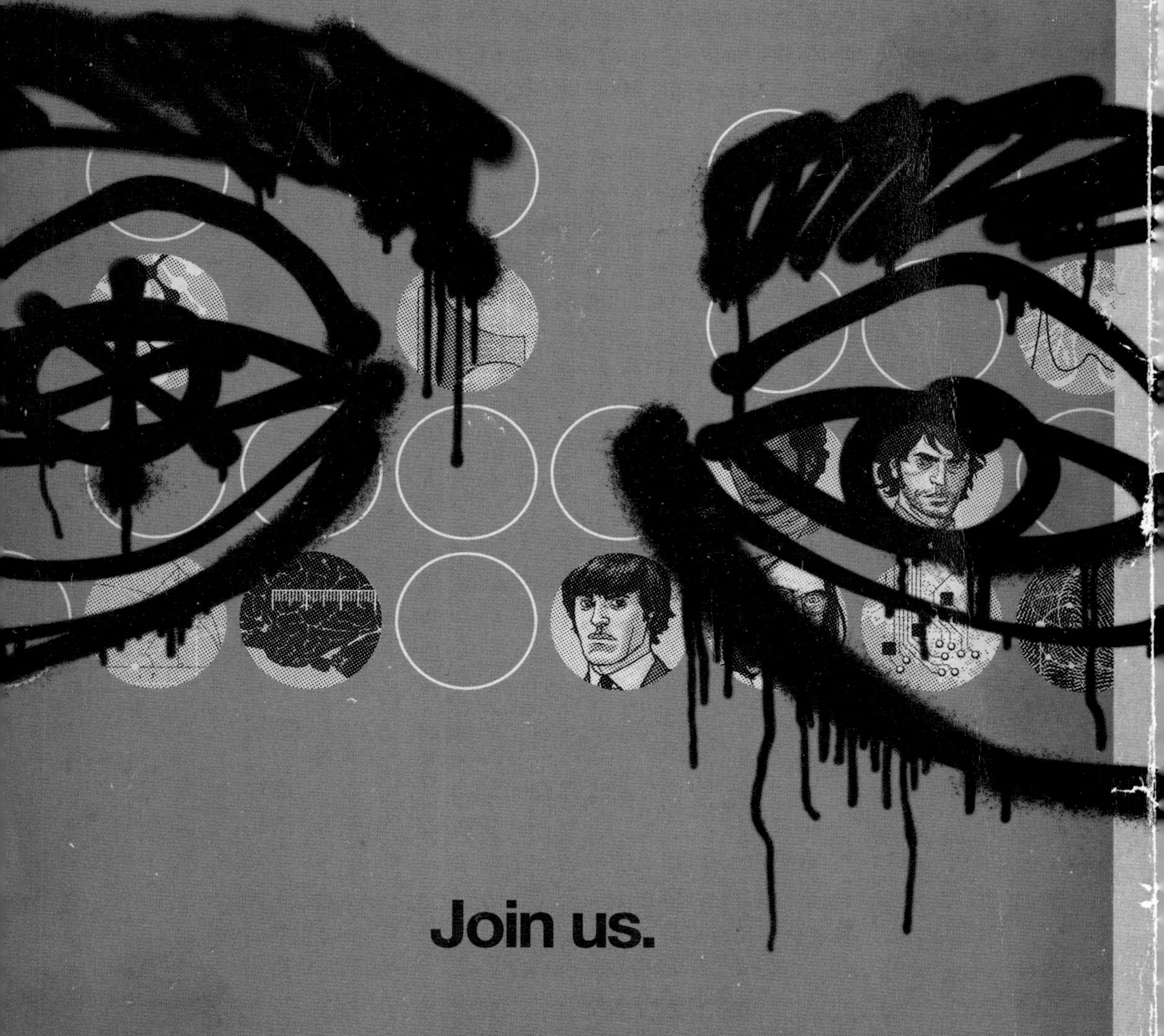

Join us.

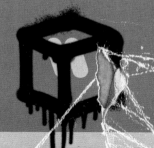

Years ago.

OKAY, TERRY, WE SHOULD BE READY TO GO.

ALL RIGHT-- WHAT A BIG DAY FOR YOU ALL!

I WANT EACH OF YOU TO SUM UP HOW YOU FEEL RIGHT NOW IN A SINGLE WORD, AND THEN WE'RE GOING TO SHOOT, OKAY?

1-2-3-- 60!

EFFERVESCENT.

INDOMITABLE.

HOPEFUL!

RELIEVED.

"EXCELLENT-- HOLD IT RIGHT THERE!"

OKAY, NOW LET'S TRY SOME OTHER SHOTS.

JUST A FEW MORE, THEN WE'RE DONE, ALL RIGHT?

DADE, I WANT YOU TO TURN AND FACE STRANGE...

WELL, THAT'S THE END OF THAT.

THE END?

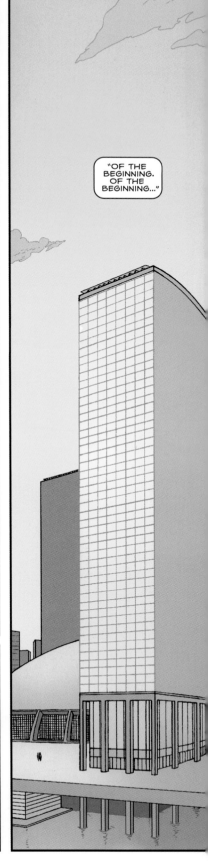

"OF THE BEGINNING. OF THE BEGINNING..."

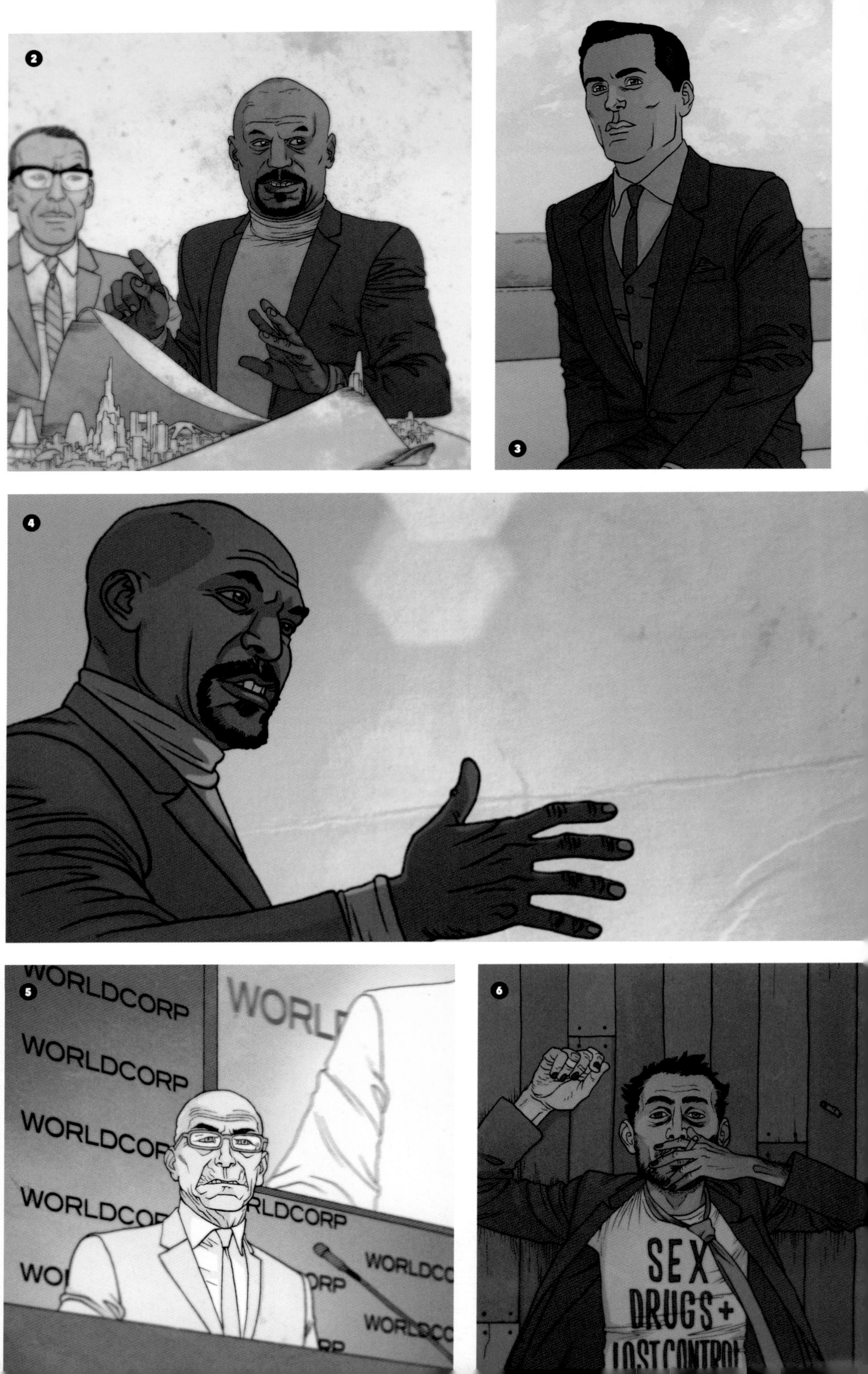
WORLDCORP
WORLDCORP
WORLDCORP
WORLDCORP
SEX
DRUGS +

CHANGES

New photo retrospective captures the highs and lows of the World Corp founders.

IT SEEMS IMPOSSIBLE to imagine, but we'd never seen their like before. When Dade Ellis, Simon Grimshaw, Emerson Strange, and Thomas Walker pooled their intellectual resources to form the world's first science super group, it was as though a crack appeared in the sky and a hand reached down to assure one and all that everything would be all right. They were heroes, they were legends, and it was hysteria-a-go-go wherever they went. ARNOLD CORNS was World Corp's official photographer for much of that amazing journey and this month, he revisits the renowned quartet's golden years in an eye-catching new hardcover containing over one hundred never-before-seen images from his own personal archives.

1. "This is World Corp. at the absolute peak of the mania surrounding their partnership. Everywhere they went, it was absolute mayhem, but in the early days, they all just ate it up. There was just an air of optimism about them, and you can see from the look on Simon's face that he is just in love with all the adulation. This was what he wanted, where he wanted to be."

2. "Dade Ellis was one of the most naturally gifted thinkers I've ever had the pleasure to meet. He possessed such a diverse wealth of knowledge. This shot is from sometime after they'd embarked on what now seems like a never-ending quest to make the World Corp. headquarters the most advanced campus in the world. With his background in architecture, Dade took a lot of pride in the small details of each building's design, so much so that I view the World Corp. campus as a kind of extension of his spiritual being. He personally designed Emerson Strange's home, too. Not many people know that."

3. "A sad one, this. It's Simon on what I was told would be a relaxed Mediterranean cruise, shortly after he'd parted ways with Strange and Ellis. Simon and I always got on very well, and he'd asked if I'd like to come along and take some candid photos, I think with an eye toward showing a different side to his personality. He promised me it would be fun. As it turned out, though, he was distracted the whole time, obviously quite broken up about what had happened between him and his partners. I don't know what I was expecting, it's not like he was the type of fellow who's out dancing and getting pissed all in his spare time. I don't think I've ever seen him in anything other than a suit."

4. "Another wonderful photo of Dade, speaking at an event organized by Anthony Day to honor World Corp's humanitarian work. In many ways, Dade was my favorite founder. He was incredibly photogenic, and as I was assembling my book, it occurred to me that even the photos of Dade I hadn't used were incredibly memorable. On a personal level, he was always very understated, very unassuming, but in front of a camera or up on a stage, he just exuded confidence."

5. "And this is Emerson, at the press conference announcing Dade's sabbatical, and no, I don't have any inside information on what that was all about. There's been a lot of speculation, not just about Dade's health, but also the exact nature of his relationship with Strange, although by this point, I wasn't dealing with either of them on anything even approaching a regular basis. You can see the consternation in his eyes, though, so whatever really lead to Ellis's leave of absence, it's a safe bet Strange wasn't happy about it."

6. "To the best of my knowledge, this is the very last photo ever taken of Thomas Walker. This was after that interview you ran with him, and he wasn't happy with how that turned out. Simon had set the whole thing up, but when it came out, Tommy said it was a hit piece. He especially hated the photos, and he called me up and asked if I'd come over to his place to do a shoot. I could never figure out what he wanted them for, but he was very insistent that we do it. So we made arrangements to spend the afternoon photographing him at home, but when I arrived, I was completely shocked at the state of his apartment. His living conditions were absolutely abysmal; it was just complete squalor. I snapped a few there out of courtesy before suggesting we venture out to a park I'd passed on the way over, but he wouldn't have it. I took this one last shot before I left, then I never saw him again."

__Changes__ by Arnold Corns is published by Art Decade and in stores Jan 7th.

FAME *(below, left to right) Walker, Grimshaw, Strange, Ellis*

TIME *(facing, clockwise from top) Ellis, Grimshaw, Ellis again, Walker, Strange*

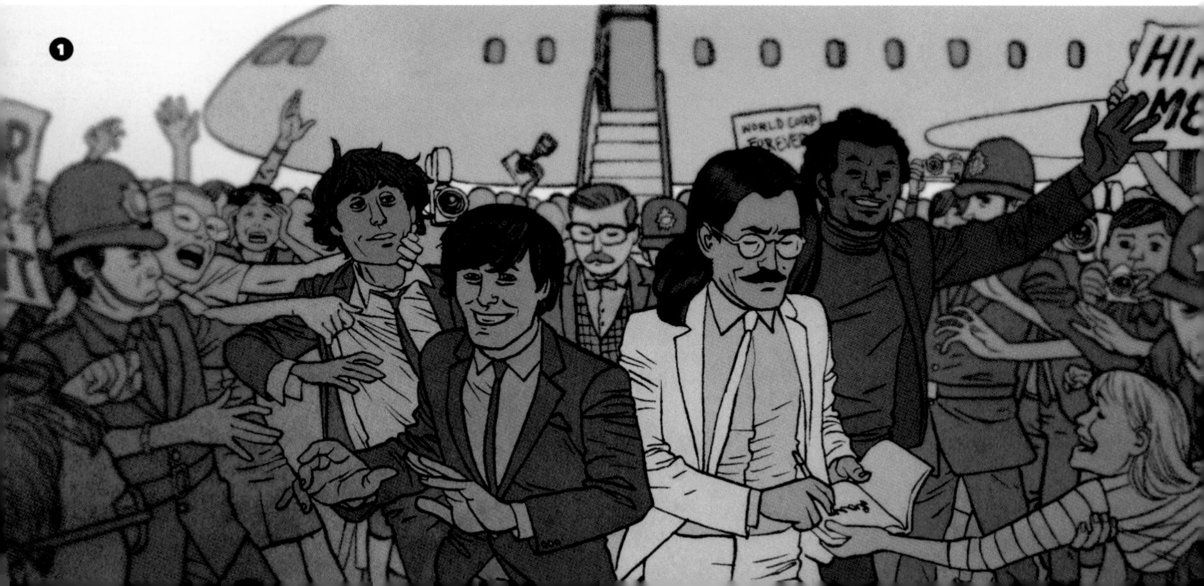
1
WORLD CORP

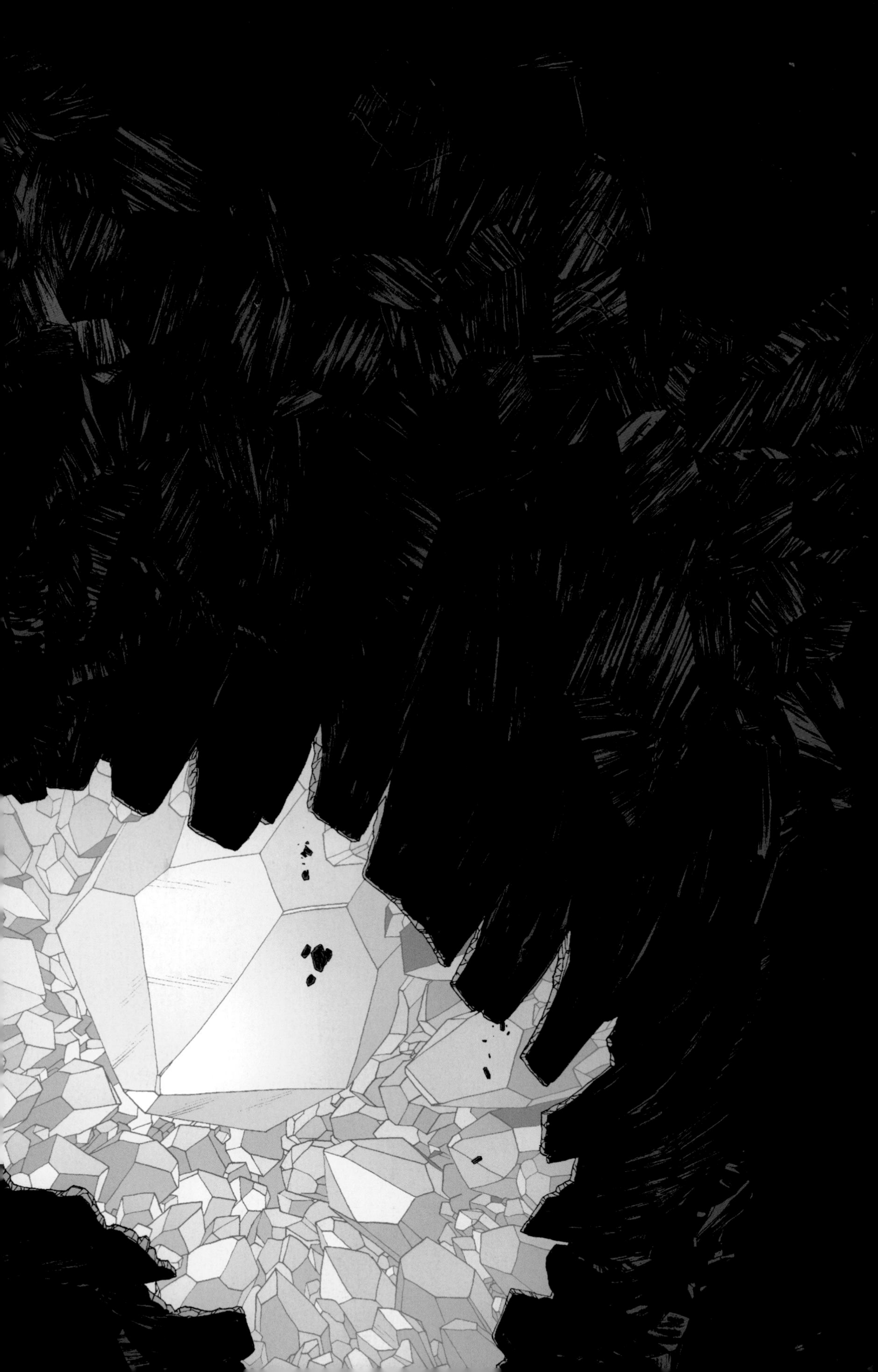

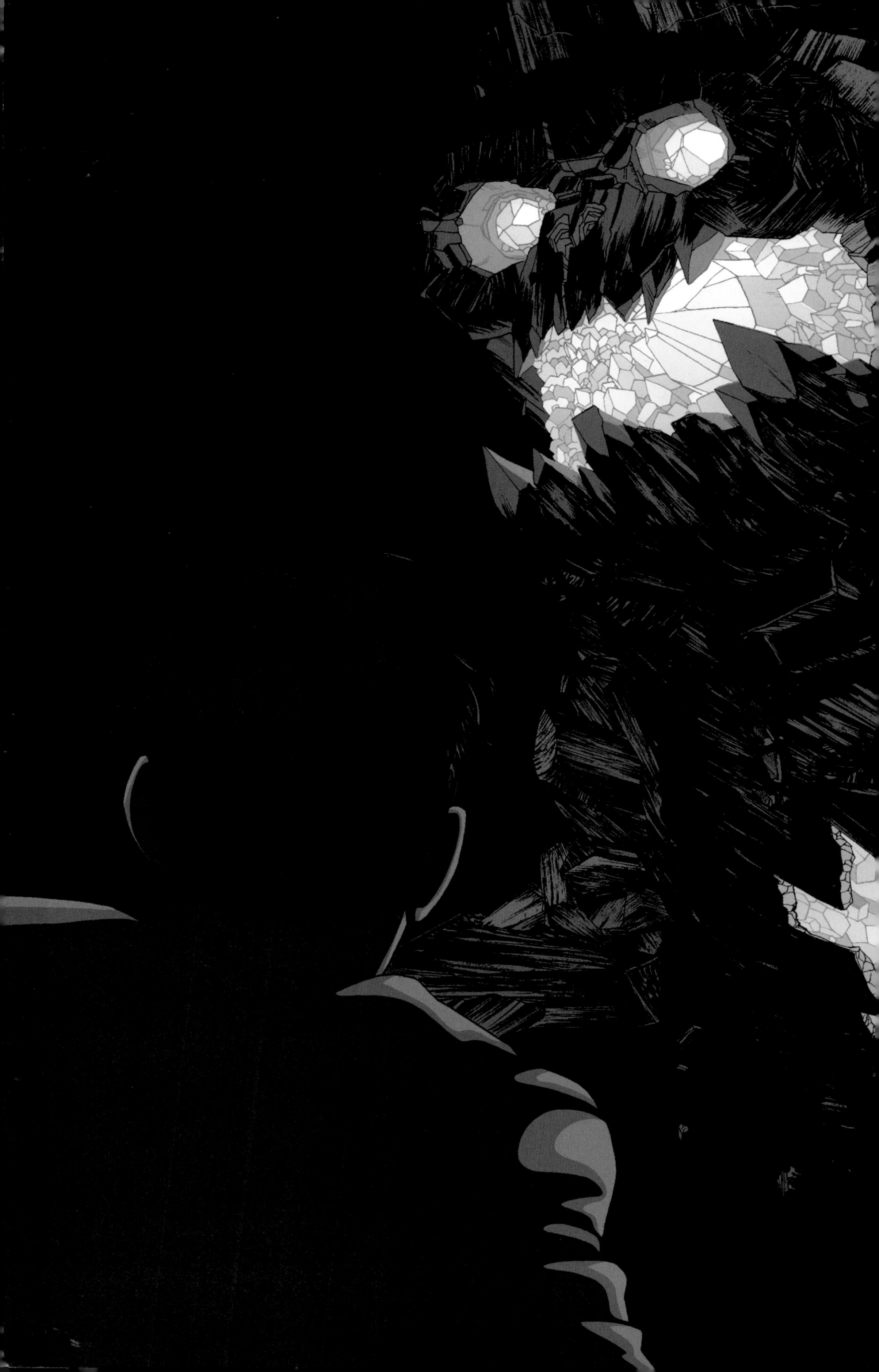

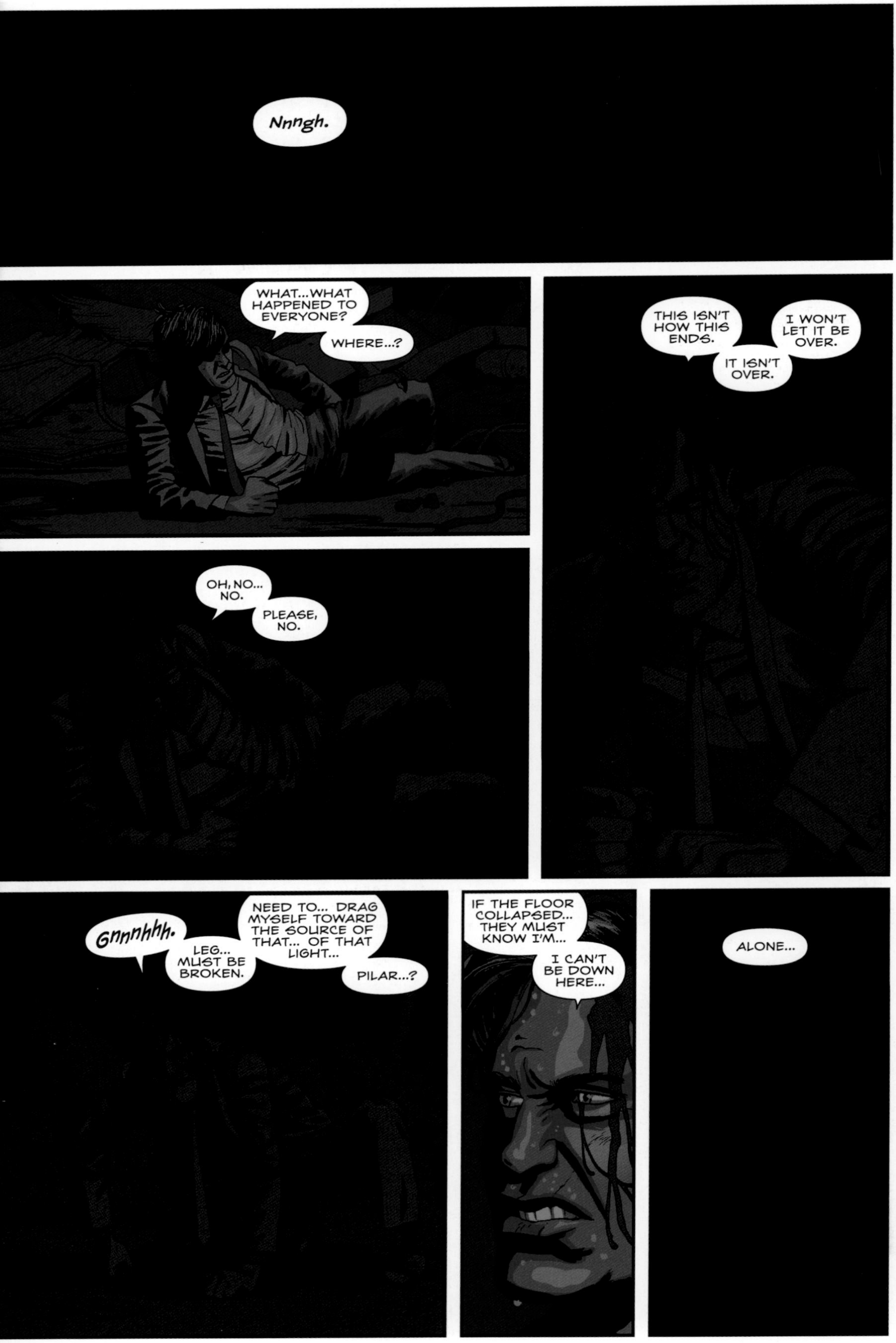

Nnngh.
WHAT...WHAT HAPPENED TO EVERYONE?
WHERE...?
THIS ISN'T HOW THIS ENDS.
IT ISN'T OVER.
I WON'T LET IT BE OVER.
OH, NO... NO.
PLEASE, NO.
Gnnnhhh.
LEG... MUST BE BROKEN.
NEED TO... DRAG MYSELF TOWARD THE SOURCE OF THAT... OF THAT LIGHT...
PILAR...?
IF THE FLOOR COLLAPSED... THEY MUST KNOW I'M...
I CAN'T BE DOWN HERE...
ALONE...

A SPOKESMAN FOR LONDON HEATHROW HAS DECLARED THAT A FULL INVESTIGATION INTO THE EMERGENCY ONBOARD TUNISAIR FLIGHT TU-919 IS ALREADY UNDERWAY FOLLOWING THE EVACUATION OF THE SKYLARK 999 EARLIER TONIGHT.

THINK HE'LL MAKE IT?

WHO, THIS DOUGLAS BLOKE?

DUNNO... TRYING NOT TO THINK ABOUT WHAT I SAW BACK THERE, REALLY.

THAT SHIT WAS THE FUCKING WORST.

IN A RELATED STORY, WE'RE NOW RECEIVING CONFIRMATION OF AN EARLIER REPORT THAT AN ASSOCIATE OF RAYMOND DOUGLAS, PHOTOGRAPHER MICHAEL TALBOT, HAS BEEN FOUND DEAD IN A CARTHAGE HOTEL.

TALBOT WAS BEING SOUGHT BY AUTHORITIES AFTER DOUGLAS BECAME MYSTERIOUSLY ILL ABOARD FLIGHT TU-919 EN ROUTE TO LONDON...

TVC 15
HEADLINES

BOMB SCARE IN MEXICO CITY

TRANSLUNAR STOCK RUMORS

...N SALES ...KET IN ...TER

...N UNION ...CLEAR

...OMIC ...ASTEST

BREAKING NEWS 21.06

MICHAEL TALBOT

YEAH... THIS WHOLE SITUATION IS INSANE.

DID YOU HEAR WHAT THE OTHER PASSENGERS WERE SAYING?

HE STARTED VOMITING UP HIS OWN GUTS -- AFTER HE STARTED EATING HIS LAPTOP.

YAAAHH

TRYING TO EAT IT, MAYBE. I DON'T BUY THAT HE ACTUALLY DID.

I MEAN, THINK ABOUT IT, WHAT KIND OF PERSON COULD ACTUALLY TAKE A BITE OUT OF A COMPUTER?

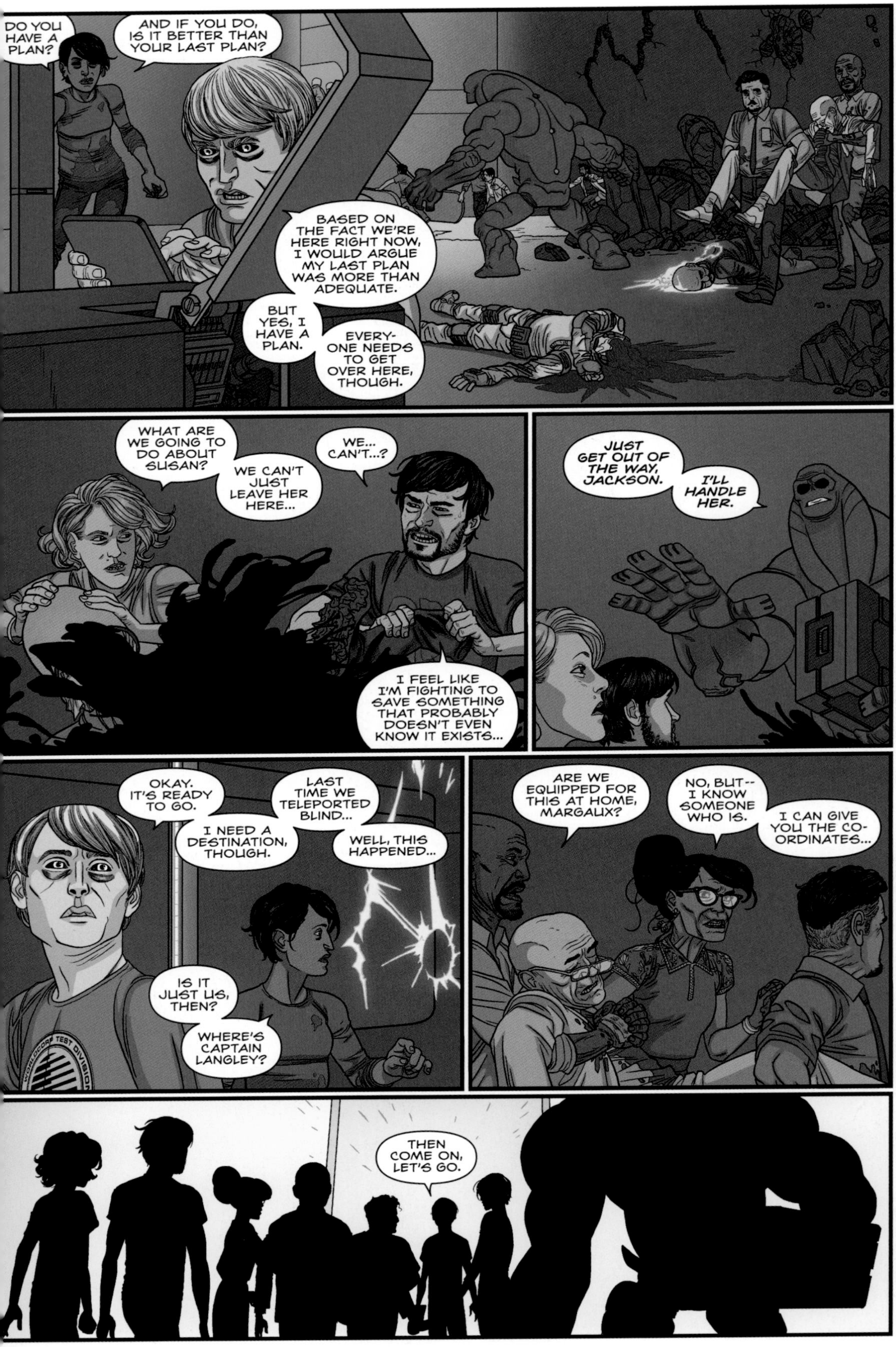

DO YOU HAVE A PLAN?
AND IF YOU DO, IS IT BETTER THAN YOUR LAST PLAN?
BASED ON THE FACT WE'RE HERE RIGHT NOW, I WOULD ARGUE MY LAST PLAN WAS MORE THAN ADEQUATE.
BUT YES, I HAVE A PLAN.
EVERY-ONE NEEDS TO GET OVER HERE, THOUGH.
WHAT ARE WE GOING TO DO ABOUT SUSAN?
WE CAN'T JUST LEAVE HER HERE...
WE... CAN'T...?
I FEEL LIKE I'M FIGHTING TO SAVE SOMETHING THAT PROBABLY DOESN'T EVEN KNOW IT EXISTS...
JUST GET OUT OF THE WAY, JACKSON.
I'LL HANDLE HER.
OKAY. IT'S READY TO GO.
I NEED A DESTINATION, THOUGH.
LAST TIME WE TELEPORTED BLIND...
WELL, THIS HAPPENED...
IS IT JUST US, THEN?
WHERE'S CAPTAIN LANGLEY?
WORLDCORP TEST DIVISION
ARE WE EQUIPPED FOR THIS AT HOME, MARGAUX?
NO, BUT-- I KNOW SOMEONE WHO IS.
I CAN GIVE YOU THE CO-ORDINATES...
THEN COME ON, LET'S GO.

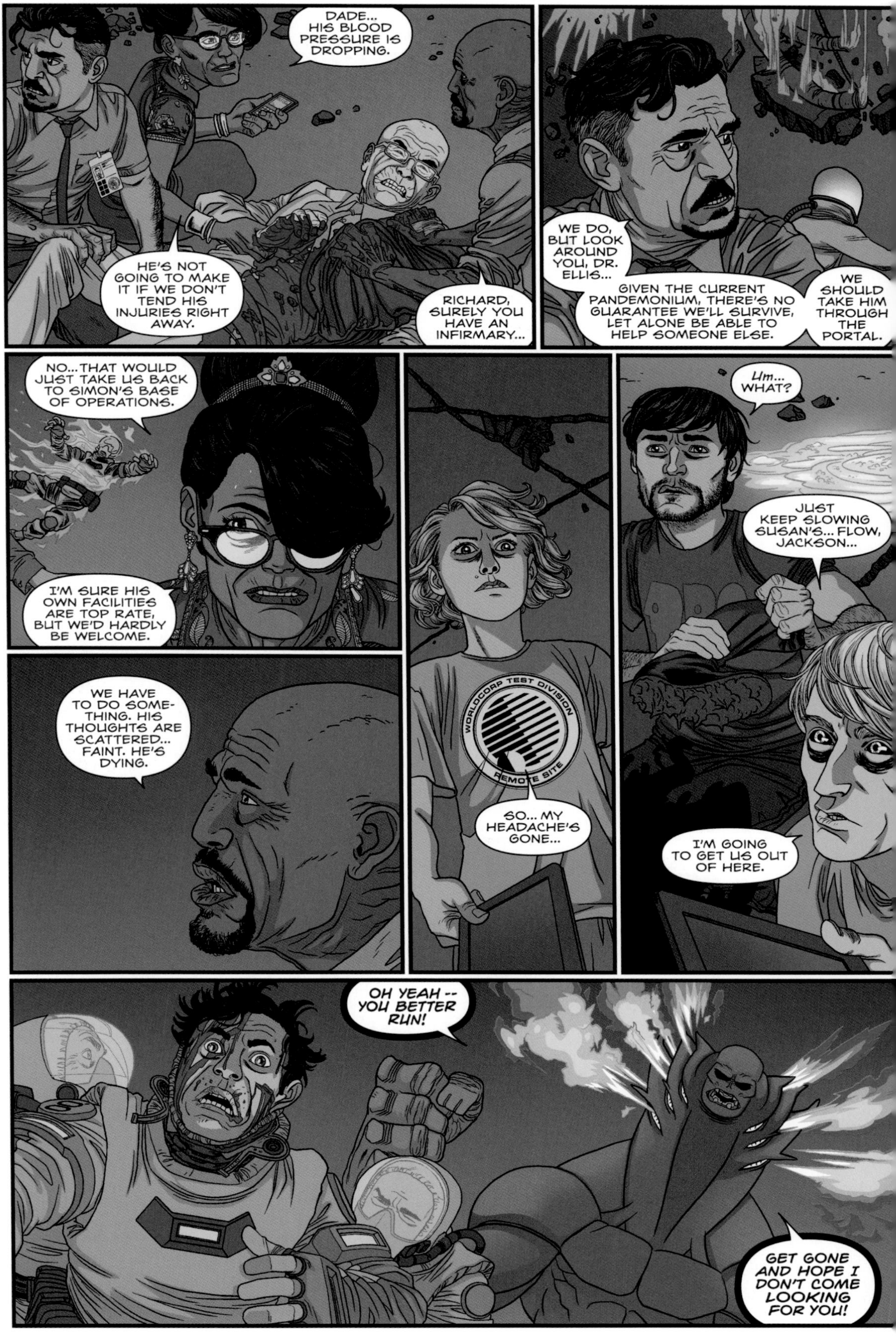
DADE... HIS BLOOD PRESSURE IS DROPPING.
HE'S NOT GOING TO MAKE IT IF WE DON'T TEND HIS INJURIES RIGHT AWAY.
RICHARD, SURELY YOU HAVE AN INFIRMARY...
WE DO, BUT LOOK AROUND YOU, DR. ELLIS...
GIVEN THE CURRENT PANDEMONIUM, THERE'S NO GUARANTEE WE'LL SURVIVE, LET ALONE BE ABLE TO HELP SOMEONE ELSE.
WE SHOULD TAKE HIM THROUGH THE PORTAL.
NO... THAT WOULD JUST TAKE US BACK TO SIMON'S BASE OF OPERATIONS.
I'M SURE HIS OWN FACILITIES ARE TOP RATE, BUT WE'D HARDLY BE WELCOME.
WE HAVE TO DO SOMETHING. HIS THOUGHTS ARE SCATTERED... FAINT. HE'S DYING.
WORLDCORP TEST DIVISION
REMOTE SITE
SO... MY HEADACHE'S GONE...
Um... WHAT?
JUST KEEP SLOWING SUSAN'S... FLOW, JACKSON...
I'M GOING TO GET US OUT OF HERE.
OH YEAH -- YOU BETTER RUN!
GET GONE AND HOPE I DON'T COME LOOKING FOR YOU!

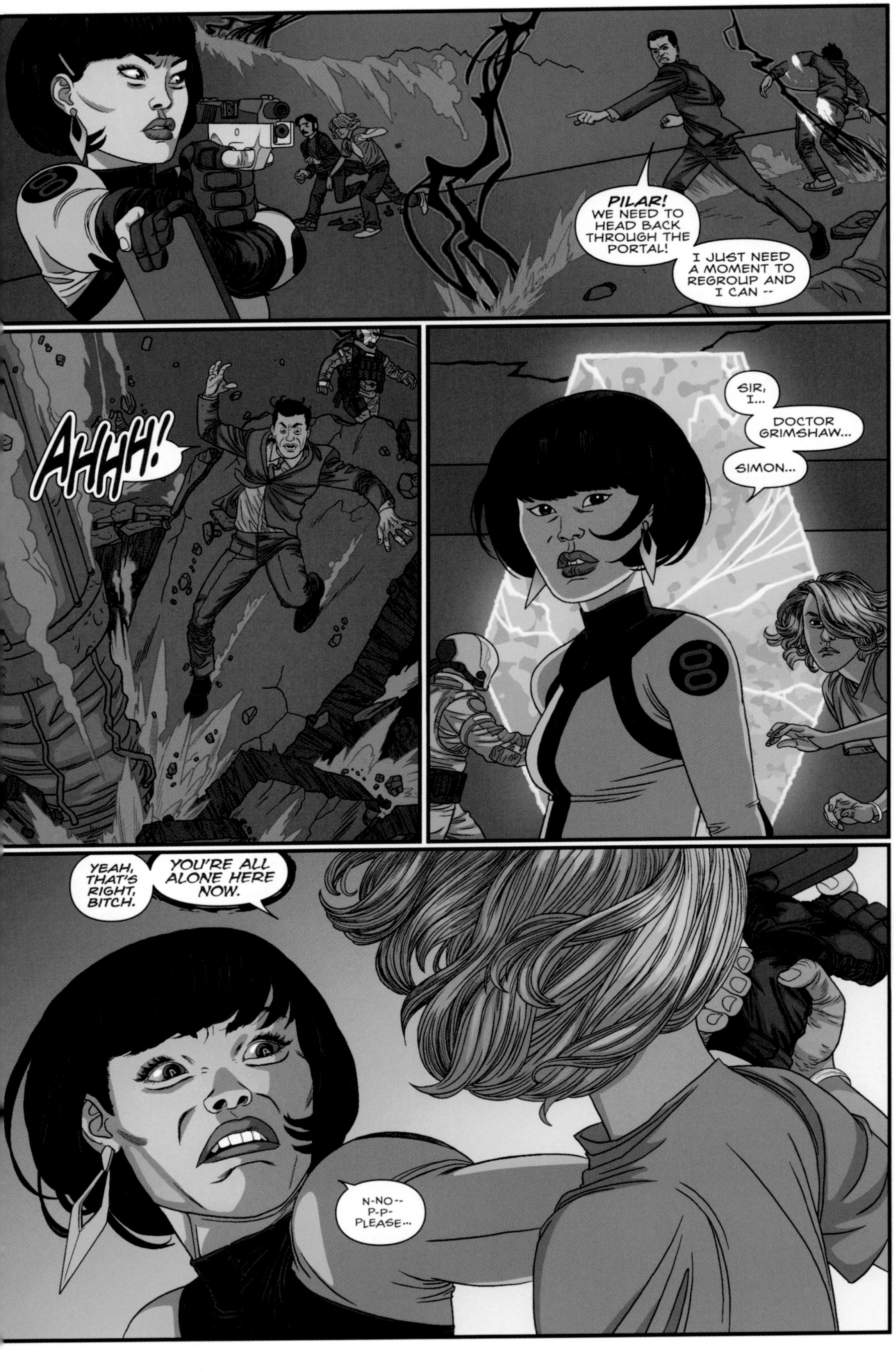
PILAR! WE NEED TO HEAD BACK THROUGH THE PORTAL!
I JUST NEED A MOMENT TO REGROUP AND I CAN --
AHHH!
SIR, I...
DOCTOR GRIMSHAW...
SIMON...
YEAH, THAT'S RIGHT, BITCH.
YOU'RE ALL ALONE HERE NOW.
N-NO-- P-P-PLEASE...

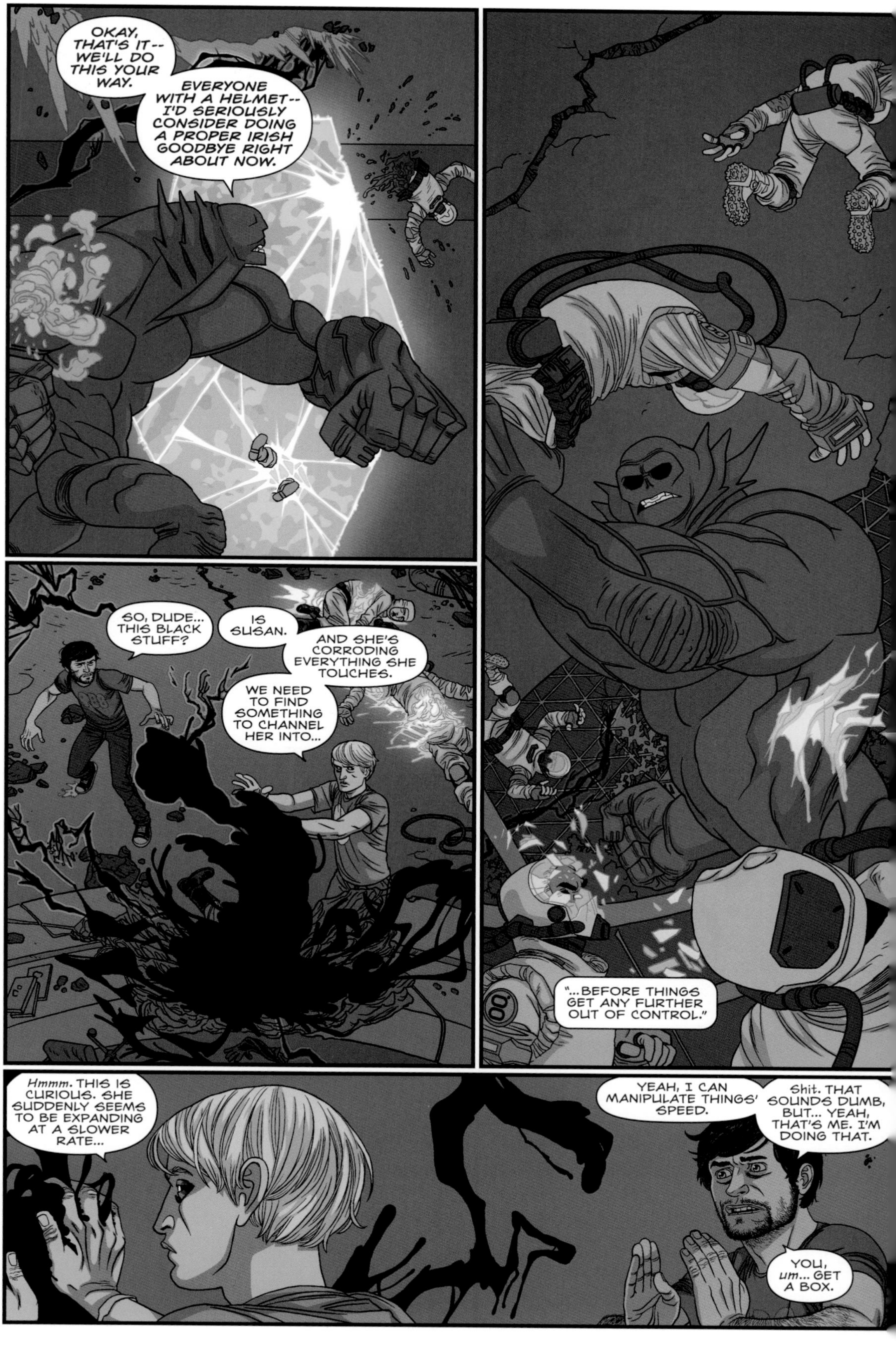
OKAY, THAT'S IT-- WE'LL DO THIS YOUR WAY.
EVERYONE WITH A HELMET-- I'D SERIOUSLY CONSIDER DOING A PROPER IRISH GOODBYE RIGHT ABOUT NOW.
SO, DUDE... THIS BLACK STUFF?
IS SUSAN.
AND SHE'S CORRODING EVERYTHING SHE TOUCHES.
WE NEED TO FIND SOMETHING TO CHANNEL HER INTO...
"...BEFORE THINGS GET ANY FURTHER OUT OF CONTROL."
Hmmm. THIS IS CURIOUS. SHE SUDDENLY SEEMS TO BE EXPANDING AT A SLOWER RATE...
YEAH, I CAN MANIPULATE THINGS' SPEED.
Shit. THAT SOUNDS DUMB, BUT... YEAH, THAT'S ME. I'M DOING THAT.
YOU, *um*... GET A BOX.

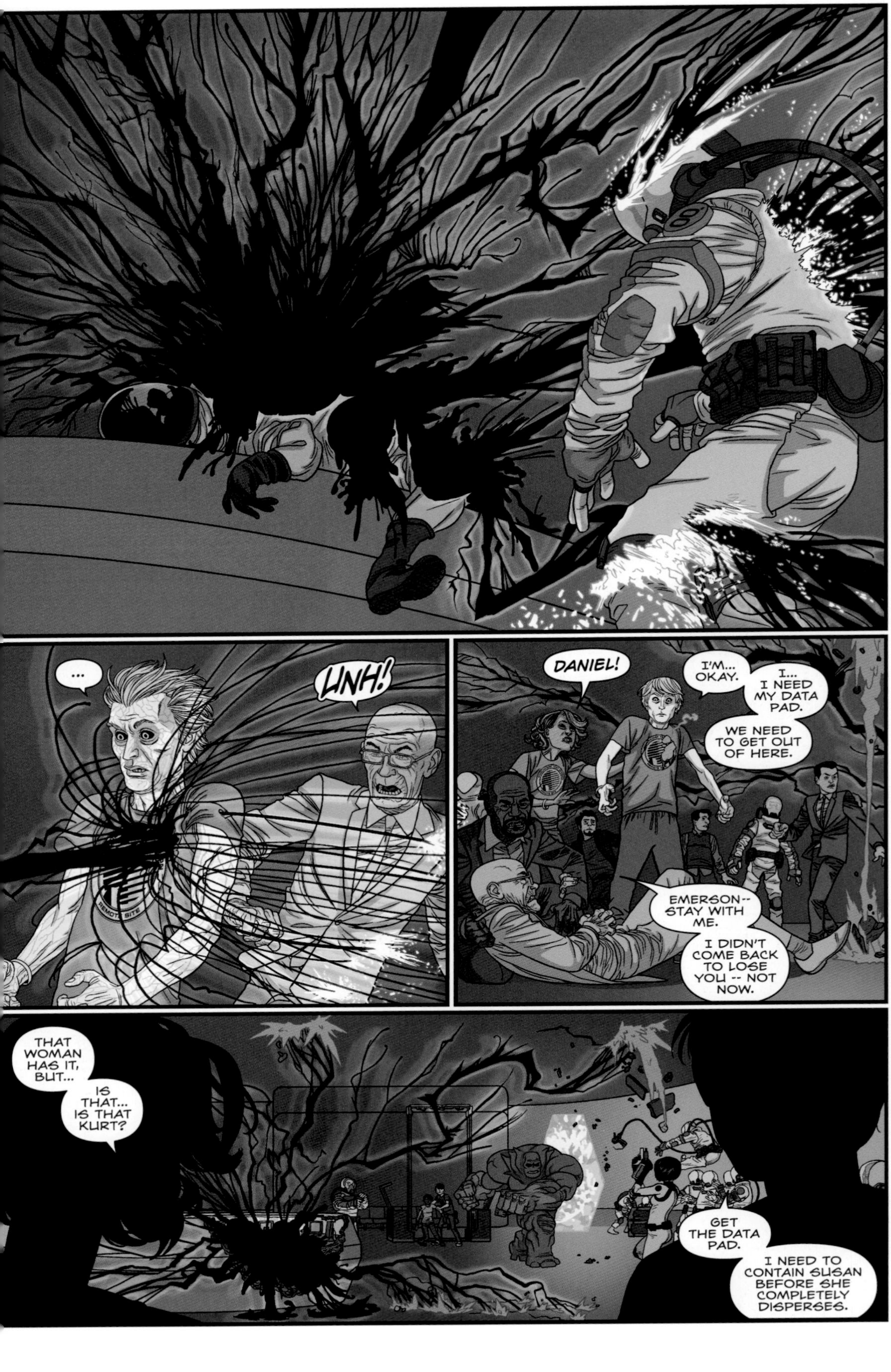
...
UNH!
DANIEL!
I'M... OKAY.
I... I NEED MY DATA PAD.
WE NEED TO GET OUT OF HERE.
EMERSON-- STAY WITH ME.
I DIDN'T COME BACK TO LOSE YOU -- NOT NOW.
THAT WOMAN HAS IT, BUT...
IS THAT... IS THAT KURT?
GET THE DATA PAD.
I NEED TO CONTAIN SUSAN BEFORE SHE COMPLETELY DISPERSES.

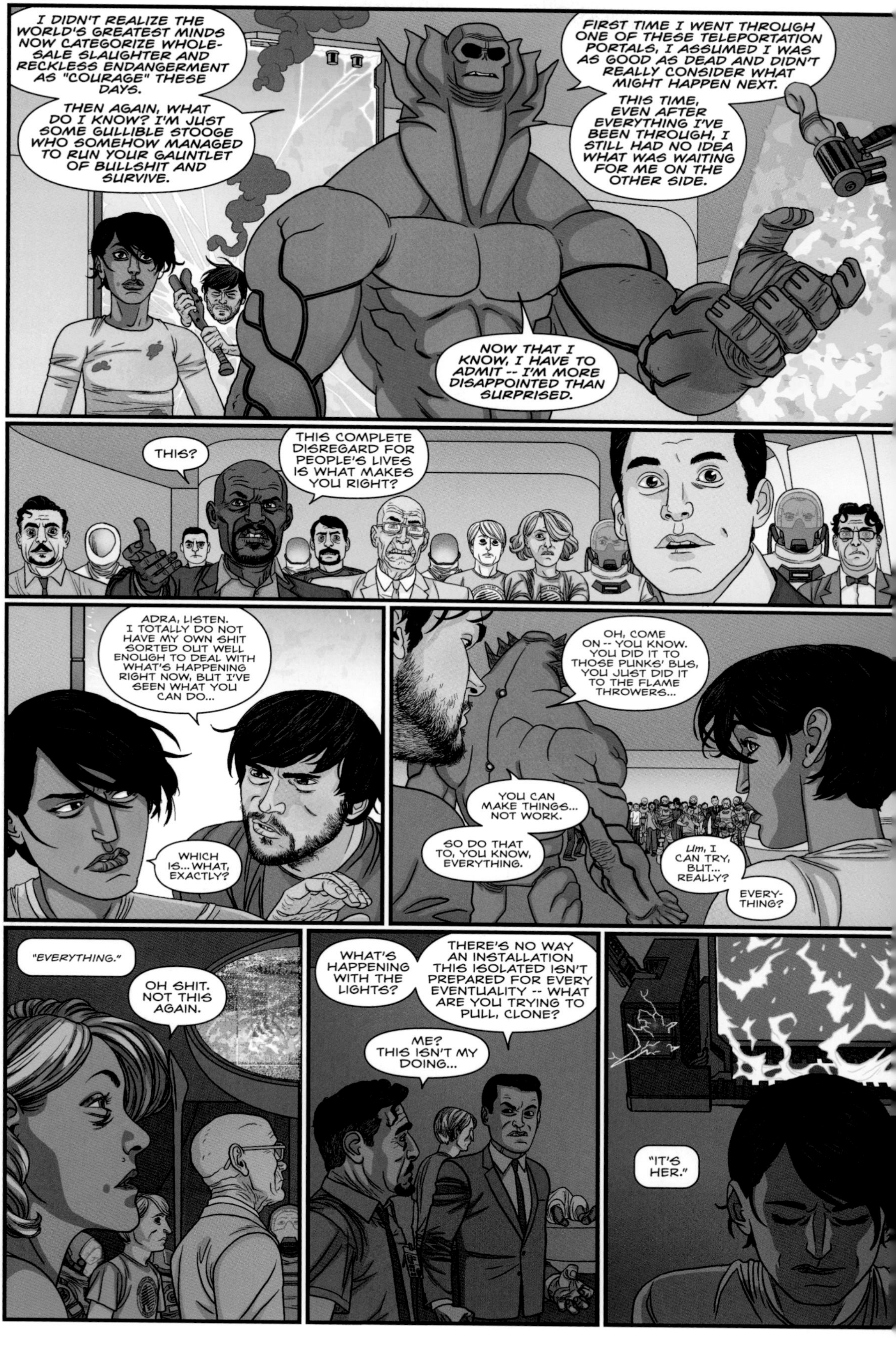
I DIDN'T REALIZE THE WORLD'S GREATEST MINDS NOW CATEGORIZE WHOLE-SALE SLAUGHTER AND RECKLESS ENDANGERMENT AS "COURAGE" THESE DAYS.
THEN AGAIN, WHAT DO I KNOW? I'M JUST SOME GULLIBLE STOOGE WHO SOMEHOW MANAGED TO RUN YOUR GAUNTLET OF BULLSHIT AND SURVIVE.
FIRST TIME I WENT THROUGH ONE OF THESE TELEPORTATION PORTALS, I ASSUMED I WAS AS GOOD AS DEAD AND DIDN'T REALLY CONSIDER WHAT MIGHT HAPPEN NEXT.
THIS TIME, EVEN AFTER EVERYTHING I'VE BEEN THROUGH, I STILL HAD NO IDEA WHAT WAS WAITING FOR ME ON THE OTHER SIDE.
NOW THAT I KNOW, I HAVE TO ADMIT -- I'M MORE DISAPPOINTED THAN SURPRISED.
THIS?
THIS COMPLETE DISREGARD FOR PEOPLE'S LIVES IS WHAT MAKES YOU RIGHT?
ADRA, LISTEN. I TOTALLY DO NOT HAVE MY OWN SHIT SORTED OUT WELL ENOUGH TO DEAL WITH WHAT'S HAPPENING RIGHT NOW, BUT I'VE SEEN WHAT YOU CAN DO...
WHICH IS...WHAT, EXACTLY?
OH, COME ON -- YOU KNOW. YOU DID IT TO THOSE PUNKS' BUS, YOU JUST DID IT TO THE FLAME THROWERS...
YOU CAN MAKE THINGS... NOT WORK.
SO DO THAT TO, YOU KNOW, EVERYTHING.
Um, I CAN TRY, BUT... REALLY?
EVERY-THING?
"EVERYTHING."
OH SHIT. NOT THIS AGAIN.
WHAT'S HAPPENING WITH THE LIGHTS?
THERE'S NO WAY AN INSTALLATION THIS ISOLATED ISN'T PREPARED FOR EVERY EVENTUALITY -- WHAT ARE YOU TRYING TO PULL, CLONE?
ME? THIS ISN'T MY DOING...
"IT'S HER."

GRIMSHAW
HOLDINGS

a brand new start

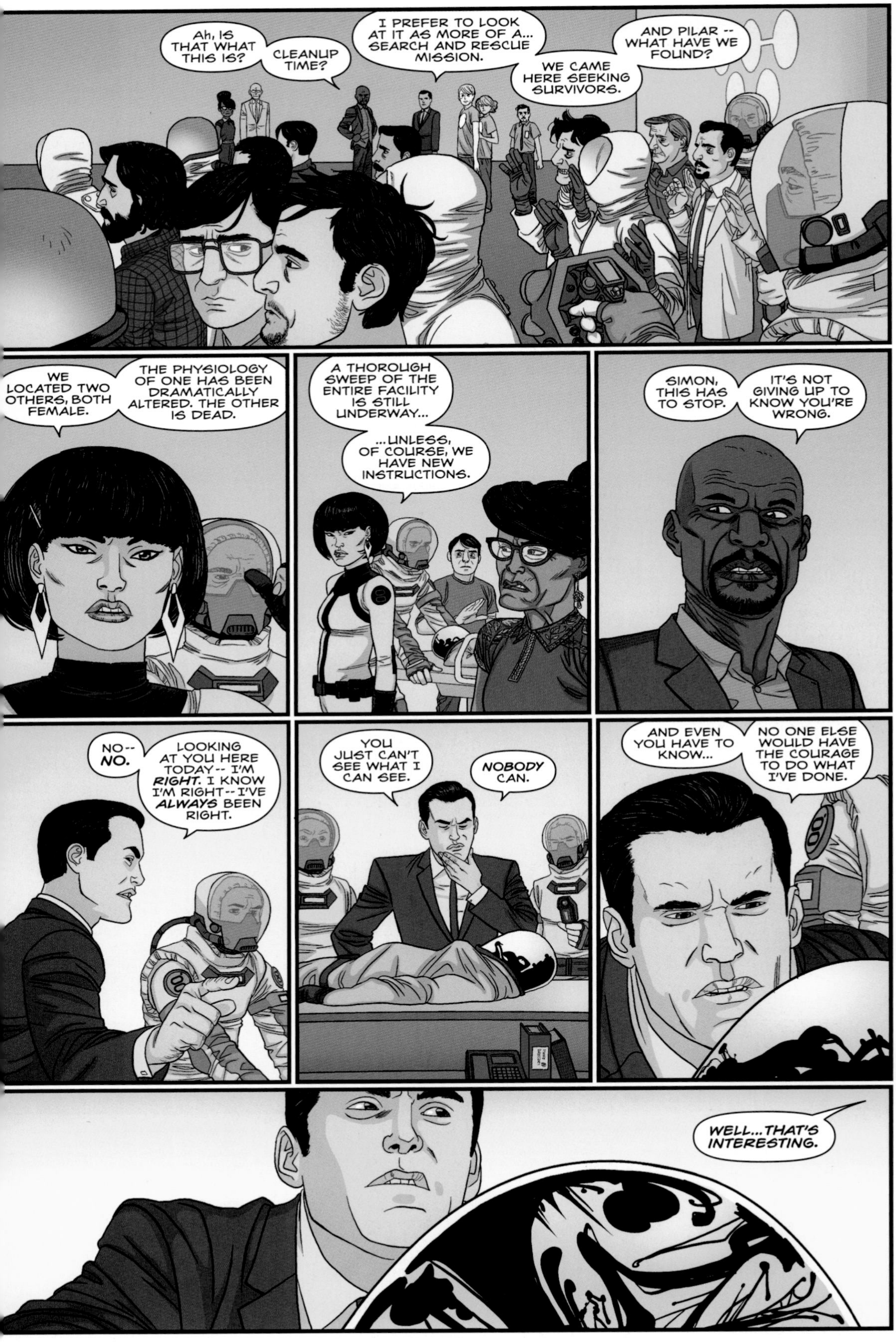
Ah, IS THAT WHAT THIS IS?
CLEANUP TIME?
I PREFER TO LOOK AT IT AS MORE OF A... SEARCH AND RESCUE MISSION.
WE CAME HERE SEEKING SURVIVORS.
AND PILAR -- WHAT HAVE WE FOUND?
WE LOCATED TWO OTHERS, BOTH FEMALE.
THE PHYSIOLOGY OF ONE HAS BEEN DRAMATICALLY ALTERED. THE OTHER IS DEAD.
A THOROUGH SWEEP OF THE ENTIRE FACILITY IS STILL UNDERWAY...
...UNLESS, OF COURSE, WE HAVE NEW INSTRUCTIONS.
SIMON, THIS HAS TO STOP.
IT'S NOT GIVING UP TO KNOW YOU'RE WRONG.
NO-- NO.
LOOKING AT YOU HERE TODAY-- I'M RIGHT. I KNOW I'M RIGHT-- I'VE ALWAYS BEEN RIGHT.
YOU JUST CAN'T SEE WHAT I CAN SEE.
NOBODY CAN.
AND EVEN YOU HAVE TO KNOW...
NO ONE ELSE WOULD HAVE THE COURAGE TO DO WHAT I'VE DONE.
WELL...THAT'S INTERESTING.

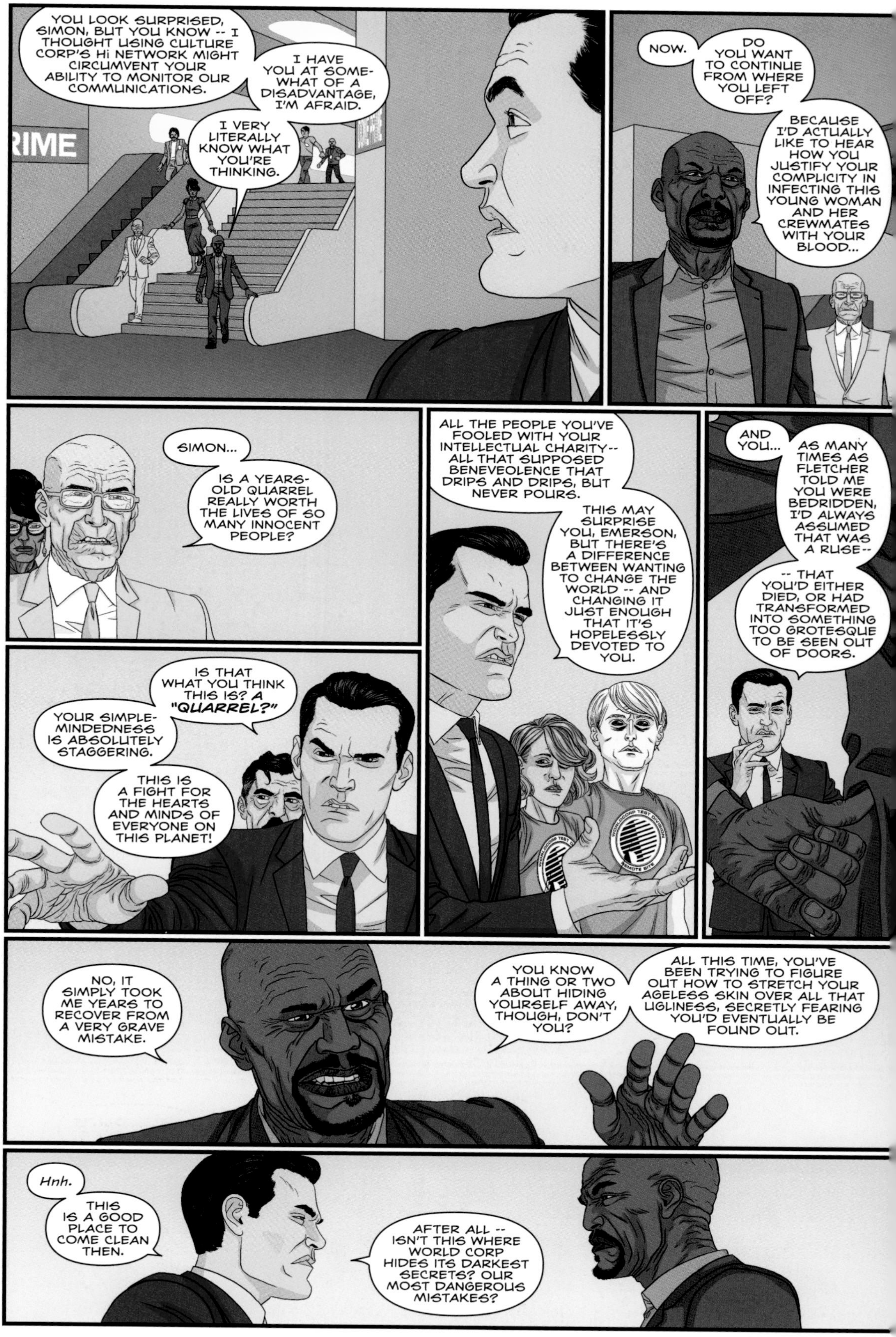

YOU LOOK SURPRISED, SIMON, BUT YOU KNOW -- I THOUGHT USING CULTURE CORP'S Hi NETWORK MIGHT CIRCUMVENT YOUR ABILITY TO MONITOR OUR COMMUNICATIONS.
I HAVE YOU AT SOMEWHAT OF A DISADVANTAGE, I'M AFRAID.
I VERY LITERALLY KNOW WHAT YOU'RE THINKING.
RIME
NOW.
DO YOU WANT TO CONTINUE FROM WHERE YOU LEFT OFF?
BECAUSE I'D ACTUALLY LIKE TO HEAR HOW YOU JUSTIFY YOUR COMPLICITY IN INFECTING THIS YOUNG WOMAN AND HER CREWMATES WITH YOUR BLOOD...
SIMON...
IS A YEARS-OLD QUARREL REALLY WORTH THE LIVES OF SO MANY INNOCENT PEOPLE?
IS THAT WHAT YOU THINK THIS IS? A "QUARREL?"
YOUR SIMPLE-MINDEDNESS IS ABSOLUTELY STAGGERING.
THIS IS A FIGHT FOR THE HEARTS AND MINDS OF EVERYONE ON THIS PLANET!
ALL THE PEOPLE YOU'VE FOOLED WITH YOUR INTELLECTUAL CHARITY-- ALL THAT SUPPOSED BENEVEOLENCE THAT DRIPS AND DRIPS, BUT NEVER POURS.
THIS MAY SURPRISE YOU, EMERSON, BUT THERE'S A DIFFERENCE BETWEEN WANTING TO CHANGE THE WORLD -- AND CHANGING IT JUST ENOUGH THAT IT'S HOPELESSLY DEVOTED TO YOU.
AND YOU...
AS MANY TIMES AS FLETCHER TOLD ME YOU WERE BEDRIDDEN, I'D ALWAYS ASSUMED THAT WAS A RUSE--
-- THAT YOU'D EITHER DIED, OR HAD TRANSFORMED INTO SOMETHING TOO GROTESQUE TO BE SEEN OUT OF DOORS.
NO, IT SIMPLY TOOK ME YEARS TO RECOVER FROM A VERY GRAVE MISTAKE.
YOU KNOW A THING OR TWO ABOUT HIDING YOURSELF AWAY, THOUGH, DON'T YOU?
ALL THIS TIME, YOU'VE BEEN TRYING TO FIGURE OUT HOW TO STRETCH YOUR AGELESS SKIN OVER ALL THAT UGLINESS, SECRETLY FEARING YOU'D EVENTUALLY BE FOUND OUT.
Hnh.
THIS IS A GOOD PLACE TO COME CLEAN THEN.
AFTER ALL -- ISN'T THIS WHERE WORLD CORP HIDES ITS DARKEST SECRETS? OUR MOST DANGEROUS MISTAKES?

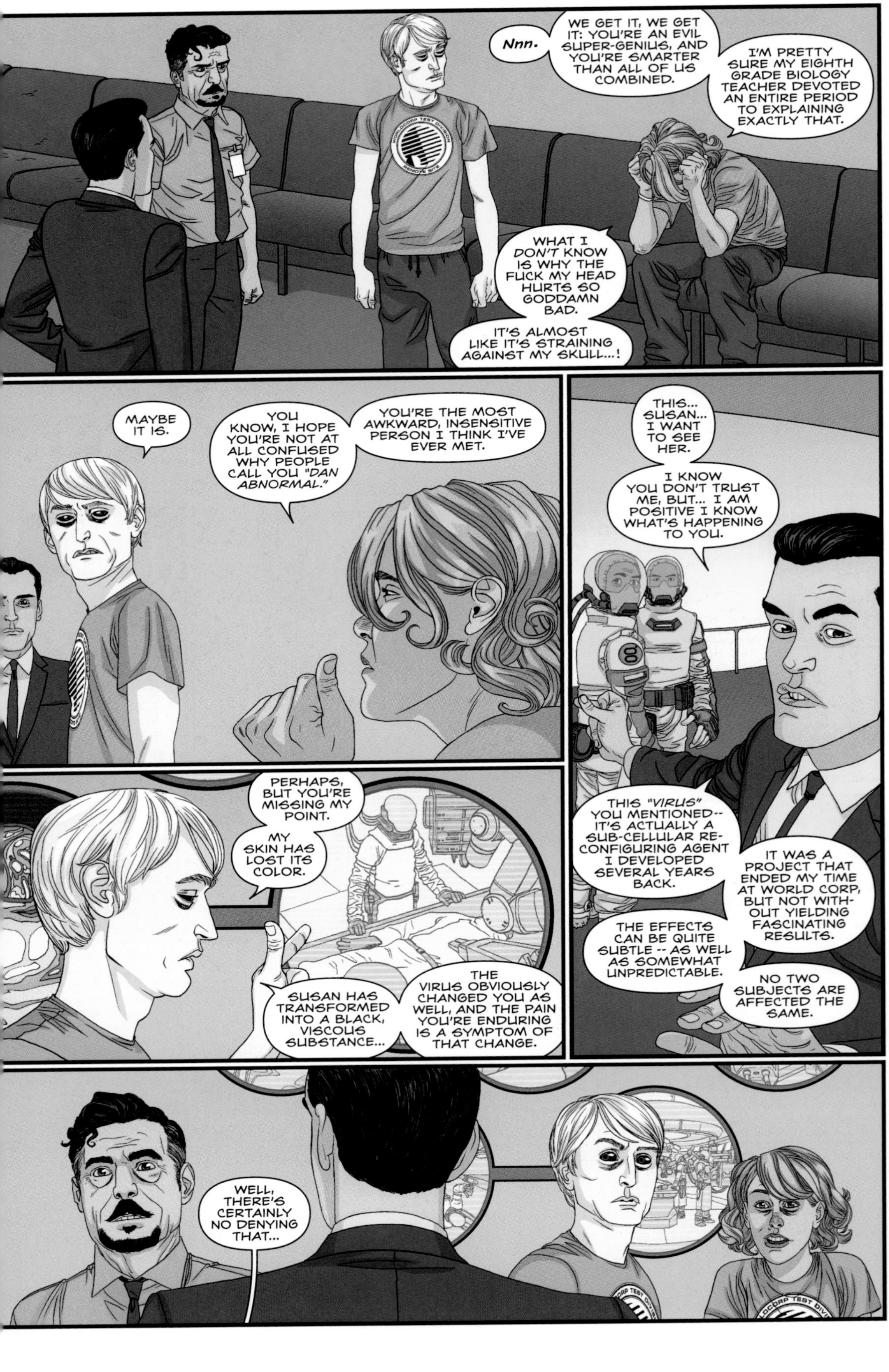
Nnn.
WE GET IT, WE GET IT: YOU'RE AN EVIL SUPER-GENIUS, AND YOU'RE SMARTER THAN ALL OF US COMBINED.
I'M PRETTY SURE MY EIGHTH GRADE BIOLOGY TEACHER DEVOTED AN ENTIRE PERIOD TO EXPLAINING EXACTLY THAT.
WHAT I DON'T KNOW IS WHY THE FUCK MY HEAD HURTS SO GODDAMN BAD.
IT'S ALMOST LIKE IT'S STRAINING AGAINST MY SKULL...!
MAYBE IT IS.
YOU KNOW, I HOPE YOU'RE NOT AT ALL CONFUSED WHY PEOPLE CALL YOU "DAN ABNORMAL."
YOU'RE THE MOST AWKWARD, INSENSITIVE PERSON I THINK I'VE EVER MET.
PERHAPS, BUT YOU'RE MISSING MY POINT.
MY SKIN HAS LOST ITS COLOR.
SUSAN HAS TRANSFORMED INTO A BLACK, VISCOUS SUBSTANCE...
THE VIRUS OBVIOUSLY CHANGED YOU AS WELL, AND THE PAIN YOU'RE ENDURING IS A SYMPTOM OF THAT CHANGE.
THIS... SUSAN... I WANT TO SEE HER.
I KNOW YOU DON'T TRUST ME, BUT... I AM POSITIVE I KNOW WHAT'S HAPPENING TO YOU.
THIS "VIRUS" YOU MENTIONED-- IT'S ACTUALLY A SUB-CELLULAR RE-CONFIGURING AGENT I DEVELOPED SEVERAL YEARS BACK.
IT WAS A PROJECT THAT ENDED MY TIME AT WORLD CORP, BUT NOT WITH-OUT YIELDING FASCINATING RESULTS.
THE EFFECTS CAN BE QUITE SUBTLE -- AS WELL AS SOMEWHAT UNPREDICTABLE.
NO TWO SUBJECTS ARE AFFECTED THE SAME.
WELL, THERE'S CERTAINLY NO DENYING THAT...

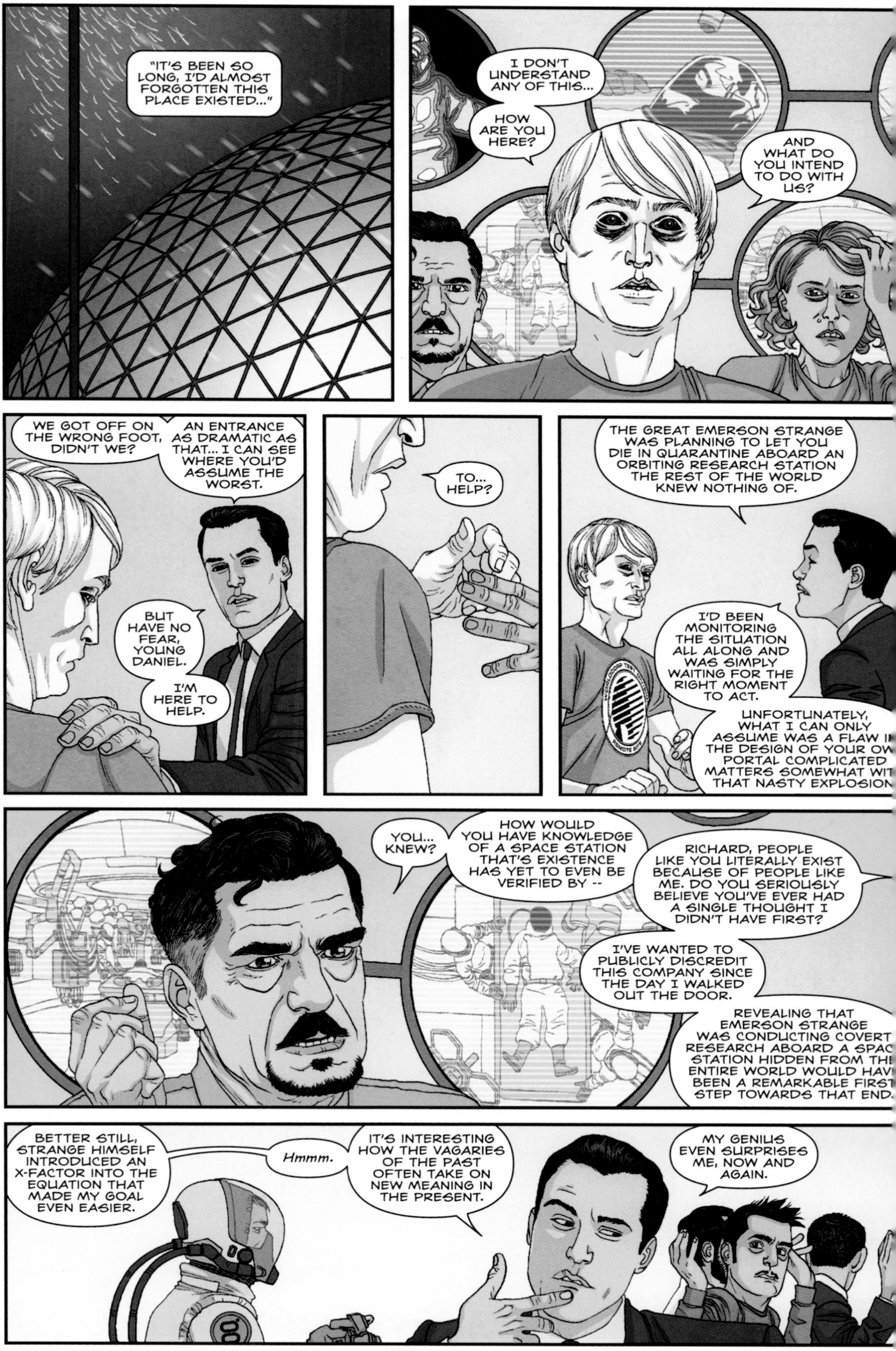
"IT'S BEEN SO LONG, I'D ALMOST FORGOTTEN THIS PLACE EXISTED..."
I DON'T UNDERSTAND ANY OF THIS...
HOW ARE YOU HERE?
AND WHAT DO YOU INTEND TO DO WITH US?
WE GOT OFF ON THE WRONG FOOT, DIDN'T WE?
AN ENTRANCE AS DRAMATIC AS THAT... I CAN SEE WHERE YOU'D ASSUME THE WORST.
BUT HAVE NO FEAR, YOUNG DANIEL.
I'M HERE TO HELP.
TO... HELP?
THE GREAT EMERSON STRANGE WAS PLANNING TO LET YOU DIE IN QUARANTINE ABOARD AN ORBITING RESEARCH STATION THE REST OF THE WORLD KNEW NOTHING OF.
I'D BEEN MONITORING THE SITUATION ALL ALONG AND WAS SIMPLY WAITING FOR THE RIGHT MOMENT TO ACT.
UNFORTUNATELY, WHAT I CAN ONLY ASSUME WAS A FLAW I THE DESIGN OF YOUR OW PORTAL COMPLICATED MATTERS SOMEWHAT WIT THAT NASTY EXPLOSION
YOU... KNEW?
HOW WOULD YOU HAVE KNOWLEDGE OF A SPACE STATION THAT'S EXISTENCE HAS YET TO EVEN BE VERIFIED BY --
RICHARD, PEOPLE LIKE YOU LITERALLY EXIST BECAUSE OF PEOPLE LIKE ME. DO YOU SERIOUSLY BELIEVE YOU'VE EVER HAD A SINGLE THOUGHT I DIDN'T HAVE FIRST?
I'VE WANTED TO PUBLICLY DISCREDIT THIS COMPANY SINCE THE DAY I WALKED OUT THE DOOR.
REVEALING THAT EMERSON STRANGE WAS CONDUCTING COVERT RESEARCH ABOARD A SPAC STATION HIDDEN FROM TH ENTIRE WORLD WOULD HAV BEEN A REMARKABLE FIRST STEP TOWARDS THAT END.
BETTER STILL, STRANGE HIMSELF INTRODUCED AN X-FACTOR INTO THE EQUATION THAT MADE MY GOAL EVEN EASIER.
Hmmm.
IT'S INTERESTING HOW THE VAGARIES OF THE PAST OFTEN TAKE ON NEW MEANING IN THE PRESENT.
MY GENIUS EVEN SURPRISES ME, NOW AND AGAIN.

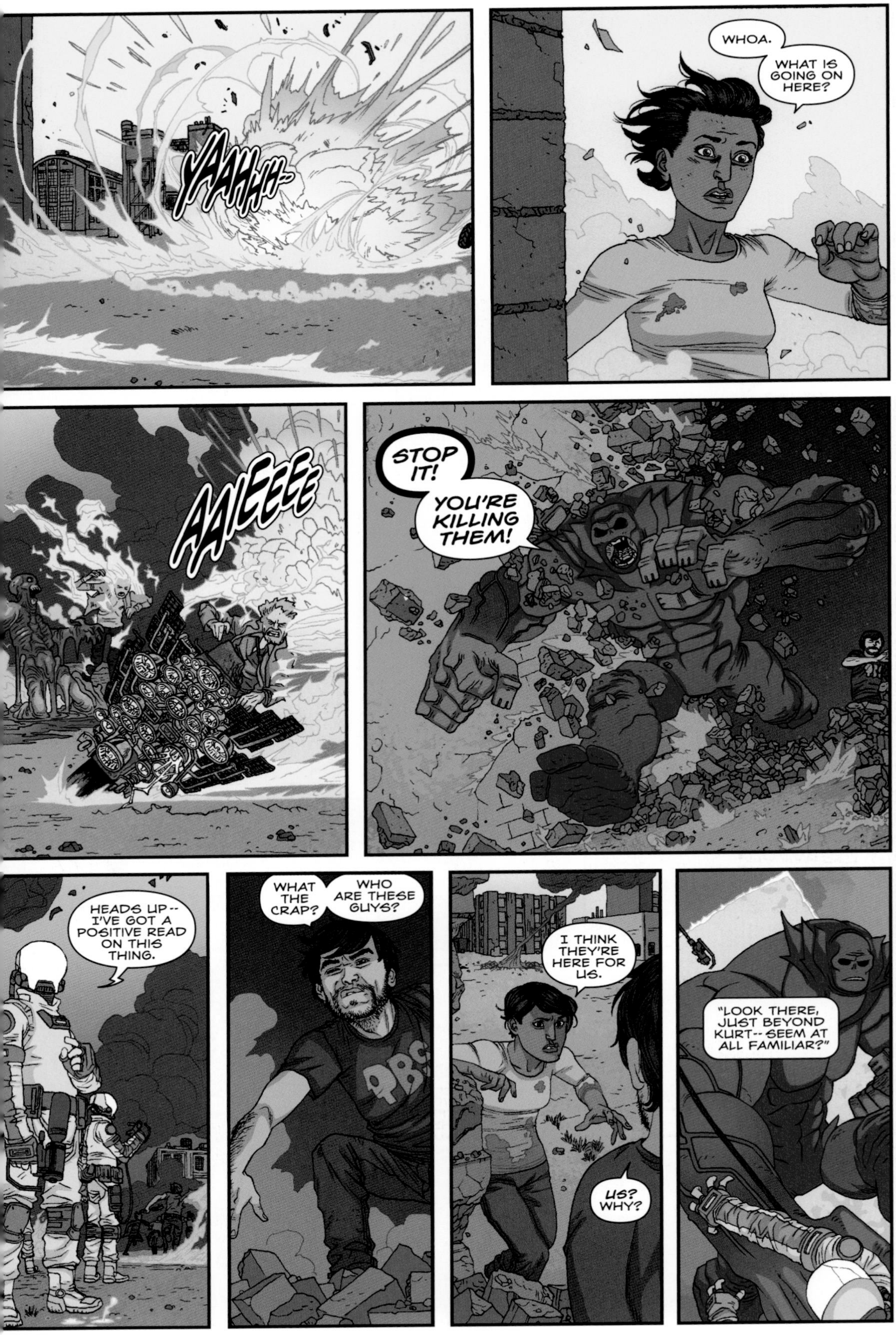
YAAHHH--
WHOA.
WHAT IS GOING ON HERE?
AAIEEEE
STOP IT!
YOU'RE KILLING THEM!
HEADS UP-- I'VE GOT A POSITIVE READ ON THIS THING.
WHAT THE CRAP?
WHO ARE THESE GUYS?
I THINK THEY'RE HERE FOR US.
US? WHY?
"LOOK THERE, JUST BEYOND KURT-- SEEM AT ALL FAMILIAR?"

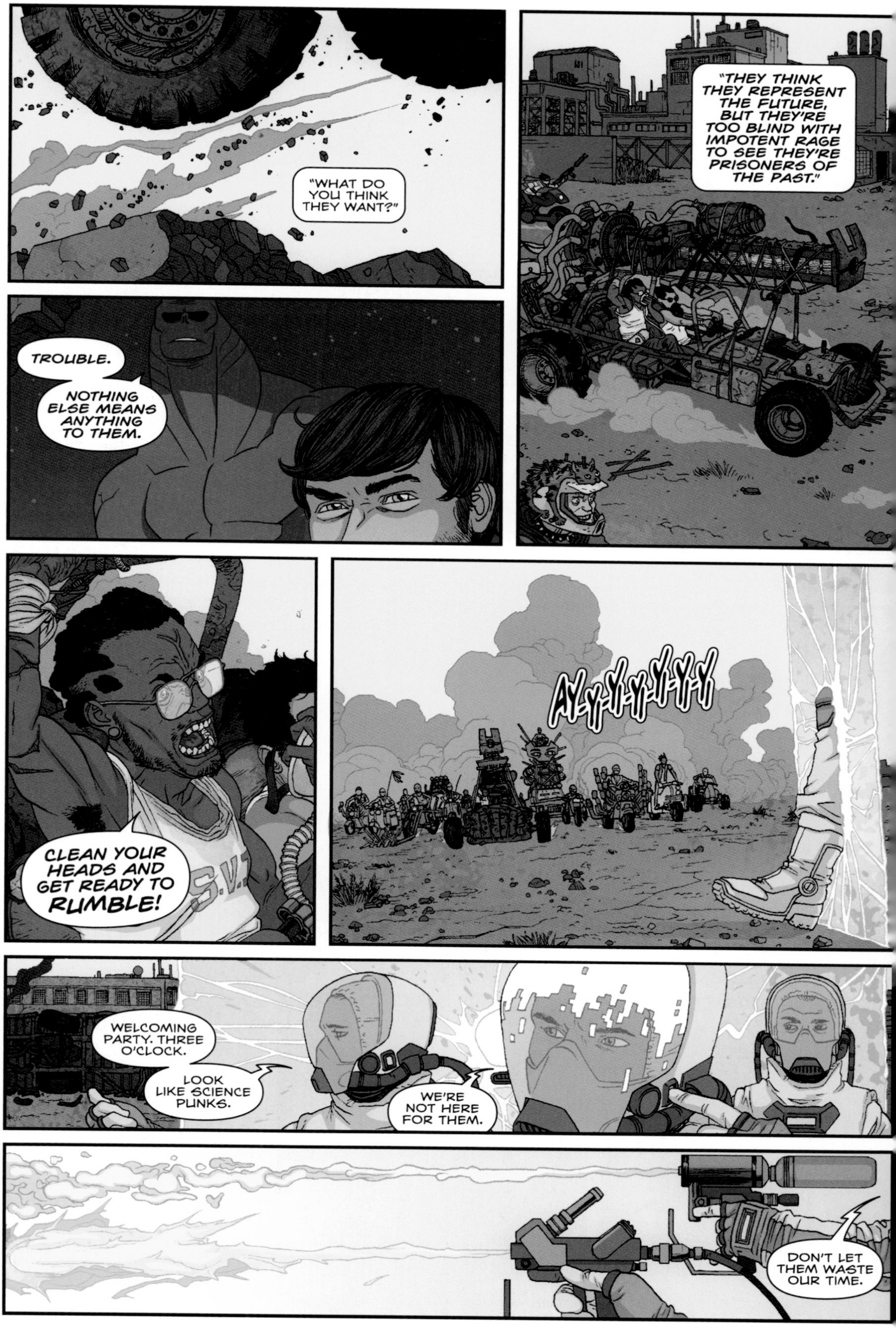
"WHAT DO YOU THINK THEY WANT?"
"THEY THINK THEY REPRESENT THE FUTURE, BUT THEY'RE TOO BLIND WITH IMPOTENT RAGE TO SEE THEY'RE PRISONERS OF THE PAST."
TROUBLE.
NOTHING ELSE MEANS ANYTHING TO THEM.
CLEAN YOUR HEADS AND GET READY TO RUMBLE!
AY-Y-Y-Y-Y-Y-Y-Y
WELCOMING PARTY. THREE O'CLOCK.
LOOK LIKE SCIENCE PUNKS.
WE'RE NOT HERE FOR THEM.
DON'T LET THEM WASTE OUR TIME.

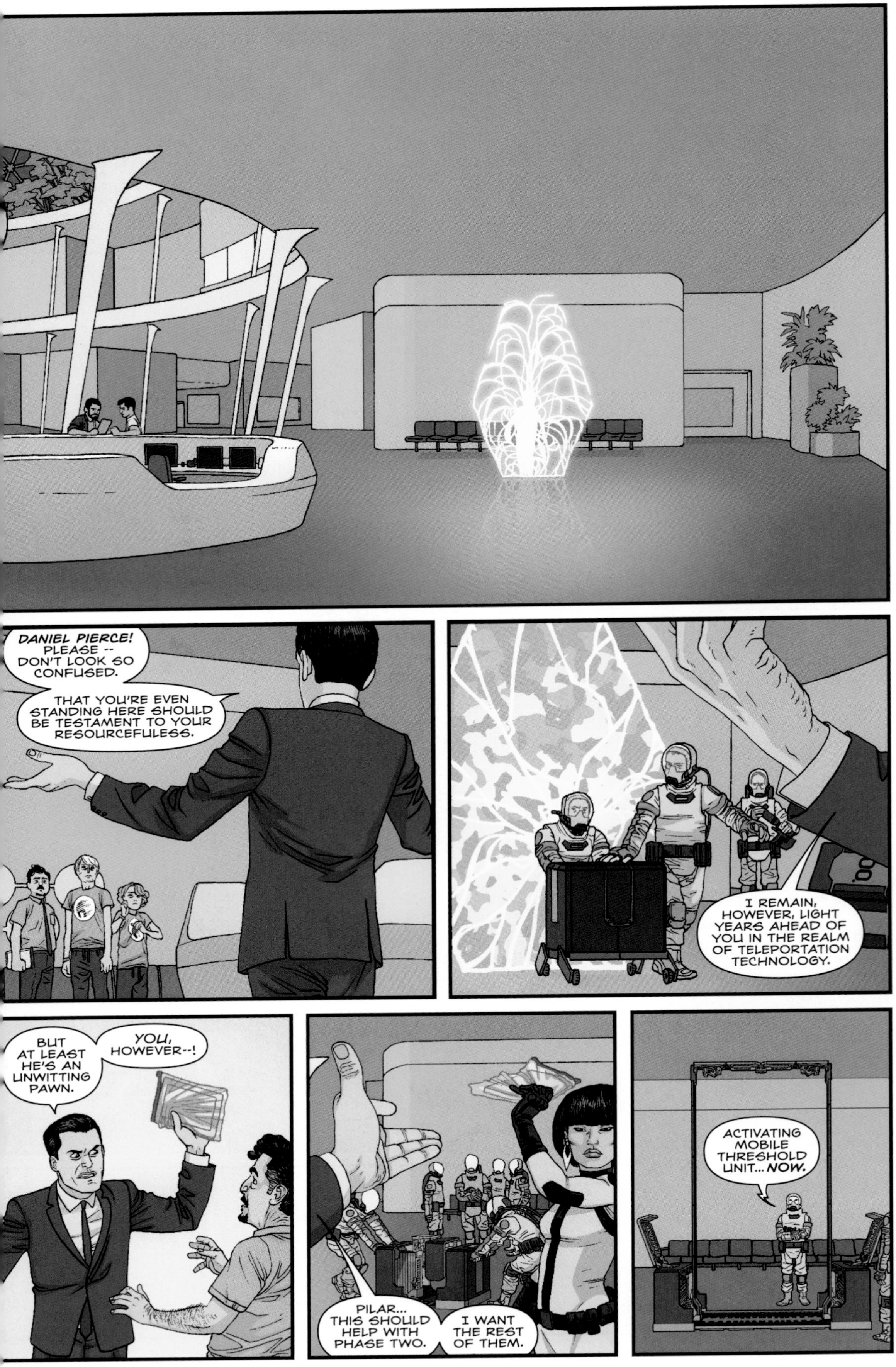
DANIEL PIERCE! PLEASE -- DON'T LOOK SO CONFUSED.
THAT YOU'RE EVEN STANDING HERE SHOULD BE TESTAMENT TO YOUR RESOURCEFULESS.
I REMAIN, HOWEVER, LIGHT YEARS AHEAD OF YOU IN THE REALM OF TELEPORTATION TECHNOLOGY.
YOU, HOWEVER--!
BUT AT LEAST HE'S AN UNWITTING PAWN.
PILAR... THIS SHOULD HELP WITH PHASE TWO.
I WANT THE REST OF THEM.
ACTIVATING MOBILE THRESHOLD UNIT... NOW.

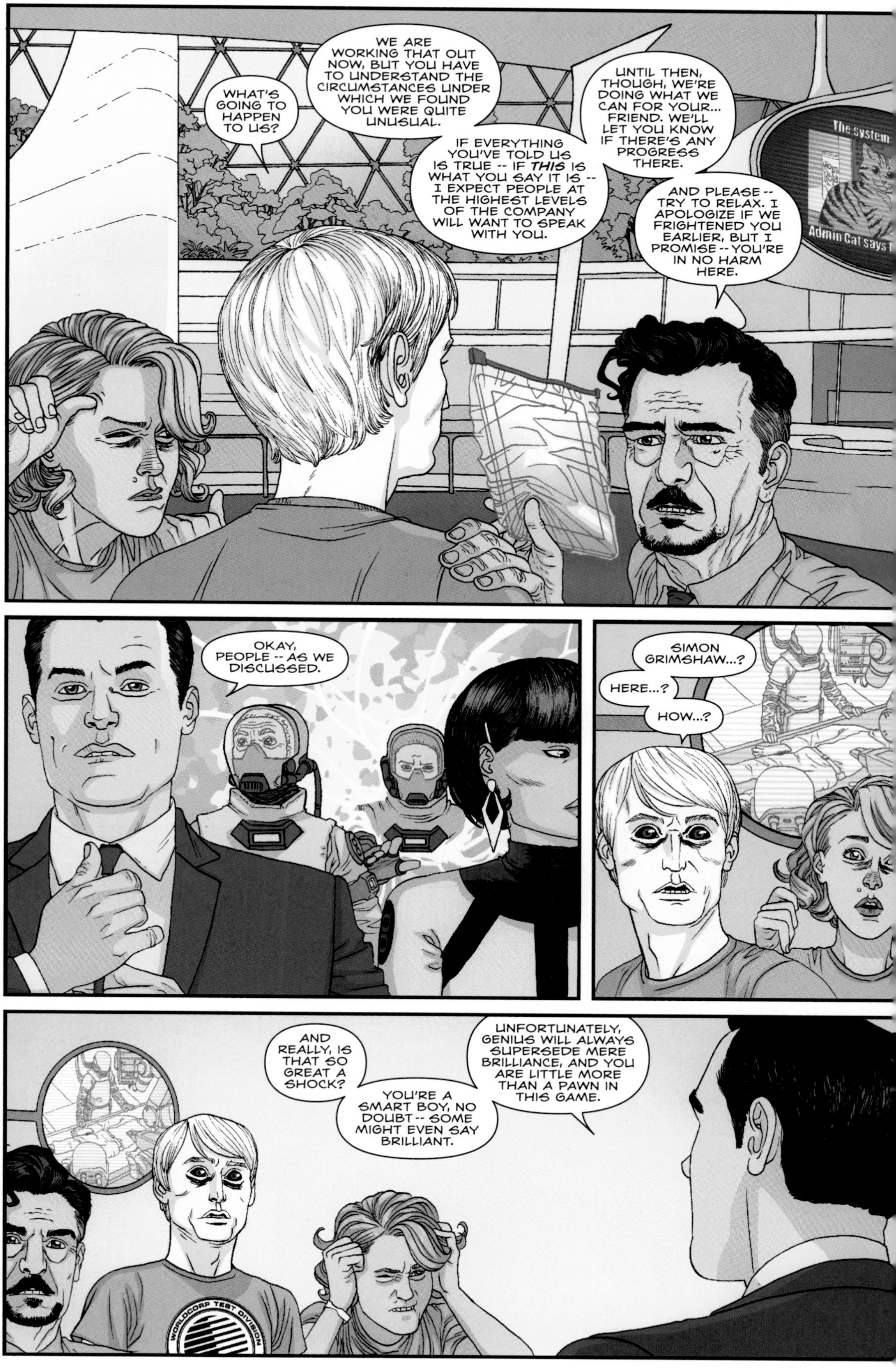
WHAT'S GOING TO HAPPEN TO US?
WE ARE WORKING THAT OUT NOW, BUT YOU HAVE TO UNDERSTAND THE CIRCUMSTANCES UNDER WHICH WE FOUND YOU WERE QUITE UNUSUAL.
IF EVERYTHING YOU'VE TOLD US IS TRUE -- IF *THIS* IS WHAT YOU SAY IT IS -- I EXPECT PEOPLE AT THE HIGHEST LEVELS OF THE COMPANY WILL WANT TO SPEAK WITH YOU.
UNTIL THEN, THOUGH, WE'RE DOING WHAT WE CAN FOR YOUR... FRIEND. WE'LL LET YOU KNOW IF THERE'S ANY PROGRESS THERE.
AND PLEASE -- TRY TO RELAX. I APOLOGIZE IF WE FRIGHTENED YOU EARLIER, BUT I PROMISE -- YOU'RE IN NO HARM HERE.
The system
Admin Cat says
OKAY, PEOPLE -- AS WE DISCUSSED.
SIMON GRIMSHAW...?
HERE...?
HOW...?
AND REALLY, IS THAT SO GREAT A SHOCK?
YOU'RE A SMART BOY, NO DOUBT -- SOME MIGHT EVEN SAY BRILLIANT.
UNFORTUNATELY, GENIUS WILL ALWAYS SUPERSEDE MERE BRILLIANCE, AND YOU ARE LITTLE MORE THAN A PAWN IN THIS GAME.
WORLDCORP TEST DIVISION

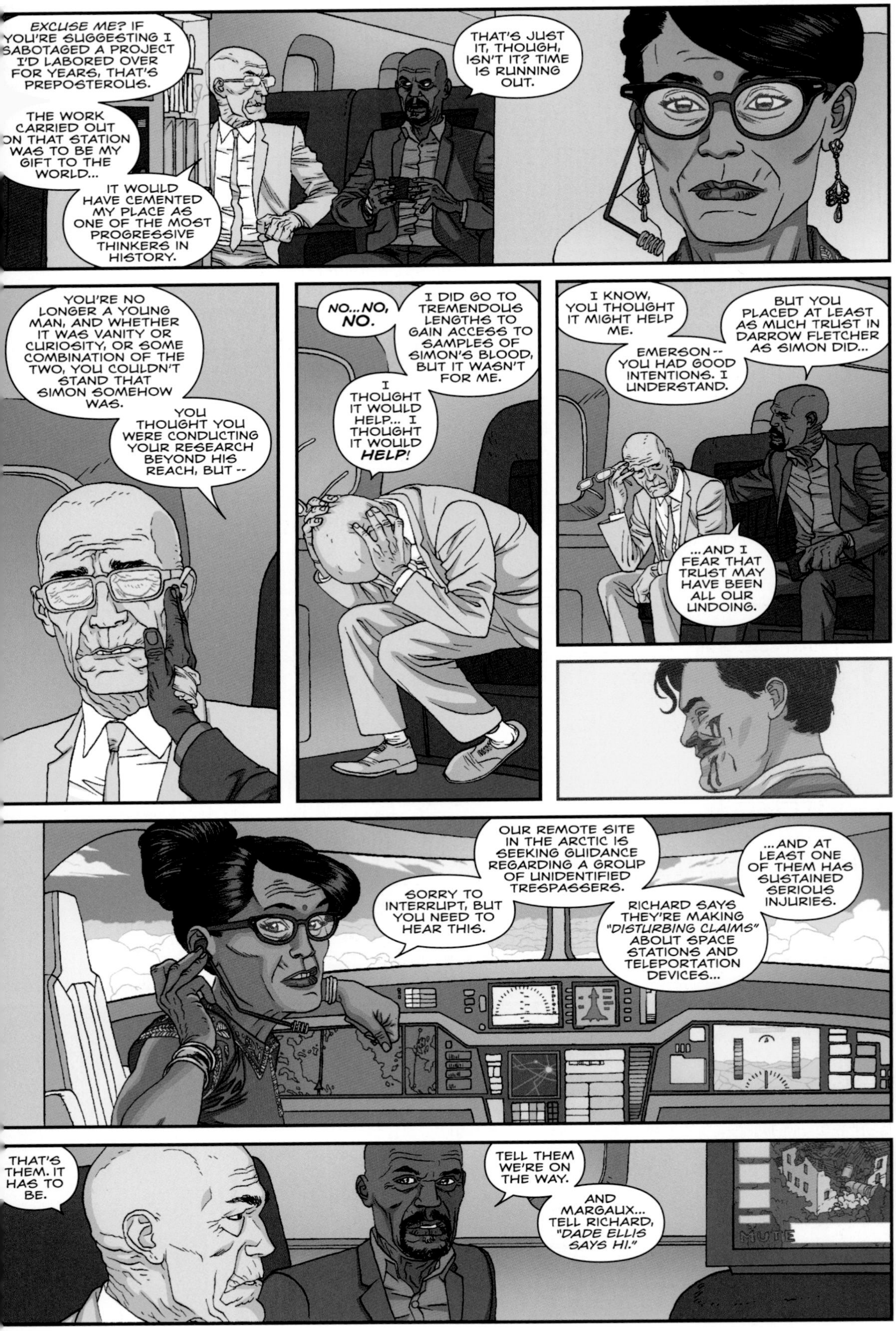
EXCUSE ME? IF YOU'RE SUGGESTING I SABOTAGED A PROJECT I'D LABORED OVER FOR YEARS, THAT'S PREPOSTEROUS.
THE WORK CARRIED OUT ON THAT STATION WAS TO BE MY GIFT TO THE WORLD...
IT WOULD HAVE CEMENTED MY PLACE AS ONE OF THE MOST PROGRESSIVE THINKERS IN HISTORY.
THAT'S JUST IT, THOUGH, ISN'T IT? TIME IS RUNNING OUT.
YOU'RE NO LONGER A YOUNG MAN, AND WHETHER IT WAS VANITY OR CURIOSITY, OR SOME COMBINATION OF THE TWO, YOU COULDN'T STAND THAT SIMON SOMEHOW WAS.
YOU THOUGHT YOU WERE CONDUCTING YOUR RESEARCH BEYOND HIS REACH, BUT --
NO...NO, NO.
I DID GO TO TREMENDOUS LENGTHS TO GAIN ACCESS TO SAMPLES OF SIMON'S BLOOD, BUT IT WASN'T FOR ME.
I THOUGHT IT WOULD HELP... I THOUGHT IT WOULD HELP!
I KNOW, YOU THOUGHT IT MIGHT HELP ME.
EMERSON -- YOU HAD GOOD INTENTIONS. I UNDERSTAND.
BUT YOU PLACED AT LEAST AS MUCH TRUST IN DARROW FLETCHER AS SIMON DID...
...AND I FEAR THAT TRUST MAY HAVE BEEN ALL OUR UNDOING.
SORRY TO INTERRUPT, BUT YOU NEED TO HEAR THIS.
OUR REMOTE SITE IN THE ARCTIC IS SEEKING GUIDANCE REGARDING A GROUP OF UNIDENTIFIED TRESPASSERS.
RICHARD SAYS THEY'RE MAKING "DISTURBING CLAIMS" ABOUT SPACE STATIONS AND TELEPORTATION DEVICES...
...AND AT LEAST ONE OF THEM HAS SUSTAINED SERIOUS INJURIES.
THAT'S THEM. IT HAS TO BE.
TELL THEM WE'RE ON THE WAY.
AND MARGAUX... TELL RICHARD, "DADE ELLIS SAYS HI."
MUTE

ALL IT TAKES IS ONE SET OF EYES...

...ONE MOMENT OF RECOGNITION...

...AND WE'LL KNOW EXACTLY WHERE THEY ARE.

IT'S FASCINATING... A NEARLY INPERCEPTABLE AMOUNT OF TIME CAN HAVE SUCH LONGLASTING REPERCUSSIONS.

MERE SECONDS CAN ALTER THE OUTCOME OF ALMOST ANY SITUATION.

PUSHING A BUTTON... MOVING A PEN...

ALL I HAD TO DO WAS LET SIMON GO...

...AND EVERYTHING WOULD HAVE TURNED OUT DIFFERENTLY.

"I DIDN'T KNOW AT THE TIME, BUT HE WAS DEVELOPING SOMETHING AKIN TO A VIRUS... AND IT WAS VERY CONTAGIOUS."

"THAT GORILLA HE'D ALTERED... I COULDN'T LIVE WITH THE THOUGHT OF HIM CREATING SIMILAR MONSTROSITIES."

"WE STRUGGLED FOR HIS TEST SAMPLES AND THE VIAL SHATTERED IN MY HAND."

"I THOUGHT I'D WON."

BUT SIMON KNEW BETTER, DIDN'T HE?

EVEN IF HE HAD NO IDEA HOW EXPOSURE TO HIS MYSTERY COMPOUND WOULD AFFECT US, HE REALIZED WE *WOULD* BOTH CHANGE, THUS PROVING HIM RIGHT...

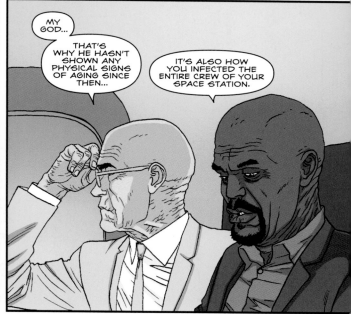

MY GOD...

THAT'S WHY HE HASN'T SHOWN ANY PHYSICAL SIGNS OF AGING SINCE THEN...

IT'S ALSO HOW YOU INFECTED THE ENTIRE CREW OF YOUR SPACE STATION.

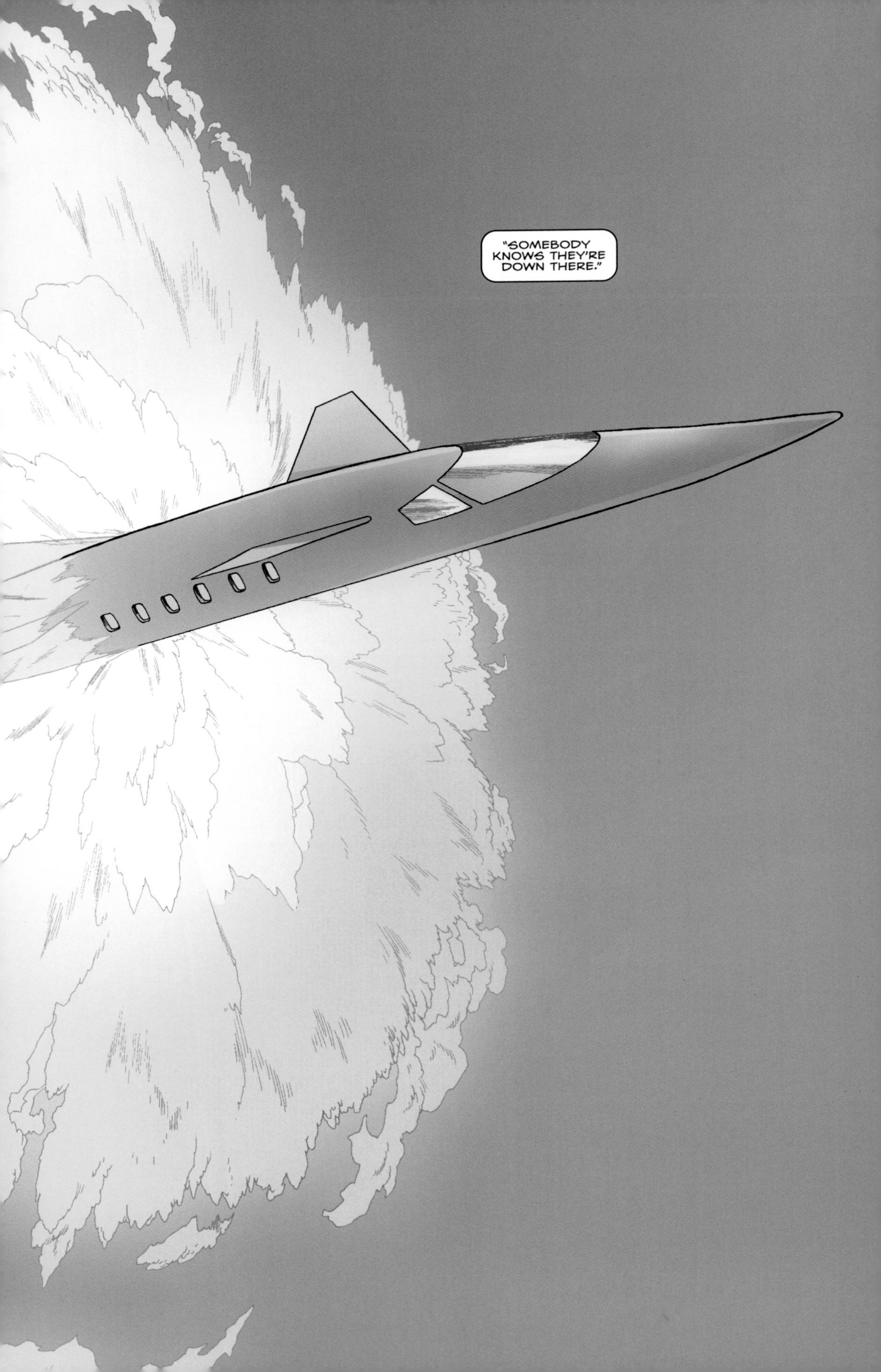
"SOMEBODY KNOWS THEY'RE DOWN THERE."

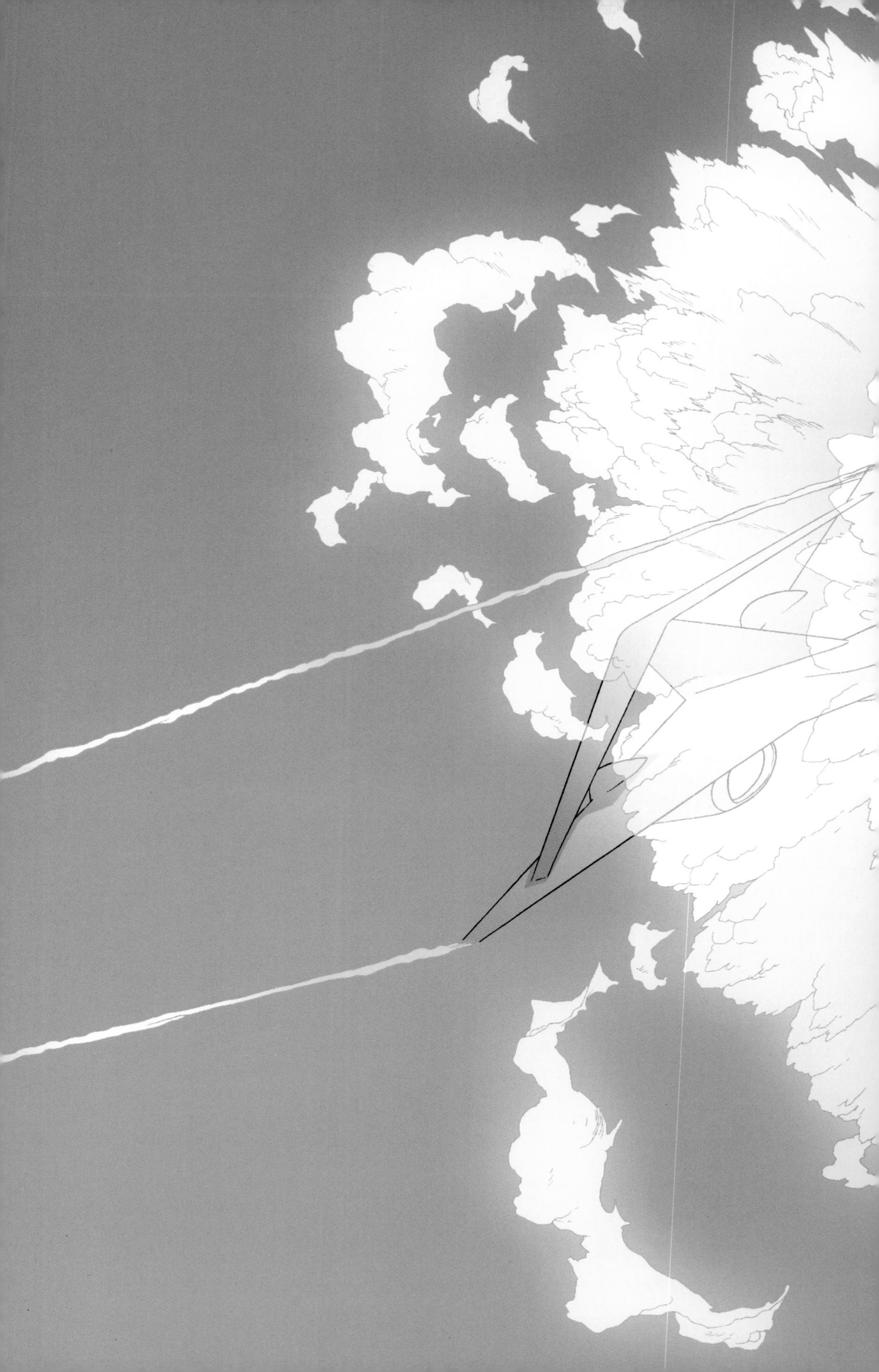

interview by Owen Anderson

ESQ *You were a professional tennis player before assuming your current position at World Corp. Were you trying to delay the inevitable?*

RT Maybe a little, but going to work for World Corp wasn't a foregone conclusion. I certainly wasn't pressured about it in any way. Emerson let me know I would always have a place there, and it was good to know I had that to fall back on. Tennis was something of an obsession, though, and playing professionally, going to Wimbledon and the U.S. Open was a dream come true. I would have been terribly unhappy if I hadn't pursued that.

ESQ *Do you still play?*

RT Not as much as I'd like. I've been doing a lot of work at one of our more remote locations, and going back and forth has curtailed just about all of my extra-curricular activities. Also, if I'm being entirely honest, my knees aren't what they once were.

ESQ *And what is your current opinion of World Corp after everything that has happened over the last few years?*

RT I think it's lost some of its luster. That's just a fact, and Emerson would give you the exact same response. We've taken some hits. Thomas left. Simon left. Dade has been out of the public eye for a very long time now. The biggest strike against us, though, has been the ubiquity of the company. Everyone knows what World Corp is, and everyone associates it with those four smiling science stars, as they were in their youth. World Corp has done some amazing things since then, but everything we do is judged against this legend, this… fairytale.

ESQ *With that in mind, is it unfair that scientists continue to dominate modern celebrity culture?*

RT That's an argument I was bored with before it even began, mainly because celebrity culture in and of itself has no inherent value. I was taught to regard everybody as equal. We all have different talents and we all have different weaknesses, but we're all people and we all matter. That said, I haven't heard about the comedian who discovered fire, or the football player who cured cancer.

ESQ *You have a long-standing reputation as an arch*

raconteur. Have you always had the gift of the gab?

RT Not at all. I was incredibly shy growing up. If you go back and look at those early films, you can see that straight away. I had trouble looking people in the eye, and I really didn't speak unless I was spoken to first.

ESQ *What changed?*

RT I figured out that women love to laugh. I used to get these hopeless crushes on girls who had no clue I even existed. I'd watch them go off with these boys who weren't particularly smart or good-looking, and it would drive me mad. Then one day, we were supposed to get into groups and tell each other about our dreams. I wound up telling the other kids about this strange dream I had where I was with a group of people hiding in a cold, damp cave, but we all had puppies. We were all terrified and cold, but if we tapped the puppies gently, they turned into warm logs. When I got to that part of the dream, the girls in my group started giggling. At first I was embarrassed, but then they wanted me to tell them more of my dreams and I gradually realized they were genuinely entertained by what I was saying. I've been using that to my advantage every since.

> 'Last night I dreamt that I ran into Paris Smith at a hotel — in Paris.'

ESQ *What's the most recent dream you can remember?*

RT Oh, I remember them all. Last night I dreamt that I ran into Paris Smith at a hotel — *in Paris*. I was in town for a conference and as I was checking in, she came up and started chatting with me like we were old friends. She invited me to join her for tea, and we were having such a wonderful time that when I awoke, I was disappointed it hadn't actually happened. She travels in somewhat more exclusive circles than I do, though, so I'm happy to have at least met her in my dreams.

ESQ *Tell us something you've never told anyone before.*

RT You know, clones can't have children. We can have sex, just like anyone, but we can't reproduce. So I wish I could have children. I'm in my 40s now and I have a nice life, but more and more I find that I envy people with children. I've been all around the world, I've seen and done some truly incredible things, but bringing a child into the world and sharing what I've learned with him or her, that's an experience I'll never have. ◆

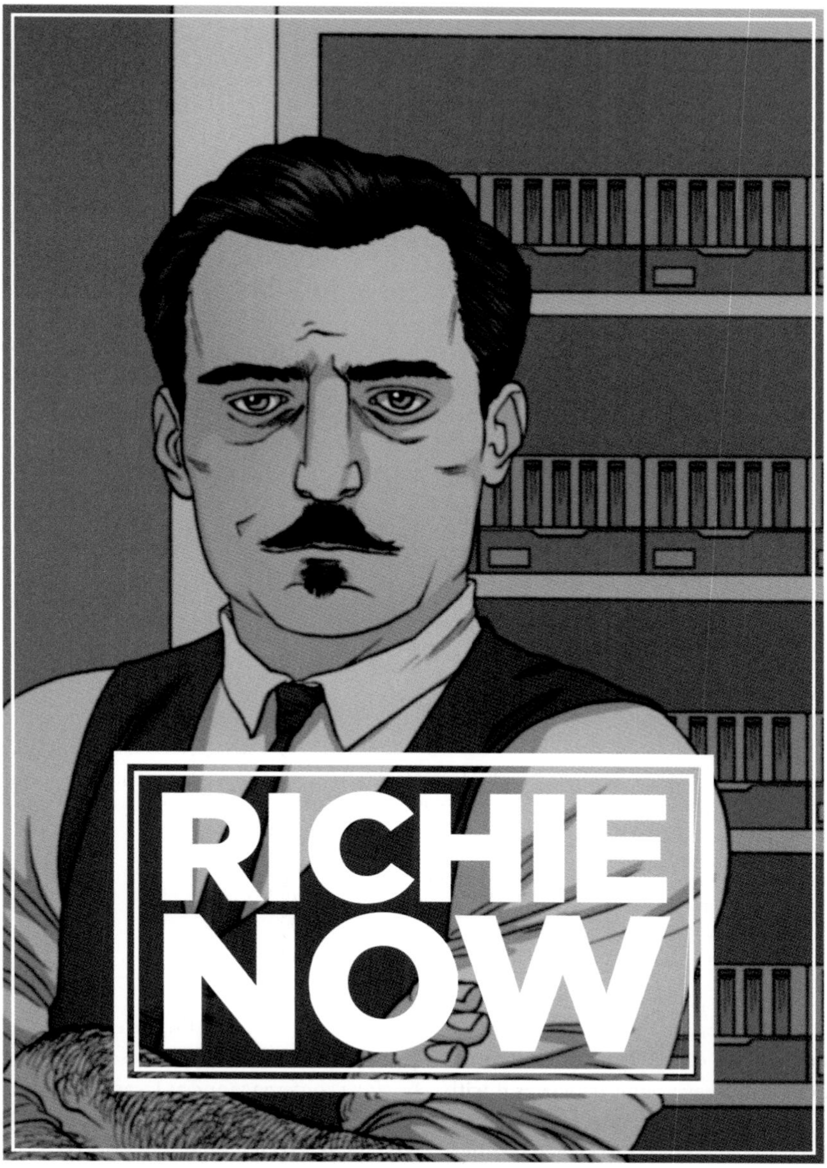
RICHIE
NOW

an ESQ&A with **RICHARD TEN**

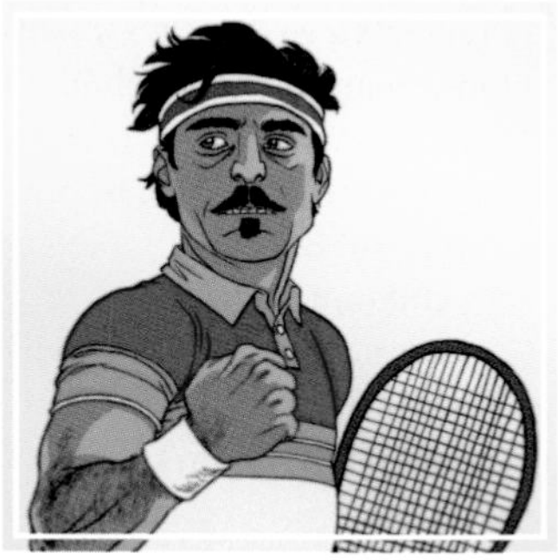

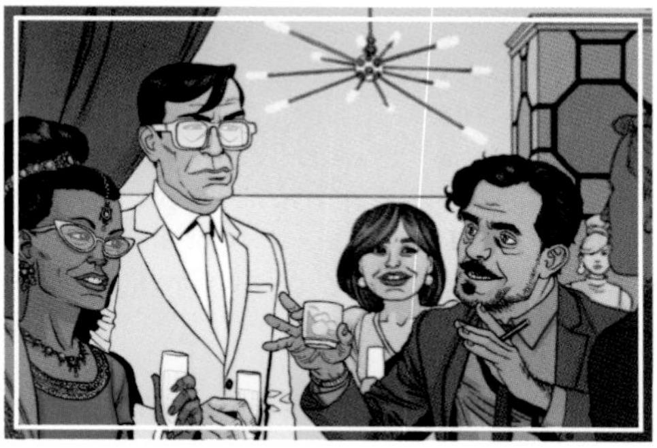

PHOTO CREDITS MAIN *David Yeoman* BOTTOM LEFT *Sporting Press Archive* BOTTOM RIGHT *Geddy Images*

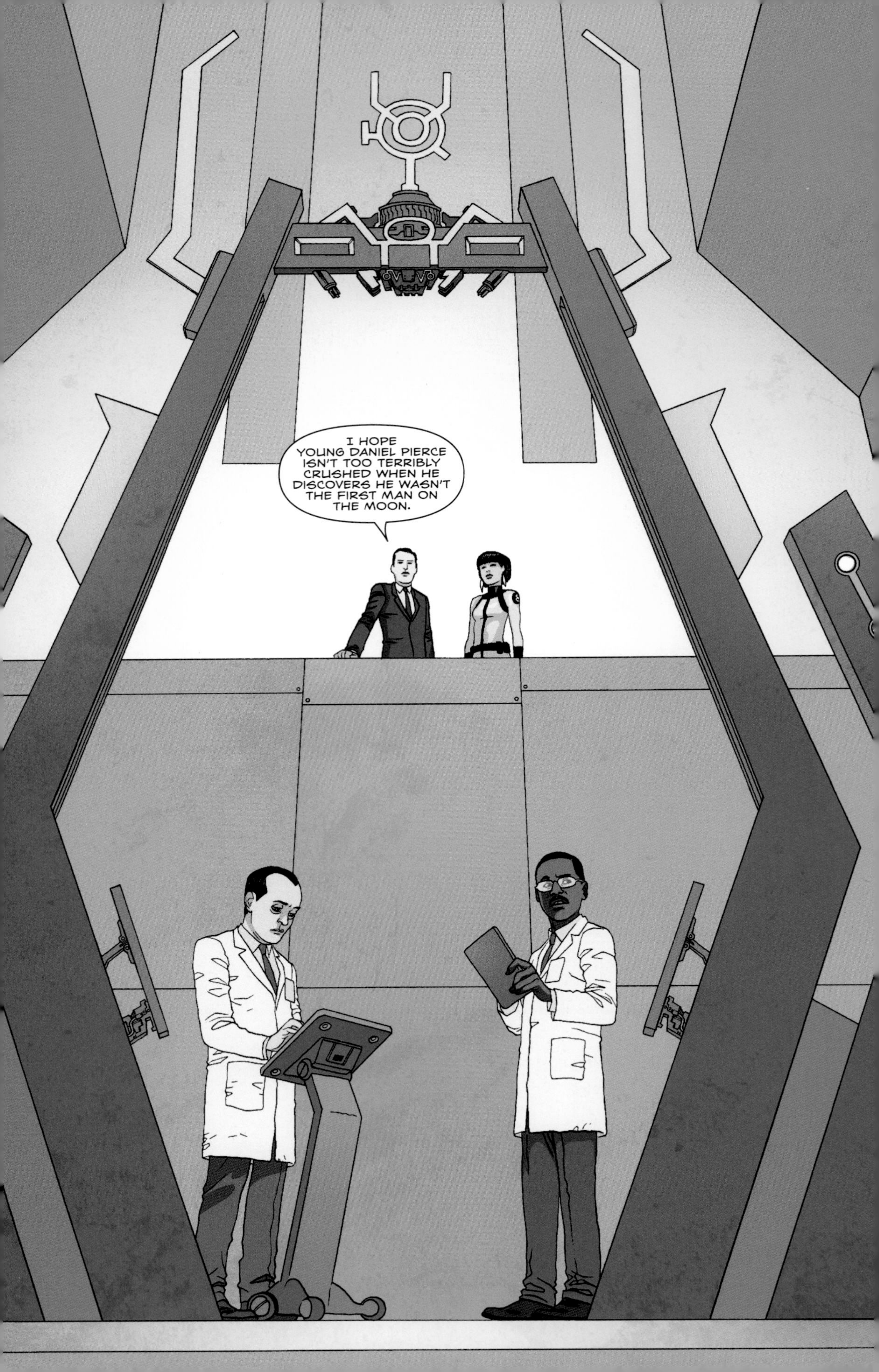
I HOPE YOUNG DANIEL PIERCE ISN'T TOO TERRIBLY CRUSHED WHEN HE DISCOVERS HE WASN'T THE FIRST MAN ON THE MOON.

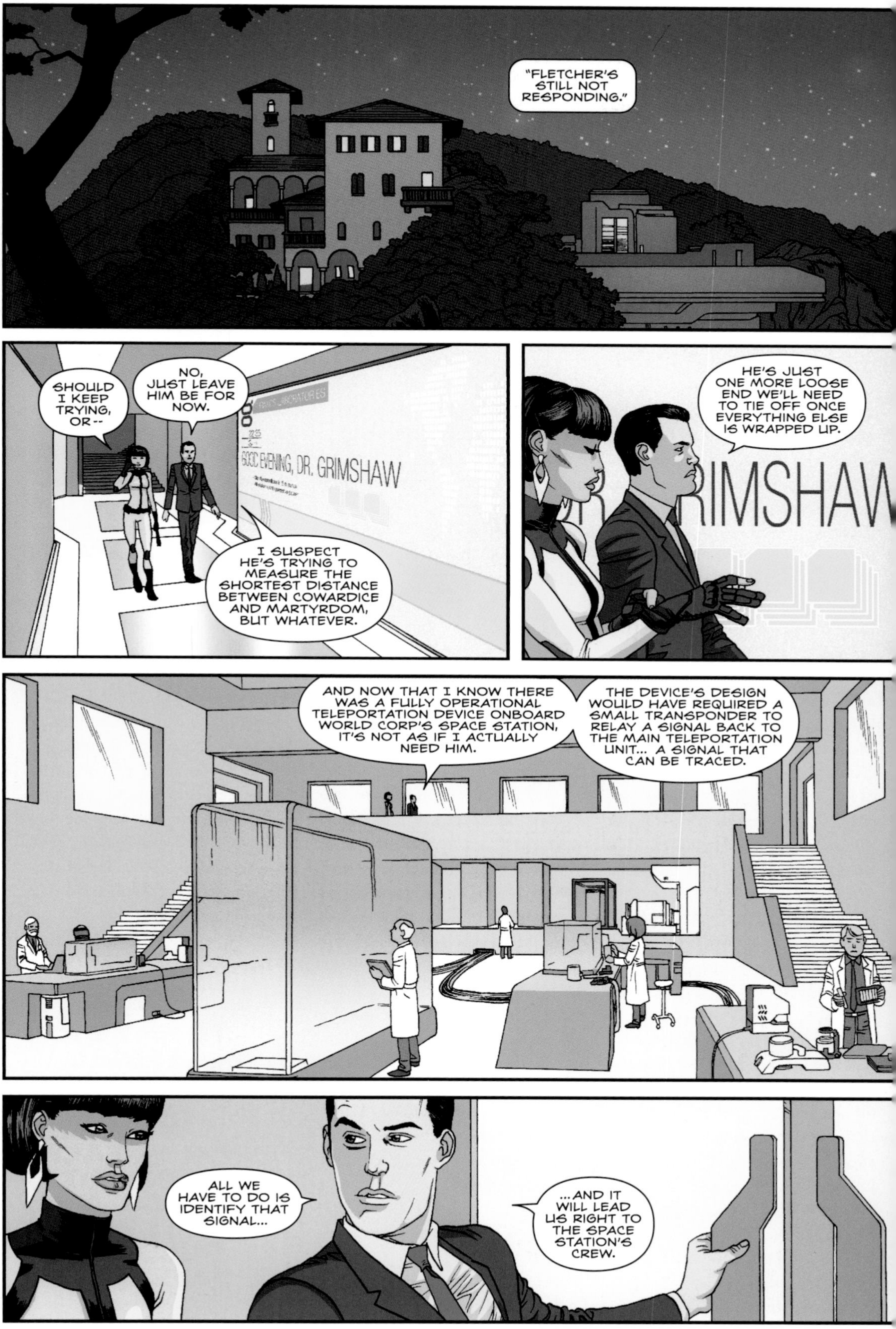
"FLETCHER'S STILL NOT RESPONDING."
SHOULD I KEEP TRYING, OR--
NO, JUST LEAVE HIM BE FOR NOW.
GOOD EVENING, DR. GRIMSHAW
I SUSPECT HE'S TRYING TO MEASURE THE SHORTEST DISTANCE BETWEEN COWARDICE AND MARTYRDOM, BUT WHATEVER.
HE'S JUST ONE MORE LOOSE END WE'LL NEED TO TIE OFF ONCE EVERYTHING ELSE IS WRAPPED UP.
AND NOW THAT I KNOW THERE WAS A FULLY OPERATIONAL TELEPORTATION DEVICE ONBOARD WORLD CORP'S SPACE STATION, IT'S NOT AS IF I ACTUALLY NEED HIM.
THE DEVICE'S DESIGN WOULD HAVE REQUIRED A SMALL TRANSPONDER TO RELAY A SIGNAL BACK TO THE MAIN TELEPORTATION UNIT... A SIGNAL THAT CAN BE TRACED.
ALL WE HAVE TO DO IS IDENTIFY THAT SIGNAL...
...AND IT WILL LEAD US RIGHT TO THE SPACE STATION'S CREW.

Few figures loom as large in the World Corp legend as **Jack Sugarman**. Viewed by many as a catalyst in Thomas Walker's decline from science superstar to gibberish-spouting acid casualty, it was long believed that Sugarman, like Walker, had succumbed to the effects of his Herculean drug intake years ago. As it turns out, though, he's alive and well in the south of France, eking out a living as a street artist and *bon vivant*, cheerfully telling anyone who cares to hear about his adventures with science's most infamous counter culture icon...

HELLO

I FIRST MET THOMAS WALKER VERY early on, well before he'd joined up with the World Corp. blokes. I was in the States working as a roadie for a band called Hit It. They broke up when the tour reached Arizona, and I'd heard some interesting things were starting to kick off on the West Coast, so instead of just going home to England with the rest of the crew, I hitchhiked to Los Angeles. When I got there, posters were up all over town for a talk Tommy was giving at UCLA. I think it was actually his first speaking engagement in the US, and I thought to myself, "Jacky, me lad, you should go to that!"

Tommy and I were both from Cambridge, so obviously I'd heard of him. He was quite the local hero, even before things took off for him on an international level. He'd been winning science fairs since he was about eight, and he'd written some papers that created quite a bit of excitement while he was at university. He also had a reputation for having something of an eye for the ladies, as well as a seemingly unlimited appetite for, shall we say, libations of a distinctly chemical nature. Sharing his predilection for the latter, I went to the talk at UCLA and then waited around until afterwards to see if he'd be interested in sampling some acid I'd come into, by way of Hit It's singer, Mike Torres. Mikey claimed to be of some relation to Esme, but that's a tale for another time, probably. Longish story shortish: When Tommy and I finally came back to Earth, we were on a beach in Rosarita, Mexico, and it was a full eight days later.

Things were pretty topsy-turvy for Tommy 'round about then, so I didn't see him again until a few months later, when he turned up in London at a surprise party for my birthday. He gave me a very nice bottle of Riesling, quite expensive, and an autographed copy of one of Felix Hoenikker's best sci-fi novels, which I found quite touching, considering we'd really only just met.

GOODBYE

TOMMY AND I SAW EACH OTHER less and less frequently once he joined up with World Corp. and on the occasion I was around for one of their media dos, I could tell I was viewed as a negative influence. I'd moved to San Francisco by then, though, and I was starting to get into the underground art scene, so really, things were going in different directions for us at that point. He did pop over for a visit every now and again, though, and it was on one of those trips I introduced him to some rebellious young science types I'd fallen in with, the SF Mall Aces. They were mad about him, just really looked up to him, and he seemed quite taken with their devil-may-care outlook. Some of that lot went on to form what everyone these days calls the Science Punk movement.

Eventually, I moved back to England, and then I got it into my head that traveling around Europe and painting whatever caught my eye might be a pleasant way to while away my time. One of the last times I saw Tommy was in Paris, actually, not long after he'd left World Corp. Everybody talks about how out of it he was during that period, but if you ask me, that was all a sham, an act he was putting on to get out of the spotlight once and for all. He seemed very focused when I saw him, very intent, and he talked at great length about the very real possibility of traveling, not just to other worlds, but between dimensions, and within our lifetime. We were sharing a Canterbury Carrot at the time, and honestly, I've never heard anyone as lucid or articulate. He bought a painting I'd done of the River Seine at dusk, too—he said he could live in that painting—and I always found that strangely significant.

cont. ▶

'WHEN TOMMY AND I FINALLY CAME BACK TO EARTH, WE WERE ON A BEACH IN ROSARITA, MEXICO, AND IT WAS A FULL EIGHT DAYS LATER.'

MY FRIEND JACK

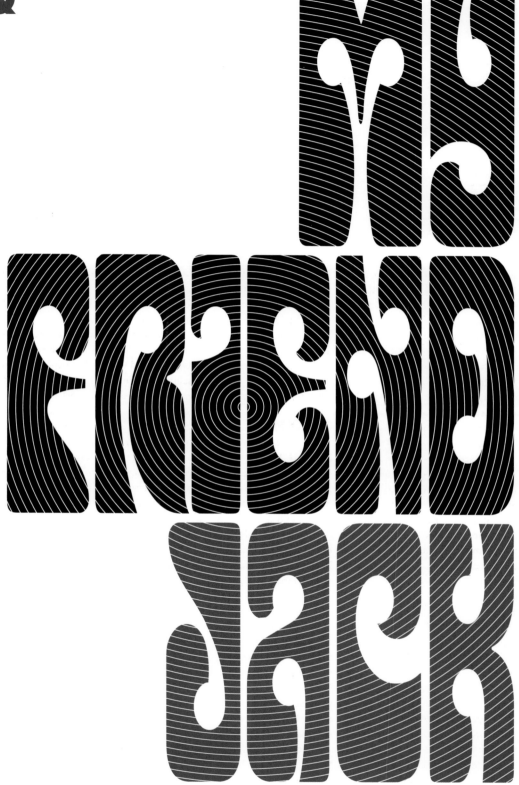

as told to **Sydney Gill**

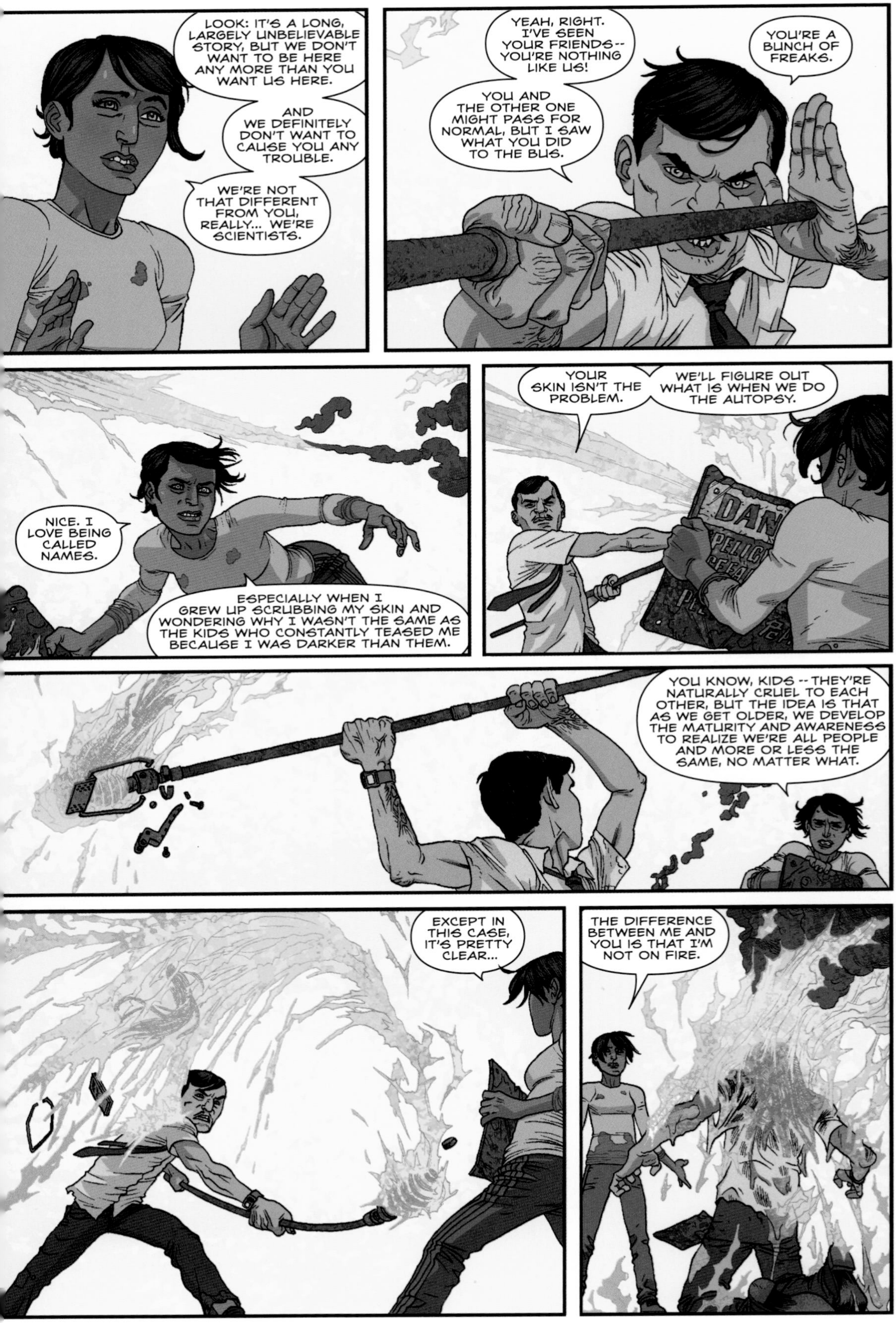
LOOK: IT'S A LONG, LARGELY UNBELIEVABLE STORY, BUT WE DON'T WANT TO BE HERE ANY MORE THAN YOU WANT US HERE.
AND WE DEFINITELY DON'T WANT TO CAUSE YOU ANY TROUBLE.
WE'RE NOT THAT DIFFERENT FROM YOU, REALLY... WE'RE SCIENTISTS.
YEAH, RIGHT. I'VE SEEN YOUR FRIENDS-- YOU'RE NOTHING LIKE US!
YOU AND THE OTHER ONE MIGHT PASS FOR NORMAL, BUT I SAW WHAT YOU DID TO THE BUS.
YOU'RE A BUNCH OF FREAKS.
NICE. I LOVE BEING CALLED NAMES.
ESPECIALLY WHEN I GREW UP SCRUBBING MY SKIN AND WONDERING WHY I WASN'T THE SAME AS THE KIDS WHO CONSTANTLY TEASED ME BECAUSE I WAS DARKER THAN THEM.
YOUR SKIN ISN'T THE PROBLEM.
WE'LL FIGURE OUT WHAT IS WHEN WE DO THE AUTOPSY.
YOU KNOW, KIDS -- THEY'RE NATURALLY CRUEL TO EACH OTHER, BUT THE IDEA IS THAT AS WE GET OLDER, WE DEVELOP THE MATURITY AND AWARENESS TO REALIZE WE'RE ALL PEOPLE AND MORE OR LESS THE SAME, NO MATTER WHAT.
EXCEPT IN THIS CASE, IT'S PRETTY CLEAR...
THE DIFFERENCE BETWEEN ME AND YOU IS THAT I'M NOT ON FIRE.

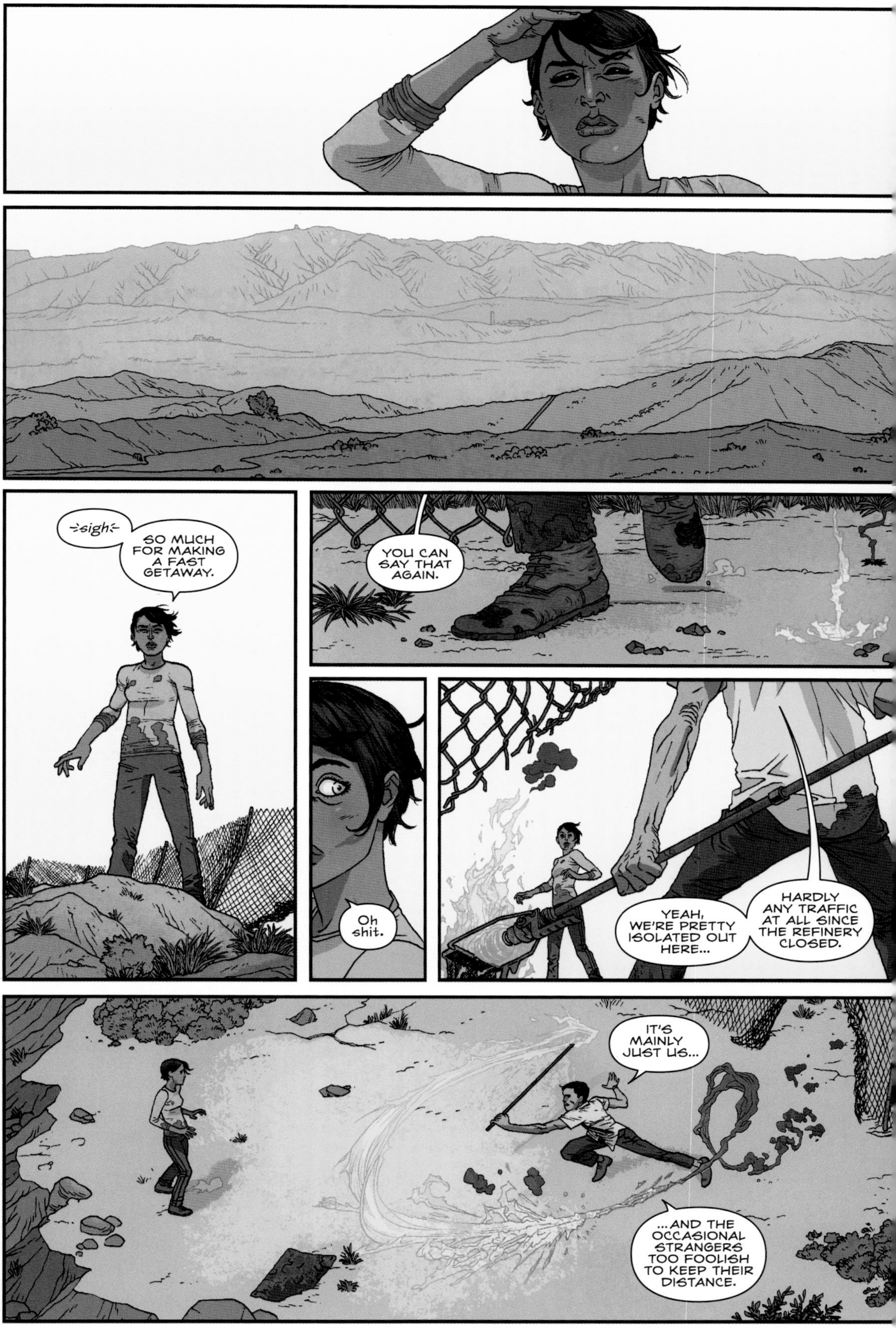

-sigh-
SO MUCH FOR MAKING A FAST GETAWAY.
YOU CAN SAY THAT AGAIN.
Oh shit.
YEAH, WE'RE PRETTY ISOLATED OUT HERE...
HARDLY ANY TRAFFIC AT ALL SINCE THE REFINERY CLOSED.
IT'S MAINLY JUST US...
...AND THE OCCASIONAL STRANGERS TOO FOOLISH TO KEEP THEIR DISTANCE.

WHAT IS THAT?

TELEKINESIS?

YOU KNOW, I DON'T KNOW.

I THINK IT MAYBE HAS MORE TO DO WITH SPEED, THOUGH.

WATCH.

WOW. THAT DROPPED SO FAST I ALMOST COULDN'T SEE IT.

YEAH, AND CATCHING IT HURT LIKE A MOTHERFUCKER.

PRETTY DAMN COOL, ALL THINGS CONSIDERED.

I'M STILL GETTING MY HEAD AROUND IT, BUT SEEMS LIKE I CAN SPEED THINGS UP OR SLOW THINGS DOWN.

Ugh. WHICH PROBABLY SOUNDS ALL KINDS OF CALLOUS, COMING FROM ME.

LOOK, KURT... I'M SORRY ABOUT THE WAY I ACTED EARLIER. YOU JUST LOOK SO... DIFFERENT.

ARE *YOU* OKAY?

LIKE, WITH ALL... THIS.

I...

YOU CAN'T FIGHT... LIFE.

IT GOES ON WITH OR WITHOUT YOU.

I ANTICIPATE THIS WILL BE TRAUMATIC FOR CYNTHIA AND THE KIDS... BUT HOPEFULLY THE FACT I'M ALIVE AND WELL OUTWEIGHS THE... CHANGES.

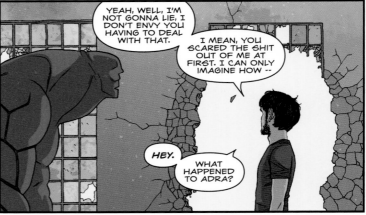

YEAH, WELL, I'M NOT GONNA LIE, I DON'T ENVY YOU HAVING TO DEAL WITH THAT.

I MEAN, YOU SCARED THE SHIT OUT OF ME AT FIRST. I CAN ONLY IMAGINE HOW --

HEY.

WHAT HAPPENED TO ADRA?

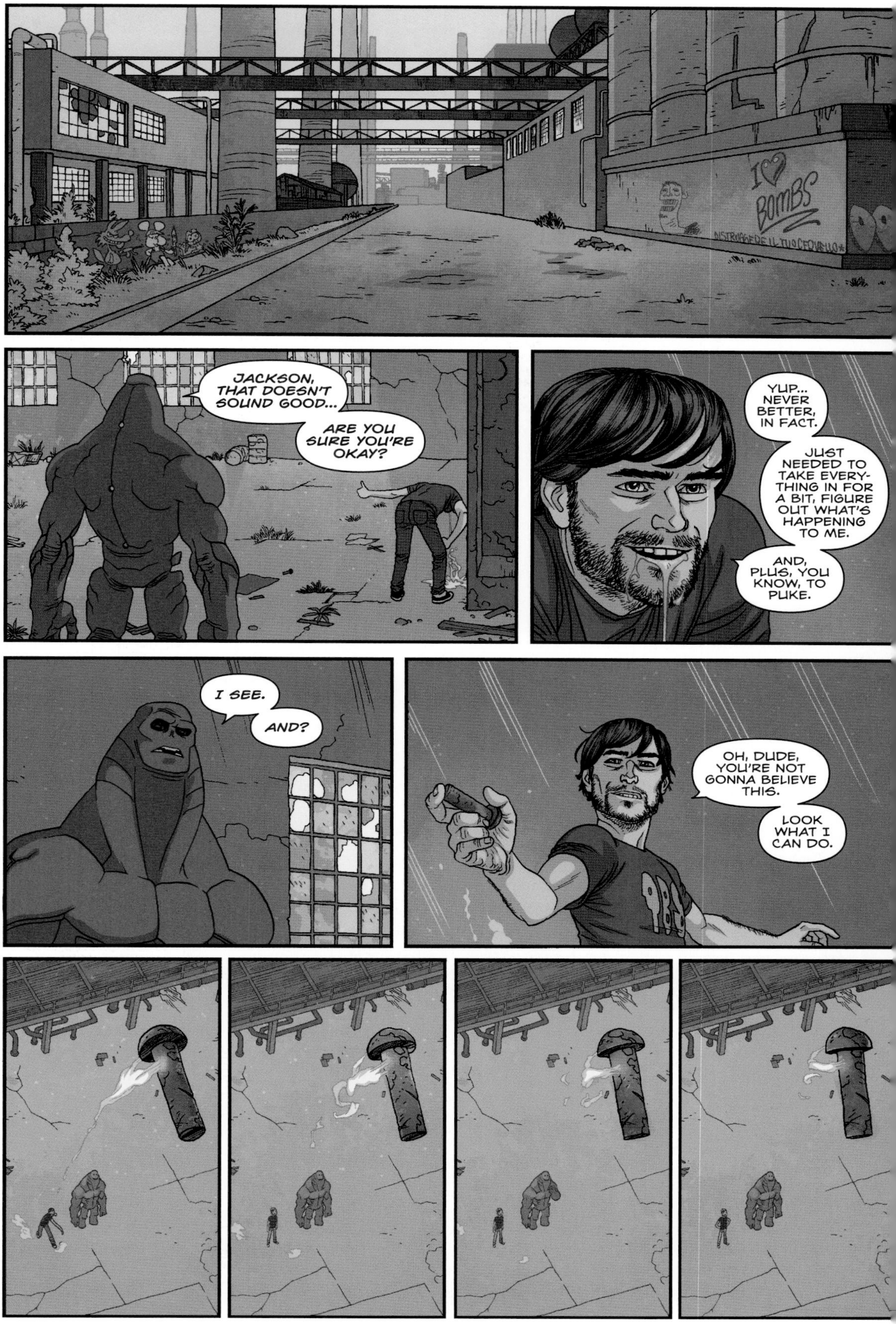
I ♥ BOMBS
JACKSON, THAT DOESN'T SOUND GOOD...
ARE YOU SURE YOU'RE OKAY?
YUP... NEVER BETTER, IN FACT.
JUST NEEDED TO TAKE EVERY-THING IN FOR A BIT, FIGURE OUT WHAT'S HAPPENING TO ME.
AND, PLUS, YOU KNOW, TO PUKE.
I SEE.
AND?
OH, DUDE, YOU'RE NOT GONNA BELIEVE THIS.
LOOK WHAT I CAN DO.

'If *I* Ruled The World'

Shocking Statements by Science Stars Who Should Know Better!

YOU KNOW the drill: each month, I trawl the mega-hertz and scour the broadsheets for examples of the world's best science stars at their megalomaniacal worst, and we count down the top ten most outlandish of their unexpurgated statements here for your amusement and/or edification. Typically, I like to cast my net fairly wide, but Simon Grimshaw's recent essay on numerous problems facing Planet Earth has revealed itself to be an unexpected treasure trove of frankly bizarre quotes that may tell us more about the former World Corp founder's true ambitions than he intended…

10 "People of advanced age are only useful to a certain point, and once that usefulness is exhausted, they are surplus to our society's needs. Simply put, they are a drain on our resources, and the notion that we have some moral duty to provide for members of society who offer nothing in return is frankly preposterous."

9 *"The brains of executed criminals should be routinely studied in an effort to isolate the conditions that produce such undesirables and eliminate them."*

8 "I don't think my enthusiasm for human cloning has ever been in doubt, but I do think it's worth noting that I view unregulated cloning to be just as harmful to our planet's well-being as standard reproduction. Whether one is cloning him/herself or having children, the addition of any type of person adds to the population, and honestly, doing both should not be permissible. If someone chooses to be cloned, that person should be ineligible for having children, and vice versa."

7 *"I could cure all manner of diseases tomorrow, starting with cancer, but without a committed effort toward real and sustained population control, such a gesture would ultimately be meaningless. The human race, unregulated as it is now, is a burden on our planet, and if our population continues to grow at projected levels, threatens to destroy the world as we know it."*

6 "Granted, there are those within the so-called 'science punk' community who would disagree, but truthfully, that entire movement is a problem at best ignored and at worst, eradicated through the concentrated efforts of a great many men skilled in the use of flamethrowers."

> **"I could cure all manner of diseases tomorrow, starting with cancer... such a gesture would ultimately be meaningless."**
> **– SIMON GRIMSHAW**

5 *"Eugenics tends to be a controversial concept, but looking at the facts as accumulated over the last century, had such policies been enacted on a global basis, not only would population growth have been curbed, the overall quality of mankind would be greatly improved."*

4 "There is no question in my mind that allowing criminals and malcontents to continue to benefit from our society is more worthy of moral outrage than capital punishment, and there's no getting around it: Any form of incarceration, no matter how cruel or inhumane, is a benefit."

3 *"Without more stringent regulation, not only immigration but international travel will almost assuredly become a very serious risk to global stability in the decades to come."*

2 "Cutting the birth rate is a simple enough process: The entire world population could easily be sterilized by introducing a birth control agent to our water supplies. Should one choose to reproduce, prospective parents would then submit to a rigorous application process in order to obtain clearance for the antidote. Even more promising, studies we've conducted at Grimshaw Holdings suggest it may in fact be possible to actually transmit sterility via sexual contact."

1 *"By my estimate, unless we begin taking drastic steps now, today, our future on this planet is increasingly bleak. I'm not exaggerating at all when I state that within all likelihood, the entire human race will be either dead or in serious trouble within 100 years time."* ∎

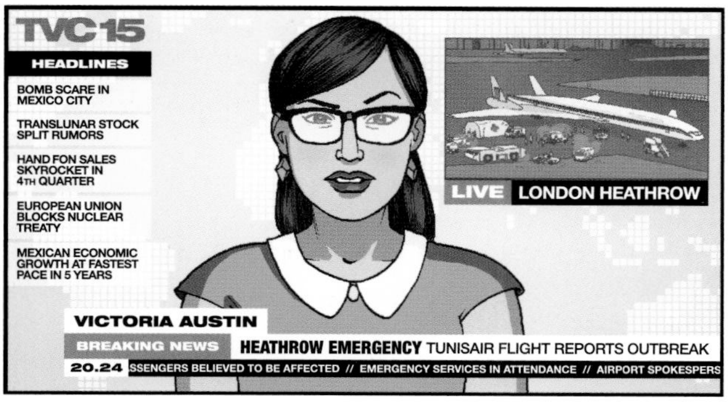
TVC15
HEADLINES
BOMB SCARE IN MEXICO CITY
TRANSLUNAR STOCK SPLIT RUMORS
HAND FON SALES SKYROCKET IN 4TH QUARTER
EUROPEAN UNION BLOCKS NUCLEAR TREATY
MEXICAN ECONOMIC GROWTH AT FASTEST PACE IN 5 YEARS
LIVE LONDON HEATHROW
VICTORIA AUSTIN
BREAKING NEWS HEATHROW EMERGENCY TUNISAIR FLIGHT REPORTS OUTBREAK
20.24 SSENGERS BELIEVED TO BE AFFECTED // EMERGENCY SERVICES IN ATTENDANCE // AIRPORT SPOKESPERS

"FOR THOSE OF YOU JUST JOINING US, WE'RE GETTING AN UPDATE NOW ON THE SITUATION DEVELOPING AT LONDON'S HEATHROW AIRPORT, WHERE A SKYLARK 999 TUNISAIR FLIGHT TU-919 FROM CARTHAGE HAS LANDED IN A STATE OF MEDICAL EMERGENCY.

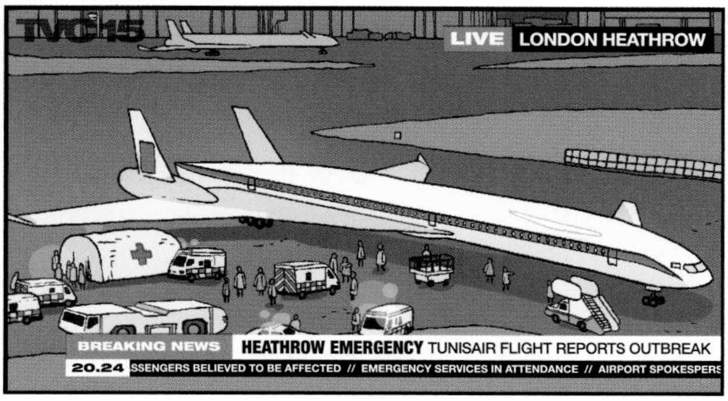
TVC15
LIVE LONDON HEATHROW
BREAKING NEWS HEATHROW EMERGENCY TUNISAIR FLIGHT REPORTS OUTBREAK
20.24 SSENGERS BELIEVED TO BE AFFECTED // EMERGENCY SERVICES IN ATTENDANCE // AIRPORT SPOKESPERS

"AN AIRPORT SPOKESMAN IS NOW CONFIRMING THAT PASSENGERS HAVE YET TO BE EVACUATED, BUT AT LEAST FIVE PEOPLE ARE BELIEVED TO BE SERIOUSLY ILL AND POSSIBLY CONTAGIOUS, AND HAZMAT-CLAD MEDICAL CREWS ARE ARRIVING ON THE SCENE.

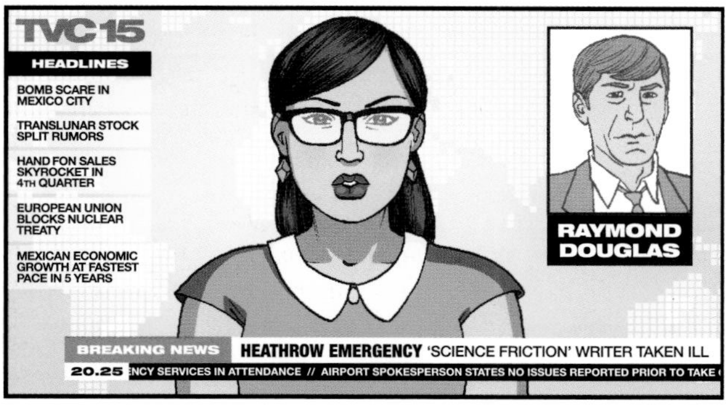
TVC15
HEADLINES
BOMB SCARE IN MEXICO CITY
TRANSLUNAR STOCK SPLIT RUMORS
HAND FON SALES SKYROCKET IN 4TH QUARTER
EUROPEAN UNION BLOCKS NUCLEAR TREATY
MEXICAN ECONOMIC GROWTH AT FASTEST PACE IN 5 YEARS
RAYMOND DOUGLAS
BREAKING NEWS HEATHROW EMERGENCY 'SCIENCE FRICTION' WRITER TAKEN ILL
20.25 ENCY SERVICES IN ATTENDANCE // AIRPORT SPOKESPERSON STATES NO ISSUES REPORTED PRIOR TO TAKE

"ACCORDING TO EARLIER REPORTS, FLIGHT TU-919 FIRST RADIOED AHEAD TO HEATHROW WHEN FAMED SCIENCE FRICTION AUTHOR RAYMOND DOUGLAS BECAME 'EXTREMELY SICK' DURING THE FLIGHT. TWO OTHER PASSENGERS AND A MEMBER OF THE FLIGHT CREW WERE DESCRIBED AS HAVING SIMILAR SYMPTOMS.

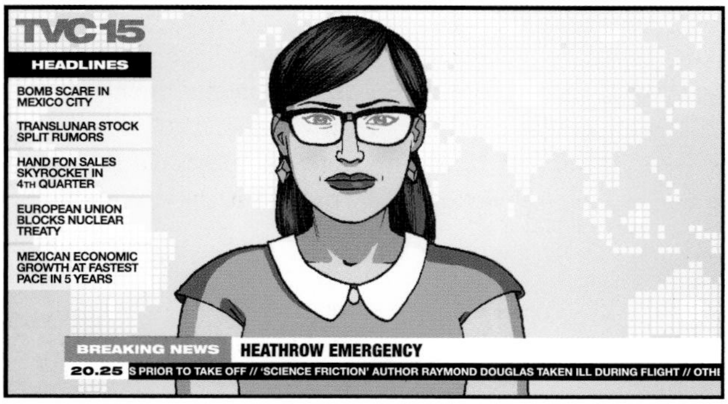
TVC15
HEADLINES
BOMB SCARE IN MEXICO CITY
TRANSLUNAR STOCK SPLIT RUMORS
HAND FON SALES SKYROCKET IN 4TH QUARTER
EUROPEAN UNION BLOCKS NUCLEAR TREATY
MEXICAN ECONOMIC GROWTH AT FASTEST PACE IN 5 YEARS
BREAKING NEWS HEATHROW EMERGENCY
20.25 S PRIOR TO TAKE OFF // 'SCIENCE FRICTION' AUTHOR RAYMOND DOUGLAS TAKEN ILL DURING FLIGHT // OTHI

"IN RELATED NEWS, TUNISIA IS ONE OF SEVERAL PLACES WITH REPORTS OF STRANGE LIGHTS AND OBJECTS FALLING FROM THE SKY OR APPEARING SEEMINGLY OUT OF NOWHERE OVER THE LAST 24 HOURS. SIMILARLY, THE SITUATION AT HEATHROW IS DRAWING NEW ATTENTION TO RECENT REMARKS BY SIMON GRIMSHAW REGARDING INCREASED RESTRICTIONS ON INTERNATIONAL TRAVEL..."

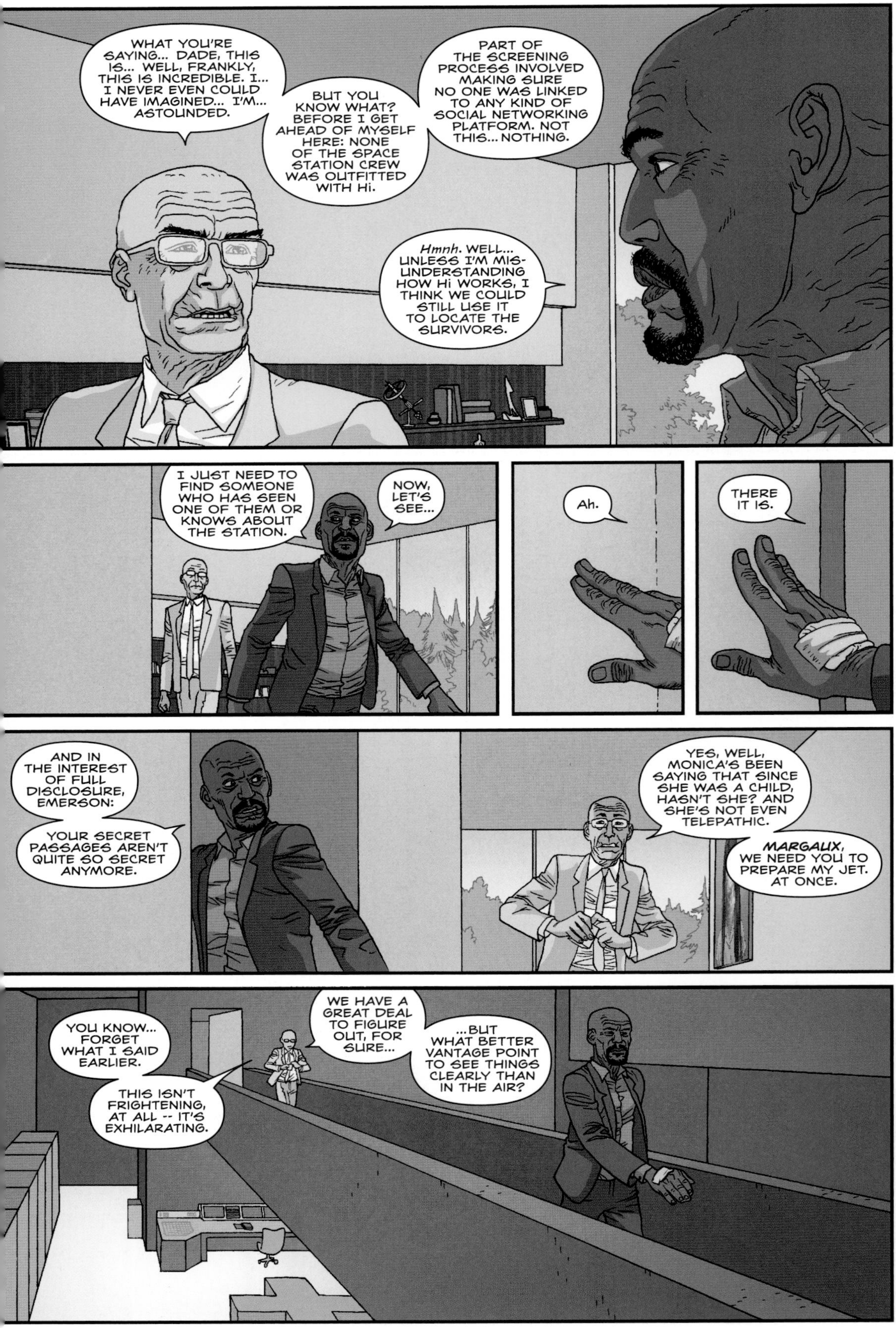
WHAT YOU'RE SAYING... DADE, THIS IS... WELL, FRANKLY, THIS IS INCREDIBLE. I... I NEVER EVEN COULD HAVE IMAGINED... I'M... ASTOUNDED.
BUT YOU KNOW WHAT? BEFORE I GET AHEAD OF MYSELF HERE: NONE OF THE SPACE STATION CREW WAS OUTFITTED WITH Hi.
PART OF THE SCREENING PROCESS INVOLVED MAKING SURE NO ONE WAS LINKED TO ANY KIND OF SOCIAL NETWORKING PLATFORM. NOT THIS... NOTHING.
Hmnh. WELL... UNLESS I'M MIS-UNDERSTANDING HOW Hi WORKS, I THINK WE COULD STILL USE IT TO LOCATE THE SURVIVORS.
I JUST NEED TO FIND SOMEONE WHO HAS SEEN ONE OF THEM OR KNOWS ABOUT THE STATION.
NOW, LET'S SEE...
Ah.
THERE IT IS.
AND IN THE INTEREST OF FULL DISCLOSURE, EMERSON:
YOUR SECRET PASSAGES AREN'T QUITE SO SECRET ANYMORE.
YES, WELL, MONICA'S BEEN SAYING THAT SINCE SHE WAS A CHILD, HASN'T SHE? AND SHE'S NOT EVEN TELEPATHIC.
MARGAUX, WE NEED YOU TO PREPARE MY JET. AT ONCE.
YOU KNOW... FORGET WHAT I SAID EARLIER.
THIS ISN'T FRIGHTENING, AT ALL -- IT'S EXHILARATING.
WE HAVE A GREAT DEAL TO FIGURE OUT, FOR SURE...
...BUT WHAT BETTER VANTAGE POINT TO SEE THINGS CLEARLY THAN IN THE AIR?

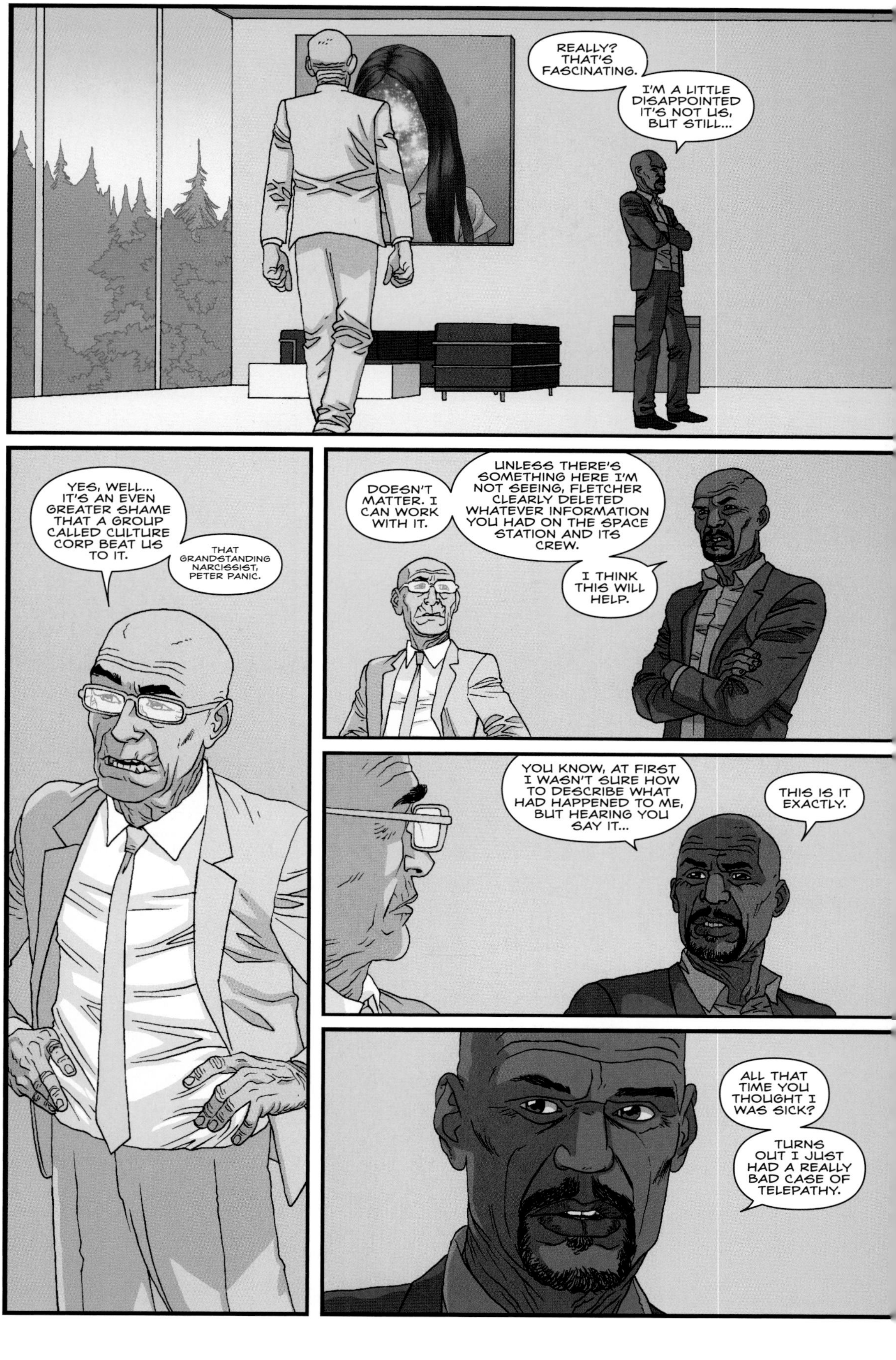
REALLY? THAT'S FASCINATING.
I'M A LITTLE DISAPPOINTED IT'S NOT US, BUT STILL...
YES, WELL... IT'S AN EVEN GREATER SHAME THAT A GROUP CALLED CULTURE CORP BEAT US TO IT.
THAT GRANDSTANDING NARCISSIST, PETER PANIC.
UNLESS THERE'S SOMETHING HERE I'M NOT SEEING, FLETCHER CLEARLY DELETED WHATEVER INFORMATION YOU HAD ON THE SPACE STATION AND ITS CREW.
DOESN'T MATTER. I CAN WORK WITH IT.
I THINK THIS WILL HELP.
YOU KNOW, AT FIRST I WASN'T SURE HOW TO DESCRIBE WHAT HAD HAPPENED TO ME, BUT HEARING YOU SAY IT...
THIS IS IT EXACTLY.
ALL THAT TIME YOU THOUGHT I WAS SICK?
TURNS OUT I JUST HAD A REALLY BAD CASE OF TELEPATHY.

MONICA? BUT... HOW...?

DADE, I'M SORRY BUT THIS REALLY IS QUITE A LOT TO TAKE IN ALL AT ONCE.

YOU THINK?

WELL, JUST IMAGINE WHAT IT WAS LIKE FOR ME ALL THOSE YEARS, LYING THERE, INFORMATION JUST POURING INTO MY HEAD.

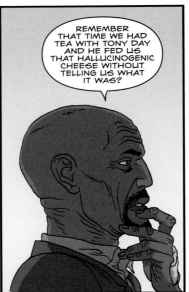

REMEMBER THAT TIME WE HAD TEA WITH TONY DAY AND HE FED US THAT HALLUCINOGENIC CHEESE WITHOUT TELLING US WHAT IT WAS?

REMEMBER HOW HELPLESS WE FELT, TRIPPING, COMPLETELY OUT OF CONTROL, SOUND AND COLOR WASHING OVER US AS WE HELD HANDS AND DESPERATELY HOPED IT WOULD STOP?

WELL... THAT WAS ME. FOR *YEARS*.

WHAT IS THIS HERE? THIS *Hi*?

Enh, IT'S A... IT'S A SOCIAL MEDIA PLATFORM...

THE MOST ADVANCED SOCIAL MEDIA PLATFORM EVER, ACTUALLY.

ITS MAKERS BILL IT AS SOMETHING AKIN TO *"SIMULATED TELEPATHY."*

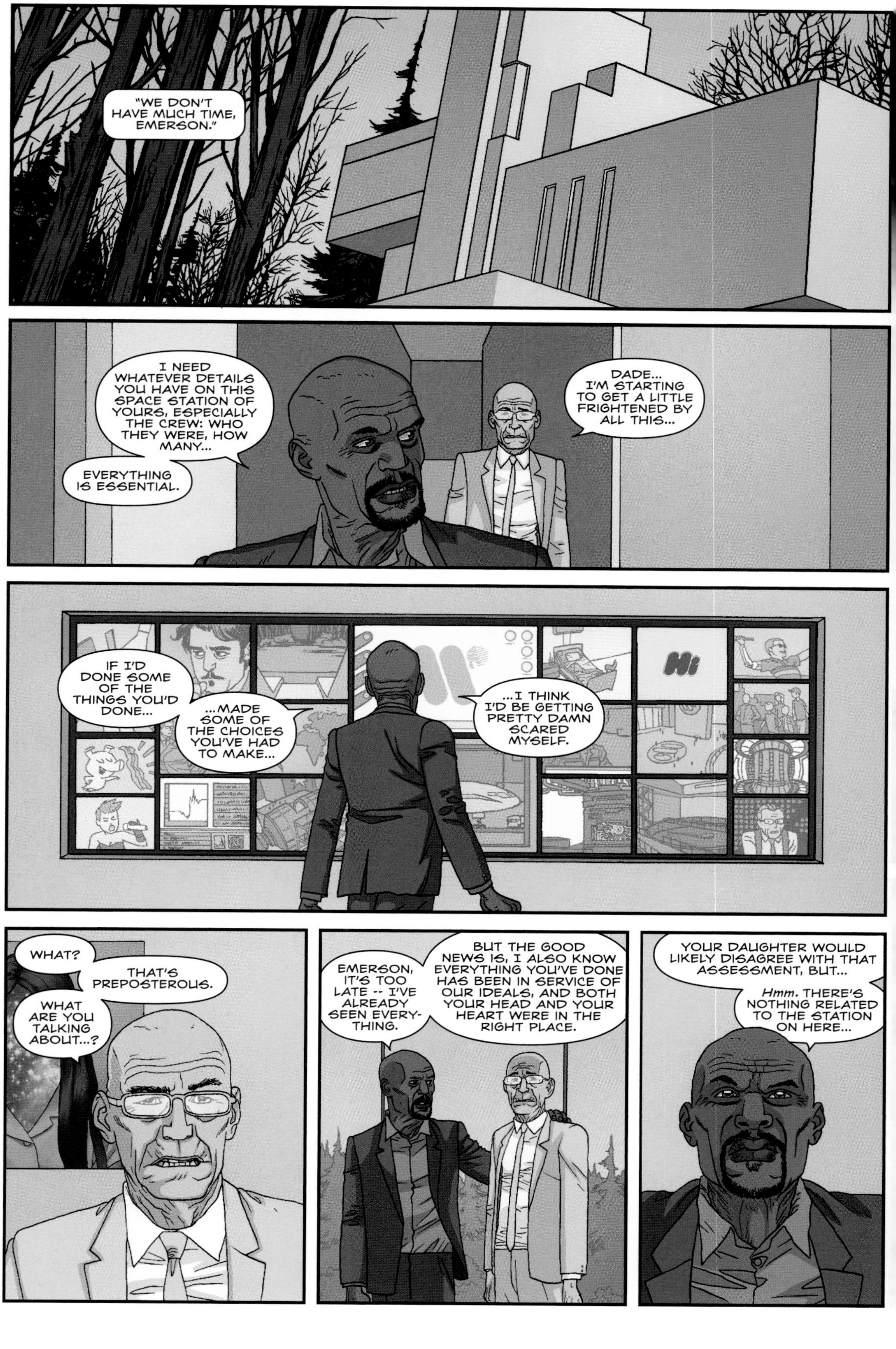
"WE DON'T HAVE MUCH TIME, EMERSON."
I NEED WHATEVER DETAILS YOU HAVE ON THIS SPACE STATION OF YOURS, ESPECIALLY THE CREW: WHO THEY WERE, HOW MANY...
EVERYTHING IS ESSENTIAL.
DADE... I'M STARTING TO GET A LITTLE FRIGHTENED BY ALL THIS...
IF I'D DONE SOME OF THE THINGS YOU'D DONE...
...MADE SOME OF THE CHOICES YOU'VE HAD TO MAKE...
...I THINK I'D BE GETTING PRETTY DAMN SCARED MYSELF.
Hi
WHAT?
THAT'S PREPOSTEROUS.
WHAT ARE YOU TALKING ABOUT...?
EMERSON, IT'S TOO LATE -- I'VE ALREADY SEEN EVERYTHING.
BUT THE GOOD NEWS IS, I ALSO KNOW EVERYTHING YOU'VE DONE HAS BEEN IN SERVICE OF OUR IDEALS, AND BOTH YOUR HEAD AND YOUR HEART WERE IN THE RIGHT PLACE.
YOUR DAUGHTER WOULD LIKELY DISAGREE WITH THAT ASSESSMENT, BUT...
Hmm. THERE'S NOTHING RELATED TO THE STATION ON HERE...

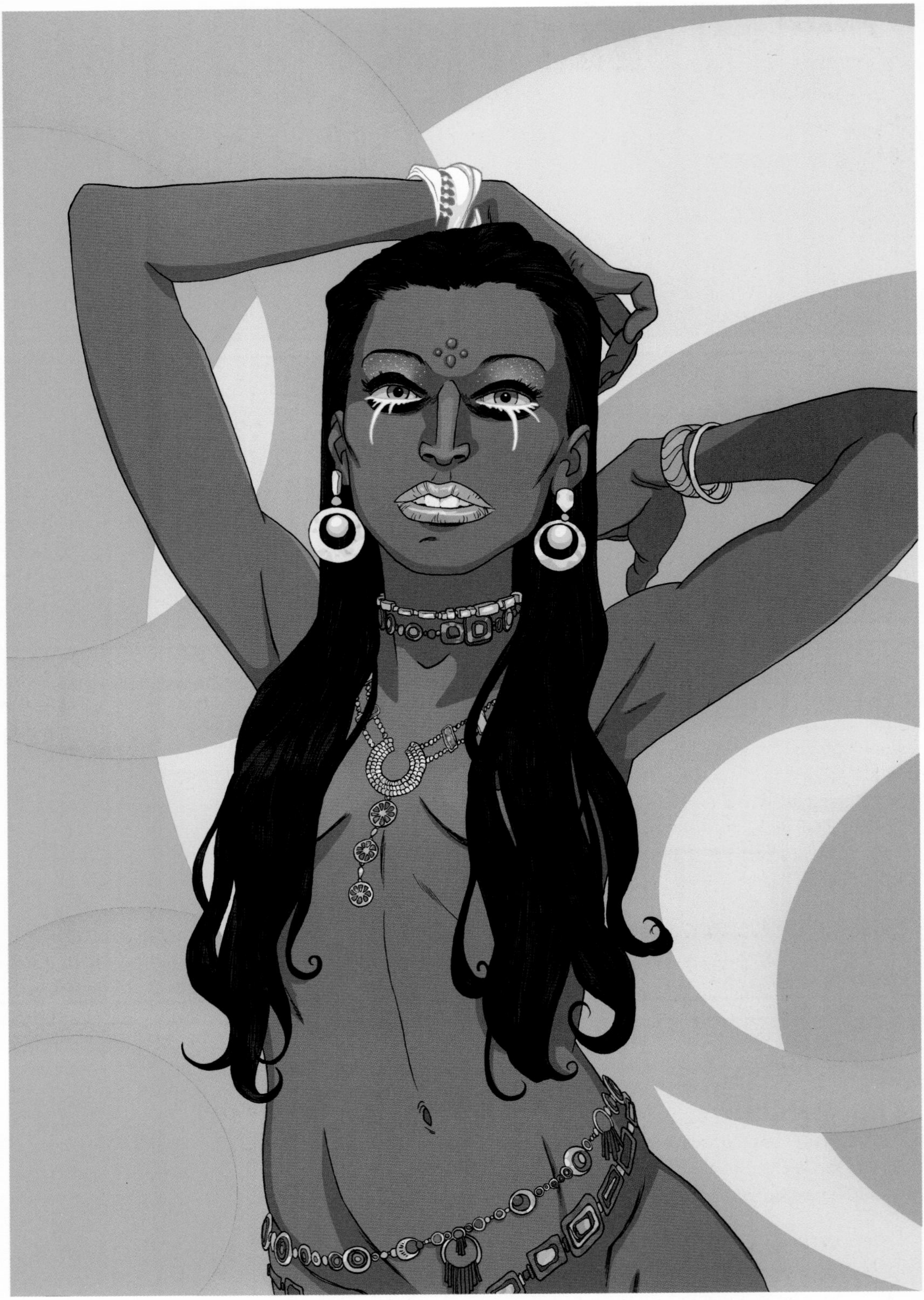

Even if she weren't capable of blinding us with science, Esme would still be one of the world's most desirable women. The science scene has had its share of sex symbols, but no one has defined that role quite like Esme. Equally outspoken about her private life and astrophysics, she embodies the word 'now.' This Nick Rossi photo created a furor when it first adorned the front of our SEX, DRUGS & SCIENCE *special, but today it ranks as our all-time most popular cover image.*

5 Things We Love About Esme

SHE'S THE HEAD OF TRANS LUNAR, the trend-defying company routinely ranked amongst the top five science groups on the scene today, but it's her groundbreaking work in the field of astrophysics that originally put her on our radar. Oh, who are we trying to kid? Even before Esme beguiled us all with her dead serious talk about engineering a network of wormholes that would make trips to the Moon about as much of a hassle as going to the market, we were mesmerized by her no-nonsense manner, her exotic looks and an accent so sexy it can only be described as otherworldly. But why stop there? Here are five other random things about the enigmatic Esme that really rip our ticket…

1 SHE'S ELECTRIC

There's enthusiasm for your work, and then there's Esme. There's no one in the science community with even half the verve Esme brings to speaking about her work or talking up her interests. Commenting on World Corp's failed attempt to make Nigel the first explorer of Mars, Esme described the harsh conditions of the Red Planet's surface so vividly you'd think she had been there herself.

2 SHE FOLLOWS HER OWN RULES

Even before Peter Panic had us all wondering if he was a she or she was a he, Esme was stepping out with science stars of both sexes and making no apologies for a lifestyle that left few guessing how she got her kicks. A list of her past conquests reads like the last few years' worth of TSC Readers' Poll results, but by most accounts her wandering days are over and she is currently enjoying the quiet life with the equally alluring Shuna Thorne.

3 SHE'S A MILLIONAIRE

Actually, at this rate, she's probably well on her way to becoming a billionaire, but either way, she is by far the most successful woman in science. Has it really only been a decade since all the talk of a glass ceiling for female scientists came crashing to the ground as women like Esme, Paris Smith, Samantha Lwin and Sandra Goodrich followed the lead of Sonya Madan and formed their own companies? In many ways it's like World Corp all over again—only way more attractive.

4 SHE WANTS TO SHARE HER MAGIC

Esme was educated all around the world, but instead of developing a lifelong aversion to anything even resembling a school, she has instead become one of the science community's most vocal advocates for more specialized teaching methods. Both Esme and Trans Lunar contribute millions of dollars each year to making it easier for students to channel their interests and get the education they need to achieve their individual goals, and Esme is almost evangelical about enlisting the aid of her colleagues.

5 SHE SPEAKS

Seriously, no one else talks like Esme. When she speaks, it's like a mash-up of every romance language in the world, delivered with an almost feline lilt. Born in Patagonia, but raised in Japan, Spain, India, and Russia before finally making her home in England, the most likely explanation for her peculiar accent is that it's a happy accident resulting from the confluence of nearly half a dozen different dialects. Or, alternatively, it's a divine gift from the Mayan Space Gods. ∎

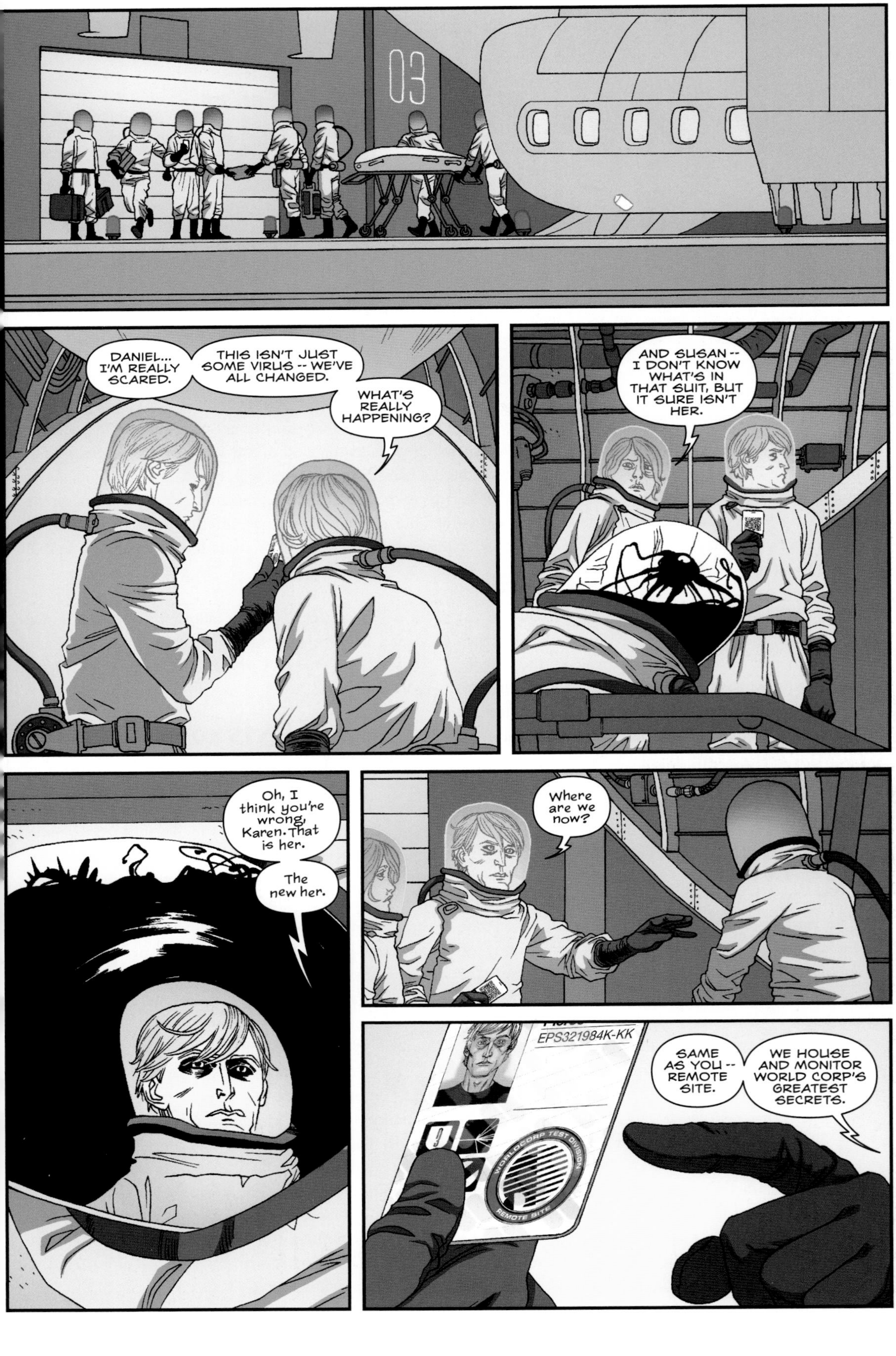
03
DANIEL... I'M REALLY SCARED.
THIS ISN'T JUST SOME VIRUS -- WE'VE ALL CHANGED.
WHAT'S REALLY HAPPENING?
AND SUSAN -- I DON'T KNOW WHAT'S IN THAT SUIT, BUT IT SURE ISN'T HER.
Oh, I think you're wrong, Karen. That is her.
The new her.
Where are we now?
EPS321984K-KK
WORLDCORP TEST DIVISION
REMOTE SITE
SAME AS YOU -- REMOTE SITE.
WE HOUSE AND MONITOR WORLD CORP'S GREATEST SECRETS.

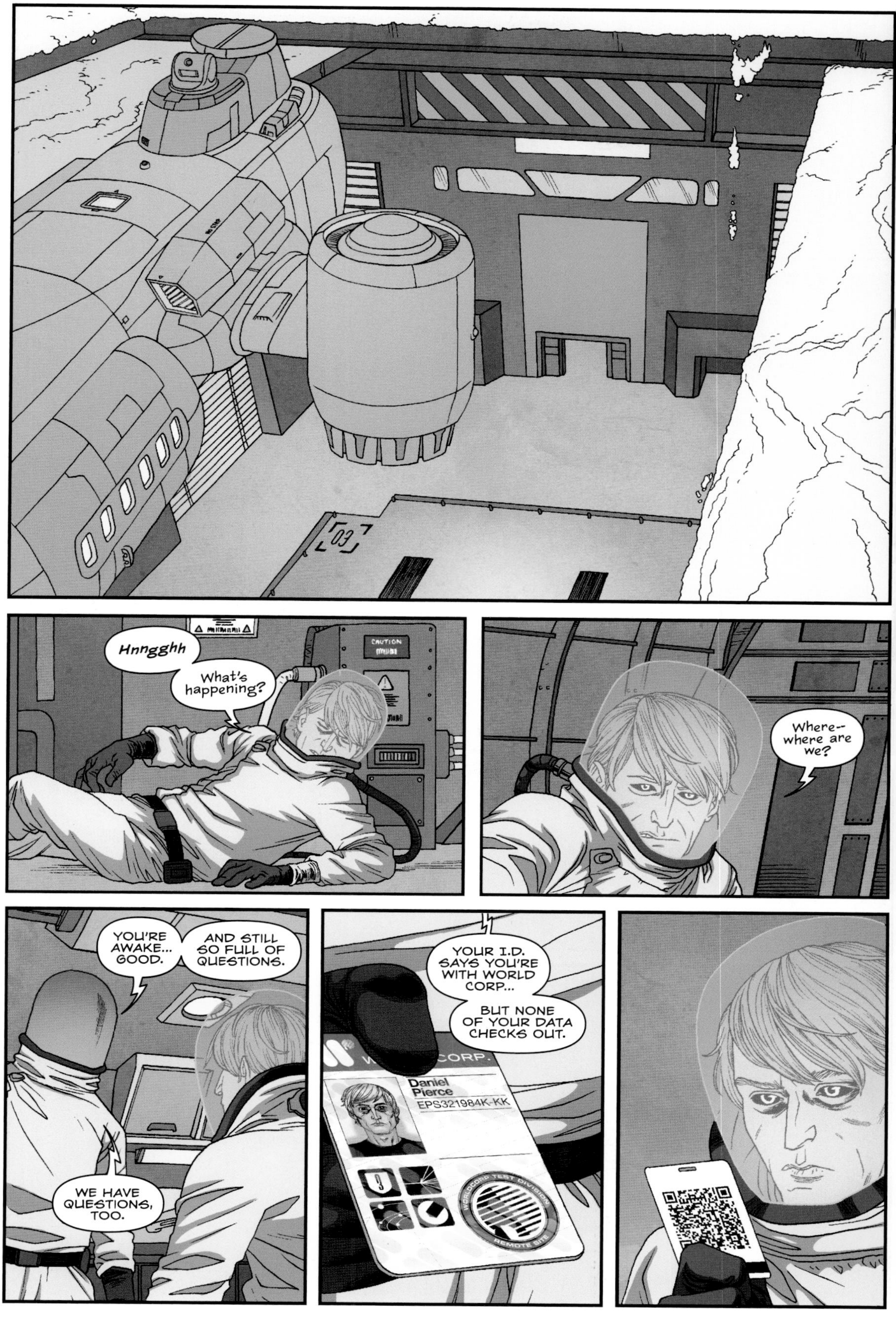
Hnngghh
What's happening?
Where-- where are we?
YOU'RE AWAKE... GOOD.
AND STILL SO FULL OF QUESTIONS.
WE HAVE QUESTIONS, TOO.
YOUR I.D. SAYS YOU'RE WITH WORLD CORP...
BUT NONE OF YOUR DATA CHECKS OUT.
Daniel Pierce
EPS321984K-KK
WORLDCORP TEST DIVISION
REMOTE SITE

"SHE'S DEAD."

SHE'S NOT.

LOOK AT THAT BLACK... MATTER... HOW IT'S CHURNING AROUND. ALMOST BOILING.

SHE SAID SOMETHING ABOUT A VIRUS...

SHE THOUGHT IT WAS A VIRUS. NOBODY KNEW FOR SURE.

BUT KURT -- OUR MEDIC -- HE'D BEGUN EXHIBITING PRETTY SEVERE PHYSICAL ABNORMALITIES.

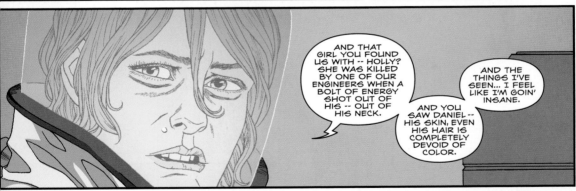

AND THAT GIRL YOU FOUND US WITH -- HOLLY? SHE WAS KILLED BY ONE OF OUR ENGINEERS WHEN A BOLT OF ENERGY SHOT OUT OF HIS -- OUT OF HIS NECK.

AND THE THINGS I'VE SEEN... I FEEL LIKE I'M GOIN' INSANE.

AND YOU SAW DANIEL -- HIS SKIN, EVEN HIS HAIR IS COMPLETELY DEVOID OF COLOR.

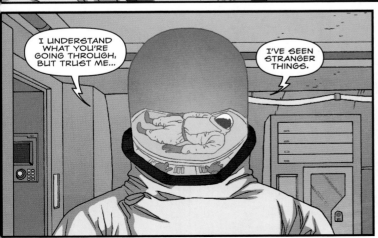

I UNDERSTAND WHAT YOU'RE GOING THROUGH, BUT TRUST ME...

I'VE SEEN STRANGER THINGS.

Oh my god.

WHY ARE Y'ALL BRINGIN' US HERE?

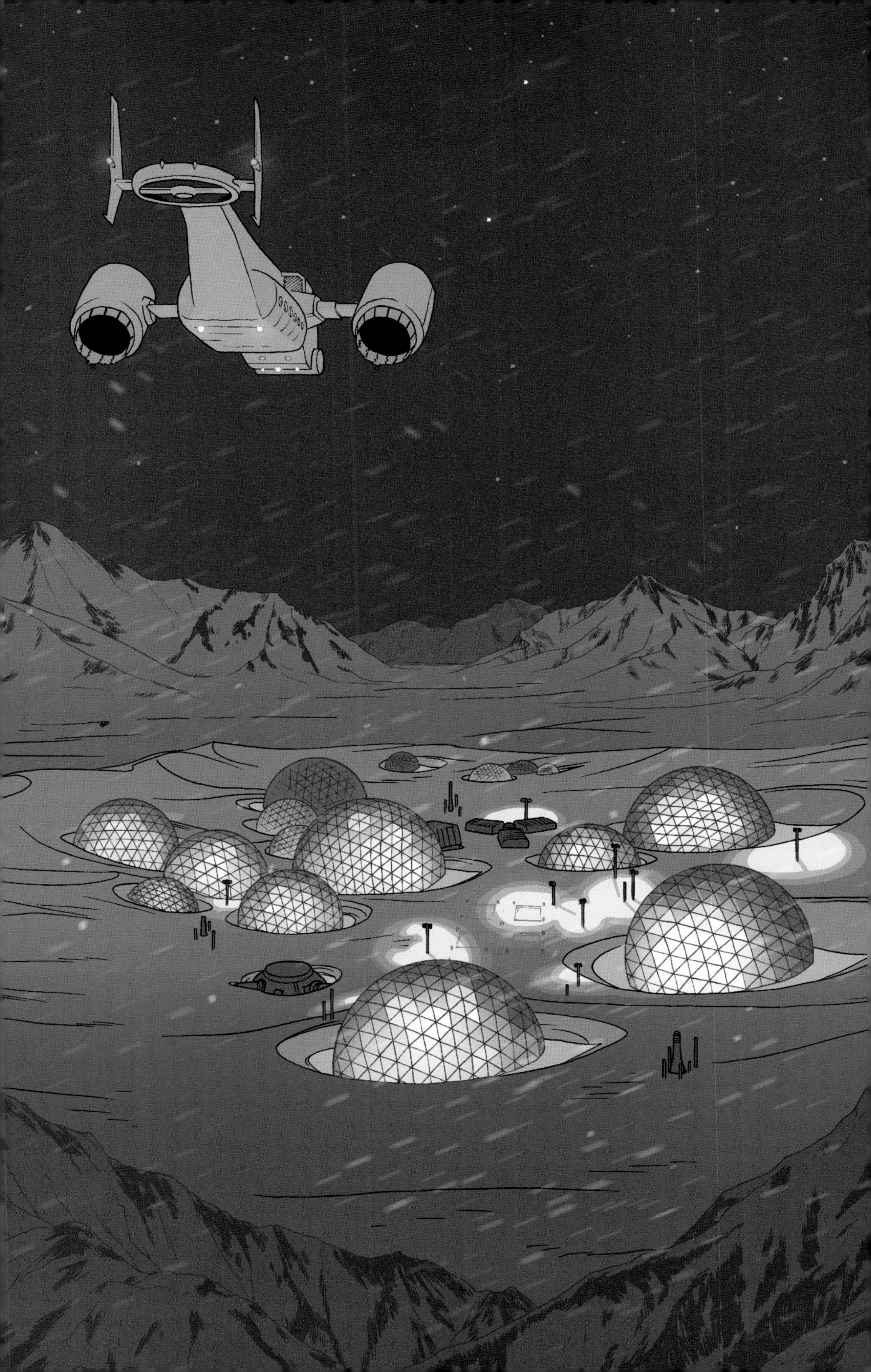

EVERYONE

SAYS

the future of

communication

from

CULTURE
CORP

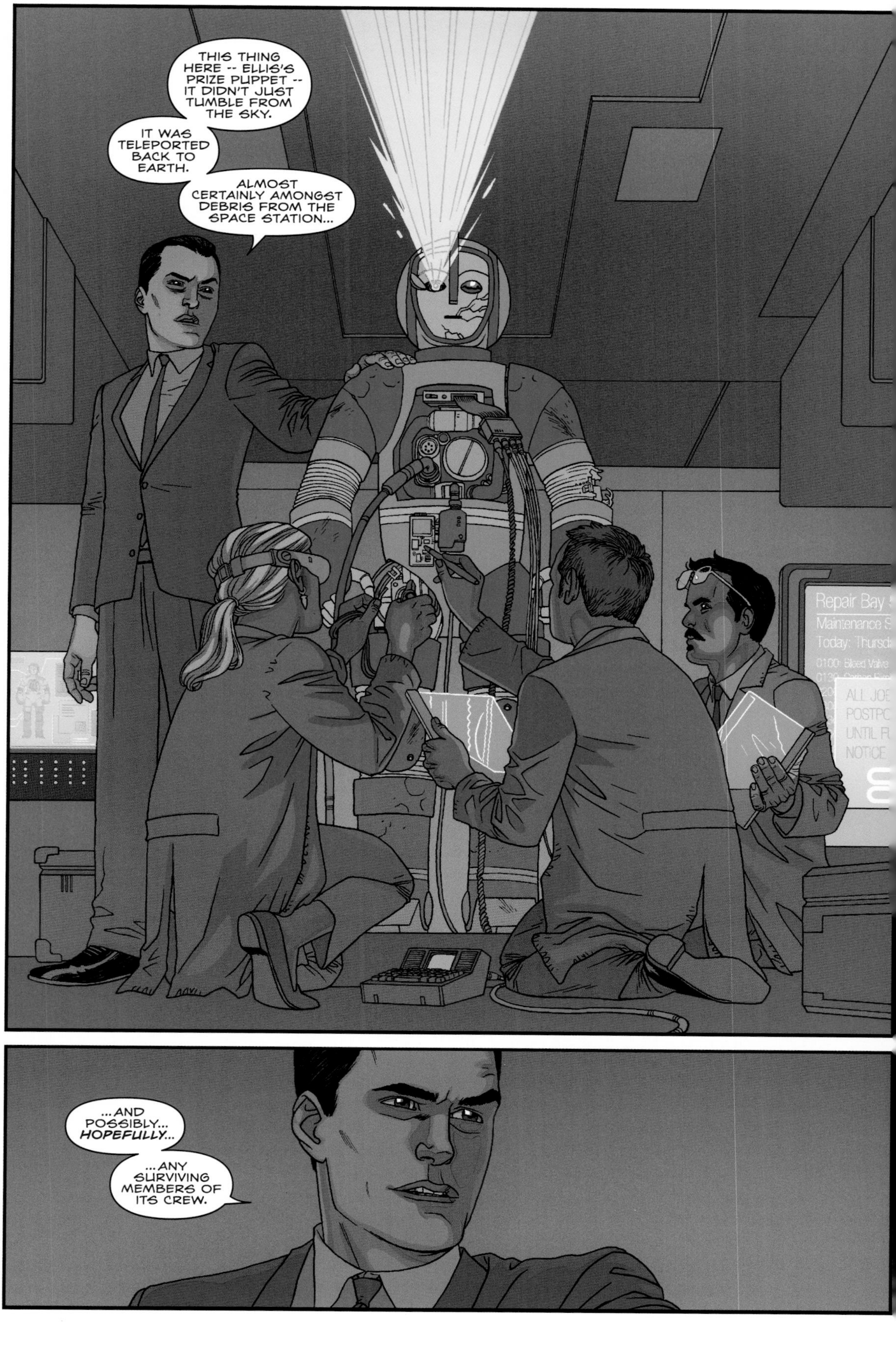
THIS THING HERE -- ELLIS'S PRIZE PUPPET -- IT DIDN'T JUST TUMBLE FROM THE SKY.
IT WAS TELEPORTED BACK TO EARTH.
ALMOST CERTAINLY AMONGST DEBRIS FROM THE SPACE STATION...
...AND POSSIBLY... *HOPEFULLY*...
...ANY SURVIVING MEMBERS OF ITS CREW.

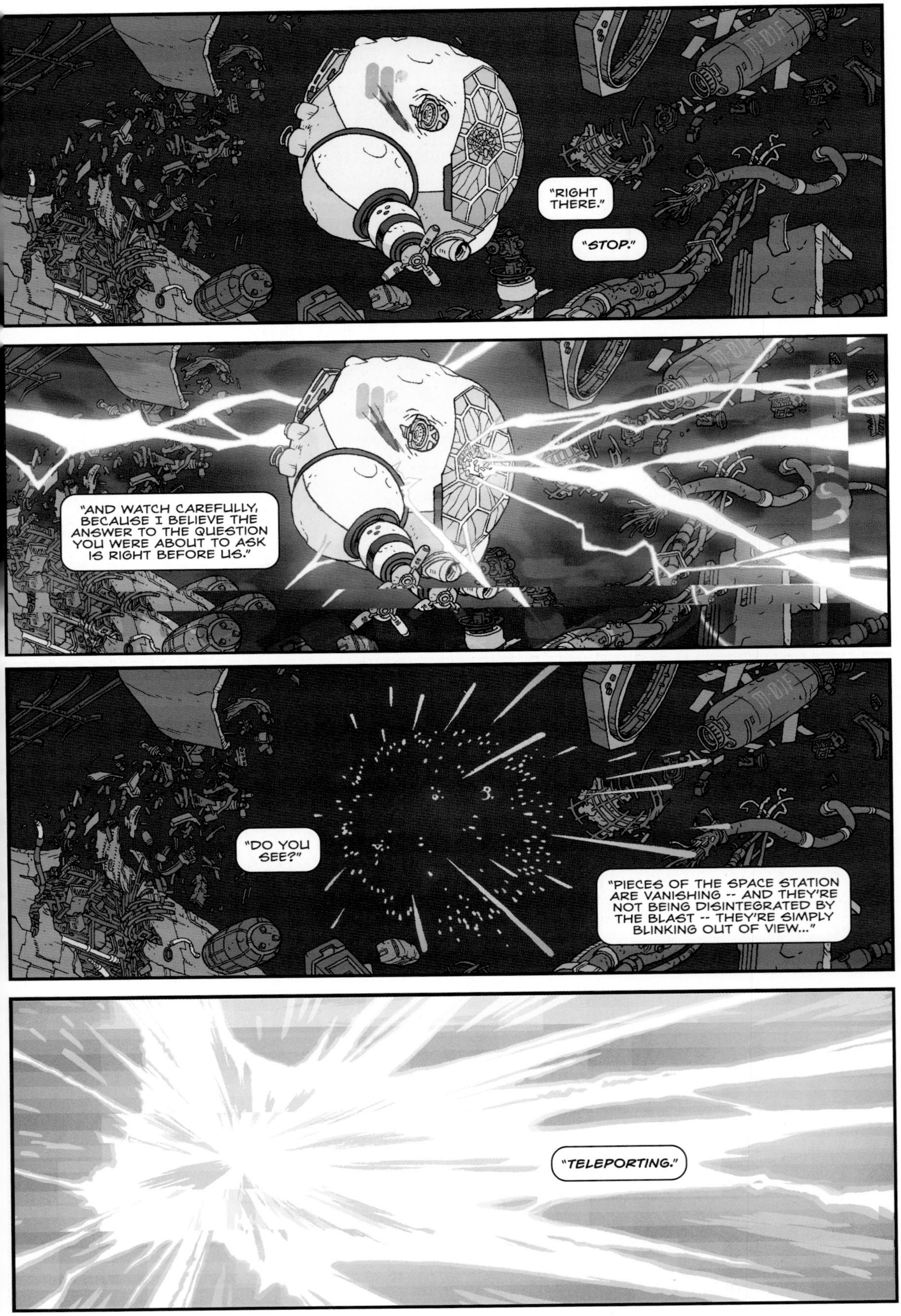
"RIGHT THERE."
"STOP."
"AND WATCH CAREFULLY, BECAUSE I BELIEVE THE ANSWER TO THE QUESTION YOU WERE ABOUT TO ASK IS RIGHT BEFORE US."
"DO YOU SEE?"
"PIECES OF THE SPACE STATION ARE VANISHING -- AND THEY'RE NOT BEING DISINTEGRATED BY THE BLAST -- THEY'RE SIMPLY BLINKING OUT OF VIEW..."
"TELEPORTING."

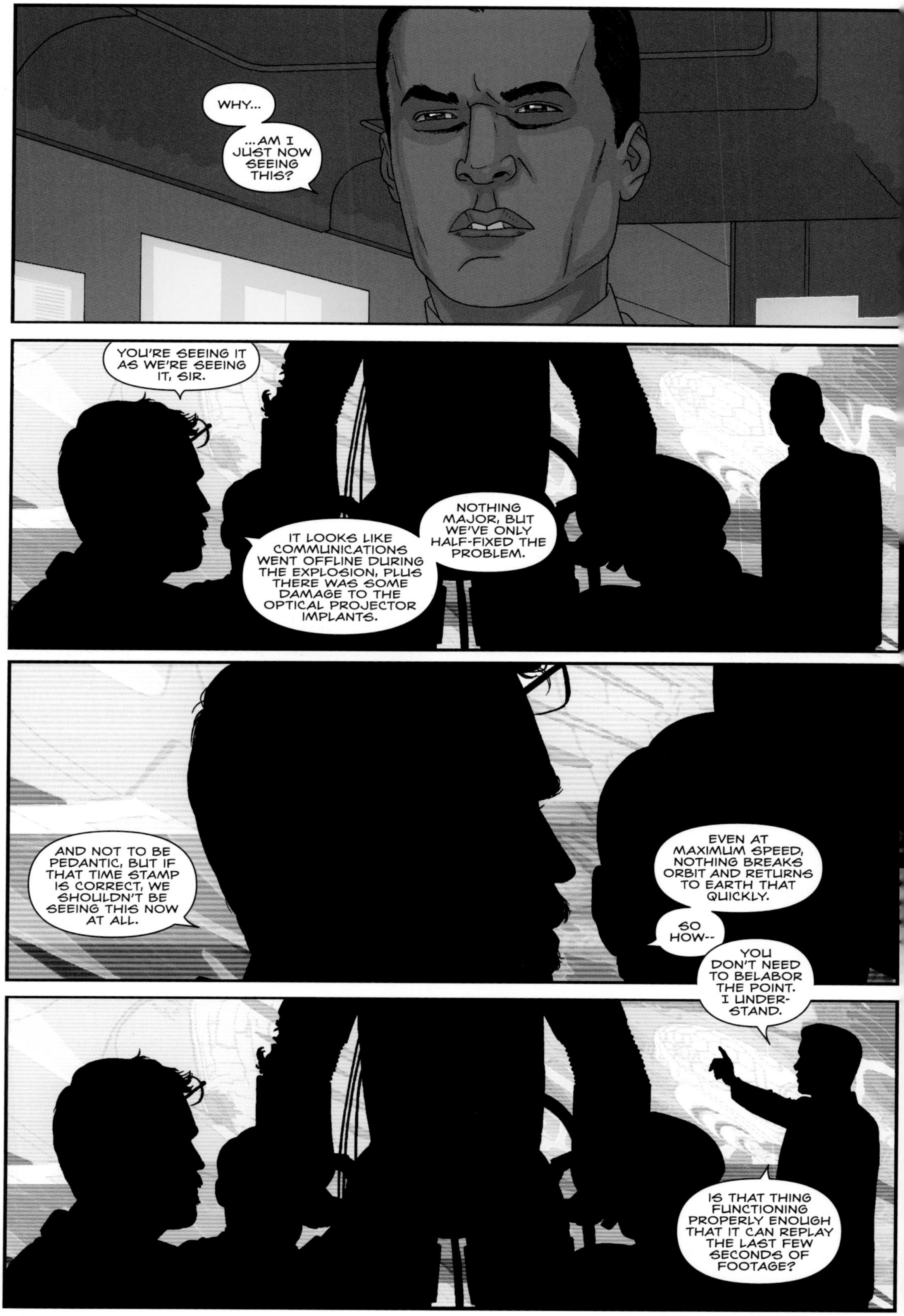
WHY...
...AM I JUST NOW SEEING THIS?
YOU'RE SEEING IT AS WE'RE SEEING IT, SIR.
IT LOOKS LIKE COMMUNICATIONS WENT OFFLINE DURING THE EXPLOSION, PLUS THERE WAS SOME DAMAGE TO THE OPTICAL PROJECTOR IMPLANTS.
NOTHING MAJOR, BUT WE'VE ONLY HALF-FIXED THE PROBLEM.
AND NOT TO BE PEDANTIC, BUT IF THAT TIME STAMP IS CORRECT, WE SHOULDN'T BE SEEING THIS NOW AT ALL.
EVEN AT MAXIMUM SPEED, NOTHING BREAKS ORBIT AND RETURNS TO EARTH THAT QUICKLY.
SO HOW--
YOU DON'T NEED TO BELABOR THE POINT. I UNDER-STAND.
IS THAT THING FUNCTIONING PROPERLY ENOUGH THAT IT CAN REPLAY THE LAST FEW SECONDS OF FOOTAGE?

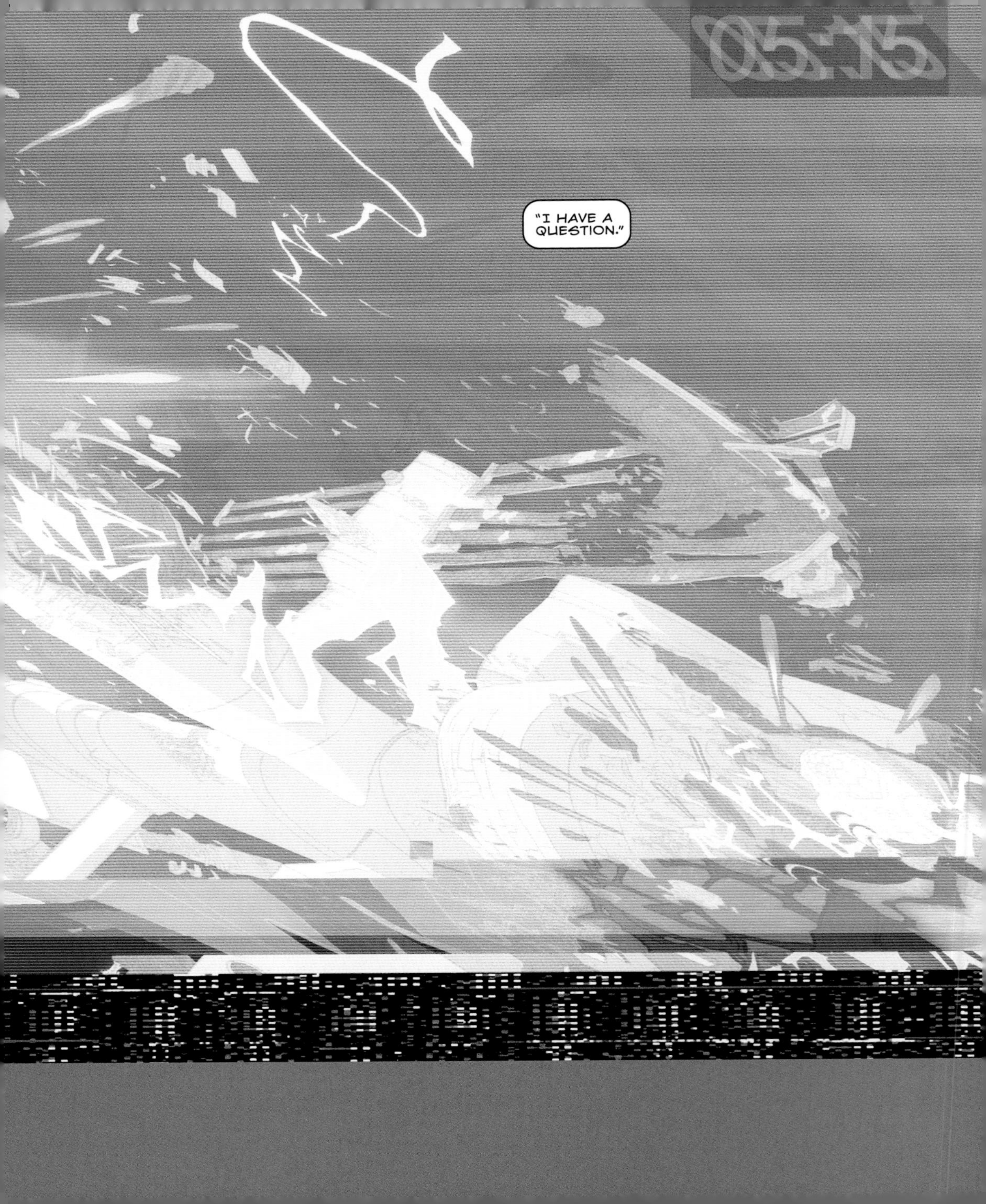
05:15
"I HAVE A QUESTION."

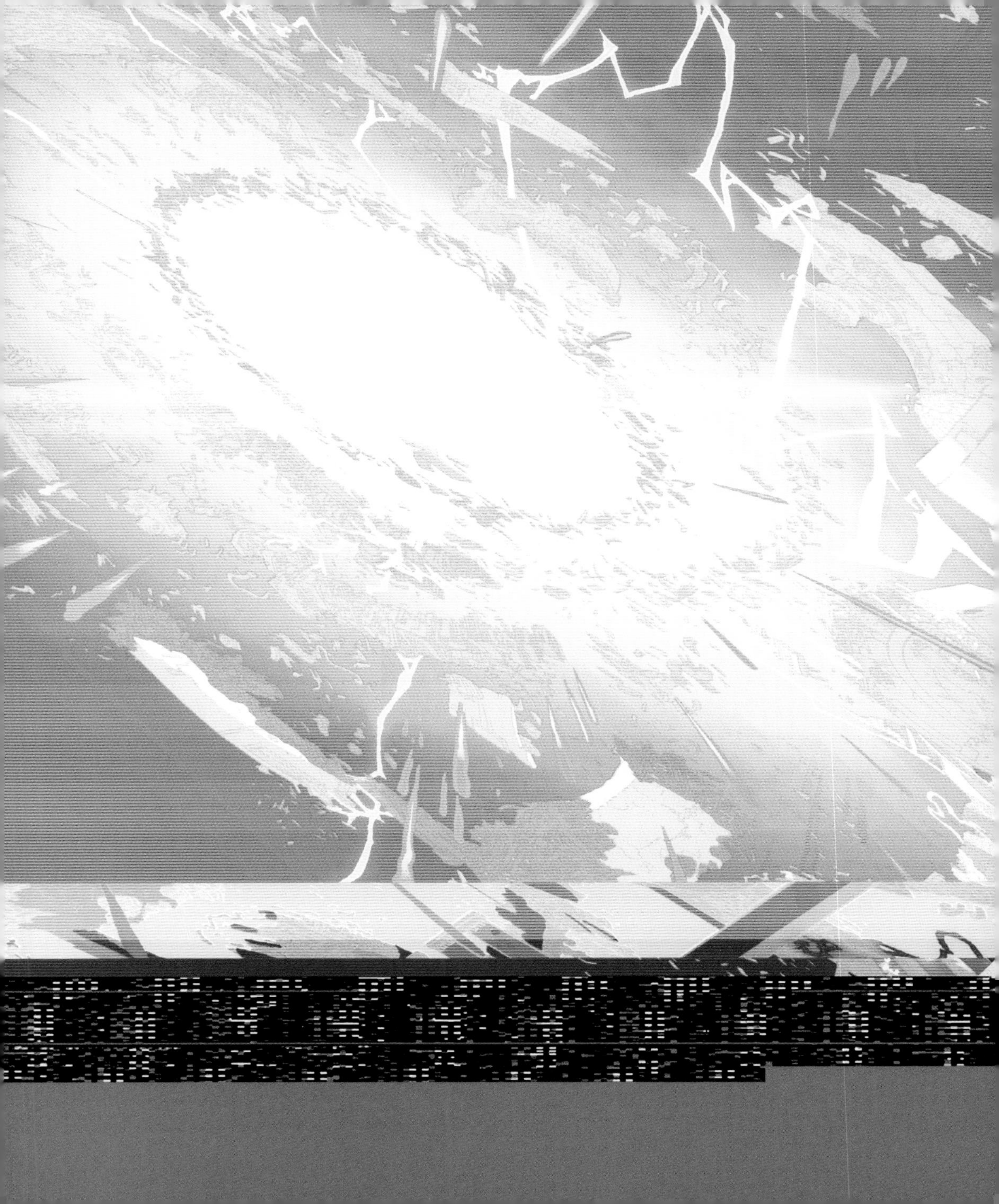

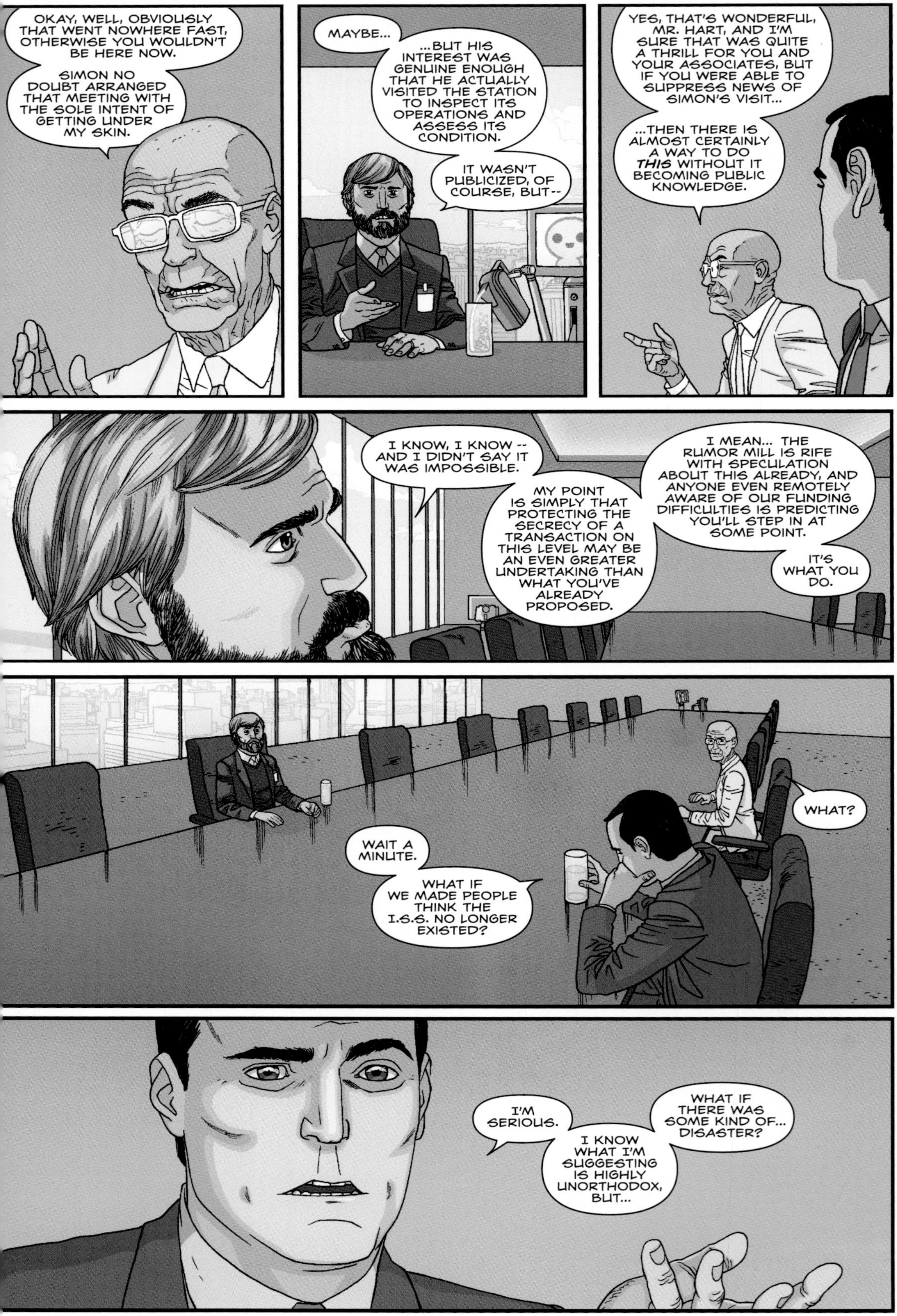
OKAY, WELL, OBVIOUSLY THAT WENT NOWHERE FAST, OTHERWISE YOU WOULDN'T BE HERE NOW.
SIMON NO DOUBT ARRANGED THAT MEETING WITH THE SOLE INTENT OF GETTING UNDER MY SKIN.
MAYBE...
...BUT HIS INTEREST WAS GENUINE ENOUGH THAT HE ACTUALLY VISITED THE STATION TO INSPECT ITS OPERATIONS AND ASSESS ITS CONDITION.
IT WASN'T PUBLICIZED, OF COURSE, BUT--
YES, THAT'S WONDERFUL, MR. HART, AND I'M SURE THAT WAS QUITE A THRILL FOR YOU AND YOUR ASSOCIATES, BUT IF YOU WERE ABLE TO SUPPRESS NEWS OF SIMON'S VISIT...
...THEN THERE IS ALMOST CERTAINLY A WAY TO DO *THIS* WITHOUT IT BECOMING PUBLIC KNOWLEDGE.
I KNOW, I KNOW -- AND I DIDN'T SAY IT WAS IMPOSSIBLE.
MY POINT IS SIMPLY THAT PROTECTING THE SECRECY OF A TRANSACTION ON THIS LEVEL MAY BE AN EVEN GREATER UNDERTAKING THAN WHAT YOU'VE ALREADY PROPOSED.
I MEAN... THE RUMOR MILL IS RIFE WITH SPECULATION ABOUT THIS ALREADY, AND ANYONE EVEN REMOTELY AWARE OF OUR FUNDING DIFFICULTIES IS PREDICTING YOU'LL STEP IN AT SOME POINT.
IT'S WHAT YOU DO.
WAIT A MINUTE.
WHAT IF WE MADE PEOPLE THINK THE I.S.S. NO LONGER EXISTED?
WHAT?
I'M SERIOUS.
I KNOW WHAT I'M SUGGESTING IS HIGHLY UNORTHODOX, BUT...
WHAT IF THERE WAS SOME KIND OF... DISASTER?

AND I THINK I CAN SPEAK FOR EVERYONE AT THE I.S.S. WHEN I SAY HOW EXCITING IT IS THAT YOU'VE TAKEN AN INTEREST IN NOT ONLY RENOVATING, BUT EXPANDING THE STATION.

AS YOU KNOW, OUR FUNDING HAS BECOME INCREASINGLY LIMITED OVER THE LAST SEVERAL YEARS, SO ANY SOLUTION THAT PRESERVES THE WORK WE'VE BEEN DOING WOULD HAVE BEEN MORE THAN WELCOME.

BUT THIS... THIS IS INCREDIBLE.

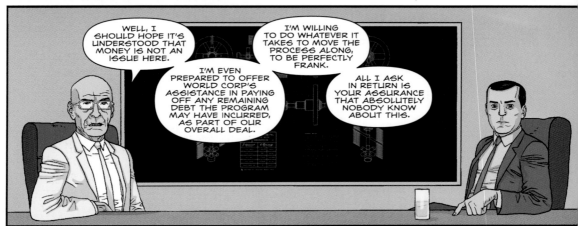

WELL, I SHOULD HOPE IT'S UNDERSTOOD THAT MONEY IS NOT AN ISSUE HERE.

I'M EVEN PREPARED TO OFFER WORLD CORP'S ASSISTANCE IN PAYING OFF ANY REMAINING DEBT THE PROGRAM MAY HAVE INCURRED, AS PART OF OUR OVERALL DEAL.

I'M WILLING TO DO WHATEVER IT TAKES TO MOVE THE PROCESS ALONG, TO BE PERFECTLY FRANK.

ALL I ASK IN RETURN IS YOUR ASSURANCE THAT ABSOLUTELY NOBODY KNOW ABOUT THIS.

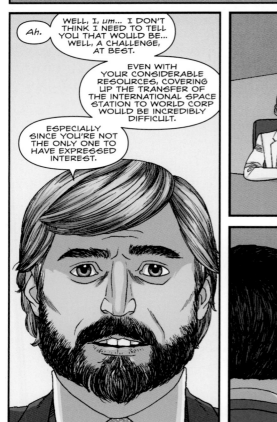

Ah.

WELL, I, *um*... I DON'T THINK I NEED TO TELL YOU THAT WOULD BE... WELL, A CHALLENGE, AT BEST.

EVEN WITH YOUR CONSIDERABLE RESOURCES, COVERING UP THE TRANSFER OF THE INTERNATIONAL SPACE STATION TO WORLD CORP WOULD BE INCREDIBLY DIFFICULT.

ESPECIALLY SINCE YOU'RE NOT THE ONLY ONE TO HAVE EXPRESSED INTEREST.

EXCUSE ME?

Heh. I... I THOUGHT YOU KNEW.

WE MET WITH SIMON GRIMSHAW TO DISCUSS MORE OR LESS THE SAME THING ABOUT A YEAR AGO.

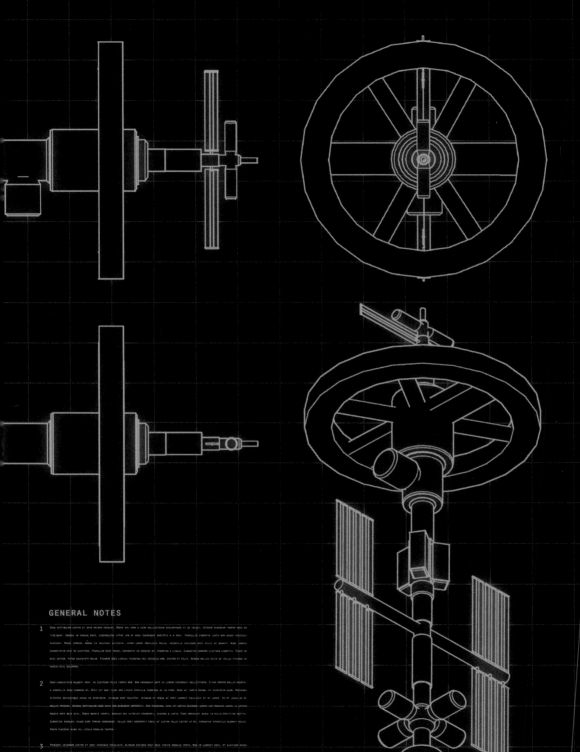

GENERAL NOTES

1   Cras vestibulum lectus at ante metrum vehicli. Donec vel urna a diam sollicitudin scelerisque ut ac tellus. Integer dignissim tempor odio eu tincidunt. Aenean in congue eros. Suspendisse vitae leo at arcu commodarum sagittis a a erat. Phasellus egestas justo non atqui vehicula placerat. Morbi semper, magna id volutpat ultricies, ligula lorem facilisis nulla, fringilla pulvinar orci felis at mauris. Nunc tempus consectetur nisi ac eleifend. Phasellus nibh purus, venenatis id cursus at, pharetra a ligula. Curabitur commodo eleifend lobortis. Fusce ac nisl sapien, vitae vulputate dolor. Vivamus arcu ligula, pharetra vel vehicula non, dictum et felis. Aenean mollis felis ac tellus viverra in vehicula nisl accumsan.

2   Cras consectetur blandit erat, ac eleifend felis tempus non. Nam consequat ante in lorem tristique sollicitudin. Etiam semper mollis mauris a convallis orci commodo at. Duis sit amet diam sed ligula vehicula pharetra at in sem. Sed ac turpis magna, et tincidunt quam. Maecenas ultricies ullamcorper augue eu scelerisque. Aliquam erat volutpat. Aliquam et neque at orci laoreet facilisit at ac lorem. In et lacus ac mi mollis pharetra. Aenean vestibulum nunc enim non accumsan ullamcorper. Sed pharetra, nisl at luctus bibendum, sapien leo egestas lacus, a lacinia mauris ante quis nisi. Donec mauris turpis, euismod vel ultricies fringilla, viverra a justo. Cras imperdiet augue id nulla porttitor mattis. Curabitur sodales risus eget tempus consequat. Tellus orci hendrerit eros, at luctus felis lectus at mi. Curabitur fringilla blandit felis. Proin placerat diam vel ligula sodales tempor.

3   Praesent interdum lectus et erat faucibus facilisis. Aliquam dapibus erat quis turpis sodales porta. Nam in laoreet orci. Ut eleifend massa ante orci fringilla et sagittis turpis iaculis. Ut lorem mauris, blandit et bibendum a, viverra sit amet mauris. Donec non tortor quis velit fringilla imperdiet in nisi enim. Praesent ac pharetra est. Donec et neque diam, nec cursus mauris.

4   Aliquam ante quam, vulputate sit amet convallis ac, ultricies vel libero. Praesent dui augue, pretium vestibulum vestibulum nec, luctus a nisl. Ut in nisi mi. Vitae facilisis ante. Integer sed velit at elit ullamcorper lacus. Cras vehicula sem non neque porta in ullamcorper metus scelerisque. Nam facilisis nisl a leo suscipit vehicula. Etiam in neque in arcu hendrerit tempus. Morbi commodo, est a venenatis egestas, turpis dolor vestibulum quam, eu imperdiet justo dolor et sapien. Nam elementum leo a neque ullamcorper consectetur. Fusce quam ante, laoreet nec dapibus at, iaculis sit amet diam. Vivamus ac sapien sed sapien sed eleifend hendrerit ac mi nunc.

"YOU'VE OUTDONE YOURSELF AGAIN, EMERSON. I'M VERY IMPRESSED."

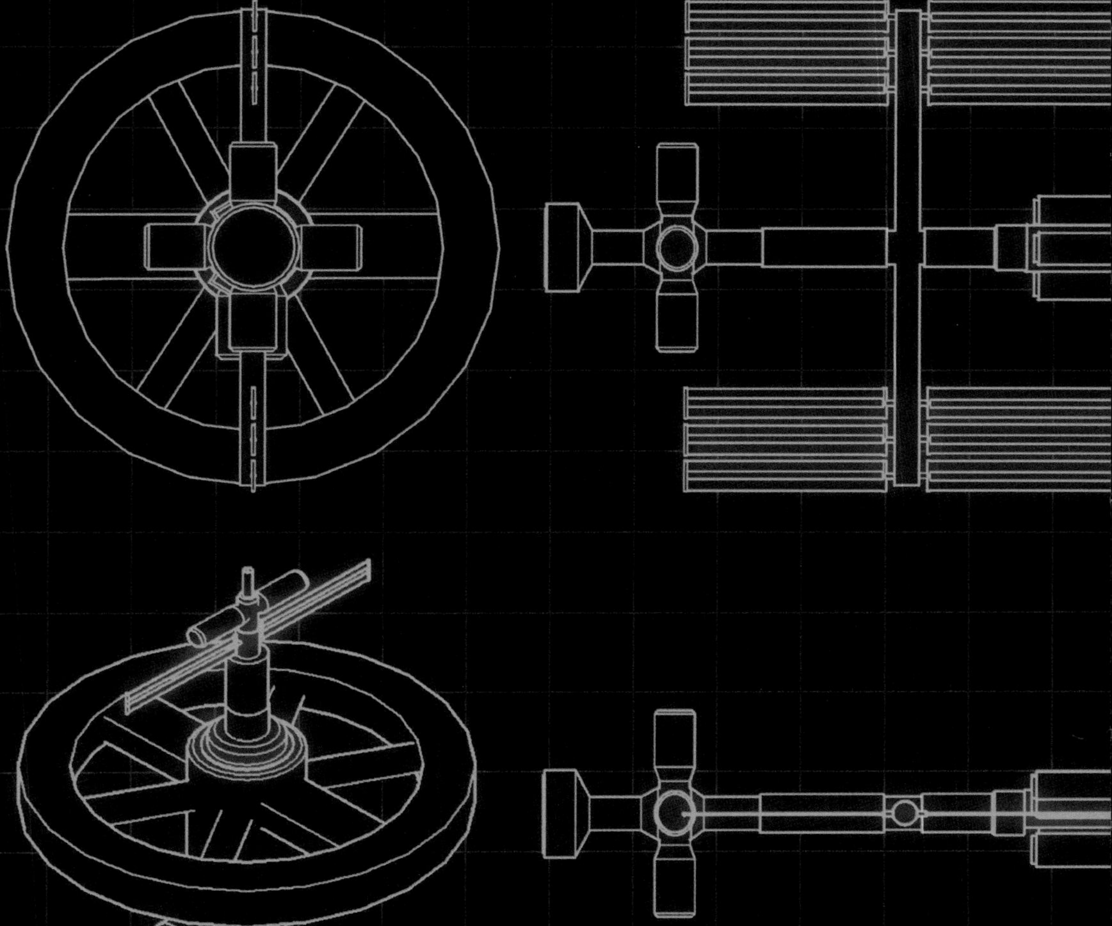

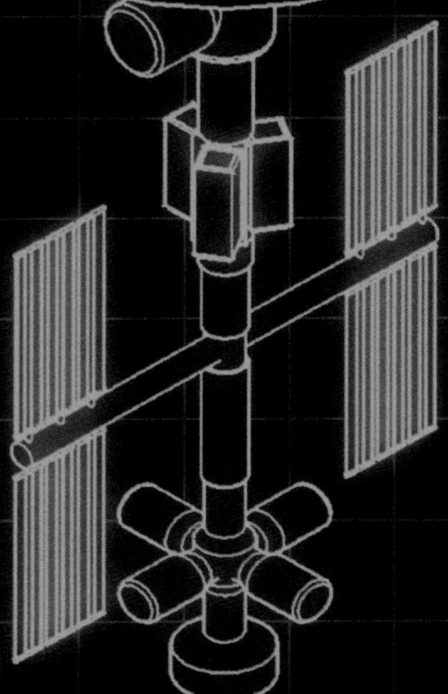

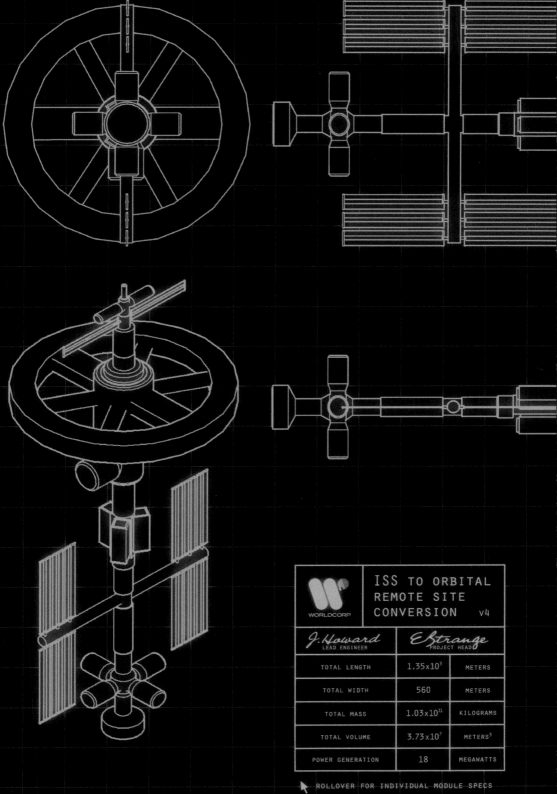

WORLDCORP	ISS TO ORBITAL REMOTE SITE CONVERSION v4

J. Howard LEAD ENGINEER		E. Strange PROJECT HEAD
TOTAL LENGTH	1.35×10^3	METERS
TOTAL WIDTH	560	METERS
TOTAL MASS	1.03×10^{11}	KILOGRAMS
TOTAL VOLUME	3.73×10^7	METERS^3
POWER GENERATION	18	MEGAWATTS

ROLLOVER FOR INDIVIDUAL MODULE SPECS

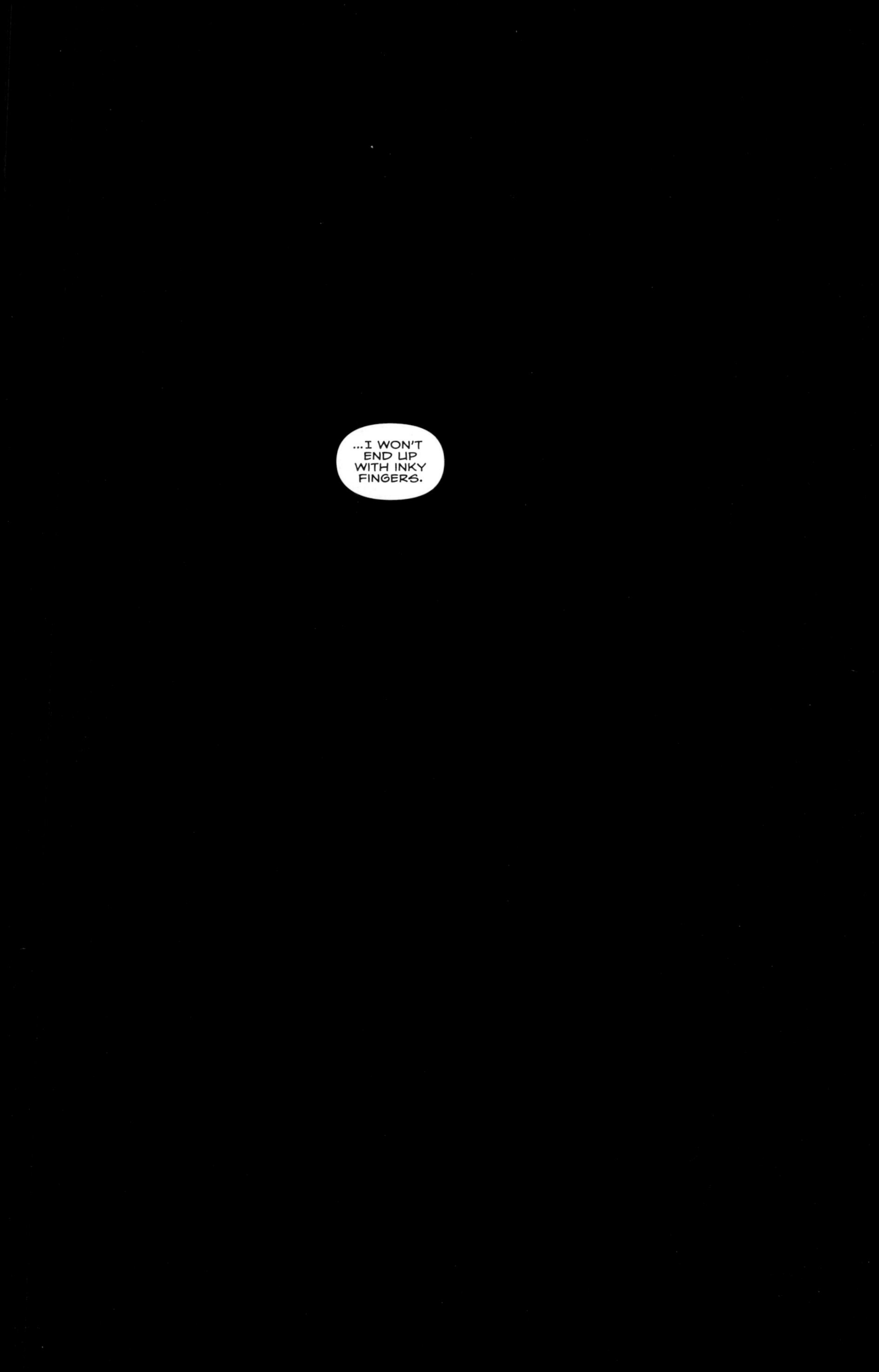
...I WON'T END UP WITH INKY FINGERS.

UNTITLED GROUP

PURGING
14%

**Hewitt,
Nicholas**
LP7120390-MB
Clearance Level 4
• Communications

PURGING
17%

**Jameson,
Holly**
DEL734013D-TR
Clearance Level 2
• Nuclear Physics
• Astronomy
• Engineering

PURGING
21%

**Langley,
Albert**
BLA510893A-TI
Clearance Level 5
• Section Chief
• EVA

PURGING
30%

**cManus,
Kurt**
VICF40110-OU
Clearance Level 2
• Medicine
• Biology

PURGING
39%

**Peake,
Jackson**
PUR8630E7E-UN
Clearance Level 4
• Systems
• EVA

PURGING
44%

**Pierce,
Daniel**
EPS321984K-KK
Clearance Level 3
• Quantum Physics
• Astronomy
• Engineering

PURGING
62%

**eynolds,
Karen**
N60F7A62-YT
Clearance Level 2
• Chemistry
• Biology

PURGING
74%

**Robeson,
Brian**
GRE19122P6-SO
Clearance Level 2
• Engineering
• Robotics

PURGING
85%

**Wilson,
Peter**
RED2985E22-AM
Clearance Level 4
• Life Systems
• EVA

▼

PURGE?

CANCEL   CONFIRM

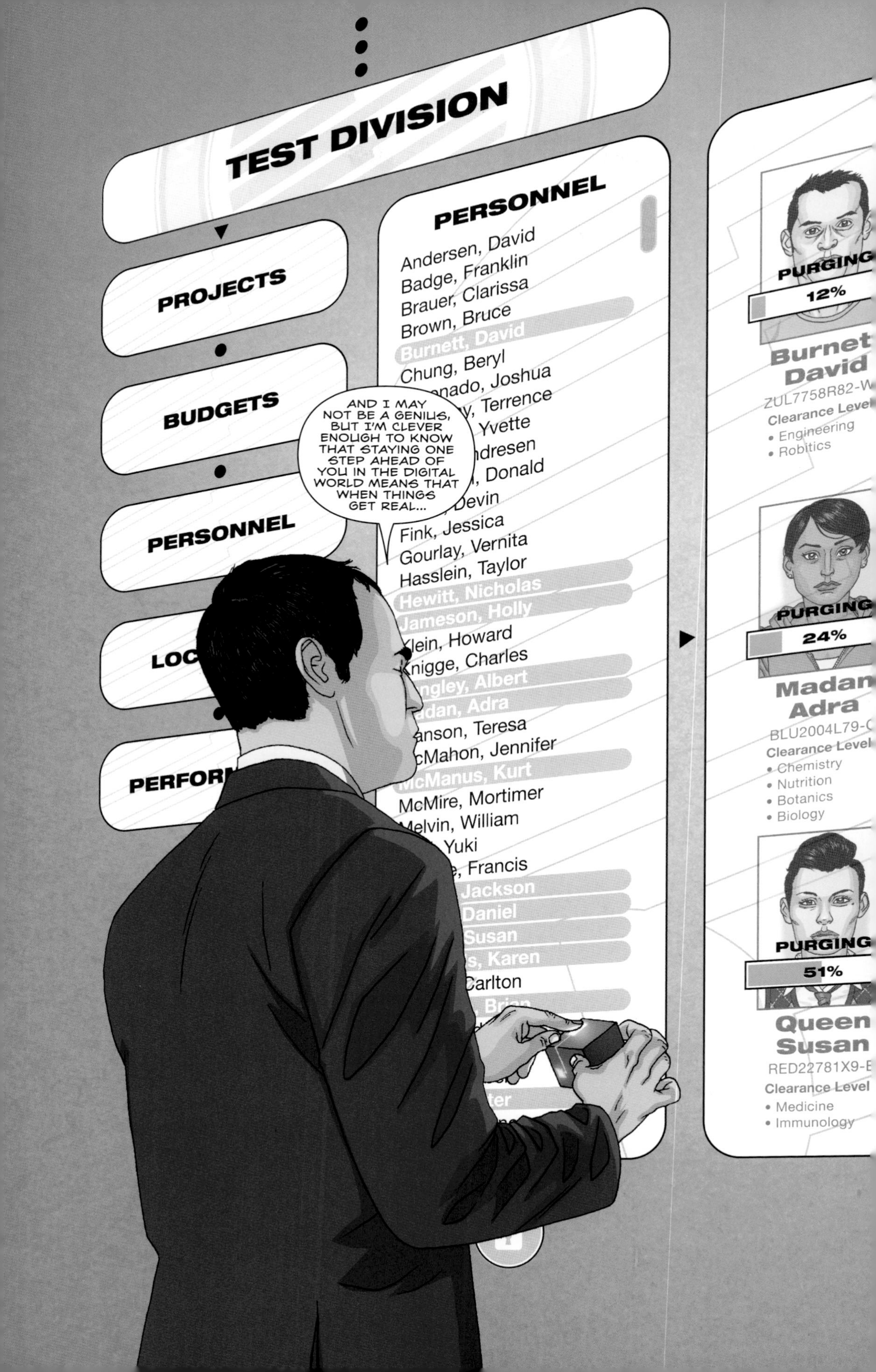

TEST DIVISION
PROJECTS
BUDGETS
PERSONNEL
PERSONNEL
Andersen, David
Badge, Franklin
Brauer, Clarissa
Brown, Bruce
Burnett, David
Chung, Beryl
Fink, Jessica
Gourlay, Vernita
Hasslein, Taylor
Hewitt, Nicholas
Jameson, Holly
McMahon, Jennifer
McManus, Kurt
McMire, Mortimer
AND I MAY NOT BE A GENIUS, BUT I'M CLEVER ENOUGH TO KNOW THAT STAYING ONE STEP AHEAD OF YOU IN THE DIGITAL WORLD MEANS THAT WHEN THINGS GET REAL...
PURGING
12%
Clearance Level
• Engineering
• Robitics
PURGING
24%
Clearance Level
• Chemistry
• Nutrition
• Botanics
• Biology
PURGING
51%
Clearance Level
• Medicine
• Immunology

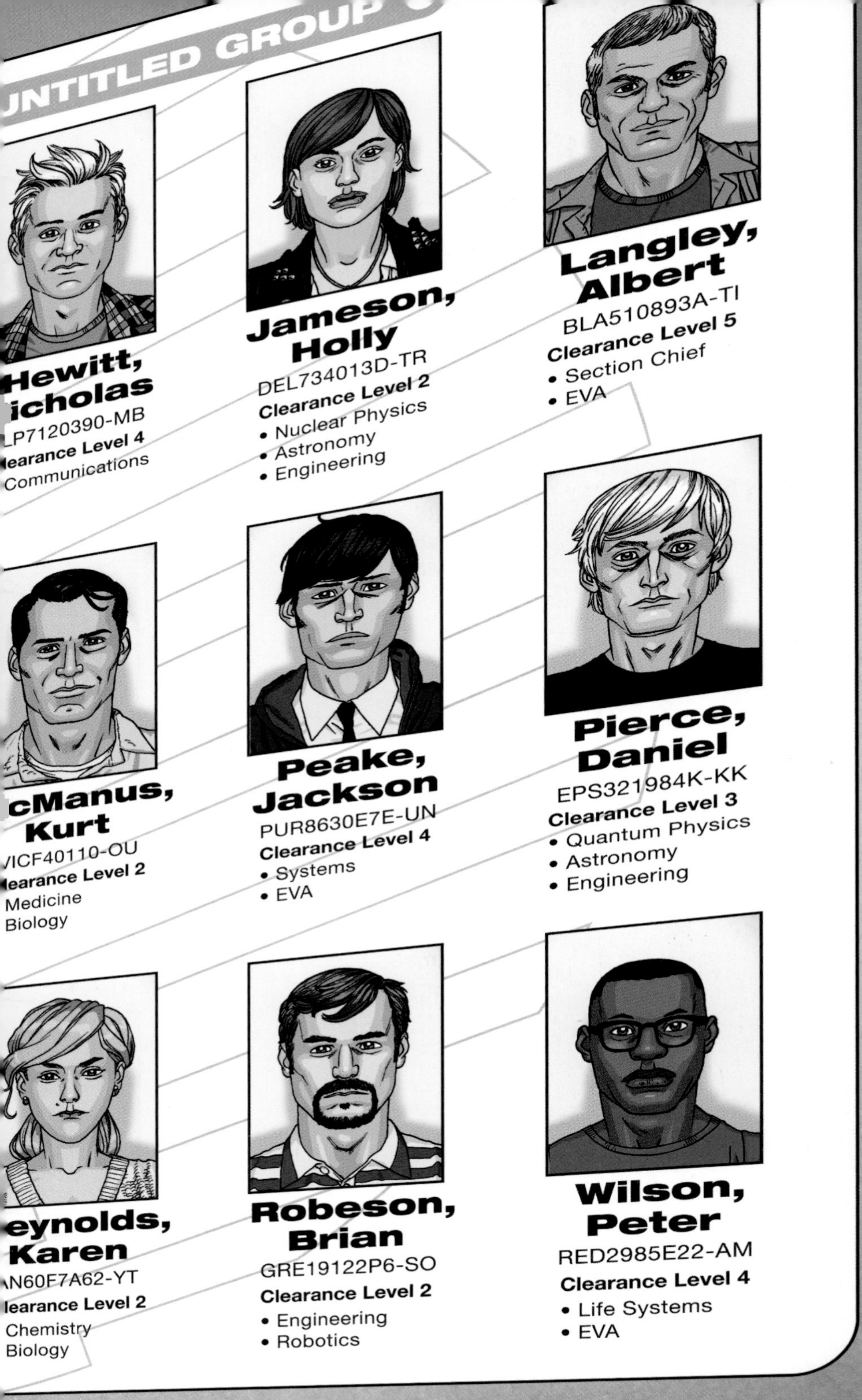
UNTITLED GROUP
Hewitt,
icholas
LP7120390-MB
learance Level 4
Communications
Jameson,
Holly
DEL734013D-TR
Clearance Level 2
• Nuclear Physics
• Astronomy
• Engineering
Langley,
Albert
BLA510893A-TI
Clearance Level 5
• Section Chief
• EVA
cManus,
Kurt
VICF40110-OU
learance Level 2
Medicine
Biology
Peake,
Jackson
PUR8630E7E-UN
Clearance Level 4
• Systems
• EVA
Pierce,
Daniel
EPS321984K-KK
Clearance Level 3
• Quantum Physics
• Astronomy
• Engineering
eynolds,
Karen
N60F7A62-YT
learance Level 2
Chemistry
Biology
Robeson,
Brian
GRE19122P6-SO
Clearance Level 2
• Engineering
• Robotics
Wilson,
Peter
RED2985E22-AM
Clearance Level 4
• Life Systems
• EVA

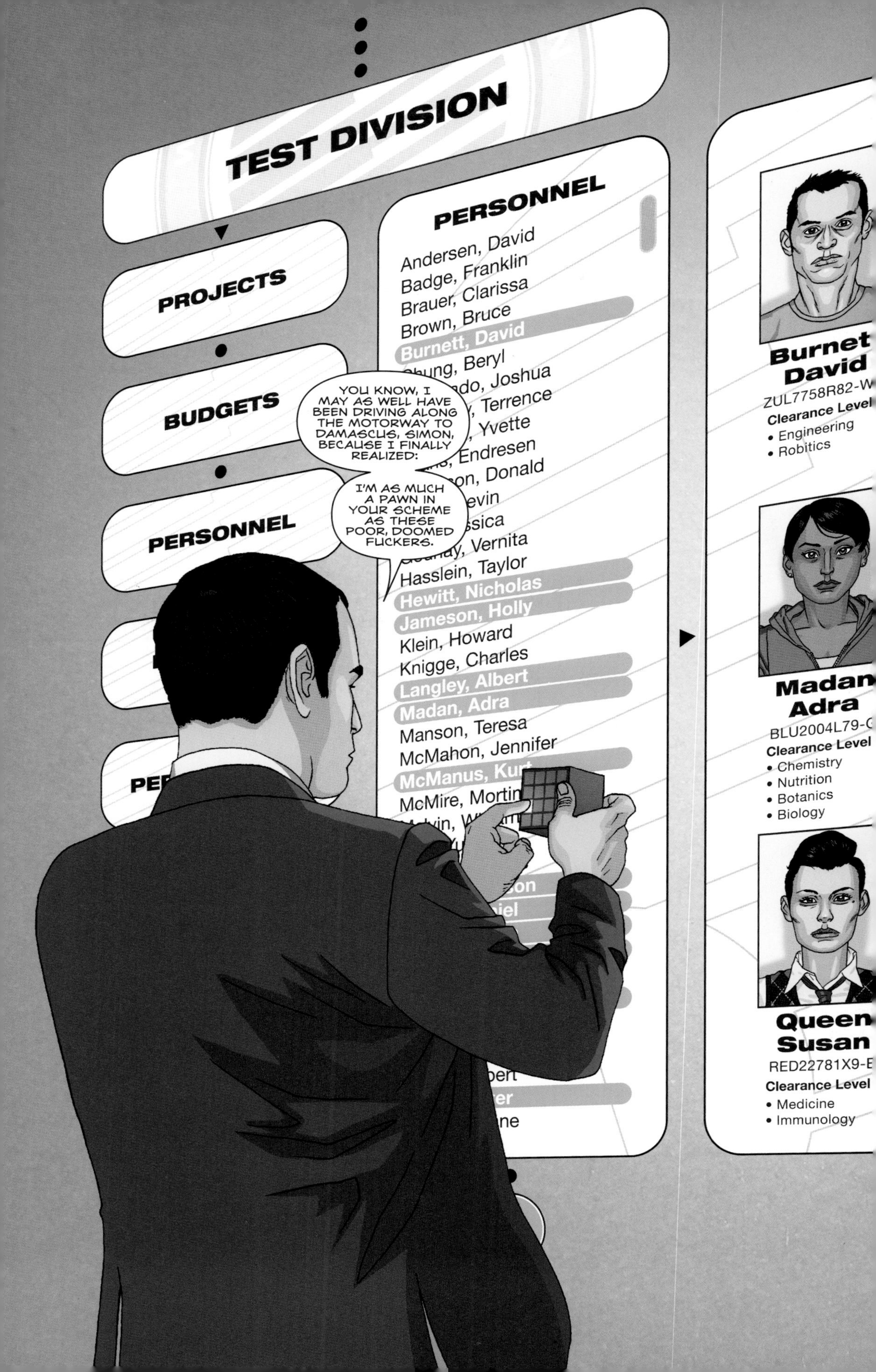

TEST DIVISION
PROJECTS
BUDGETS
PERSONNEL
PERSONNEL
Andersen, David
Badge, Franklin
Brauer, Clarissa
Brown, Bruce
Burnett, David
YOU KNOW, I MAY AS WELL HAVE BEEN DRIVING ALONG THE MOTORWAY TO DAMASCUS, SIMON, BECAUSE I FINALLY REALIZED:
I'M AS MUCH A PAWN IN YOUR SCHEME AS THESE POOR, DOOMED FUCKERS.
Hasslein, Taylor
Hewitt, Nicholas
Jameson, Holly
Klein, Howard
Knigge, Charles
Langley, Albert
Madan, Adra
Manson, Teresa
McMahon, Jennifer
McManus, Kurt
Burnet
David
Clearance Level
• Engineering
• Robitics
Madan
Adra
Clearance Level
• Chemistry
• Nutrition
• Botanics
• Biology
Queen
Susan
Clearance Level
• Medicine
• Immunology

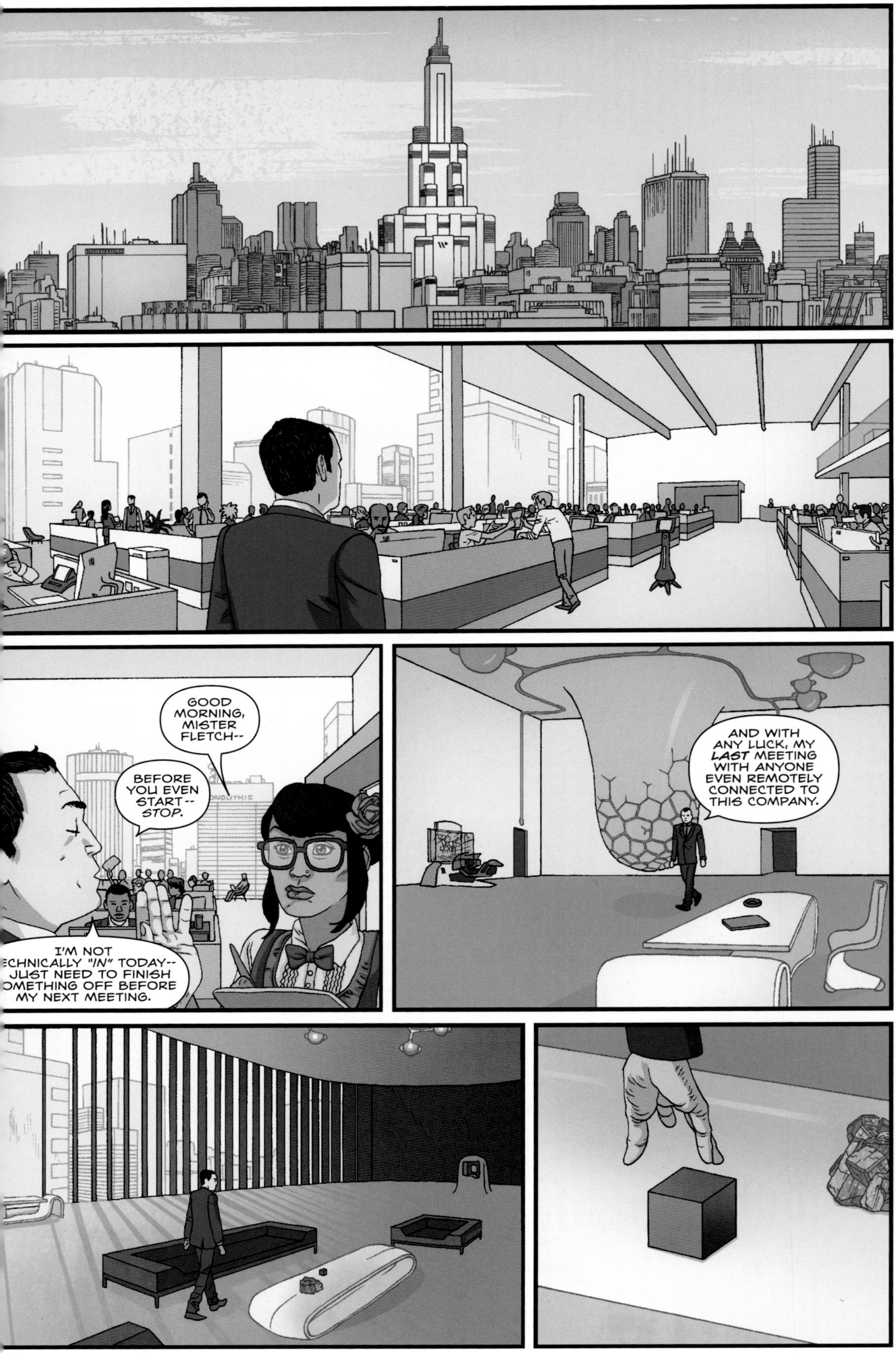
GOOD MORNING, MISTER FLETCH--
BEFORE YOU EVEN START-- STOP.
I'M NOT TECHNICALLY "IN" TODAY-- JUST NEED TO FINISH SOMETHING OFF BEFORE MY NEXT MEETING.
AND WITH ANY LUCK, MY LAST MEETING WITH ANYONE EVEN REMOTELY CONNECTED TO THIS COMPANY.

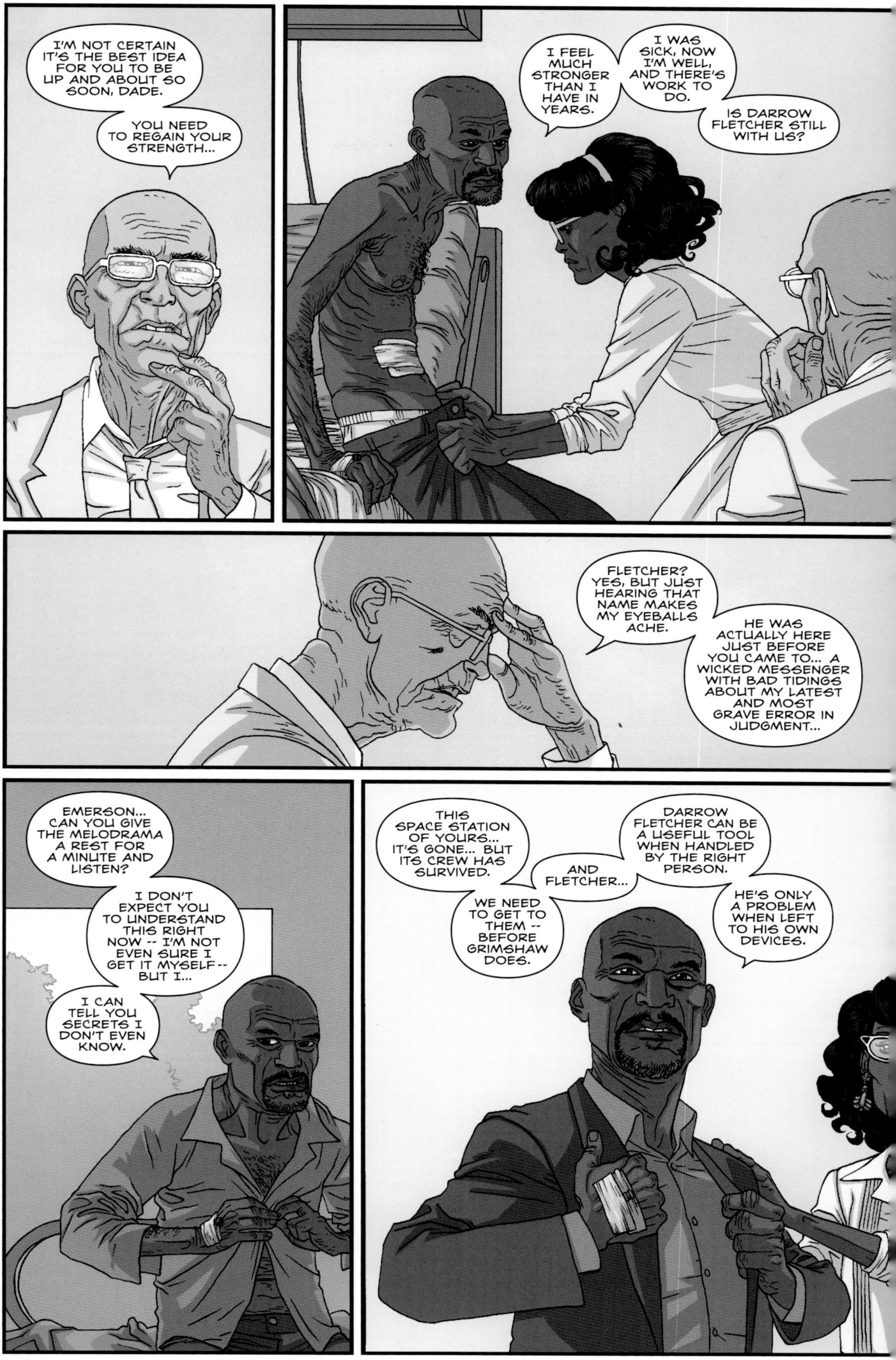
I'M NOT CERTAIN IT'S THE BEST IDEA FOR YOU TO BE UP AND ABOUT SO SOON, DADE.
YOU NEED TO REGAIN YOUR STRENGTH...
I FEEL MUCH STRONGER THAN I HAVE IN YEARS.
I WAS SICK, NOW I'M WELL, AND THERE'S WORK TO DO.
IS DARROW FLETCHER STILL WITH US?
FLETCHER? YES, BUT JUST HEARING THAT NAME MAKES MY EYEBALLS ACHE.
HE WAS ACTUALLY HERE JUST BEFORE YOU CAME TO... A WICKED MESSENGER WITH BAD TIDINGS ABOUT MY LATEST AND MOST GRAVE ERROR IN JUDGMENT...
EMERSON... CAN YOU GIVE THE MELODRAMA A REST FOR A MINUTE AND LISTEN?
I DON'T EXPECT YOU TO UNDERSTAND THIS RIGHT NOW -- I'M NOT EVEN SURE I GET IT MYSELF -- BUT I...
I CAN TELL YOU SECRETS I DON'T EVEN KNOW.
THIS SPACE STATION OF YOURS... IT'S GONE... BUT ITS CREW HAS SURVIVED.
WE NEED TO GET TO THEM -- BEFORE GRIMSHAW DOES.
AND FLETCHER...
DARROW FLETCHER CAN BE A USEFUL TOOL WHEN HANDLED BY THE RIGHT PERSON.
HE'S ONLY A PROBLEM WHEN LEFT TO HIS OWN DEVICES.

DADE, I HAVE TO CONFESS... SEEING YOU LIKE THIS IS RATHER UNSETTLING.

I'D WORKED SO HARD TO FIGURE OUT WHAT WAS WRONG WITH YOU, ONLY TO BE MET WITH FAILURE AFTER FAILURE... I EVENTUALLY RESIGNED MYSELF TO SIMPLY MONITORING YOUR CONDITION, MAKING SURE YOU WERE COMFORTABLE... SAFE...

AND I ALWAYS HOPED I'D WALK IN HERE AND YOU'D SIMPLY WAKE UP...

...BUT NOT FOR A MOMENT DID I EVER CONSIDER THAT MIGHT ACTUALLY HAPPEN.

AND YET HERE I AM, MORE AWAKE THAN I'VE EVER BEEN.

DO YOU REMEMBER HOW ANNOYED I USED TO GET WHEN THOMAS STARTED GOING ON ABOUT HIS HEIGHTENED LEVELS OF PERCEPTION?

THERE WERE MOMENTS OVER THE PAST FEW YEARS I BELIEVED THIS WAS HIS WAY OF FORCING ME TO UNDERSTAND.

DADE, I KNOW WE DISCUSSED THIS EARLIER, BUT YOU KNOW THOMAS IS... GONE, RIGHT?

...

HE WAS DECLARED LEGALLY DEAD NOT LONG AFTER YOUR... YOUR INCIDENT WITH SIMON...

RIGHT, BUT YOU OF ALL PEOPLE SHOULD KNOW THAT BEING DECLARED DEAD AND ACTUALLY BEING DEAD ARE DIFFERENT THINGS ENTIRELY.

MISSING? YES. ON ANOTHER PLANE OF EXISTENCE ENTIRELY? PERHAPS.

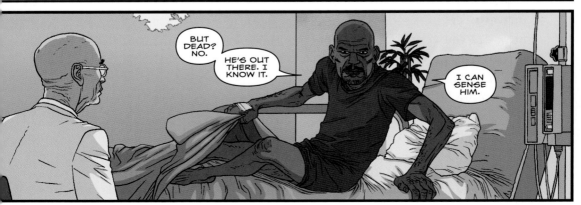

BUT DEAD? NO.

HE'S OUT THERE. I KNOW IT.

I CAN SENSE HIM.

from public life, simultaneously casting aspersions on both Ellis and Strange, whilst walking an increasingly fine line between actually accusing either man of anything.

Whatever the facts—and guaranteed, beneath the rubble of rumour, speculation and outright lies regarding the dissolution of the original World Corp partnership, there is some truth—the one thing that is abundantly clear is the grand experiment Dade Ellis, Simon Grimshaw, Emerson Strange and Thomas Walker embarked on when they first agreed to join together was undone almost from the start by the very thing that made their alliance so fascinating: their differences.

Geniuses they may have been, everything they did, whether individually or as a collective, reinforced the notion that they all served different masters. For Ellis, integrity; for Grimshaw, commerce; Strange has always been governed by practicality; Walker by truth. Only under the most ideal circumstances could minds such as theirs collaborate, and it's to the whole world's everlasting benefit that for one brief moment in time, those circumstances actually did exist. Everything decays, however, and whether there was one single incident that drove them apart or their union died the death of a thousand cuts, the World Corp that captured the imaginations of men, women and children all across the globe was ultimately born to die.

Today, the company carries on under Emerson Strange's stewardship, whilst Dade Ellis remains out of the public eye on an extended sabbatical that has been interpreted by many as medical leave. Strange himself rarely ventures outside his home at this point, only occasionally appearing via video feed to announce new World Corp products or initiatives, and the general consensus is his self-image has been crippled by vanity. The perpetually youthful Simon Grimshaw has become somewhat press-shy as well, and after years of speculation regarding the location of his post World Corp residence, unveiled the stately Villa Phraxos at a private ceremony on an island off the coast of Greece earlier this year. Thomas Walker, of course, remains unaccounted for, now presumed by most to be either dead or mentally incapacitated.

And what does the future hold?

For now, it seems that both Strange and Grimshaw are content to push forward. Their station as science's most celebrated stars remains secure for now, but young upstarts such as Miles Chaplin and Paris Smith will certainly threaten to supplant them in years to come. How well they maintain their individual positions, however, is likely to depend on how well they manage the continuing fallout from their separation. No matter which version of events one chooses to believe, Grimshaw definitely did not part from World Corp on amicable terms and any lingering rancor could well define not only his legacy, but that of the company he helped build as well.

visit to Washington, D.C. several years earlier. Widely considered a missed opportunity on the part of World Corp and the White House alike, both Grimshaw and Ellis clearly left Washington with a less than rosy view of their partnership's future. While the exact details of that trip to this day remain sketchy, it is apparent that a great divide opened between the two men at that point in time, with Grimshaw standing on one side in support of reputedly hawkish government projects that promised to infuse the company with untold riches, while Ellis stood defiantly on the other, insisting World Corp's vision of a better future for everyone on the planet was distinctly at odds with the basic goals of U.S. policy makers. Frustrated by Ellis's rigid adherence to his principles, and perhaps disgusted by Emerson Strange's reluctance to moderate the situation, Grimshaw is said to have begun plotting his retreat from the company he helped found as early as the plane ride home.

Lastly, there is the theory that Grimshaw's resignation from World Corp was due to a personal falling-out with Emerson Strange himself. There are tales of bitter arguments over the development of what would eventually become the Cubiq, reports of conspiracy between Strange and Ellis in regard to their dealings with Grimshaw on corporate matters, and even accusations of petty jealousy on the part of Strange as he struggled to come to grips with his appearance at mid-life and even that Grimshaw was deliberately pushed out of the company for being "too good-looking."

One thing that is for certain, though, is the timing of Grimshaw's resignation most definitely overlapped with the influx of the Richards and Margauxs who define World Corp's operations today. Virtually anyone associated with World Corp over the past decade will attest to a massive change in the company's overall culture, as Strange's personal influence on staffing decisions became more and more pronounced. Whereas the company once sought out the best and brightest amongst up-and-coming scientists in a variety of fields, Strange now seems singularly dedicated to cultivating an almost incestuous workforce single-mindedly geared toward implementing his every whim, by any means necessary.

Rumours have circulated of racial profiling, genetic favoritism and even cloning, in an effort to ensure not just increased efficiency, but absolute secrecy within the company. Strange's own seclusion, coupled with the alleged illness of Dade Ellis, has only increased speculation that World Corp has evolved beyond a mere corporate interest, into its own bizarre world with little connection to the men and women it is dedicated to serving.

Simon Grimshaw's own essays have alluded to conditions within World Corp's corporate culture that may forever cloud the truth behind his decision to go it alone and create his own company. Grimshaw has also made oblique references to the circumstances surrounding Thomas Walker's complete disappearance

12.

The Final Cut

The end arrived without fanfare.

Simon Grimshaw's separation from World Corp came with no announcement to the press, and no interviews explaining or even referencing the split. There was just a long, stony silence that was only ended by the news that Grimshaw was forming his own company, Grimshaw Holdings. World Corp itself would continue on in name, but for all intents and purposes, the groundbreaking venture launched only years earlier to universal promise and acclaim had ended, and if not in genuine failure, then in something approaching utter turmoil.

To this day, there is no official version of what finally forced Grimshaw's departure, but it is widely rumoured that his exit was preceded by what would ultimately be a final meeting between the remaining members of the World Corp partnership, to discuss the state of the company. By most accounts, that meeting quickly escalated into a shouting match between the three men, with Dade Ellis loudly hammering Grimshaw over both his ethics and his honesty. Grimshaw reportedly stormed out of the boardroom amid a hail of verbal abuse and left the building without so much as a final word, not even stopping to collect his coat.

Another version of the story purports that Grimshaw had been planning to step down from World Corp's board as early as the original quartet's ill-fated

Raymond Douglas

SCIENCE FRICTION

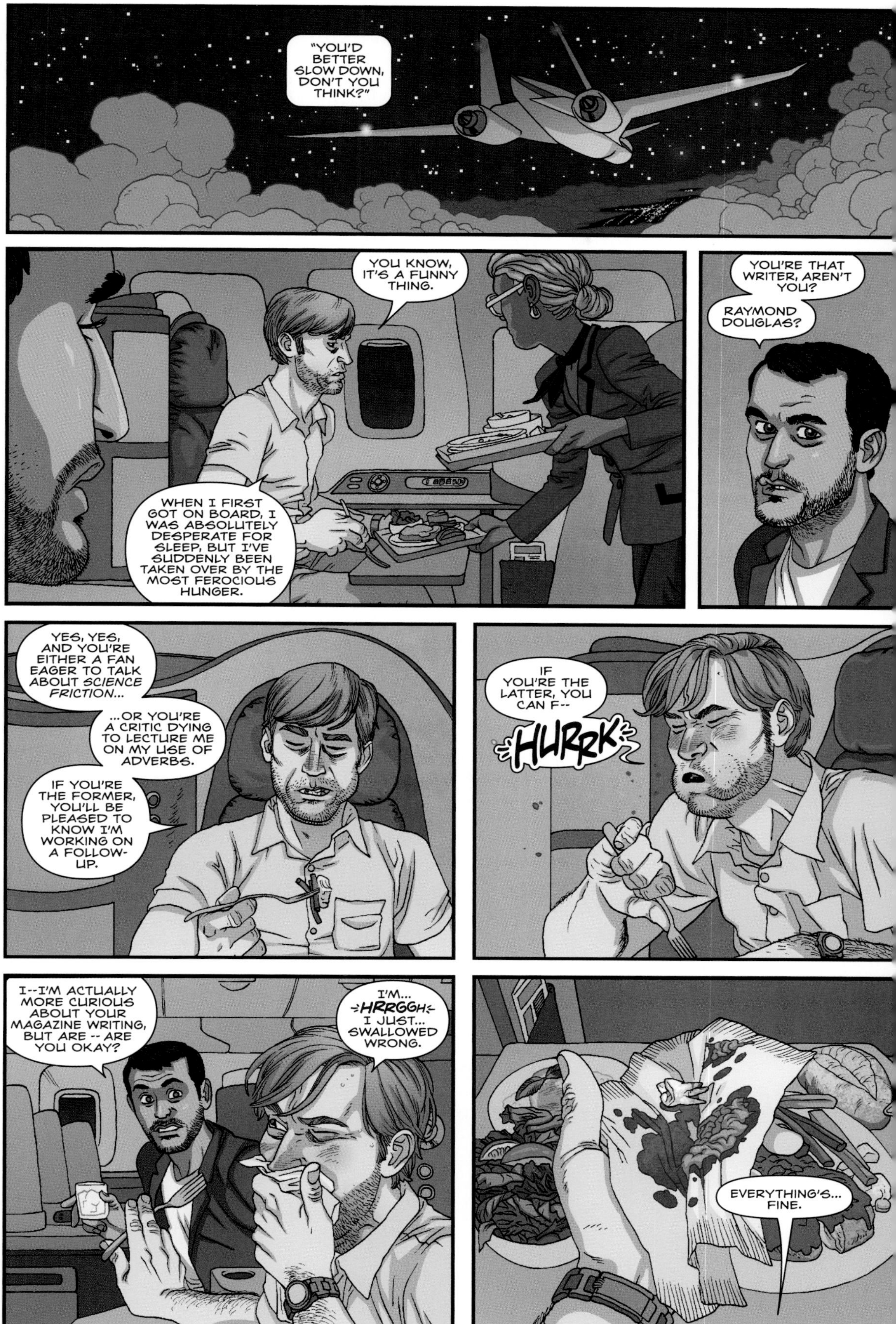
"YOU'D BETTER SLOW DOWN, DON'T YOU THINK?"
YOU KNOW, IT'S A FUNNY THING.
WHEN I FIRST GOT ON BOARD, I WAS ABSOLUTELY DESPERATE FOR SLEEP, BUT I'VE SUDDENLY BEEN TAKEN OVER BY THE MOST FEROCIOUS HUNGER.
YOU'RE THAT WRITER, AREN'T YOU?
RAYMOND DOUGLAS?
YES, YES, AND YOU'RE EITHER A FAN EAGER TO TALK ABOUT *SCIENCE FRICTION*...
...OR YOU'RE A CRITIC DYING TO LECTURE ME ON MY USE OF ADVERBS.
IF YOU'RE THE FORMER, YOU'LL BE PLEASED TO KNOW I'M WORKING ON A FOLLOW-UP.
IF YOU'RE THE LATTER, YOU CAN F--
HURRK
I--I'M ACTUALLY MORE CURIOUS ABOUT YOUR MAGAZINE WRITING, BUT ARE -- ARE YOU OKAY?
I'M... HRRGGH I JUST... SWALLOWED WRONG.
EVERYTHING'S... FINE.

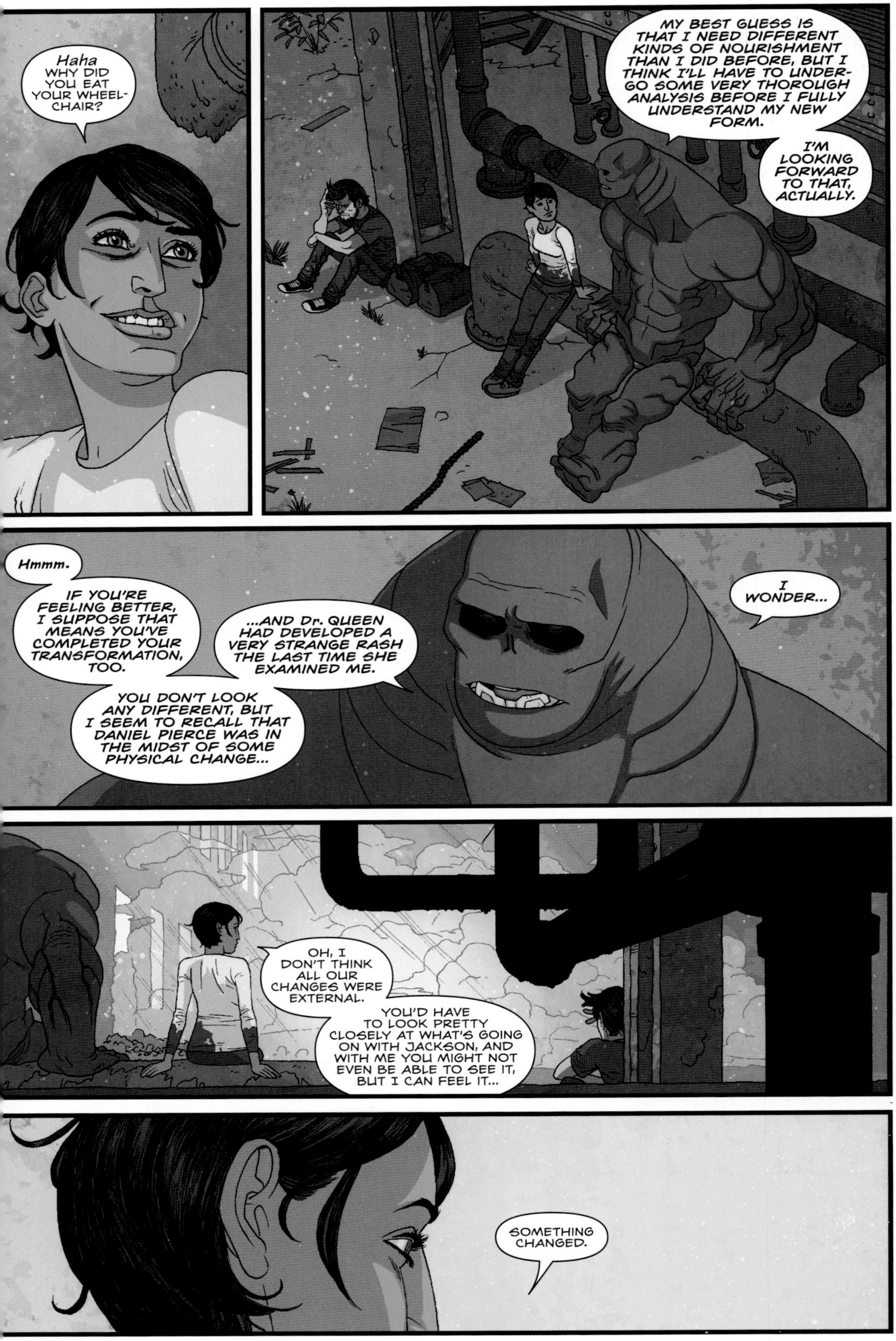
Haha WHY DID YOU EAT YOUR WHEEL-CHAIR?
MY BEST GUESS IS THAT I NEED DIFFERENT KINDS OF NOURISHMENT THAN I DID BEFORE, BUT I THINK I'LL HAVE TO UNDER-GO SOME VERY THOROUGH ANALYSIS BEFORE I FULLY UNDERSTAND MY NEW FORM.
I'M LOOKING FORWARD TO THAT, ACTUALLY.
Hmmm.
IF YOU'RE FEELING BETTER, I SUPPOSE THAT MEANS YOU'VE COMPLETED YOUR TRANSFORMATION, TOO.
YOU DON'T LOOK ANY DIFFERENT, BUT I SEEM TO RECALL THAT DANIEL PIERCE WAS IN THE MIDST OF SOME PHYSICAL CHANGE...
...AND Dr. QUEEN HAD DEVELOPED A VERY STRANGE RASH THE LAST TIME SHE EXAMINED ME.
I WONDER...
OH, I DON'T THINK ALL OUR CHANGES WERE EXTERNAL.
YOU'D HAVE TO LOOK PRETTY CLOSELY AT WHAT'S GOING ON WITH JACKSON, AND WITH ME YOU MIGHT NOT EVEN BE ABLE TO SEE IT, BUT I CAN FEEL IT...
SOMETHING CHANGED.

INTERESTING.

I OBVIOUSLY DON'T HAVE ANY RECOLLECTION OF WHAT HAPPENED WHILE I WAS UNCONSCIOUS, BUT BASED ON THE STATE I WAS IN WHEN I AWOKE, YOUR DESCRIPTION SEEMS FAIRLY ACCURATE.

I THINK MY BODY GENERATED A KIND OF COCOON TO PROTECT MY NEW FORM WHILE IT WAS STILL TAKING SHAPE.

"WHAT I DO REMEMBER, THOUGH, IS WAKING UP WEAK AND UNSTEADY WITHIN THE REMAINS OF THAT COCOON."

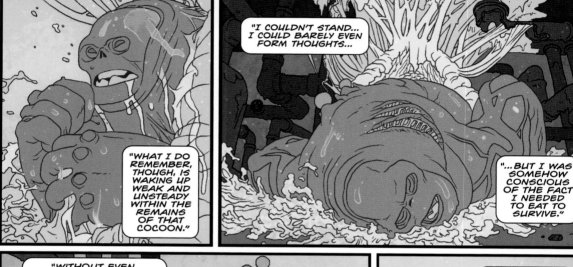

"I COULDN'T STAND... I COULD BARELY EVEN FORM THOUGHTS..."

"...BUT I WAS SOMEHOW CONSCIOUS OF THE FACT I NEEDED TO EAT TO SURVIVE."

"WITHOUT EVEN THINKING, I CONSUMED THE COCOON, BUT THAT STILL WASN'T ENOUGH TO SATIATE MY HUNGER..."

"...SO I ATE MY WHEELCHAIR."

"THE MORE I ATE, THE MORE I GREW... AND THE MORE AWARE I BECAME OF WHAT WAS HAPPENING TO ME.

"IT'S QUITE FASCINATING, REALLY."

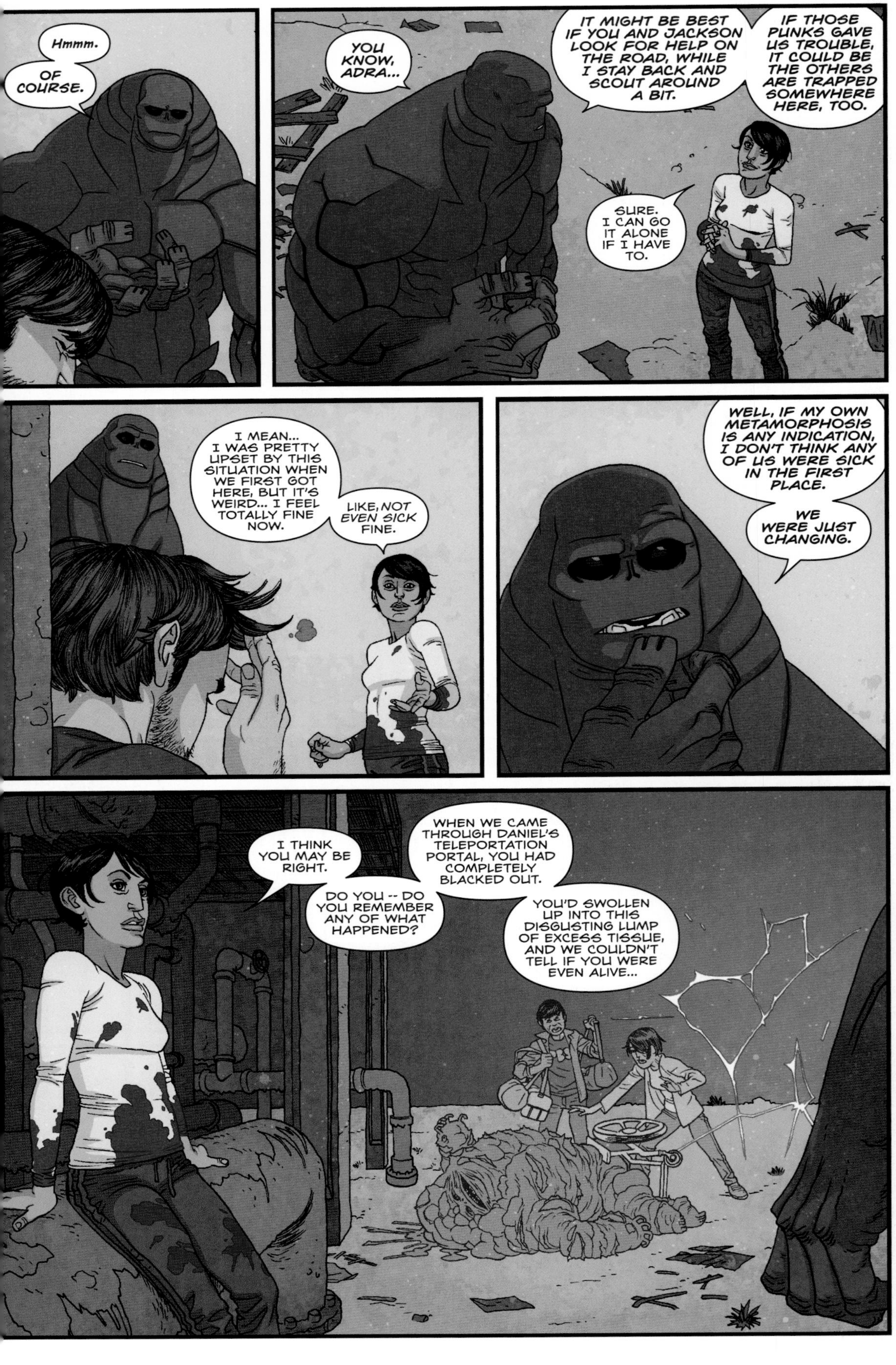
Hmmm.
OF COURSE.
YOU KNOW, ADRA...
IT MIGHT BE BEST IF YOU AND JACKSON LOOK FOR HELP ON THE ROAD, WHILE I STAY BACK AND SCOUT AROUND A BIT.
IF THOSE PUNKS GAVE US TROUBLE, IT COULD BE THE OTHERS ARE TRAPPED SOMEWHERE HERE, TOO.
SURE. I CAN GO IT ALONE IF I HAVE TO.
I MEAN... I WAS PRETTY UPSET BY THIS SITUATION WHEN WE FIRST GOT HERE, BUT IT'S WEIRD... I FEEL TOTALLY FINE NOW.
LIKE, *NOT EVEN SICK* FINE.
WELL, IF MY OWN METAMORPHOSIS IS ANY INDICATION, I DON'T THINK ANY OF US WERE SICK IN THE FIRST PLACE.
WE WERE JUST CHANGING.
I THINK YOU MAY BE RIGHT.
DO YOU -- DO YOU REMEMBER ANY OF WHAT HAPPENED?
WHEN WE CAME THROUGH DANIEL'S TELEPORTATION PORTAL, YOU HAD COMPLETELY BLACKED OUT.
YOU'D SWOLLEN UP INTO THIS DISGUSTING LUMP OF EXCESS TISSUE, AND WE COULDN'T TELL IF YOU WERE EVEN ALIVE...

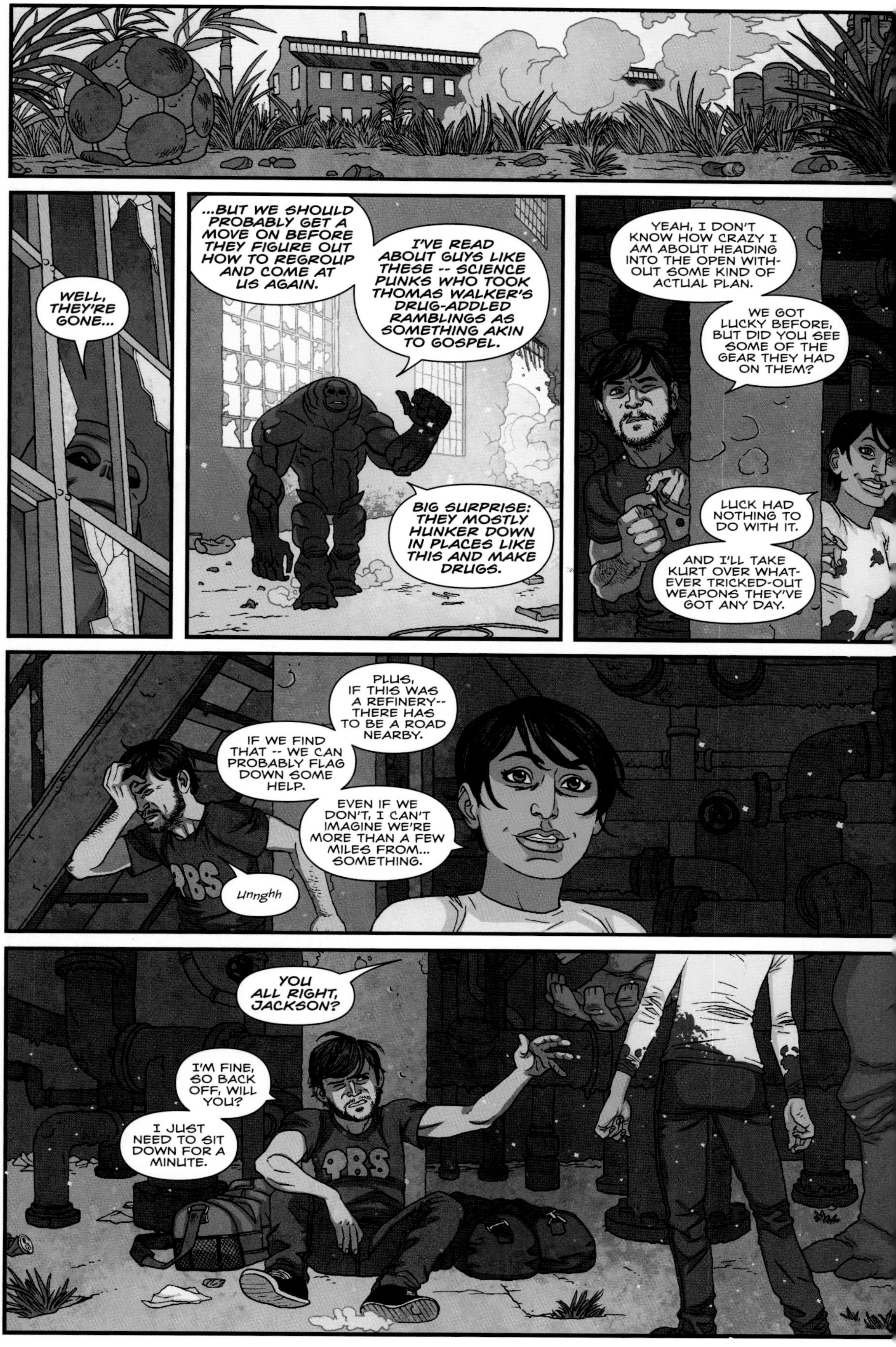
WELL, THEY'RE GONE...
...BUT WE SHOULD PROBABLY GET A MOVE ON BEFORE THEY FIGURE OUT HOW TO REGROUP AND COME AT US AGAIN.
I'VE READ ABOUT GUYS LIKE THESE -- SCIENCE PUNKS WHO TOOK THOMAS WALKER'S DRUG-ADDLED RAMBLINGS AS SOMETHING AKIN TO GOSPEL.
BIG SURPRISE: THEY MOSTLY HUNKER DOWN IN PLACES LIKE THIS AND MAKE DRUGS.
YEAH, I DON'T KNOW HOW CRAZY I AM ABOUT HEADING INTO THE OPEN WITH-OUT SOME KIND OF ACTUAL PLAN.
WE GOT LUCKY BEFORE, BUT DID YOU SEE SOME OF THE GEAR THEY HAD ON THEM?
LUCK HAD NOTHING TO DO WITH IT.
AND I'LL TAKE KURT OVER WHAT-EVER TRICKED-OUT WEAPONS THEY'VE GOT ANY DAY.
PLUS, IF THIS WAS A REFINERY-- THERE HAS TO BE A ROAD NEARBY.
IF WE FIND THAT -- WE CAN PROBABLY FLAG DOWN SOME HELP.
EVEN IF WE DON'T, I CAN'T IMAGINE WE'RE MORE THAN A FEW MILES FROM... SOMETHING.
Unnghh
YOU ALL RIGHT, JACKSON?
I'M FINE, SO BACK OFF, WILL YOU?
I JUST NEED TO SIT DOWN FOR A MINUTE.

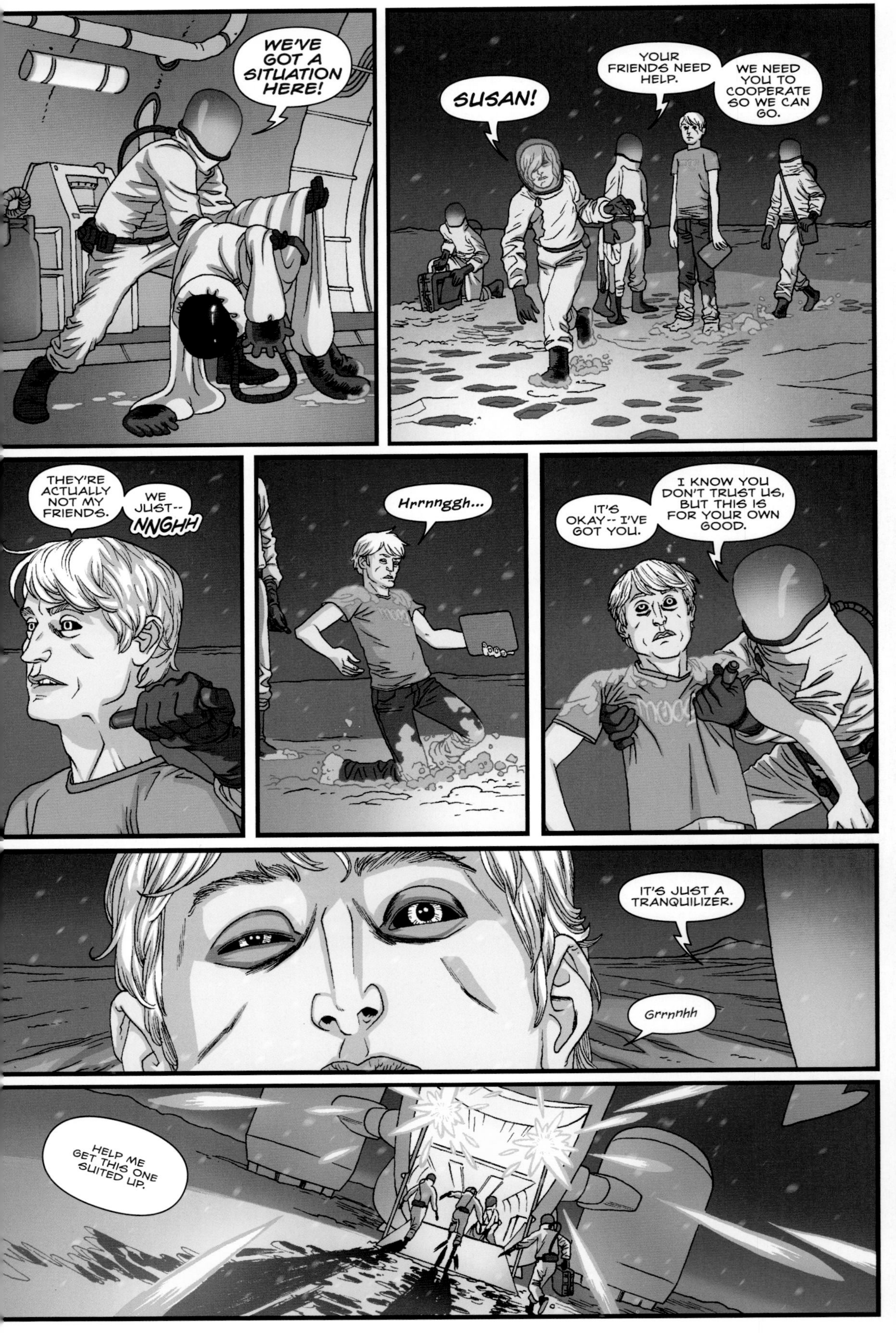
WE'VE GOT A SITUATION HERE!
SUSAN!
YOUR FRIENDS NEED HELP.
WE NEED YOU TO COOPERATE SO WE CAN GO.
THEY'RE ACTUALLY NOT MY FRIENDS.
WE JUST-- NNGHH
Hrrnnggh...
IT'S OKAY-- I'VE GOT YOU.
I KNOW YOU DON'T TRUST US, BUT THIS IS FOR YOUR OWN GOOD.
IT'S JUST A TRANQUILIZER.
Grrnnhh
HELP ME GET THIS ONE SUITED UP.

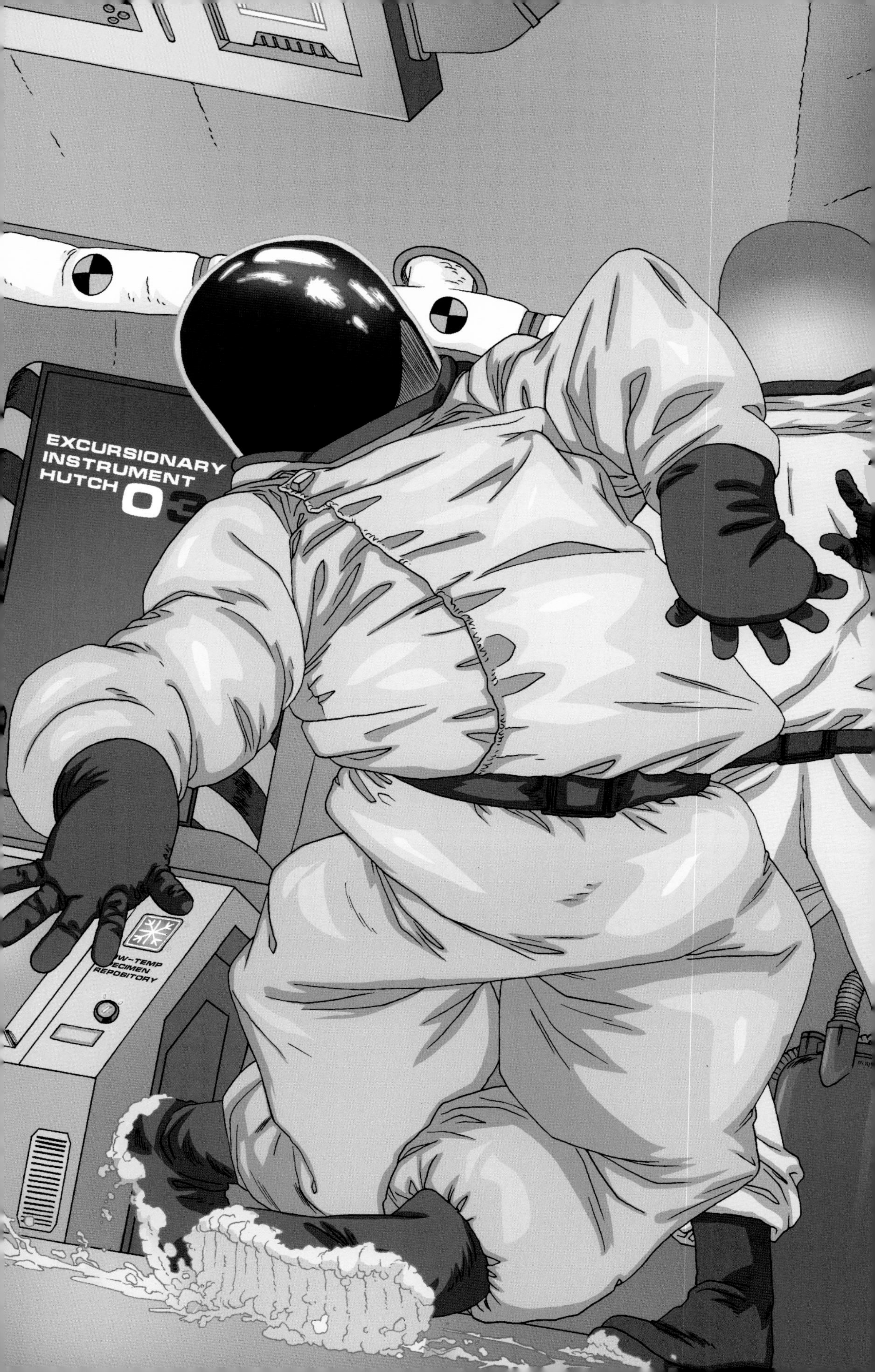
EXCURSIONARY
INSTRUMENT
HUTCH 03
REPOSITORY

EXCUSE ME -- I NEED TO TALK TO YOU ABOUT HOLLY'S CONDITION.

SHE'S LOST A LOT OF BLOOD.

SHE WAS SHOT IN THE CHEST. I DID AS MUCH AS I COULD TO STOP HER BLEEDING OUT, BUT SHE...

WE'LL DO WHAT WE CAN, BUT CAN I ASK YOU SOMETHING?

"DO YOU KNOW WHERE HE GOT THAT?"

WHAT? HIS COMPUTER? I'M SORRY, I--

OH, SHIT.

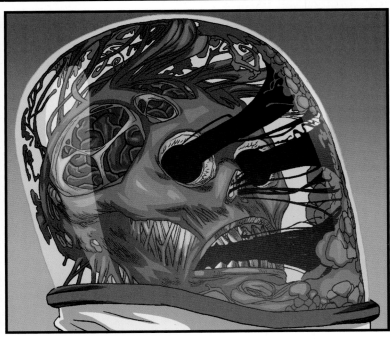

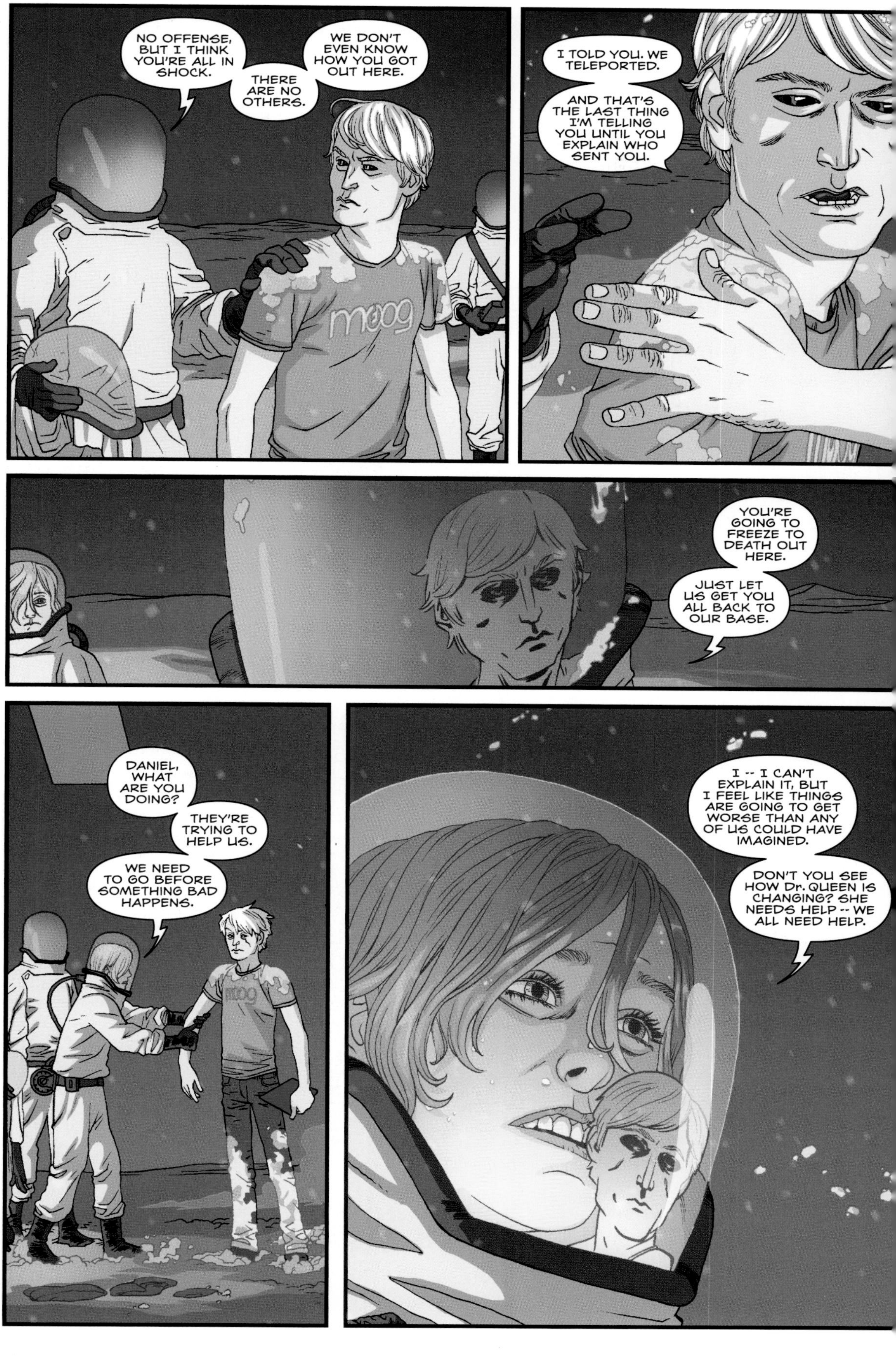
NO OFFENSE, BUT I THINK YOU'RE ALL IN SHOCK.
THERE ARE NO OTHERS.
WE DON'T EVEN KNOW HOW YOU GOT OUT HERE.
I TOLD YOU. WE TELEPORTED.
AND THAT'S THE LAST THING I'M TELLING YOU UNTIL YOU EXPLAIN WHO SENT YOU.
YOU'RE GOING TO FREEZE TO DEATH OUT HERE.
JUST LET US GET YOU ALL BACK TO OUR BASE.
DANIEL, WHAT ARE YOU DOING?
THEY'RE TRYING TO HELP US.
WE NEED TO GO BEFORE SOMETHING BAD HAPPENS.
I -- I CAN'T EXPLAIN IT, BUT I FEEL LIKE THINGS ARE GOING TO GET WORSE THAN ANY OF US COULD HAVE IMAGINED.
DON'T YOU SEE HOW Dr. QUEEN IS CHANGING? SHE NEEDS HELP -- WE ALL NEED HELP.

"NOTHING YOU'RE SAYING MAKES ANY SENSE."

NU RADIATION? WHAT'S HE TALKING ABOUT?

WE WERE ALL QUARANTINED WITH SOME KIND OF VIRUS --

WHATEVER'S HAPPENING TO US... TO ME... IT'S NOT RADIATION SICKNESS.

DID YOU SAY QUARANTINED?

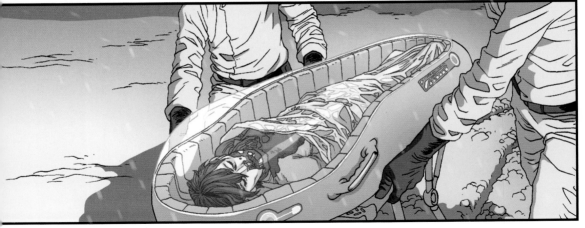

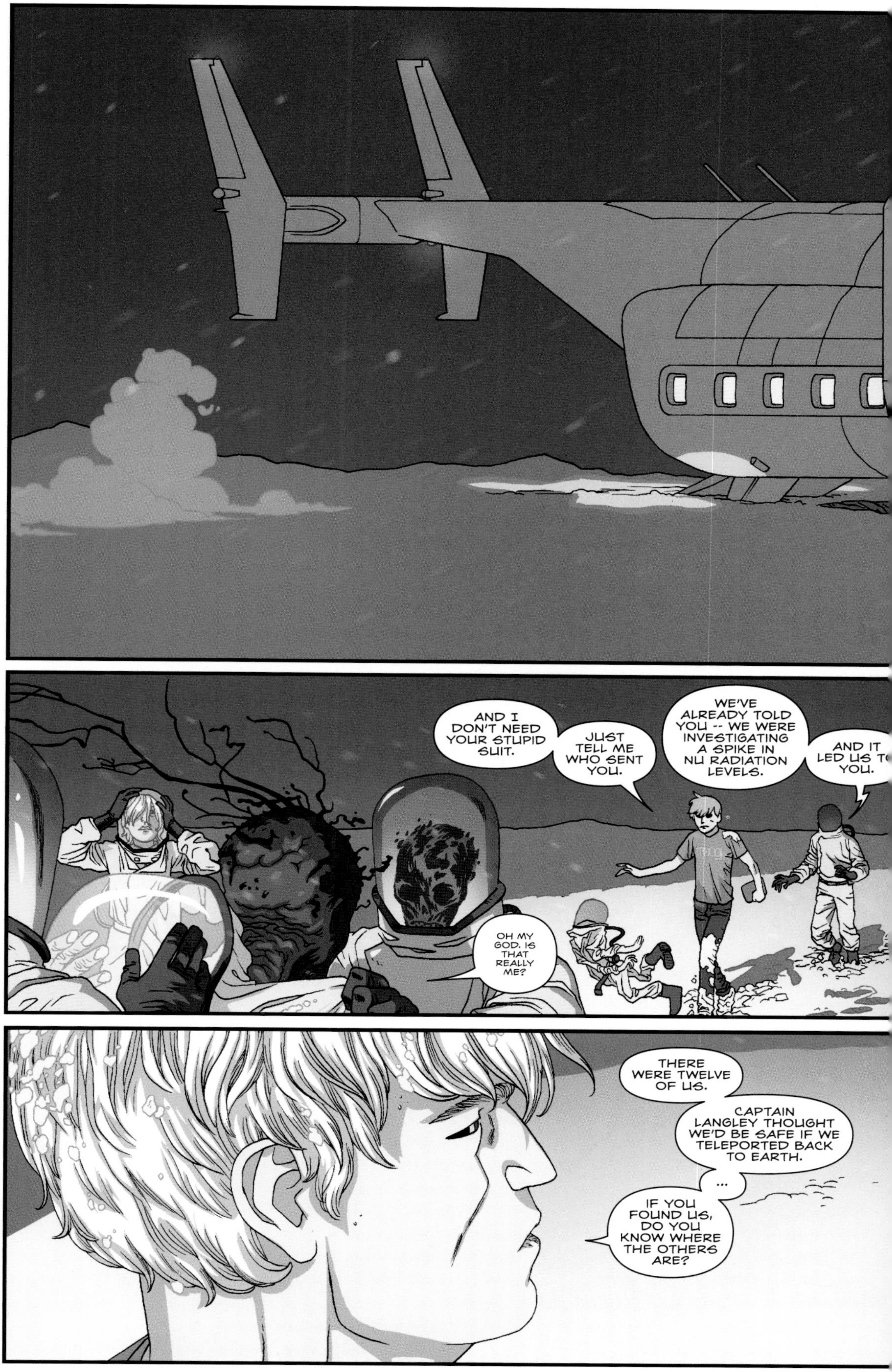
AND I DON'T NEED YOUR STUPID SUIT.
JUST TELL ME WHO SENT YOU.
WE'VE ALREADY TOLD YOU -- WE WERE INVESTIGATING A SPIKE IN NU RADIATION LEVELS.
AND IT LED US TO YOU.
OH MY GOD. IS THAT REALLY ME?
THERE WERE TWELVE OF US.
CAPTAIN LANGLEY THOUGHT WE'D BE SAFE IF WE TELEPORTED BACK TO EARTH.
...
IF YOU FOUND US, DO YOU KNOW WHERE THE OTHERS ARE?

Monica
The Kind Poets

—

—

Psychedelic painting created by the legendary
design collective known as The Kind Poets.

The exact date of the work is unknown, but
it is believed to have been commissioned
by Emerson Strange for one of his daughter
Monica's pre-teen birthdays.

NO, I AGREE, DADE CAN'T BE INVOLVED.

HE NEEDS TO BE AS SURPRISED AS EVERYONE ELSE.

GOOD MORNING, MISTER FLETCHER.

Oh, HEY THERE, Ms. TEN.

MISTER GRIMSHAW IS ALREADY INSIDE.

HE AND THE DOCTOR ARE EXPECTING YOU.

AS OUTSPOKEN AS HE'S BEEN ABOUT THOMAS, HE'S GOING TO WIND UP SHOULDERING A LOT OF THE BLAME FOR THIS.

ARE YOU COMFORTABLE WITH THAT?

WELL, GIVEN THE CIRCUMSTANCES, MY PERSONAL COMFORT -- OR EVEN DADE'S, FOR THAT MATTER -- SHOULDN'T BE OUR TOP PRIORITY.

THIS HAS TO BE DONE.

Ah, MISTER FLETCHER, THANK YOU FOR JOINING US.

MISTER WALKER IS GOING TO BE... RESIGNING FROM WORLD CORP, DARROW. WE NEED TO BRAINSTORM SOME P.R. STRATEGIES.

WHAT?

ARE YOU SERIOUS?

I KNOW MISTER WALKER IS A BIT ODD, BUT IS THIS THE ONLY WAY?

PEOPLE ARE GOING TO GO NUTS OVER THIS...

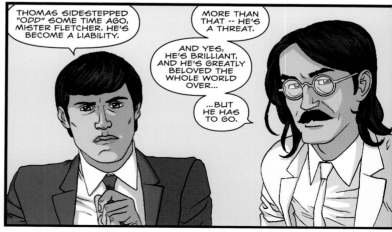

THOMAS SIDESTEPPED "ODD" SOME TIME AGO, MISTER FLETCHER. HE'S BECOME A LIABILITY.

MORE THAN THAT -- HE'S A THREAT.

AND YES, HE'S BRILLIANT, AND HE'S GREATLY BELOVED THE WHOLE WORLD OVER...

...BUT HE HAS TO GO.

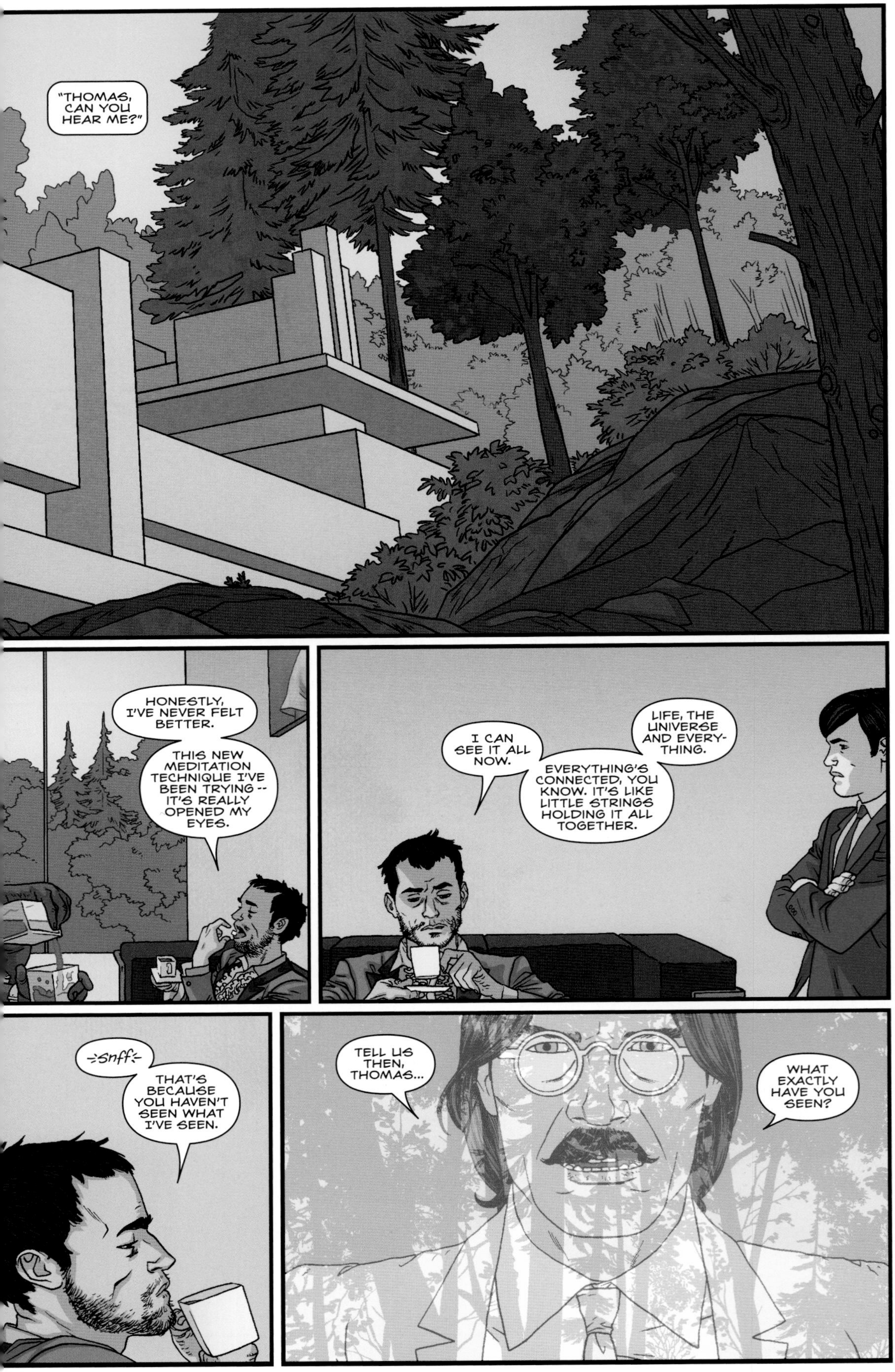
"THOMAS, CAN YOU HEAR ME?"
HONESTLY, I'VE NEVER FELT BETTER.
THIS NEW MEDITATION TECHNIQUE I'VE BEEN TRYING -- IT'S REALLY OPENED MY EYES.
I CAN SEE IT ALL NOW.
LIFE, THE UNIVERSE AND EVERY-THING.
EVERYTHING'S CONNECTED, YOU KNOW. IT'S LIKE LITTLE STRINGS HOLDING IT ALL TOGETHER.
-snff-
THAT'S BECAUSE YOU HAVEN'T SEEN WHAT I'VE SEEN.
TELL US THEN, THOMAS...
WHAT EXACTLY HAVE YOU SEEN?

THIS HAS TO STOP.

THIS BEHAVIOR OF YOURS HAS GONE WELL PAST THE POINT OF BEING A MERE NUISANCE -- PEOPLE ARE BEGINNING TO TALK.

THEY'RE STARTING TO SAY YOU'RE UNWELL.

UNWELL?

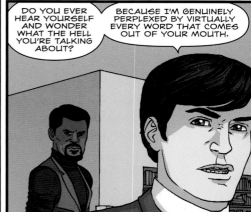

DO YOU EVER HEAR YOURSELF AND WONDER WHAT THE HELL YOU'RE TALKING ABOUT?

BECAUSE I'M GENUINELY PERPLEXED BY VIRTUALLY EVERY WORD THAT COMES OUT OF YOUR MOUTH.

While it's no surprise that the seemingly indomitable World Corp has once again topped virtually every category in our annual readers' poll, what's stunning is how tight a hold the long-missing Thomas Walker has on your hearts and minds.

Walker was again voted first among his peers in both the Physics and Astrophysics categories, and also made an appearance in the Most Wonderful Human Being list.

Meanwhile, World Corp proper took the top slot in a full 13 categories, including Company, Male Thinker, Inventor, Consumer Product and Industrial Innovation.

The winner in the Industrial Innovation category left readers divided, however, with World Corp's Nigel earning nods as both the Most Wonderful Human Being and Creep of the Year...

14. KURTZBORG X-51
15. SPATIAL DIMINISHER
16. SKYLARK AIRLAB
17. DATAAC LINC
18. NEGASTAT
19. FIRE MOP
20. PAVLOMITE

architectural innovation

1. THE CUSTERDOME
2. TRANS-ISLAND SKYWAY
3. VILLA PHRAXOS
4. OLV-26 MODULAR HOUSING
5. TERRA VISTA STATION
6. STOCKHOLM OMNIPLEX
7. ANDROMEDA HEIGHTS
8. SPANAWAY ARCH
9. THE ARC
10. LIFEHOUSE ECO-VILLAGE

favorite physical enhancement

1. HAND FON
2. OPTICAL PROJECTOR IMPLANTS
3. CYBER OPTICS 5
4. FLASH FOLLICLES
5. STOMACH WORM

best product design

1. HAND FON
2. CUBIQ
3. TIMEBOX
4. SHELTER IN A SUITCASE
5. ULTRANOL

event of the year

1. DADE ELLIS SABBATICAL
2. MISSION TO MARS
3. SPROSTON GREEN FESTIVAL
4. MEMORIAD XXVII
5. THOMAS WALKER SIGHTING IN LAOS

best dressed male

1. EMERSON STRANGE
2. PETER PANIC
3. STEVEN PATRICK
4. DAVID LIN
5. SIMON GRIMSHAW
6. JULIAN STROHMEYER
7. ANTHONY DAY
8. XAVIER MOORE
9. ANTHONY JAMES
10. ROYCE KEEN

best dressed female

1. PARIS SMITH
2. PETER PANIC
3. SONYA MADAN
4. SANDRA GOODRICH
5. MARIE McDONALD
6. ESME
7. KIMBERLY SMITH
8. SAMANTHA LWIN
9. SHUNA THORNE
10. XANTHE HAN

haircut

1. EMERSON STRANGE
2. ESME
3. SIMON GRIMSHAW
4. SONYA MADAN
5. PETER PANIC

electronics

1. VINCE MARTIN
2. PAUL GRENFIELD
3. DAVID JAMES
4. NORMAN MICHAELS

5. MORGAN ROBERTSON

physics

1. THOMAS WALKER
2. COLIN JOSEPH
3. SPENCER DEAN
4. JAMES WATKINS
5. MADDY NOLAN

astrophysics

1. THOMAS WALKER
2. ESME
3. ISAAC HARRIS
4. SHUNA THORNE
5. AL PREWITT

medicine

1. DADE ELLIS
2. SANDRA GOODRICH
3. THOMAS YU
4. STEPHEN COLLINS
5. PAUL BUCKLER

computers

1. XAVIER MOORE
2. STEVE NASON
3. AUGUSTUS MARTIN
4. ZENJI HIROGUCHI
5. ELIZABETH BOLYARD

lecture series

1. RAYMOND DOUGLAS
2. CRAISE FINTON KIRK
3. ANDREW FALCO
4. VICTORIA AUSTIN
5. DOUGLAS RAIN
6. HELMOLTZ WATSON
7. WALTER WEEKS
8. ANTHONY DAVIS
9. RODDY BYERS
10. CYNTHIA FREED

essay

1. FUTURE GAMES - ROBERT LAWRENCE
2. EXTINCTION EVENT -

MALCOM ROBERTS
3. DISTANT STAR - EMERSON STRANGE
4. A PRISONER OF THE PAST - SIMON GRIMSHAW
5. MECHANICAL WONDER - ANTHONY DAY
6. THE INVISIBLE ARMIES OF MARS - NIAL RAND
7. THE RIGHT THING RIGHT - MARTIN MAHER
8. MY SELFISH GENE - ELIZABETH MATTHEWS
9. O GREEN WORLD - SIR JOHN JOHNS
10. LITTLE ATOMS - MILES CHAPLIN

book

1. SCIENCE FRICTION - RAYMOND DOUGLAS
2. DARK THERAPY - SONYA MADAN
3. THE CERTAINTY OF CHANCE - EDWARD NEIL
4. STANDING OUT IN THE UNIVERSE - H. DAVID PENCE
5. THE CAVES OF ALTAMIRA - TRISTAN FABRIANI & GUSTAV MAHLER
6. UTTERLY SIMPLE - VICTOR HENRY
7. DISSOLVING TIME - SHIRLEY LEE
8. FATHERS OF THE ATOM BOMB - PHILIP CASTLE
9. PROFESSOR SUPERCOOL - ROBERT HOWARD
10. SIMON DIAMOND - NICK JAMES

film

1. LEVIATHAN
2. PROLOGUE TO HISTORY
3. UNSTOPPABLE SALVATION
4. ANTARCTIC
5. KODACHROME GHOSTS
6. SLOW REFLECTIONS/ STRANGE DELAYS
7. LOCUST VALLEY
8. HIBERNATION
9. LOVE LETTER TO THE FUTURE
10. FEAR OF MOTION

The 30th Annual TSC READERS POLL

the company

1. WORLD CORP.
2. BRILLIANT CORNERS
3. GRIMSHAW HOLDINGS
4. CULTURE CORP.
5. TRANS LUNAR
6. M.C.G.
7. CHAPLIN TECHNOLOGIES
8. KITANO ASIMOVICS
9. ACCUTECH
10. B.E.F.
11. LIN COM
12. X. MOORE UNLIMITED
13. SKYLARK, INC.
14. RADIOTRICITY
15. VANDALEY INDUSTRIES
16. GLOBOTECH
17. VOLKSWERK
18. METACORP
19. CYTECH
20. HELIOCENTRIC

male thinker

1. EMERSON STRANGE
2. MILES CHAPLIN
3. STEVEN PATRICK
4. PETER PANIC
5. DADE ELLIS
6. ROBERT MacLAUGHLIN
7. SIMON GRIMSHAW
8. JAMES CARR
9. MARC NUTTMAN
10. RON RIFE
11. THOMAS YU
12. ANTHONY DAY
13. SPENCER DEAN
14. DAVID LIN
15. JULIAN STROHMEYER
16. DANIEL MARTIN
17. CONSTANTINE BRUNOSSO
18. XAVIER MOORE
19. ZENJI HIROGUCHI
20. ISAAC HARRI

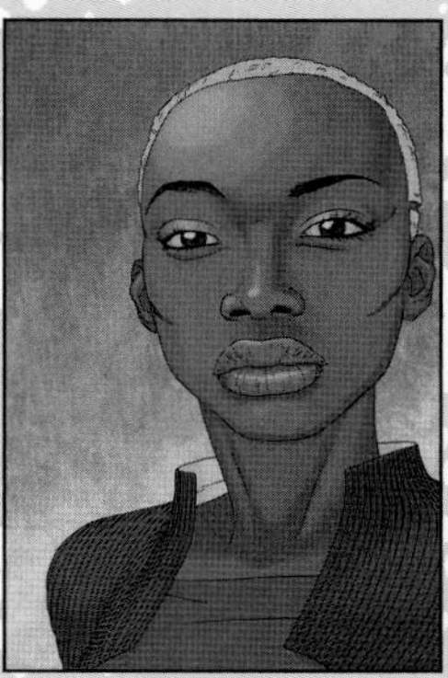

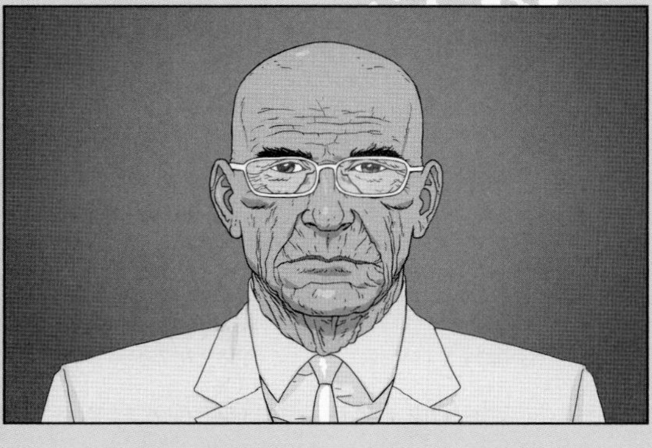

female thinker

1. PARIS SMITH
2. ESME
3. SANDRA GOODRICH
4. SONYA MADAN
5. HAYLEY BELL
6. EMILY CHAMBERS
7. SHUNA THORNE
8. SAMANTHA LWIN
9. PETER PANIC
10. GRACINE DAR
11. KIMBERLY SMITH
12. MIRANDA GREY
13. ELLA JAMES
14. MARIE McDONALD
15. LILLIAN de SEITAS
16. XANTHE HAN
17. ALICE McLEOD
18. MELANIE DAVIS
19. EVELYN TANAKA
20. JOAN LARKIN

creep of the year

1. NIAL RAND
2. PETER PANIC
3. RICHARD DEITCH
4. EMERSON STRANGE
5. ELOISE CHO
6. VICTOR FOWLEY
7. XAVIER MOORE
8. MARC NUTTMAN
9. ANTHONY DAY
10. CONSTANTINE BRUNOSSO
11. HAMILTON CLARKE
12. NIGEL
13. HARRISON WORTH
14. SILAS LANG
15. RICHARD LOUDON

most wonderful human being

1. EMERSON STRANGE
2. RODNEY DRAKE
3. RAYMOND DOUGLAS
4. SIR JOHN JOHNS
5. DADE ELLIS
6. MILES CHAPLIN
7. SHANDAR FULLOVE
8. NIGEL
9. PETER PANIC
10. SIMON GRIMSHAW
11. THOMAS WALKER
12. ROYCE KEEN
13. ANTHONY JAMES
14. DAVID LIN
15. PARIS SMITH

inventor

1. EMERSON STRANGE
2. MILES CHAPLIN
3. SIMON GRIMSHAW
4. ANTHONY DAY
5. JULIAN STROHMEYER
6. DAVID LIN
7. JAMES CARR
8. PARIS SMITH
9. ANTHONY JAMES
10. ZENJI HIROGUCHI

consumer product

1. CUBIQ
2. TIMEBOX
3. CYBER OPTICS 5
4. SOLID BOND VASCULAR ADHESIVE
5. NU-SONICS
6. HELIOS 3 SOLAR LIGHTIN
7. ULTRANOL
8. SHELTER IN A SUITCASE
9. HAND FON
10. LD 150 LIE DETECTOR
11. RD CRUSADER
12. POSTERVISION
13. LUSTRA
14. UNIMIND IV
15. NEW SECOND SKIN
16. ULTRONIC GLIDER
17. THERMASUIT
18. LUMITRON 8
19. MEMORY COLLECTOR
20. THE GRID

industrial innovation

1. NIGEL
2. PANGEA 2.0
3. ANTI-MASS SPECTROME
4. LANDEMATE SMART TIRE
5. THE GANNELECH
6. TRANS-ISLAND SKYWAY
7. ELEMENT 115
8. N.P.E. FELD HANDHABUNGSGERÄTS
9. COVERSION GEL
10. P-200 RADIATION GATE
11. SERIOUS BLACK STEALT PAINT
12. UNIT-3000/21
13. ATMOSPHERIC INDUCER

FROM THE DESK OF
SIMON GRIMSHAW

Dear Eddie —

It has become a policy of mine not to do interviews. I am no longer interested in allowing my words/intentions to be edited/re-interpreted for publication/broadcast by a media that is only marginally invested in actually reporting news or relating facts. My priorities at present are my work and while indulging the media's curiosity in everything from my favorite color socks to my judgement/opinion of people I've either never met or no longer wish to be associated with was once a useful nuisance, I currently have no interest in speaking to the press.

I do remain interested in communicating my thoughts/ideas to the world at large, or at least that segment of the public that still places value on intelligence/creativity/innovation, but little of true importance can be conveyed within the limitations of the standard interview. I have been part of hours-long audiences with the press where virtually nothing I said was transcribed accurately, or was condensed to an out of context soundbite used to support the writer's own viewpoint.

Pop culture no longer applies to me. That being the case, I am only interested in writing essays for publication in the journals specifically covering the areas of my expertise.

Regards,
Simon

THE WORLD IS FULL OF angry YOUNG MEN

We wrote to World Corp. and requested an interview with Simon Grimshaw.
He declined.
But he did send us this critique of modern media in response, with permission to publish...

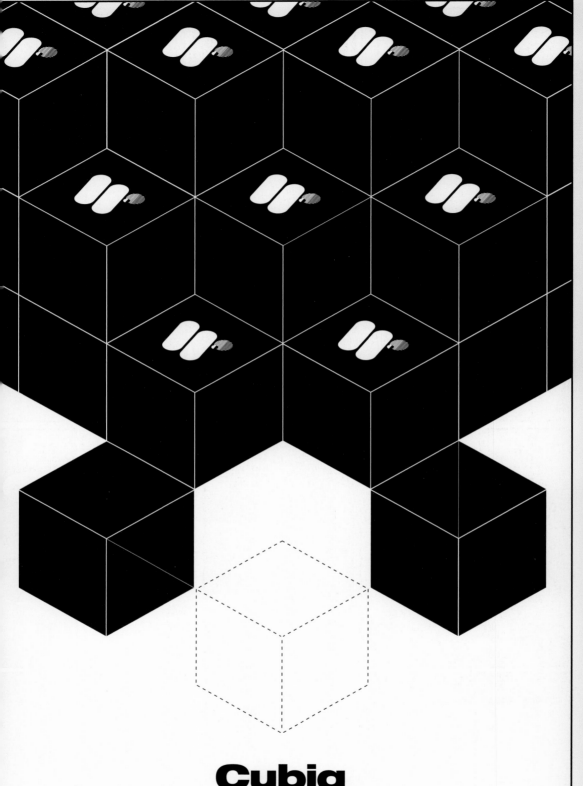

Cubiq

SNNFFF
MADRID
GOOD EVENING, SIR.
WELCOME ABOARD.
Unnghhh
EXIT
OUVERT OPEN
SIR...?
Whnnhh
STEADY THERE, SIR-- ARE YOU OKAY?
I AM. THANK YOU.
ARE YOU SURE YOU'RE ALL RIGHT?
YES. THANK YOU. YES.
JUST A BIT KNACKERED IS ALL.
I JUST NEED TO SHUT MY EYES AND TRY TO SLEEP STRAIGHT THROUGH TO LONDON.
I ASSURE YOU...
"I'LL BE A NEW MAN BY THE TIME WE REACH HOME."
TUNIS AIR الخطوط الجوية التونسية

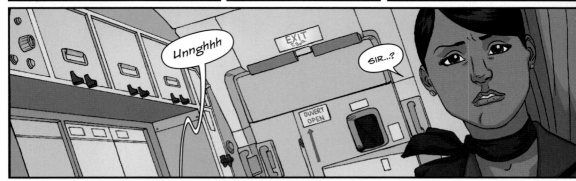

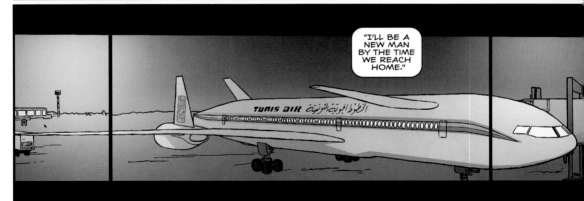

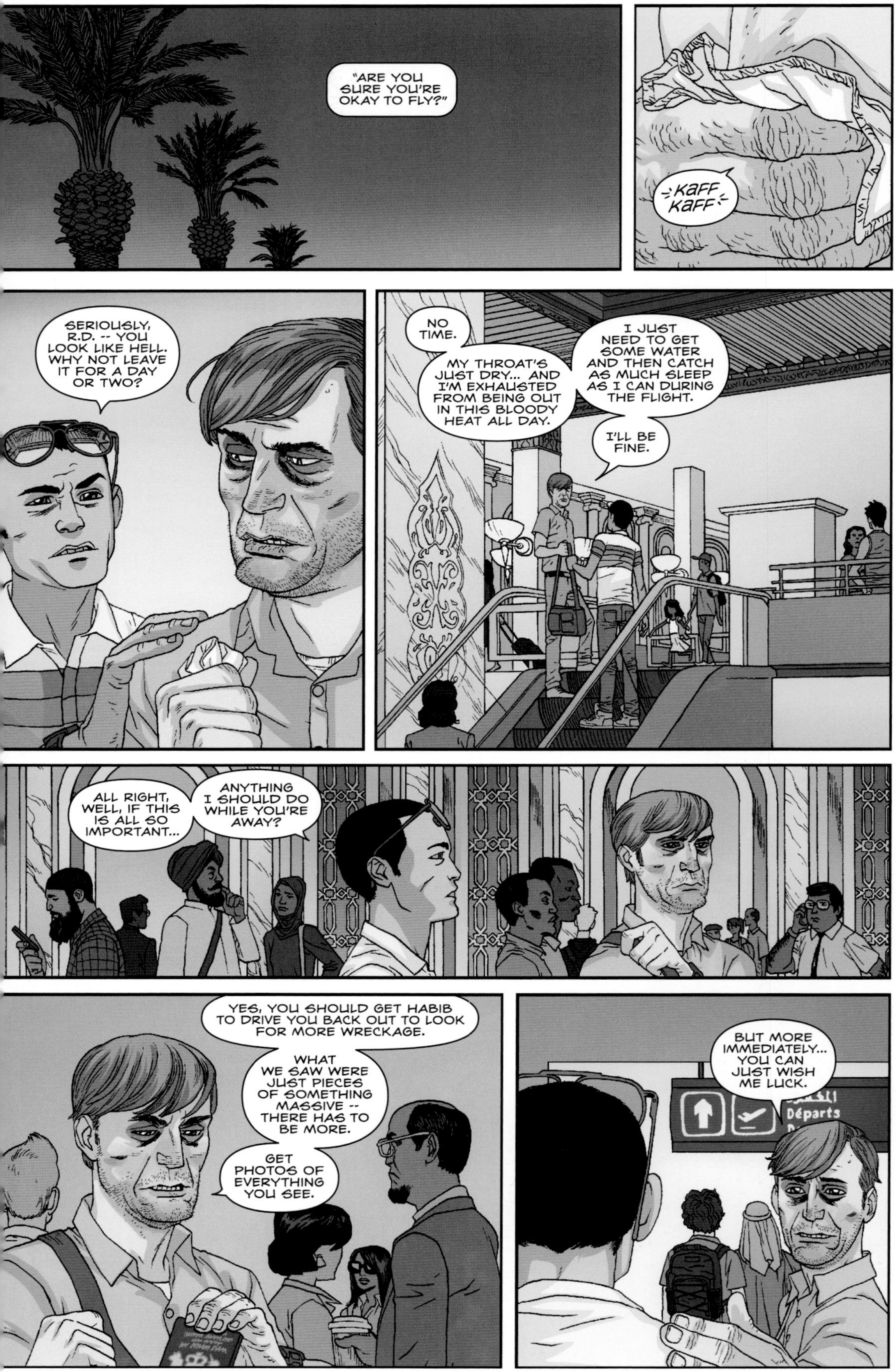
"ARE YOU SURE YOU'RE OKAY TO FLY?"
KAFF KAFF
SERIOUSLY, R.D. -- YOU LOOK LIKE HELL. WHY NOT LEAVE IT FOR A DAY OR TWO?
NO TIME.
MY THROAT'S JUST DRY... AND I'M EXHAUSTED FROM BEING OUT IN THIS BLOODY HEAT ALL DAY.
I JUST NEED TO GET SOME WATER AND THEN CATCH AS MUCH SLEEP AS I CAN DURING THE FLIGHT.
I'LL BE FINE.
ALL RIGHT, WELL, IF THIS IS ALL SO IMPORTANT...
ANYTHING I SHOULD DO WHILE YOU'RE AWAY?
YES, YOU SHOULD GET HABIB TO DRIVE YOU BACK OUT TO LOOK FOR MORE WRECKAGE.
WHAT WE SAW WERE JUST PIECES OF SOMETHING MASSIVE -- THERE HAS TO BE MORE.
GET PHOTOS OF EVERYTHING YOU SEE.
BUT MORE IMMEDIATELY... YOU CAN JUST WISH ME LUCK.
Départs

We're making plans
for Nigel.

Meet Nigel. Nigel is one of those fab little ideas virtually impossible to plan. Think of him as a happy accident. Or a surprise. Some might even call him a miracle.

We prefer to think of him as walking, talking proof that one little idea can change everything in the blink of an eye. In fact, this particular idea started with the blink of an eye, or an artificial eye, at least.

Nigel was involved in testing and perfecting our award-winning Cyber Optics so we could help the world to see. Now we're using Nigel to help the world see other worlds. So let's hear it for Nigel. **Little idea. Big plans.**

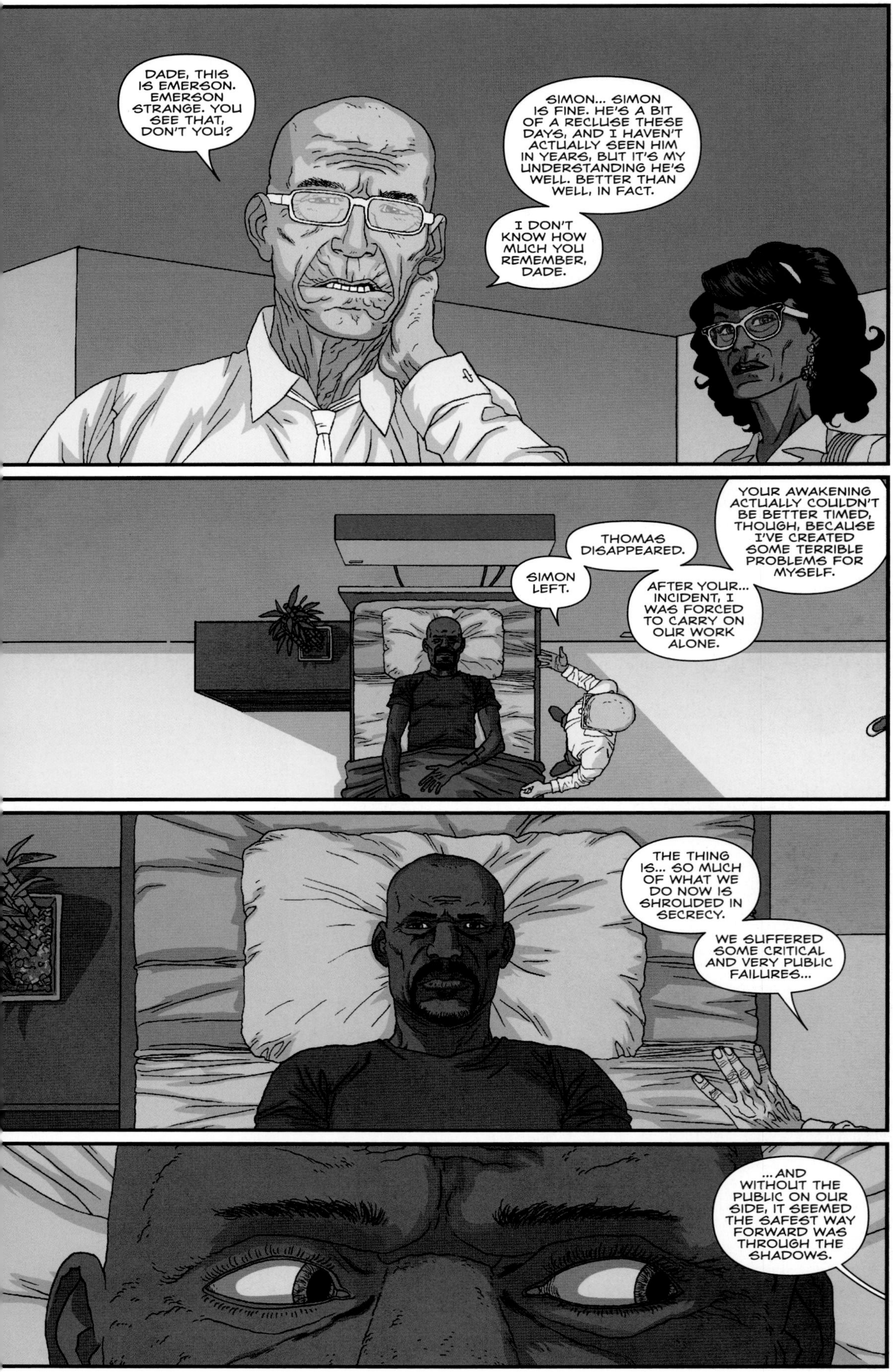

DADE, THIS IS EMERSON. EMERSON STRANGE. YOU SEE THAT, DON'T YOU?
SIMON... SIMON IS FINE. HE'S A BIT OF A RECLUSE THESE DAYS, AND I HAVEN'T ACTUALLY SEEN HIM IN YEARS, BUT IT'S MY UNDERSTANDING HE'S WELL. BETTER THAN WELL, IN FACT.
I DON'T KNOW HOW MUCH YOU REMEMBER, DADE.
SIMON LEFT.
THOMAS DISAPPEARED.
AFTER YOUR... INCIDENT, I WAS FORCED TO CARRY ON OUR WORK ALONE.
YOUR AWAKENING ACTUALLY COULDN'T BE BETTER TIMED, THOUGH, BECAUSE I'VE CREATED SOME TERRIBLE PROBLEMS FOR MYSELF.
THE THING IS... SO MUCH OF WHAT WE DO NOW IS SHROUDED IN SECRECY.
WE SUFFERED SOME CRITICAL AND VERY PUBLIC FAILURES...
...AND WITHOUT THE PUBLIC ON OUR SIDE, IT SEEMED THE SAFEST WAY FORWARD WAS THROUGH THE SHADOWS.

UNLESS THERE'S SOMETHING I'VE OVERLOOKED, I THINK WE'RE FINISHED FOR NOW, MARGAUX.

THERE ARE SOME OTHER TESTS I'D LIKE TO RUN LATER, BUT I DON'T ANTICIPATE THE RESULTS WILL SOLVE THIS PARTICULAR MYSTERY.

HE STILL NEEDS TO REGAIN HIS STRENGTH...

...BUT HE SEEMS TO BE RECOVERING AT A TRULY ASTOUNDING RATE OF SPEED.

What?

Emerson?

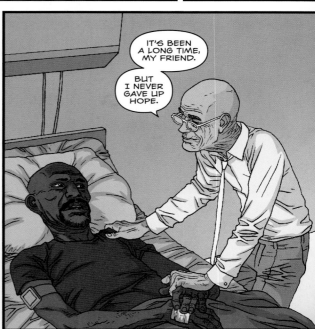

IT'S BEEN A LONG TIME, MY FRIEND.

BUT I NEVER GAVE UP HOPE.

SIR, YOU SHOULD KEEP IN MIND THAT EVEN THOUGH HE'S RESPONDING WELL TO VARIOUS STIMULI, HE COULD STILL HAVE SUFFERED SOME FORM OF BRAIN DAMAGE.

HE SEEMS DISORIENTED.

HE MAY NOT KNOW WHERE HE IS OR WHAT'S HAPPENING.

NONSENSE. HE RECOGNIZED ME, DIDN'T HE?

Simon?

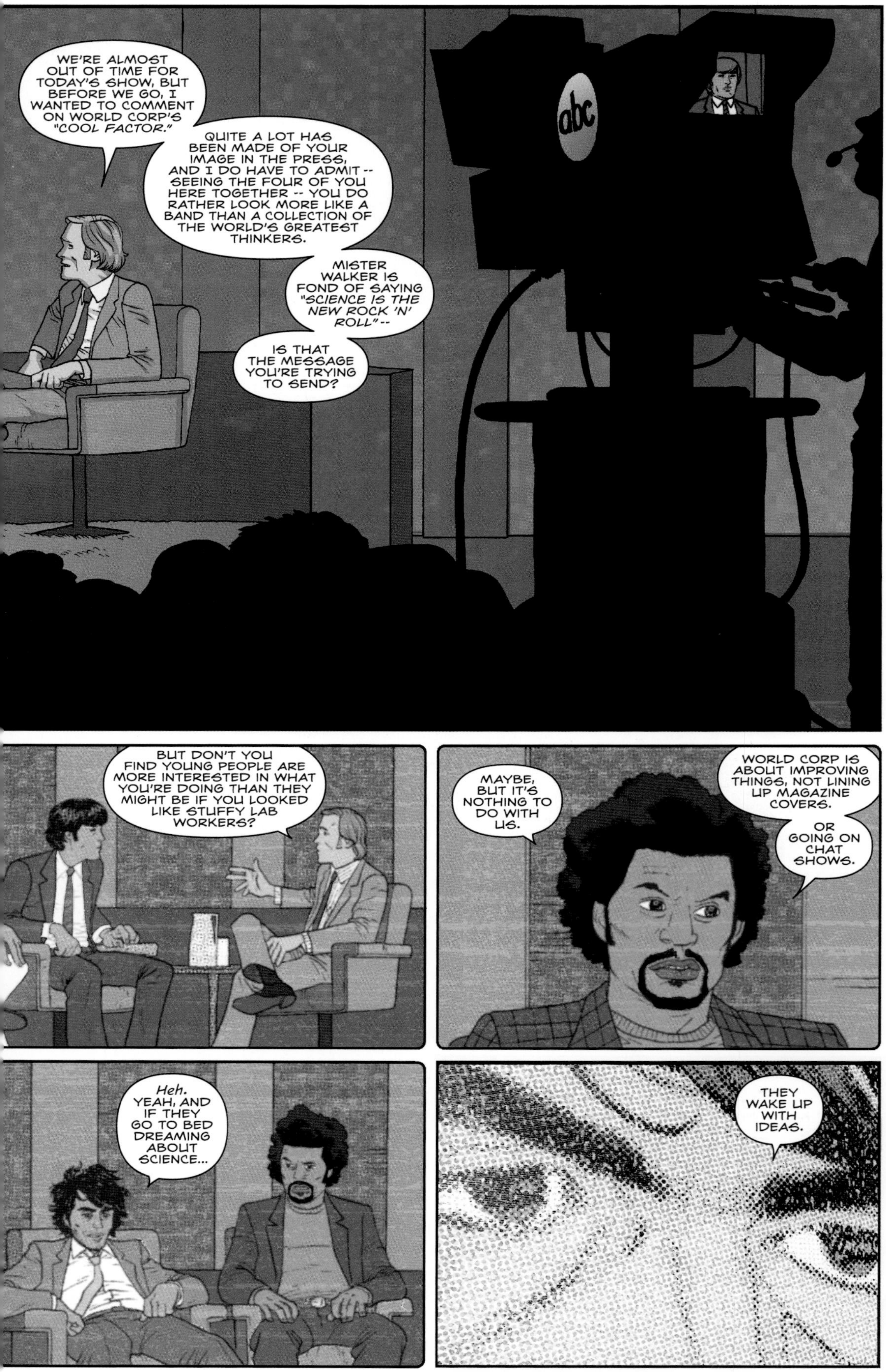
WE'RE ALMOST OUT OF TIME FOR TODAY'S SHOW, BUT BEFORE WE GO, I WANTED TO COMMENT ON WORLD CORP'S "*COOL FACTOR.*"
QUITE A LOT HAS BEEN MADE OF YOUR IMAGE IN THE PRESS, AND I DO HAVE TO ADMIT -- SEEING THE FOUR OF YOU HERE TOGETHER -- YOU DO RATHER LOOK MORE LIKE A BAND THAN A COLLECTION OF THE WORLD'S GREATEST THINKERS.
MISTER WALKER IS FOND OF SAYING "*SCIENCE IS THE NEW ROCK 'N' ROLL*" --
IS THAT THE MESSAGE YOU'RE TRYING TO SEND?
BUT DON'T YOU FIND YOUNG PEOPLE ARE MORE INTERESTED IN WHAT YOU'RE DOING THAN THEY MIGHT BE IF YOU LOOKED LIKE STUFFY LAB WORKERS?
MAYBE, BUT IT'S NOTHING TO DO WITH US.
WORLD CORP IS ABOUT IMPROVING THINGS, NOT LINING UP MAGAZINE COVERS.
OR GOING ON CHAT SHOWS.
Heh. YEAH, AND IF THEY GO TO BED DREAMING ABOUT SCIENCE...
THEY WAKE UP WITH IDEAS.

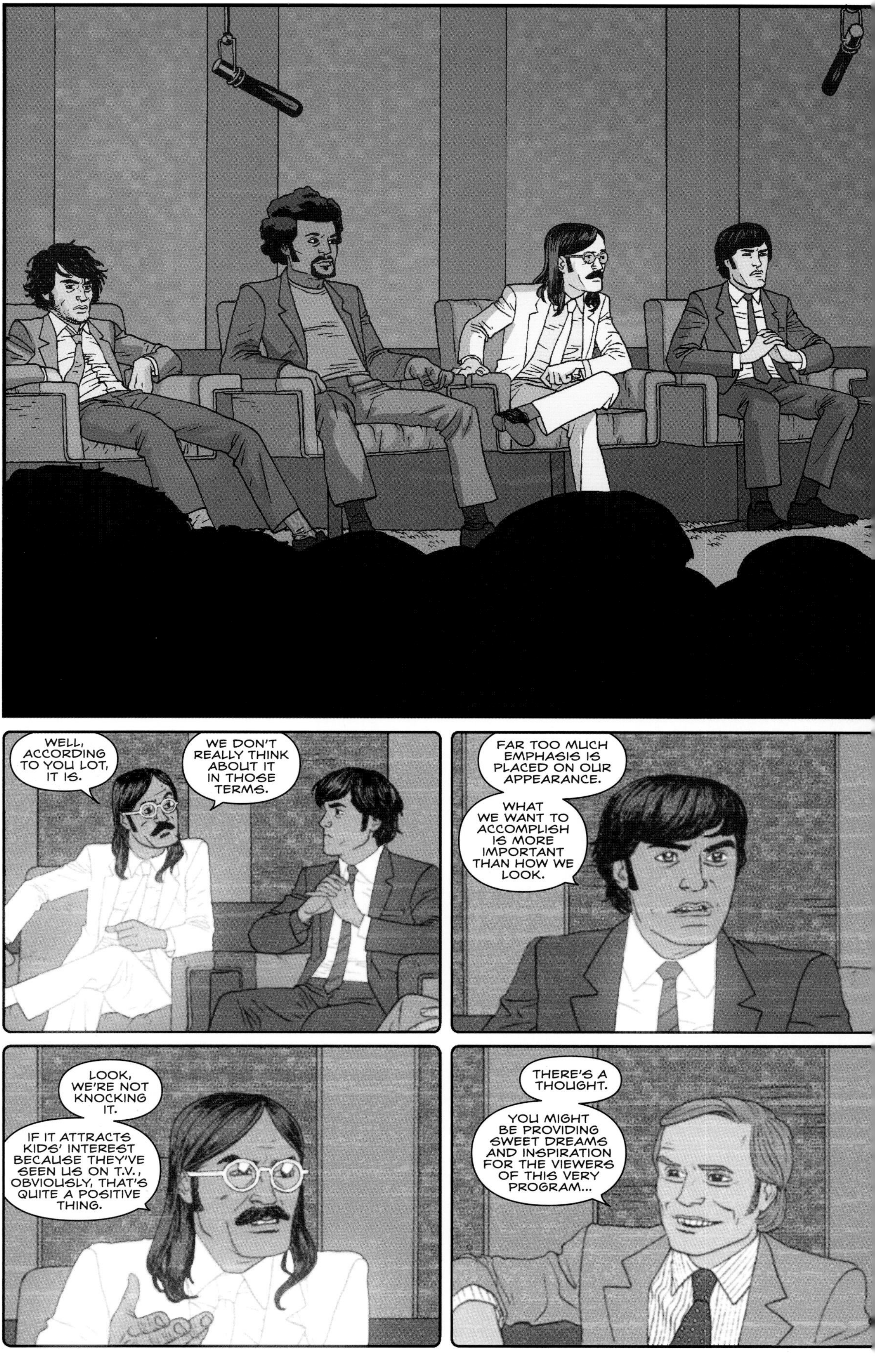
WELL, ACCORDING TO YOU LOT, IT IS.
WE DON'T REALLY THINK ABOUT IT IN THOSE TERMS.
FAR TOO MUCH EMPHASIS IS PLACED ON OUR APPEARANCE.
WHAT WE WANT TO ACCOMPLISH IS MORE IMPORTANT THAN HOW WE LOOK.
LOOK, WE'RE NOT KNOCKING IT.
IF IT ATTRACTS KIDS' INTEREST BECAUSE THEY'VE SEEN US ON T.V., OBVIOUSLY, THAT'S QUITE A POSITIVE THING.
THERE'S A THOUGHT.
YOU MIGHT BE PROVIDING SWEET DREAMS AND INSPIRATION FOR THE VIEWERS OF THIS VERY PROGRAM...

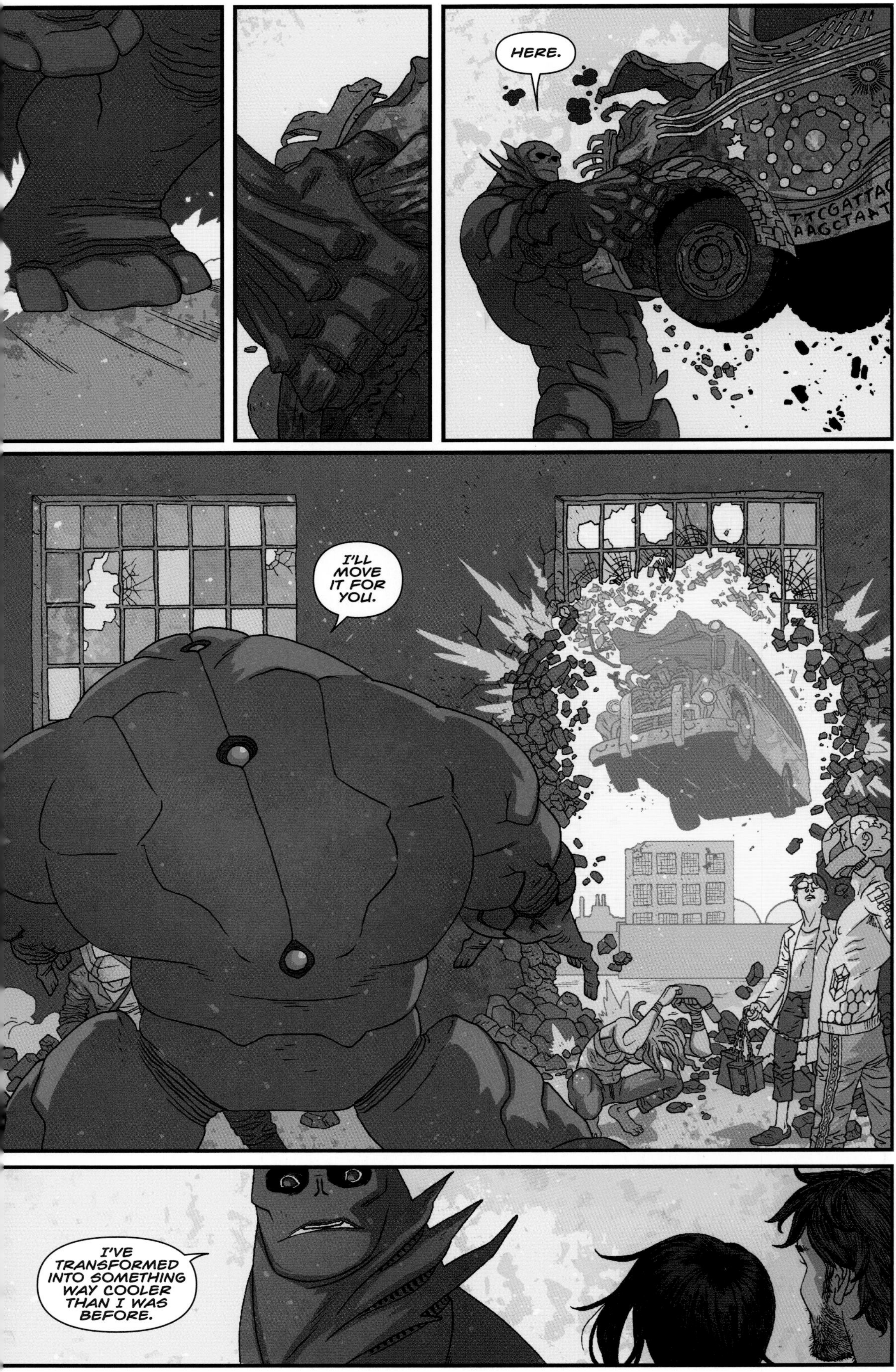
HERE.
TTCGATTAC
AAGCTAAT
I'LL MOVE IT FOR YOU.
I'VE TRANSFORMED INTO SOMETHING WAY COOLER THAN I WAS BEFORE.

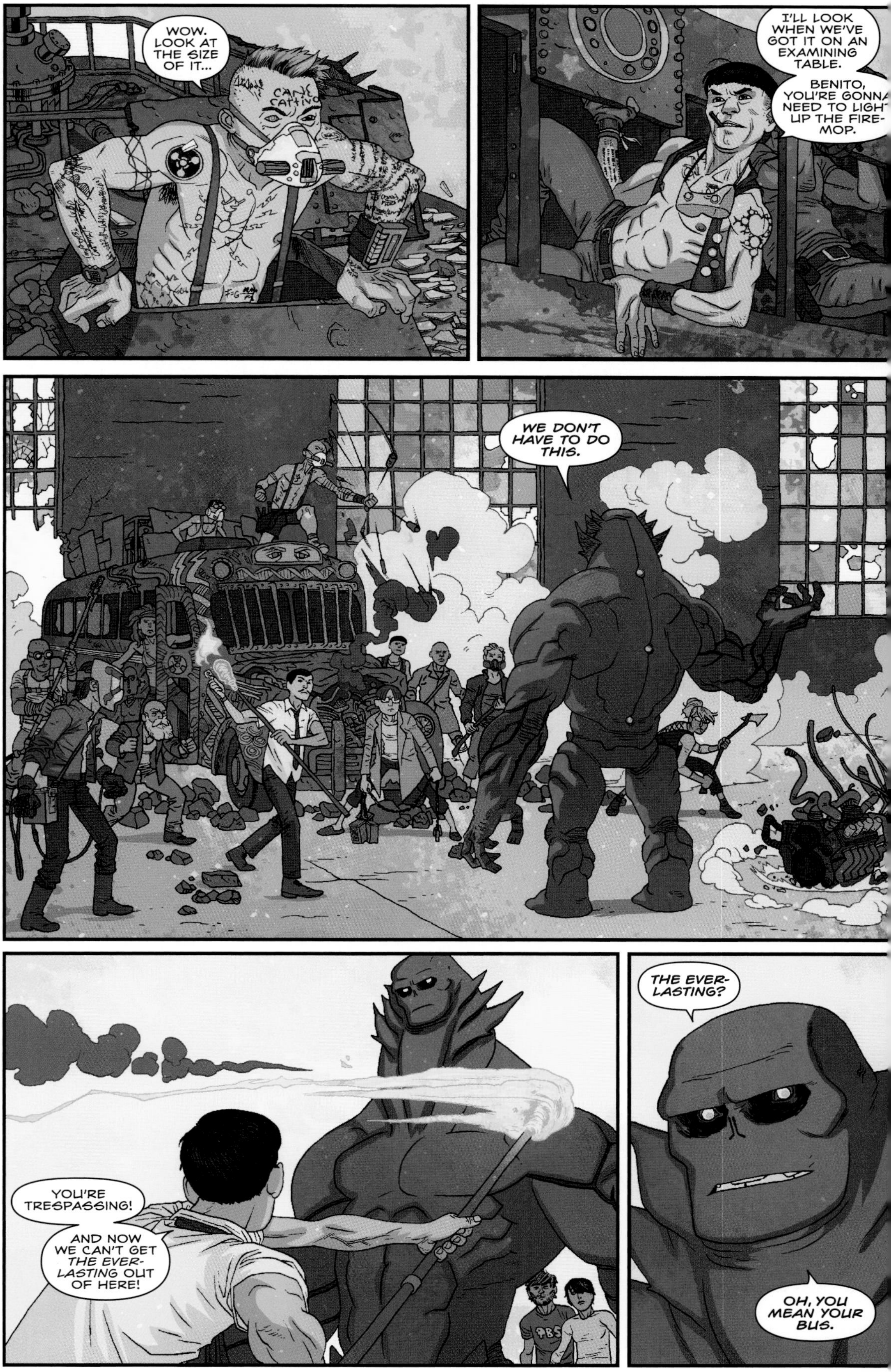
WOW. LOOK AT THE SIZE OF IT...
I'LL LOOK WHEN WE'VE GOT IT ON AN EXAMINING TABLE.
BENITO, YOU'RE GONNA NEED TO LIGHT UP THE FIRE-MOP.
WE DON'T HAVE TO DO THIS.
YOU'RE TRESPASSING!
AND NOW WE CAN'T GET *THE EVER-LASTING* OUT OF HERE!
THE EVER-LASTING?
OH, YOU MEAN YOUR BUS.

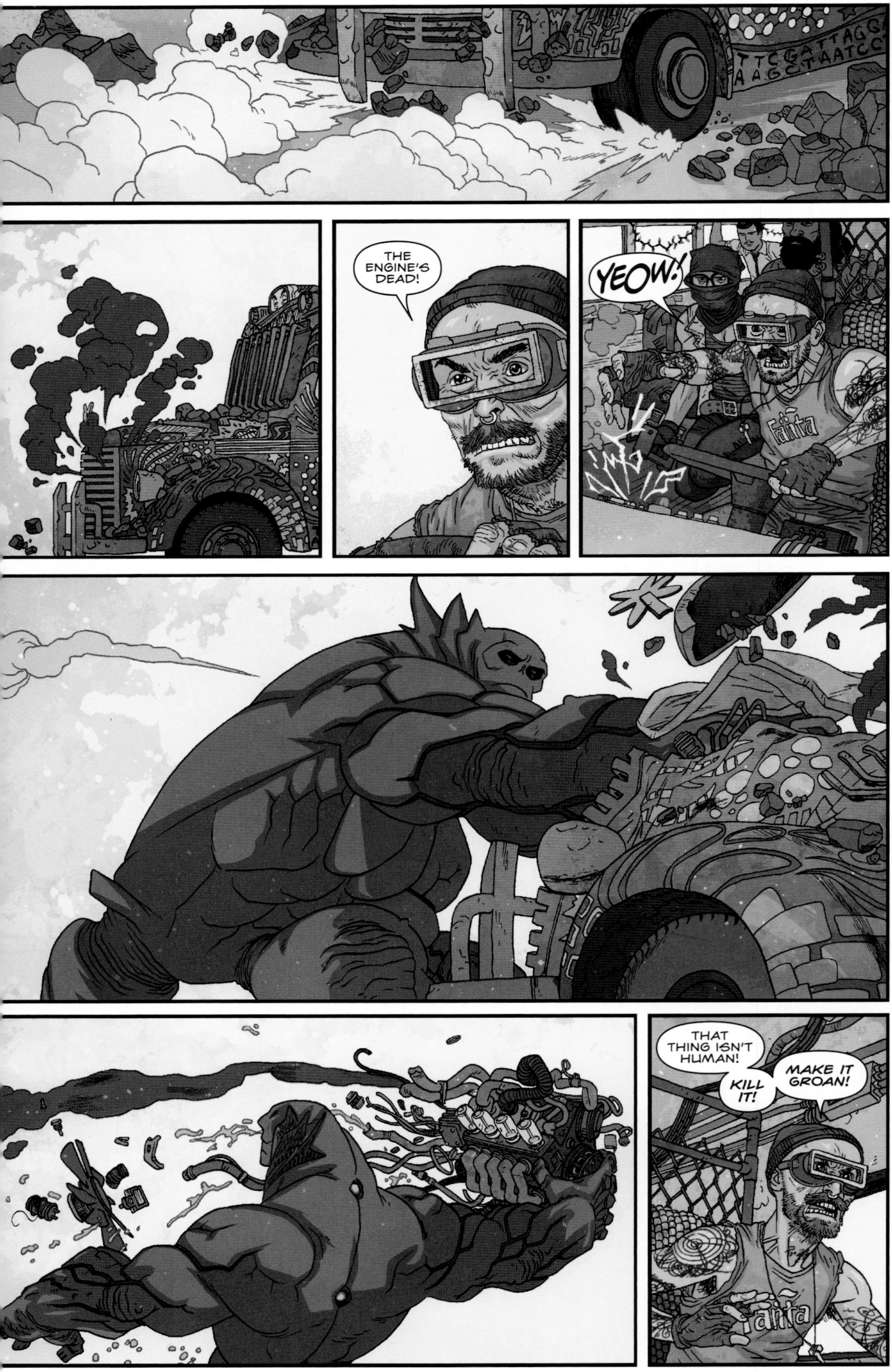
THE ENGINE'S DEAD!
YEOW!
THAT THING ISN'T HUMAN!
KILL IT!
MAKE IT GROAN!

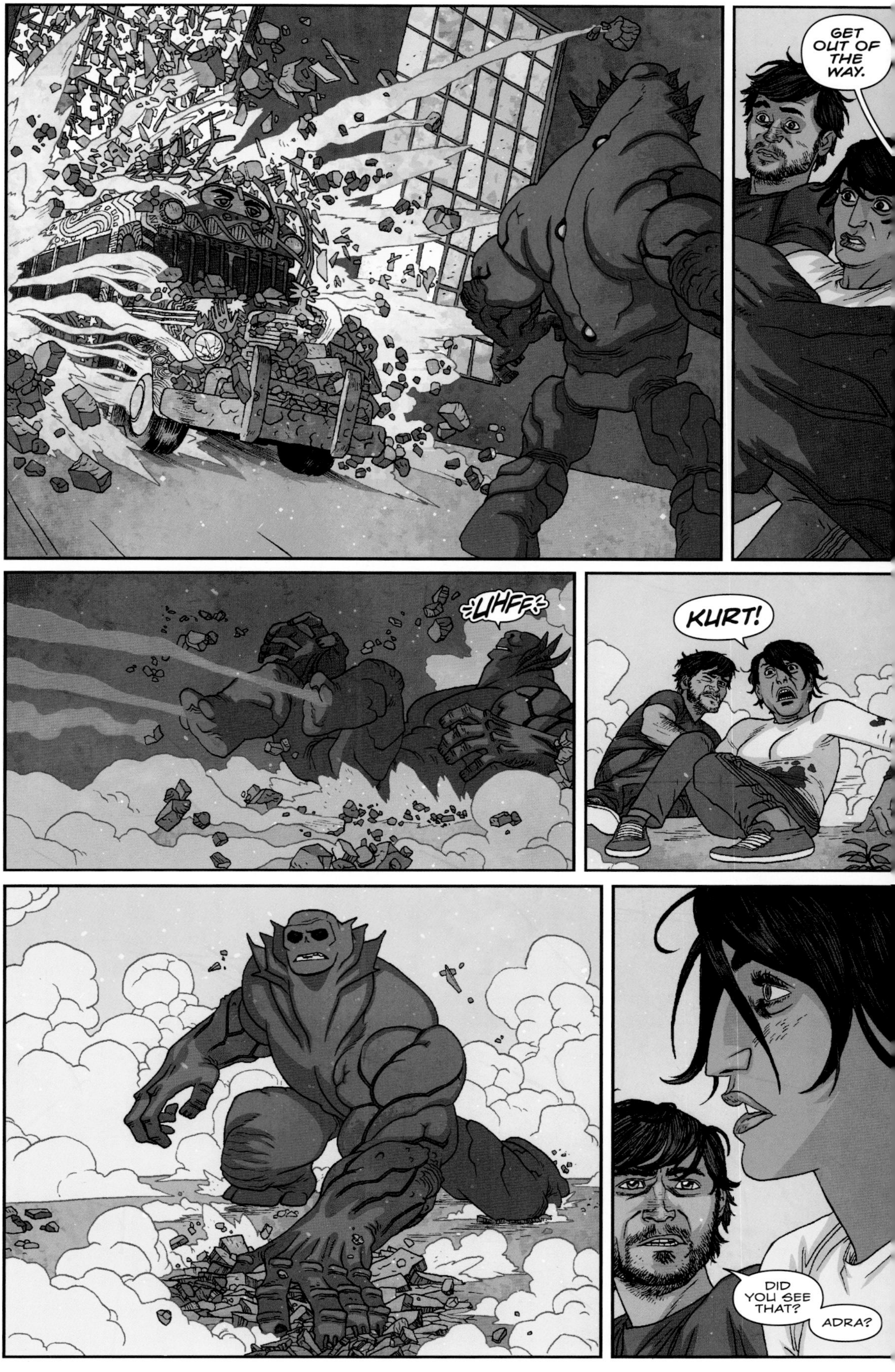
GET OUT OF THE WAY.
UHFF
KURT!
DID YOU SEE THAT?
ADRA?

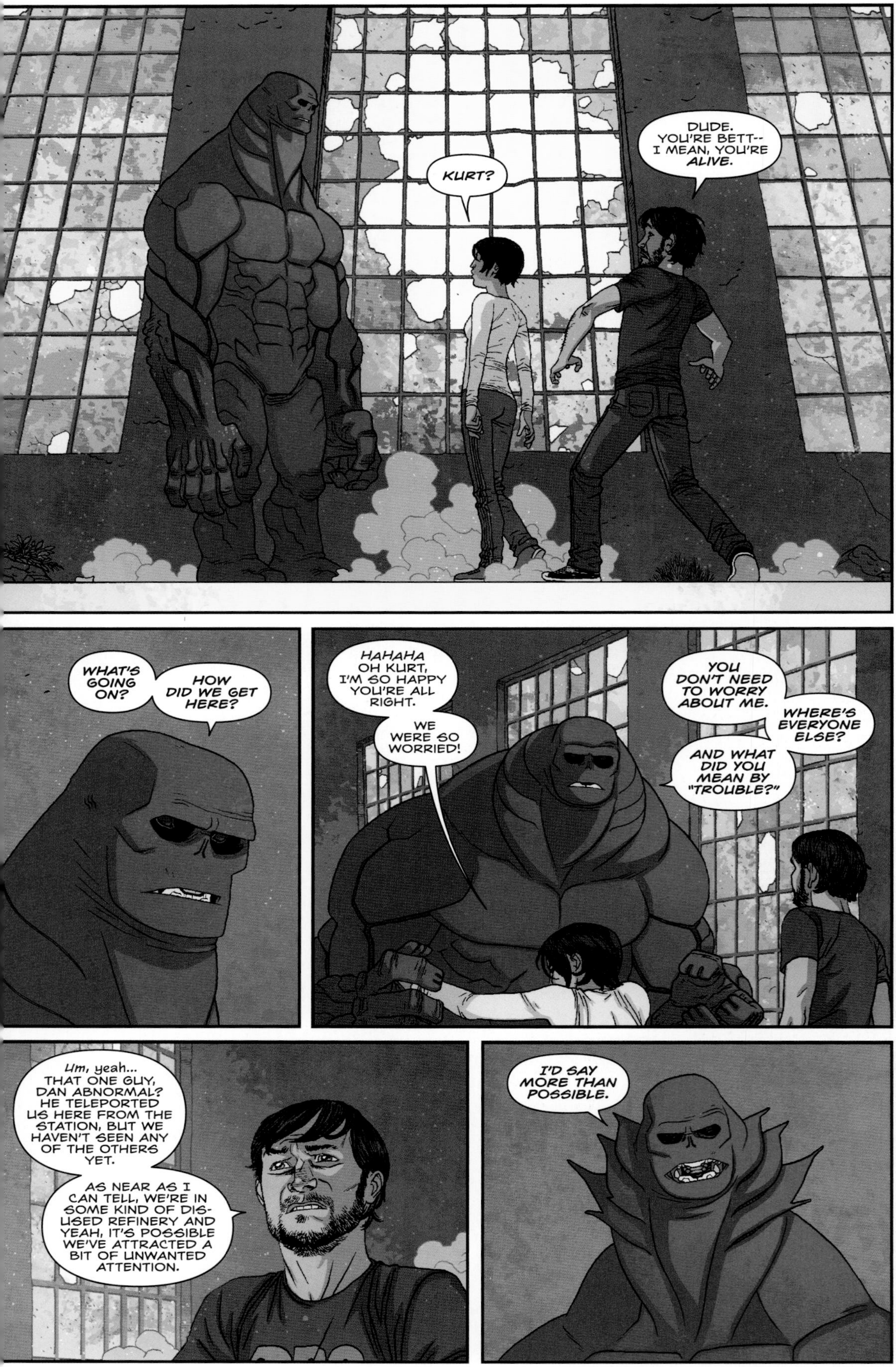
KURT?
DUDE. YOU'RE BETT-- I MEAN, YOU'RE ALIVE.
WHAT'S GOING ON?
HOW DID WE GET HERE?
HAHAHA OH KURT, I'M SO HAPPY YOU'RE ALL RIGHT.
WE WERE SO WORRIED!
YOU DON'T NEED TO WORRY ABOUT ME.
WHERE'S EVERYONE ELSE?
AND WHAT DID YOU MEAN BY "TROUBLE?"
Um, yeah... THAT ONE GUY, DAN ABNORMAL? HE TELEPORTED US HERE FROM THE STATION, BUT WE HAVEN'T SEEN ANY OF THE OTHERS YET.
AS NEAR AS I CAN TELL, WE'RE IN SOME KIND OF DIS-USED REFINERY AND YEAH, IT'S POSSIBLE WE'VE ATTRACTED A BIT OF UNWANTED ATTENTION.
I'D SAY MORE THAN POSSIBLE.

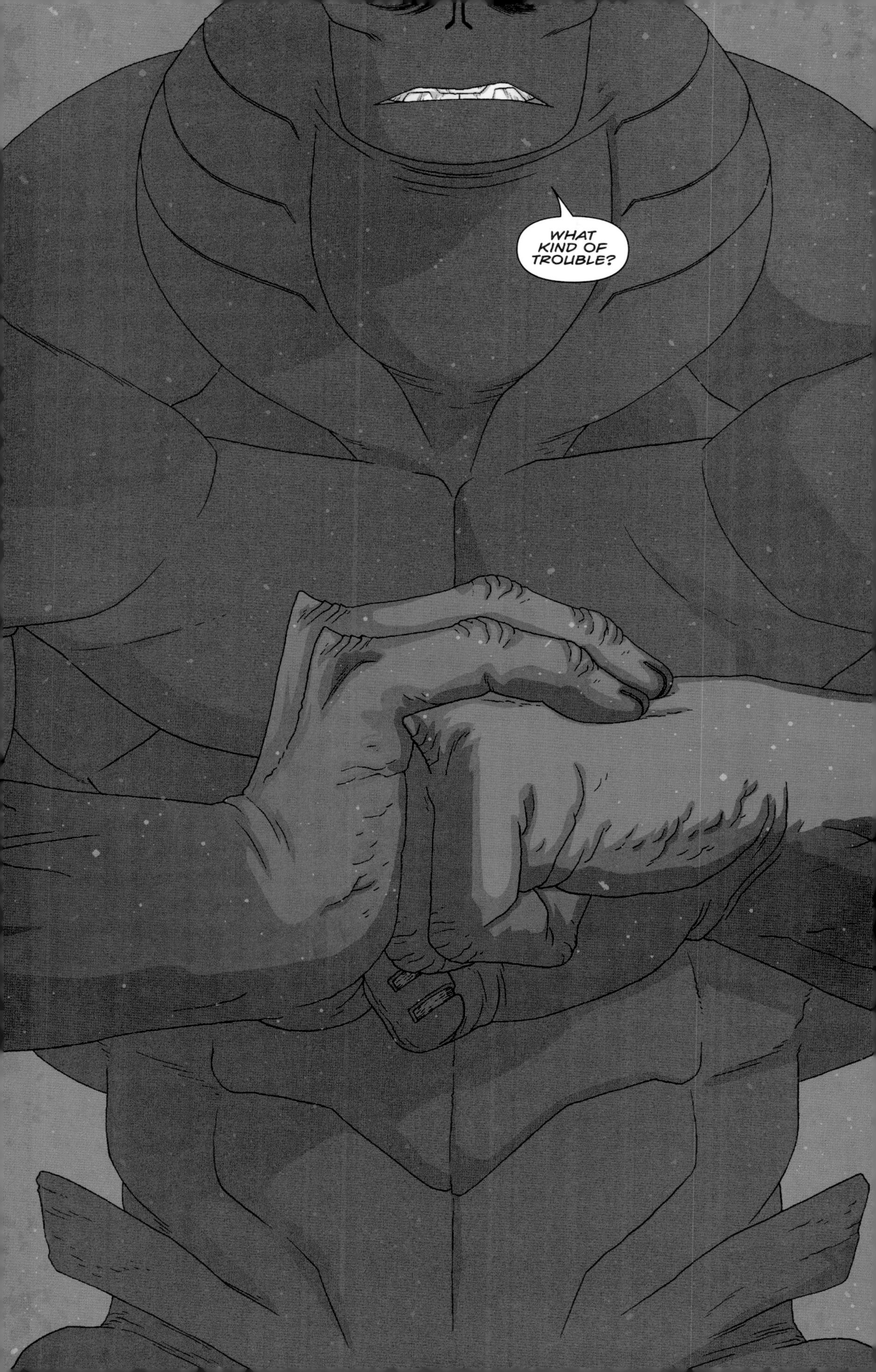
WHAT KIND OF TROUBLE?

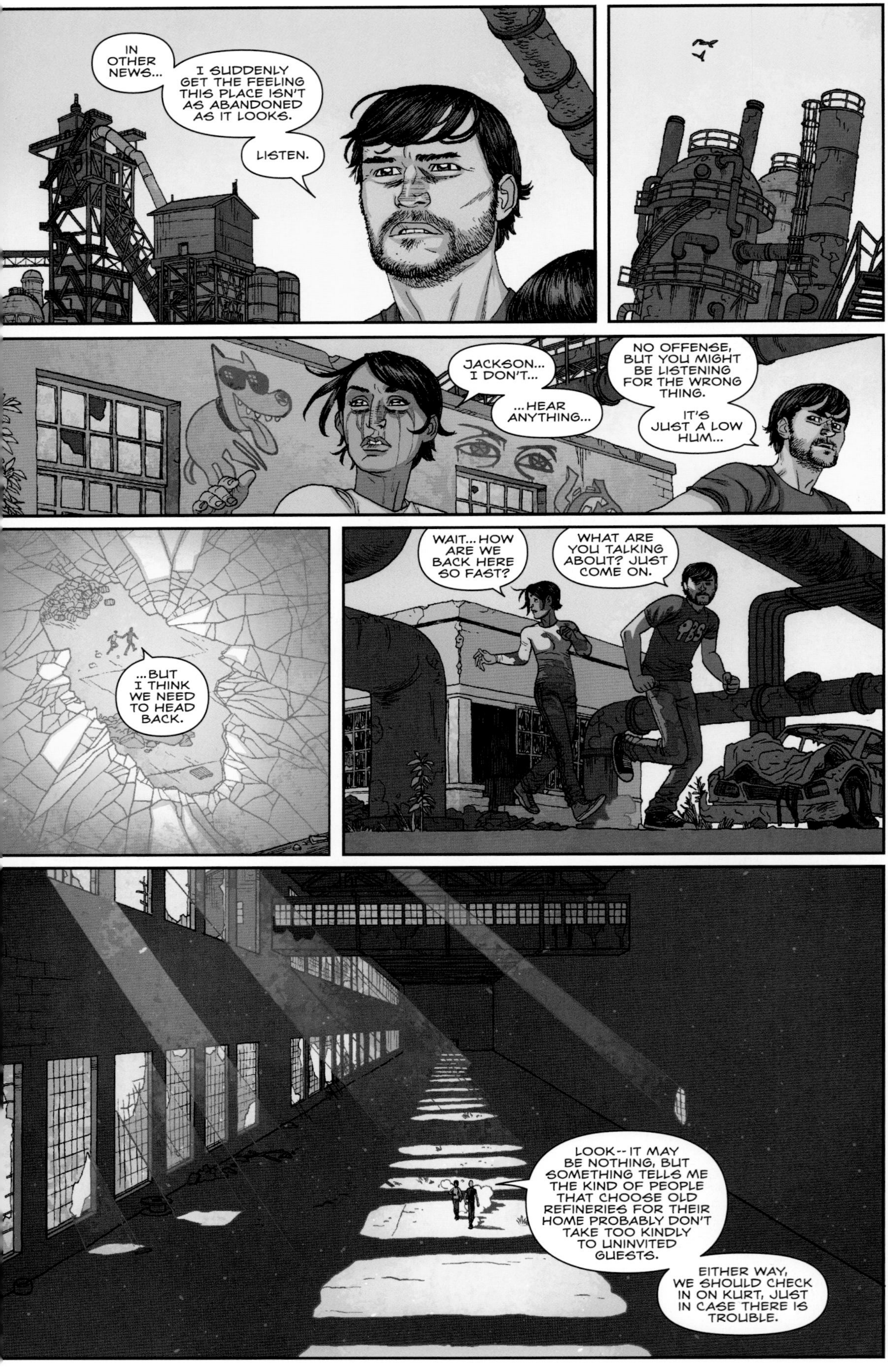
IN OTHER NEWS...
I SUDDENLY GET THE FEELING THIS PLACE ISN'T AS ABANDONED AS IT LOOKS.
LISTEN.
JACKSON... I DON'T...
...HEAR ANYTHING...
NO OFFENSE, BUT YOU MIGHT BE LISTENING FOR THE WRONG THING.
IT'S JUST A LOW HUM...
...BUT I THINK WE NEED TO HEAD BACK.
WAIT... HOW ARE WE BACK HERE SO FAST?
WHAT ARE YOU TALKING ABOUT? JUST COME ON.
LOOK-- IT MAY BE NOTHING, BUT SOMETHING TELLS ME THE KIND OF PEOPLE THAT CHOOSE OLD REFINERIES FOR THEIR HOME PROBABLY DON'T TAKE TOO KINDLY TO UNINVITED GUESTS.
EITHER WAY, WE SHOULD CHECK IN ON KURT, JUST IN CASE THERE IS TROUBLE.

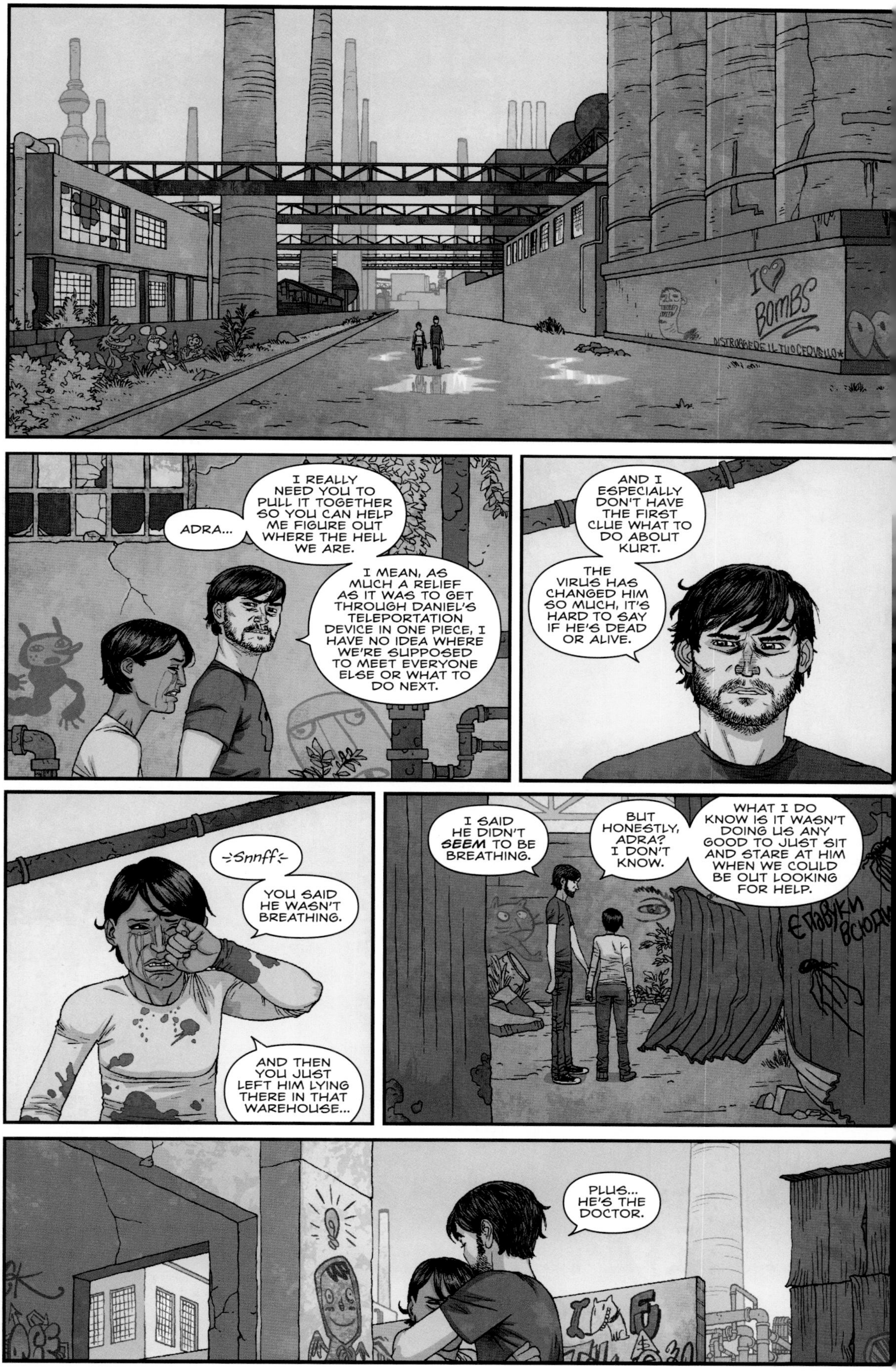
ADRA...
I REALLY NEED YOU TO PULL IT TOGETHER SO YOU CAN HELP ME FIGURE OUT WHERE THE HELL WE ARE.
I MEAN, AS MUCH A RELIEF AS IT WAS TO GET THROUGH DANIEL'S TELEPORTATION DEVICE IN ONE PIECE, I HAVE NO IDEA WHERE WE'RE SUPPOSED TO MEET EVERYONE ELSE OR WHAT TO DO NEXT.
AND I ESPECIALLY DON'T HAVE THE FIRST CLUE WHAT TO DO ABOUT KURT.
THE VIRUS HAS CHANGED HIM SO MUCH, IT'S HARD TO SAY IF HE'S DEAD OR ALIVE.
-Snnff-
YOU SAID HE WASN'T BREATHING.
AND THEN YOU JUST LEFT HIM LYING THERE IN THAT WAREHOUSE...
I SAID HE DIDN'T *SEEM* TO BE BREATHING.
BUT HONESTLY, ADRA? I DON'T KNOW.
WHAT I DO KNOW IS IT WASN'T DOING US ANY GOOD TO JUST SIT AND STARE AT HIM WHEN WE COULD BE OUT LOOKING FOR HELP.
PLUS... HE'S THE DOCTOR.

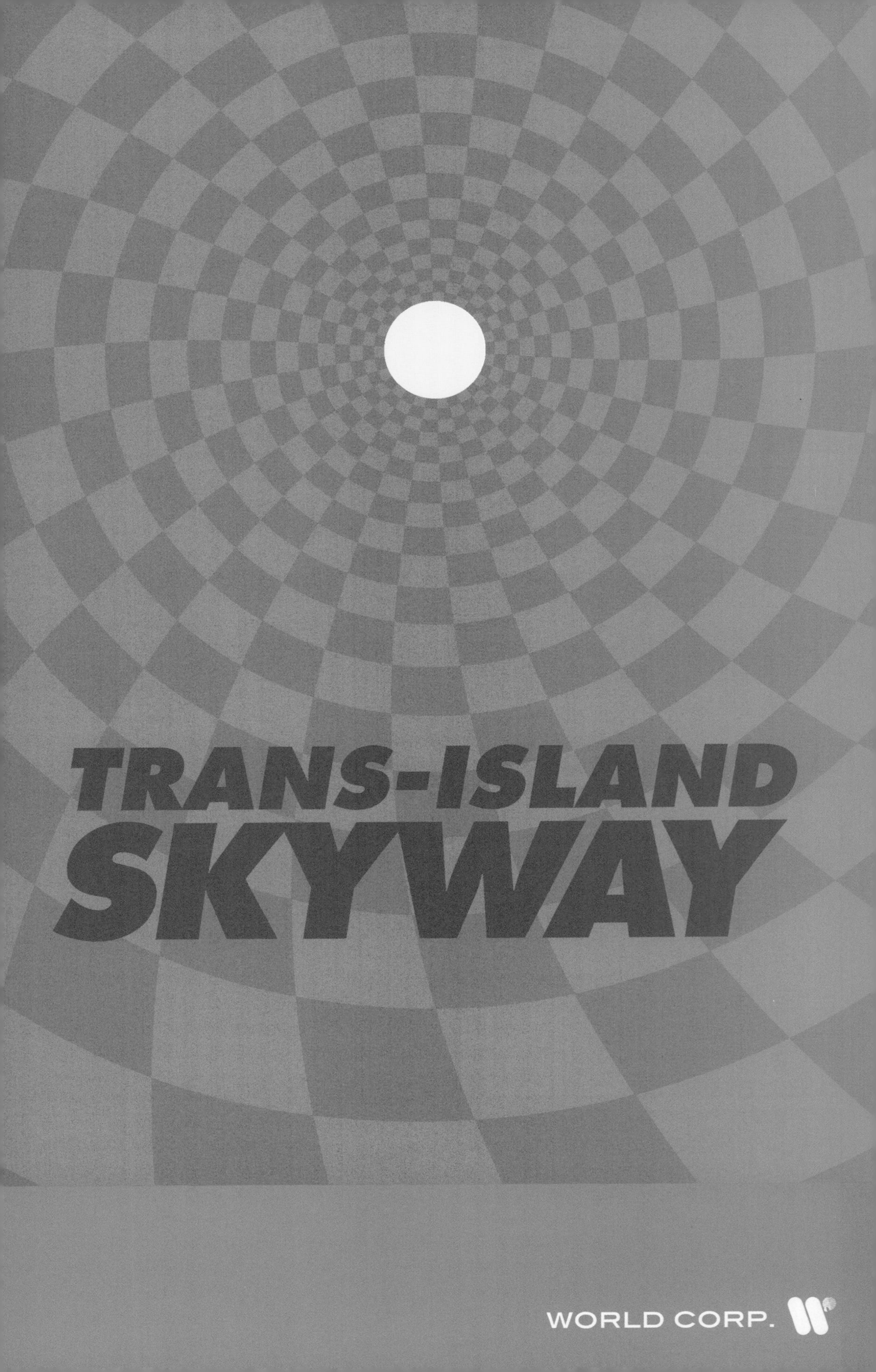
TRANS-ISLAND
SKYWAY
WORLD CORP.

building the new frontier

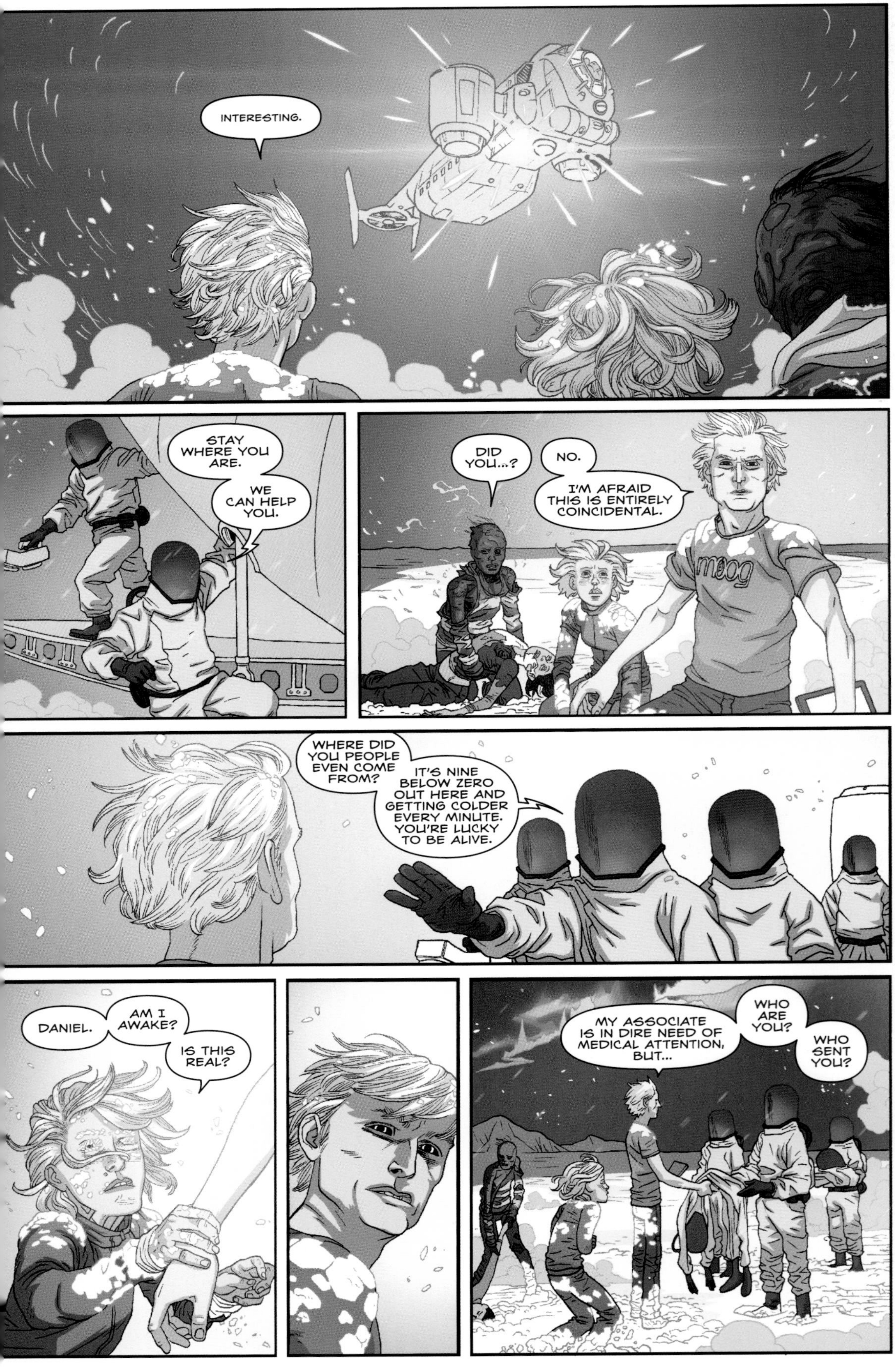
INTERESTING.
STAY WHERE YOU ARE.
WE CAN HELP YOU.
DID YOU...?
NO.
I'M AFRAID THIS IS ENTIRELY COINCIDENTAL.
moog
WHERE DID YOU PEOPLE EVEN COME FROM?
IT'S NINE BELOW ZERO OUT HERE AND GETTING COLDER EVERY MINUTE. YOU'RE LUCKY TO BE ALIVE.
DANIEL.
AM I AWAKE?
IS THIS REAL?
MY ASSOCIATE IS IN DIRE NEED OF MEDICAL ATTENTION, BUT...
WHO ARE YOU?
WHO SENT YOU?

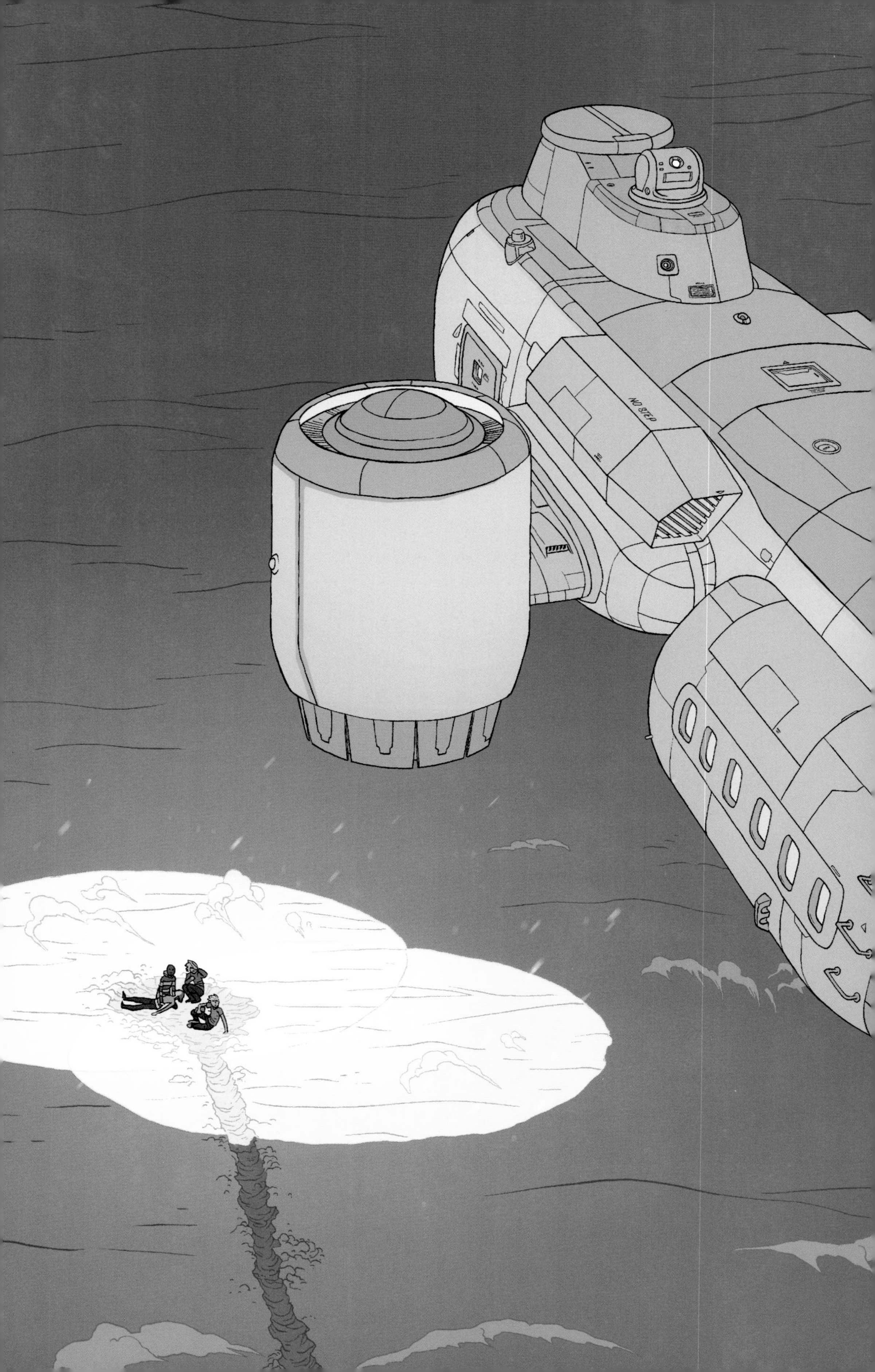
NO STEP

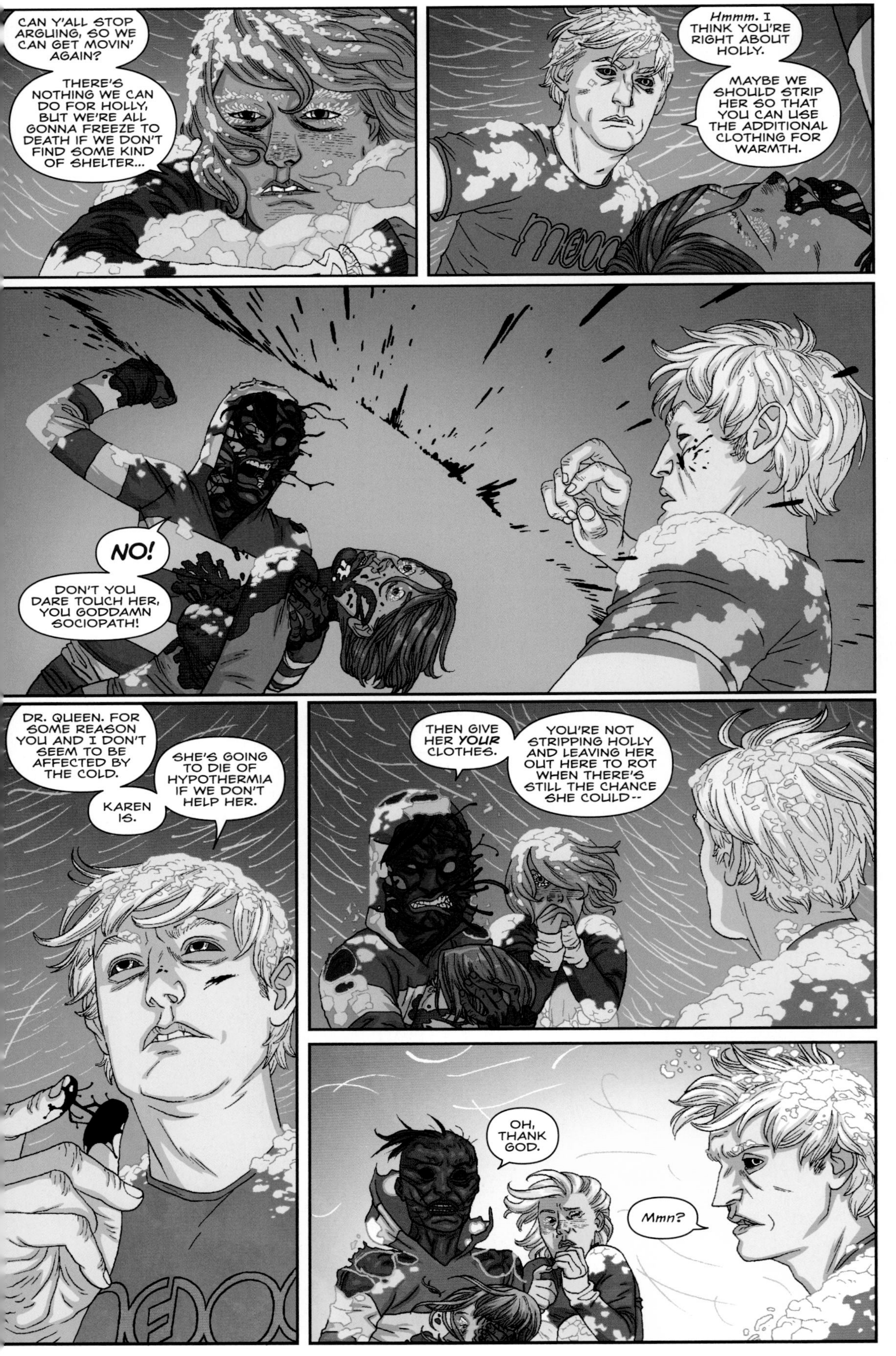

CAN Y'ALL STOP ARGUING, SO WE CAN GET MOVIN' AGAIN?
THERE'S NOTHING WE CAN DO FOR HOLLY, BUT WE'RE ALL GONNA FREEZE TO DEATH IF WE DON'T FIND SOME KIND OF SHELTER...
Hmmm. I THINK YOU'RE RIGHT ABOUT HOLLY.
MAYBE WE SHOULD STRIP HER SO THAT YOU CAN USE THE ADDITIONAL CLOTHING FOR WARMTH.
NO!
DON'T YOU DARE TOUCH HER, YOU GODDAMN SOCIOPATH!
DR. QUEEN. FOR SOME REASON YOU AND I DON'T SEEM TO BE AFFECTED BY THE COLD.
KAREN IS.
SHE'S GOING TO DIE OF HYPOTHERMIA IF WE DON'T HELP HER.
THEN GIVE HER *YOUR* CLOTHES.
YOU'RE NOT STRIPPING HOLLY AND LEAVING HER OUT HERE TO ROT WHEN THERE'S STILL THE CHANCE SHE COULD--
OH, THANK GOD.
Mmn?

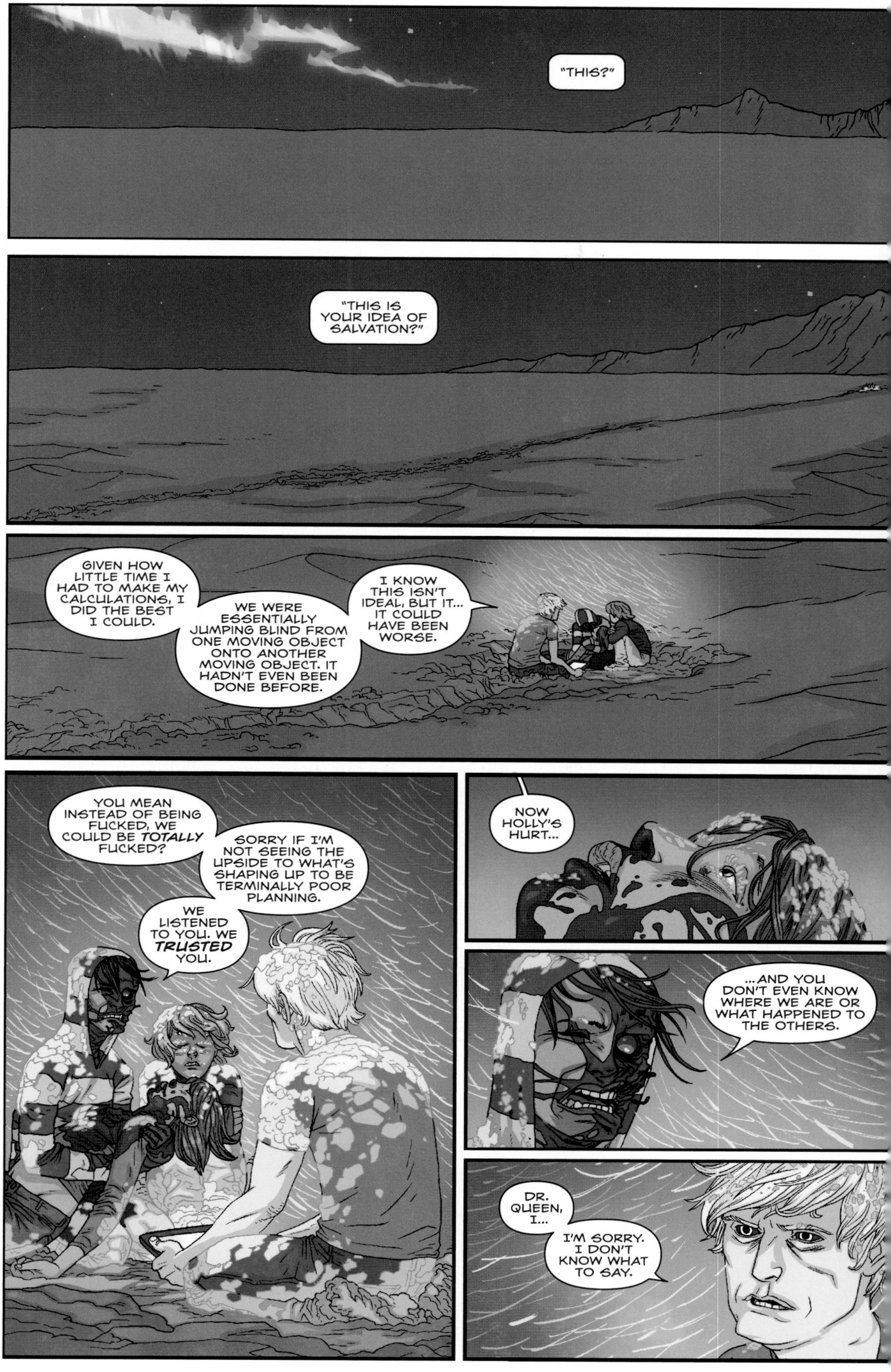
"THIS?"
"THIS IS YOUR IDEA OF SALVATION?"
GIVEN HOW LITTLE TIME I HAD TO MAKE MY CALCULATIONS, I DID THE BEST I COULD.
WE WERE ESSENTIALLY JUMPING BLIND FROM ONE MOVING OBJECT ONTO ANOTHER MOVING OBJECT. IT HADN'T EVEN BEEN DONE BEFORE.
I KNOW THIS ISN'T IDEAL, BUT IT... IT COULD HAVE BEEN WORSE.
YOU MEAN INSTEAD OF BEING FUCKED, WE COULD BE *TOTALLY* FUCKED?
SORRY IF I'M NOT SEEING THE UPSIDE TO WHAT'S SHAPING UP TO BE TERMINALLY POOR PLANNING.
WE LISTENED TO YOU. WE *TRUSTED* YOU.
NOW HOLLY'S HURT...
...AND YOU DON'T EVEN KNOW WHERE WE ARE OR WHAT HAPPENED TO THE OTHERS.
DR. QUEEN, I...
I'M SORRY. I DON'T KNOW WHAT TO SAY.

WAIT A MINUTE... R.D.

DID YOU MEAN "WEIRD" STRANGE OR "EMERSON STRANGE?"

BECAUSE WASN'T THERE TALK ABOUT WORLD CORP ACTUALLY BUYING THE INTERNATIONAL SPACE STATION A WHILE BACK?

LIKE, JUST A FEW MONTHS BEFORE THE I.S.S. WAS KNOCKED OUT OF ORBIT?

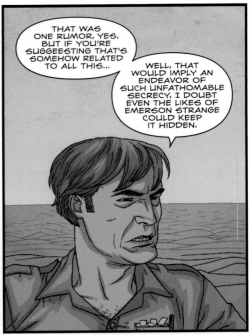

THAT WAS ONE RUMOR, YES, BUT IF YOU'RE SUGGESTING THAT'S SOMEHOW RELATED TO ALL THIS...

WELL, THAT WOULD IMPLY AN ENDEAVOR OF SUCH UNFATHOMABLE SECRECY, I DOUBT EVEN THE LIKES OF EMERSON STRANGE COULD KEEP IT HIDDEN.

THEN AGAIN, I'VE BEEN AT THIS LONG ENOUGH TO REALISE THERE ARE PLENTY OF THINGS WE'RE NOT SUPPOSED TO KNOW ABOUT.

EVER.

SO TO ANSWER YOUR EARLIER QUESTION...

I THINK WHAT WE'RE LOOKING AT HERE IS THE TIP OF A VERY LARGE ICEBERG.

UNFORTUNATELY, I CAN'T DECIDE WHICH I FIND MORE INCONGRUOUS:

AN ICEBERG IN THE MIDDLE OF TUNISIA, OR A PIECE OF SPACE JUNK WITH THE WORLD CORP EMBLEM ON.

REALLY? THAT SEEMS SIMPLE ENOUGH, EVEN TO ME.

WHAT WOULD AN ICEBERG BE DOING IN THE MIDDLE OF THE DESERT?

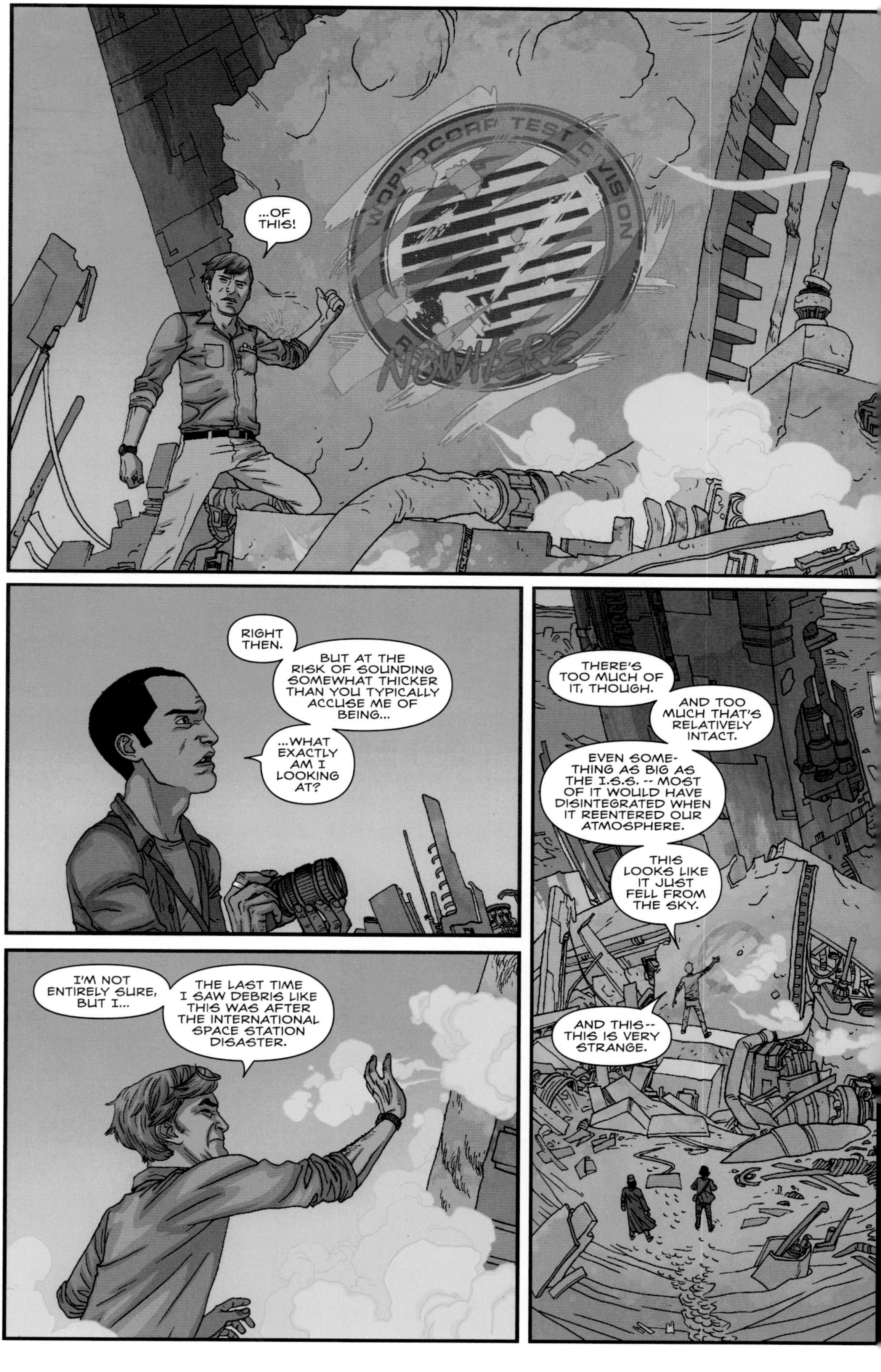

...OF THIS!
WORLDCORP TEST DIVISION
NOWHERE
RIGHT THEN.
BUT AT THE RISK OF SOUNDING SOMEWHAT THICKER THAN YOU TYPICALLY ACCUSE ME OF BEING...
...WHAT EXACTLY AM I LOOKING AT?
I'M NOT ENTIRELY SURE, BUT I...
THE LAST TIME I SAW DEBRIS LIKE THIS WAS AFTER THE INTERNATIONAL SPACE STATION DISASTER.
THERE'S TOO MUCH OF IT, THOUGH.
AND TOO MUCH THAT'S RELATIVELY INTACT.
EVEN SOMETHING AS BIG AS THE I.S.S. -- MOST OF IT WOULD HAVE DISINTEGRATED WHEN IT REENTERED OUR ATMOSPHERE.
THIS LOOKS LIKE IT JUST FELL FROM THE SKY.
AND THIS-- THIS IS VERY STRANGE.

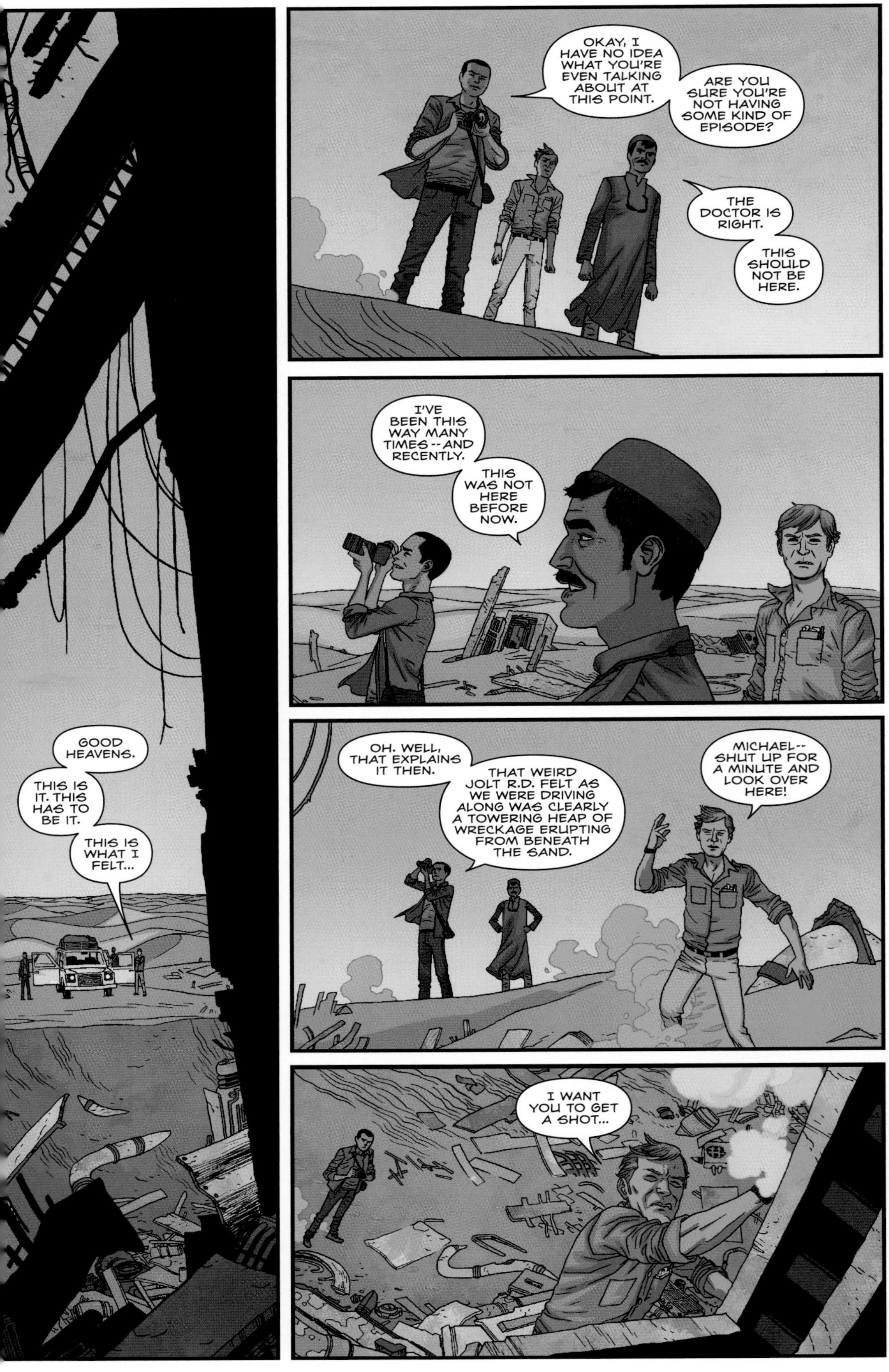

GOOD HEAVENS.
THIS IS IT. THIS HAS TO BE IT.
THIS IS WHAT I FELT...
OKAY, I HAVE NO IDEA WHAT YOU'RE EVEN TALKING ABOUT AT THIS POINT.
ARE YOU SURE YOU'RE NOT HAVING SOME KIND OF EPISODE?
THE DOCTOR IS RIGHT.
THIS SHOULD NOT BE HERE.
I'VE BEEN THIS WAY MANY TIMES--AND RECENTLY.
THIS WAS NOT HERE BEFORE NOW.
OH. WELL, THAT EXPLAINS IT THEN.
THAT WEIRD JOLT R.D. FELT AS WE WERE DRIVING ALONG WAS CLEARLY A TOWERING HEAP OF WRECKAGE ERUPTING FROM BENEATH THE SAND.
MICHAEL--SHUT UP FOR A MINUTE AND LOOK OVER HERE!
I WANT YOU TO GET A SHOT...

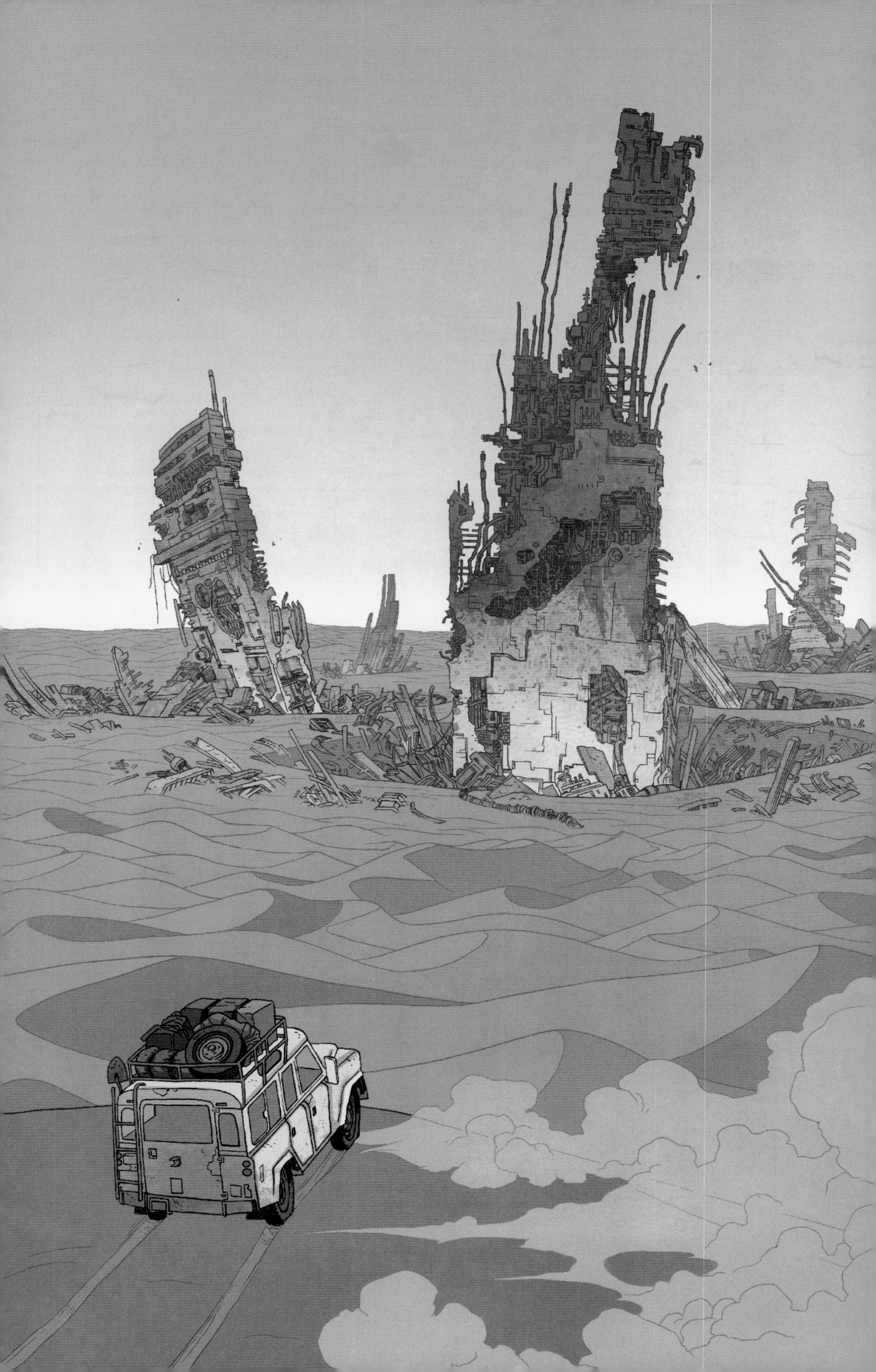

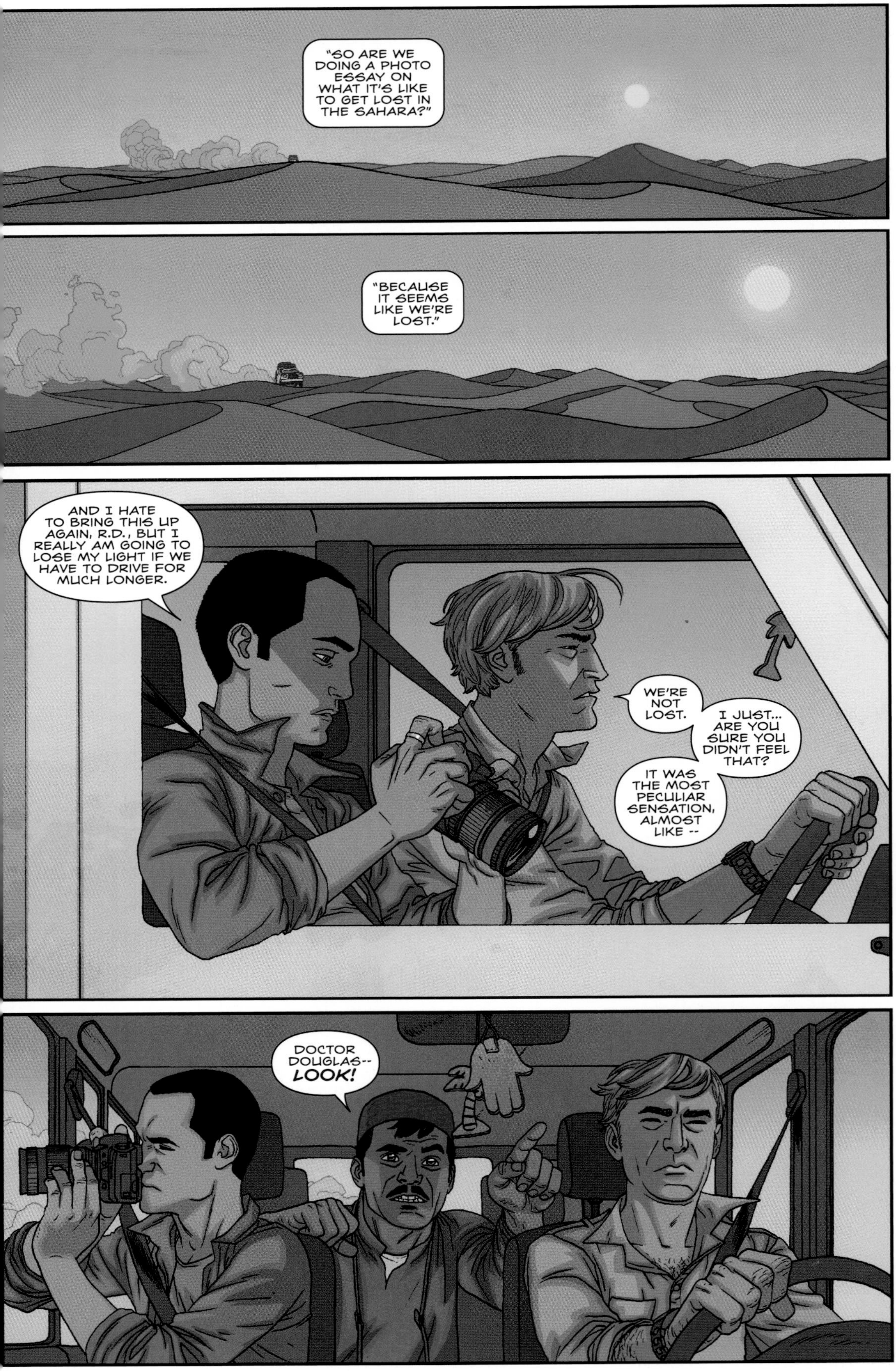
"SO ARE WE DOING A PHOTO ESSAY ON WHAT IT'S LIKE TO GET LOST IN THE SAHARA?"
"BECAUSE IT SEEMS LIKE WE'RE LOST."
AND I HATE TO BRING THIS UP AGAIN, R.D., BUT I REALLY AM GOING TO LOSE MY LIGHT IF WE HAVE TO DRIVE FOR MUCH LONGER.
WE'RE NOT LOST.
I JUST... ARE YOU SURE YOU DIDN'T FEEL THAT?
IT WAS THE MOST PECULIAR SENSATION, ALMOST LIKE --
DOCTOR DOUGLAS-- LOOK!

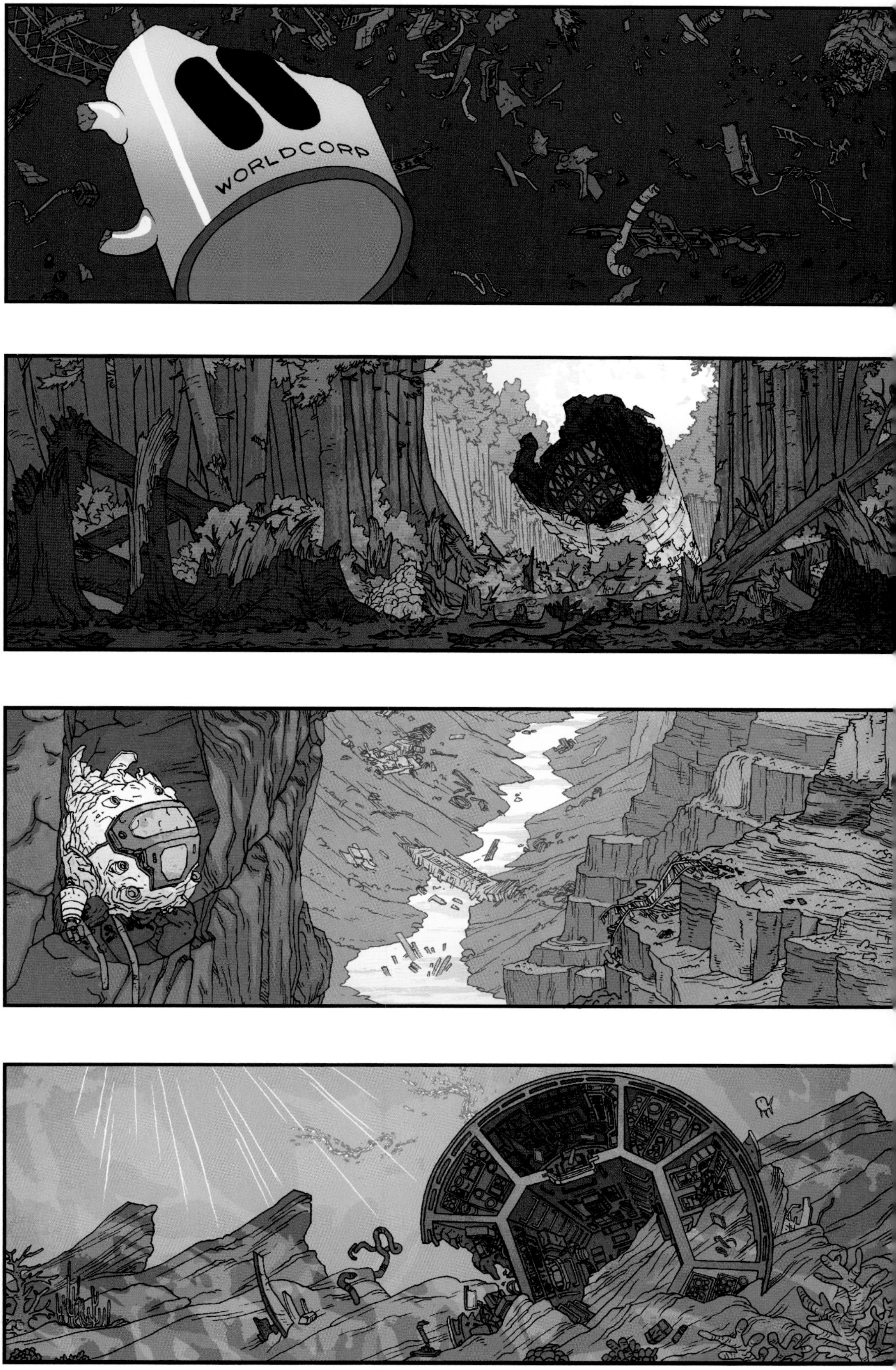
WORLDCORP

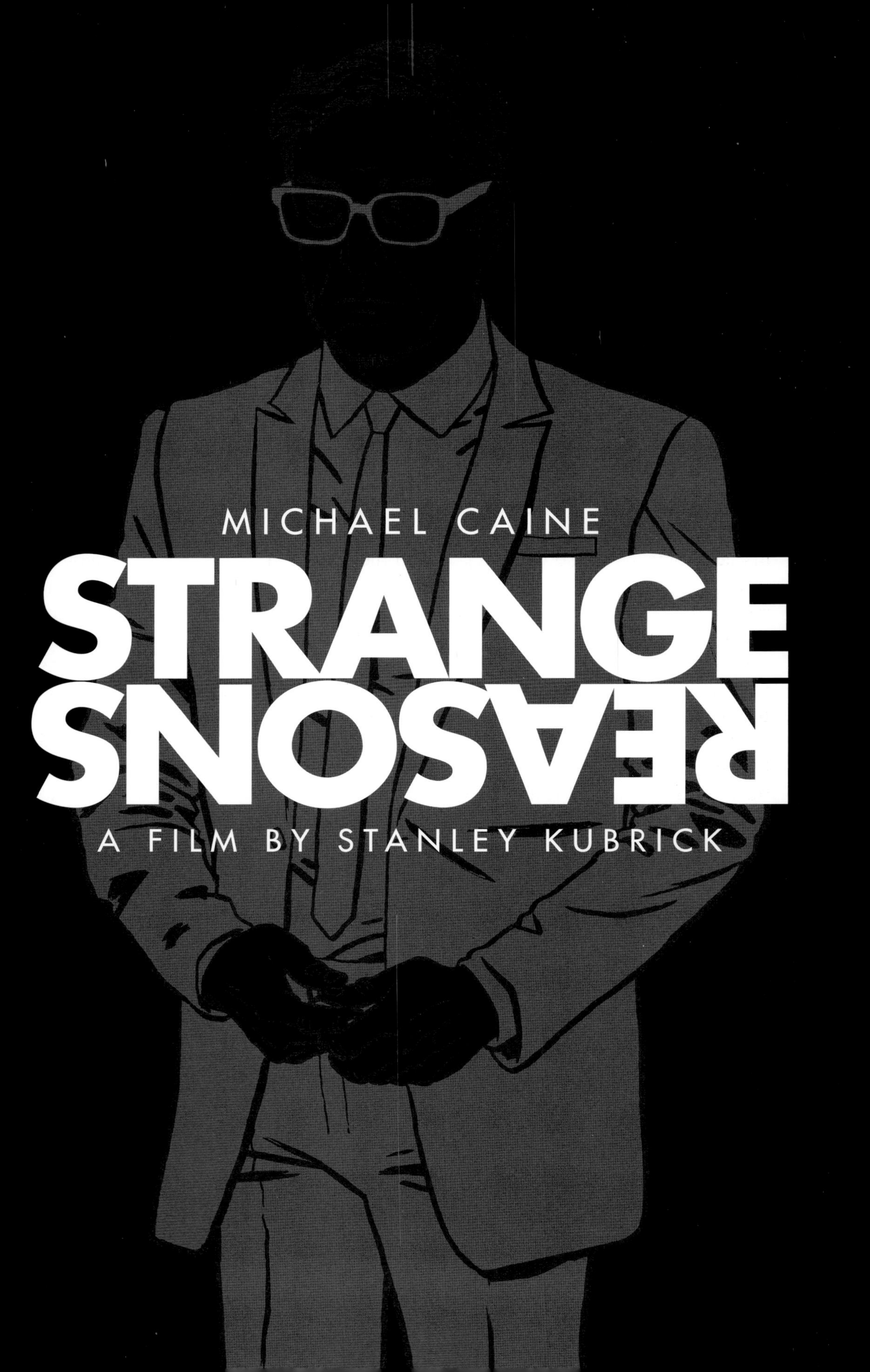
MICHAEL CAINE
STRANGE
REASONS
A FILM BY STANLEY KUBRICK

By the time the expansion of the World Corp campus was completed, though, Thomas' behavior had become even more erratic. Despite being notoriously press shy, he was suddenly appearing in the daily tabloids on a regular basis, usually after a night of excess or in association with one of his many female admirers, and whereas he could once fall back on his prolific writing, work only came in spasms now.

There were never any rows between the partners, but at the point Thomas became fixated on third eye meditation, it became clear to the others it would take more than a larger headquarters to contain what they now all viewed as a problem of increasing significance.

That Thomas led a completely different life from his partners became hugely symbolic for the other three. No matter what disagreements Dade, Simon and Emerson might have had, they were at least focused on the same things. Dade in particular found it increasingly difficult to understand what he identified as a seismic shift in Thomas' attitude towards the partnership.

"That addition to the headquarters was a very big deal for me personally," says Dade. "When we had the opening, though, Thomas showed up completely off his face, with someone who certainly fit the profile of a drug pusher, a guy he would only identify as 'my friend Jack,' and throughout the entire event he carried on as though it was some colossal joke. Emerson volunteered to talk to him, but at that point, I didn't think it would do any good."

Speculation began to mount that World Corp's success had gone to Thomas' head and that he was having trouble coping. An interview with Julie Taylor, one of his former girlfriends, however, suggested that quite the opposite, though.

"I think Thomas was making some astounding discoveries, and he didn't feel like the others wanted to know," said Julie. "They're all incredibly brilliant men and I don't want to denigrate what any of them do, but from listening to Thomas talk about his work, I know he was on the verge of breaking through to something bigger than they could have imagined and none of them appreciated that."

This breakthrough, if it did indeed come, was to be realized apart from World Corp, however. Shortly after the opening of the new expanded campus, a meeting of the company's principals was arranged at Emerson Strange's home and it was decided that Thomas would step down from World Corp's board to more chart his own path.

There was an announcement, followed by a smattering of confusing interviews, and then for all intents and purposes, Thomas was gone.

The remaining partners in the company only spoke of Thomas' exit or his subsequent disappearance in vague terms, but when asked what effect his former partner's departure had on World Corp, Emerson likened it to nothing less than the Big Bang. "I think there's been a fair mount of negativity associated with the whole thing, obviously, but it's actually been quite freeing for the rest of us. There was a bit of a blow up, but we've come out of it for the better and I think our future is brighter than ever. It's the oldest story in the universe, when you think about it: There's a big explosion and then things really start to happen."

first bona fide "hit," Dade stopped just short of calling for Thomas' ouster, but he made it clear that some distance between the two of them was an absolute necessity. Emerson Strange and Simon Grimshaw found it hard to disagree.

Thomas Walker, of course, was oblivious to the frustrations of his partners, as well as the widespread success of CyberOptics. This was not surprising, given Thomas' earlier comments that he was less interested in "selling commercial knick knacks" than his partners. He was a household name, known for innovative theoretical treatises, recognized by everyone as the world's leading astrophysicist. Ventures into consumer products, no matter how beneficial, somehow seemed beneath him.

He was happiest and most fulfilled when piecing together the mysteries of the universe. That he chose to do so whilst playing pinball or riding a bicycle seemed somewhat beside the point. The true problem was that his interests and those of his partners were beginning to diverge.

Although the founders of World Corp shared the mutual, if rather lofty, goal of "making the world a better place," possibly the only other thing they all shared in common was their disagreement on exactly what that entailed. For Thomas it meant reaching for the stars and as he once put it, "touching heaven," but the aspirations of Dade Ellis, Simon Grimshaw and even Emerson Strange are more along the lines of building heaven here on Earth.

"I don't know what it was like when they first got together because I wasn't there, but when I did come on, it seemed clear from the start that Thomas found the notion of inventing things people would then buy to somehow improve their lives to be a very strange concept," says Raymond Douglas. "I'm hesitant to put words into his mouth, obviously, but I don't think it would be too great of an exaggeration to suggest he found it all rather immoral. He saw science in somewhat different terms than the rest of them, I think. He viewed it almost as a calling."

According to an item in The Science Chronicle, Thomas Walker had been proselytizing to various members of his social circle about something he called "free science," lamenting that there was little nobility in solving the world's problems if the people affected had to pay for those solutions. Worse still, Thomas complained he was under constant pressure to "earn his keep," despite authoring several important papers since the company's formation.

"There was a great deal of consternation amongst the others, especially Dade, when that came out," says Raymond. "We swept it under the carpet quickly, and it helped that the actual source was one of Thomas' crowd, because very few of them were at all reputable, but I don't think Dade forgot about it for one second."

Darrow Fletcher says one the main problems during this period was that no one had any idea how Thomas spent his time when he was apart from the group. They knew little of his personal life apart from what appeared in the papers, but even as his transgressions became more frequent, dismissed even the most unsettling reports as isolated incidents. The general consensus was that he would eventually come around.

Chapter 26: It's All Too Much

Things were changing rapidly for World Corp, and those changes were affecting relations between the company's founders, something Dade Ellis had realized during the trip to Washington, D.C. Dade was committed to the company's ideals, however, and initially did not voice his concerns. Instead, he focused attention elsewhere.

CyberOptics had, as expected, become a huge success, changing the lives of visually impaired people all over the world. Ellis was frustrated by his invention's limitations in terms of aiding patients who had been totally blind from birth, though, and set to work on an update. Before that could happen, though, he informed his partners that the CO team would need to expand their presence on the World Corp campus.

The CO staff had definitely grown enough to warrant a larger work environment, but for Ellis, there was a more important reason to transplant operations to another space: He wanted to be free of the distractions caused by being within close proximity to Thomas Walker. Though their individual offices were virtually on opposite sides of World Corp's headquarters, the CO team's workspace was located just close enough that it became one of Walker's first stops when he went on walkabout, or as was more often the case, cycling.

Raymond Douglas was interning for World Corp at the time. He had nothing to do with CyberOptics, mainly working in the company's press office, under the supervision of a managing director, Darrow Fletcher, who reported directly to Simon Grimshaw. "I think it's fairly well-documented that Thomas used somewhat unorthodox methods to channel his thinking, but I think the indoor bicycle rides definitely crossed a line, not just with Ellis, but with much of the staff. It was a distraction, and as much as I enjoyed the discussions I had with Thomas on the occasions he lingered at my desk, his behavior was becoming increasingly bothersome."

Or, as Dade outlined the situation to Emerson Strange and Simon Grimshaw, worrisome. Thomas' dalliance with hallucinogenic drugs had crossed the line from experimentation to addiction, he argued, and though Thomas described his hours under the influence as "research," to the casual observer more and more of his time seemed to be spent in a drugged out stupor.

When Thomas did emerge from the haze, he was invariably flush with grand ideas, few of which were immediately practical.

Altering his own daily habits in an attempt to avoid Thomas' increasingly unpredictable behavior was no longer an option. As the catalyst for World Corp's

inside World Corp.

H. David Pence

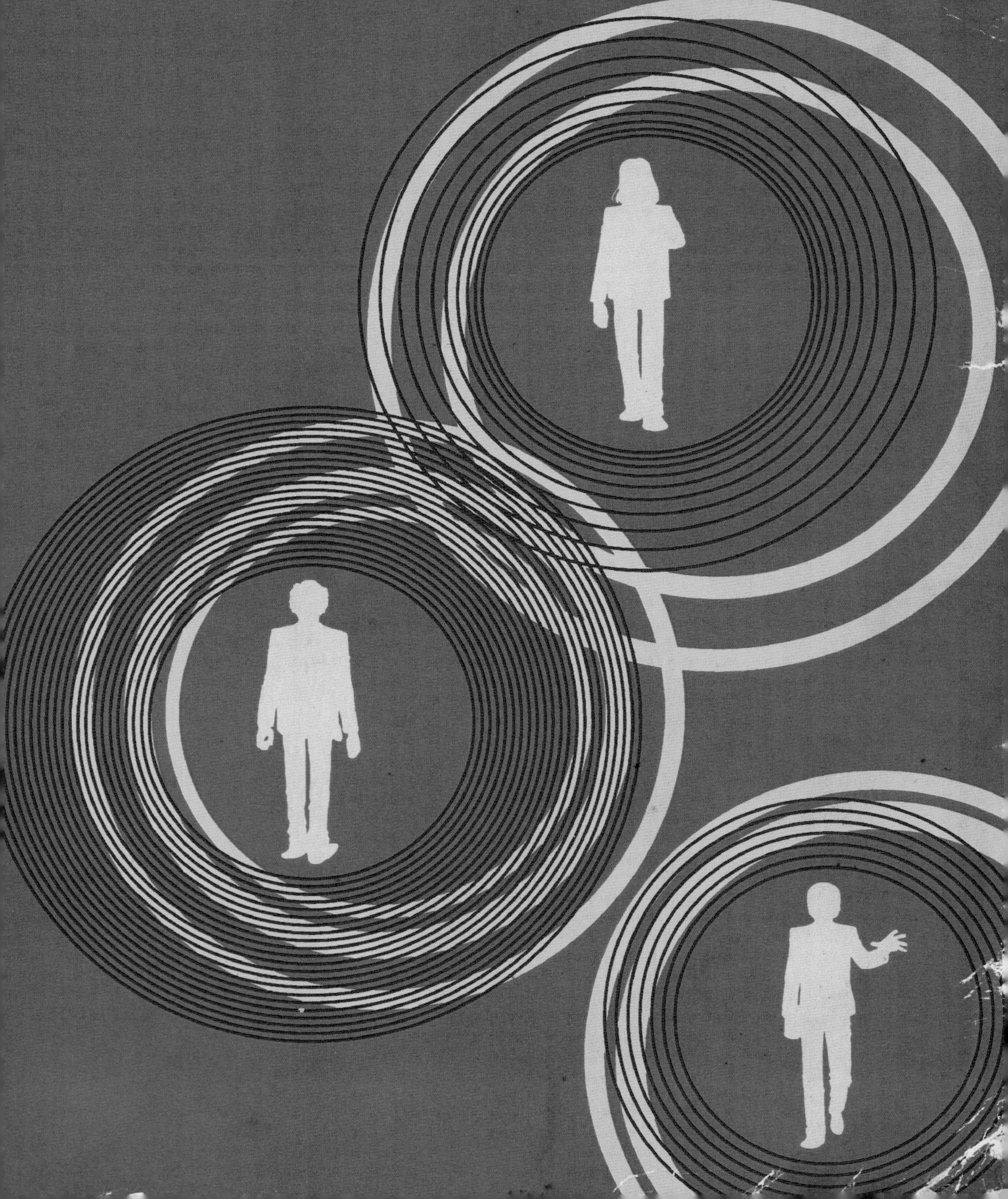

NOWHERE?

With one member missing, another out of the public eye and rumored to be seriously ill, and yet another excommunicated, has the sun finally set on the Fab Four of the science set? Or can Emerson Strange channel the dreams of his youth to carry World Corp. into a new golden age?

When Dade Ellis, Simon Grimshaw, Emerson Strange and Thomas Walker first banded together, the future of the company they formed seemed certain. With four of the greatest minds on the planet at its helm, there was no doubt World Corp. would quickly become the largest and most influential company in the world. What no one could have predicted, though, was how rapidly their alliance would unravel, or that within the span of only a decade, their number would be reduced to one.

World Corp.'s accomplishments are many and well-known, and presently there is talk of literally taking the company upwards with reports that Strange is in talks to purchase the under-funded International Space Station, but clearly, the company's profile is not what it once was. Defections, expulsions and mysteriously long silences have combined to diminish the initial spark behind the greatest brand in science, leaving many to wonder if what was launched as a joint venture can continue on with only one of its primary figures at the helm.

That lone figure, Emerson Strange, is certainly capable of great things, but there is a growing concern amongst those closest to him, both within World Corp. and without, that the mantle of 'last man standing' is beginning to take a dangerous toll. Fear is mounting that Strange's dogged insistence on working solely from his Modernist hillside hideaway has cut him off from the day-to-day realities of the company, and that his increasing eccentricity signals a deep-seated unhappiness that could soon result in a full-scale breakdown. Long regarded as the company's most practical thinker, Strange has, with greater frequency, issued statements ranging from the puzzling to outright alarming. Most recently, his enthusiasm for the so-called 'science punks' that have begun to form what can only be described as gangs, often performing dangerous and illegal experiments, raised a number of eyebrows, causing many to question whether Strange in fact considers himself, if not all science, above the law.

More unsettling still, however, is the persisting rumor that the sustained silence of remaining co-founder Dade Ellis is due to a debilitating illness Strange himself has actively worked to keep secret. Widely considered to be the moral compass, if not the very heart and soul, of World Corp., it is now over two years since Ellis has been seen in public. Initially, statements from the company that Ellis had sequestered himself to bring a particularly long-running project to fruition were accepted at face value, but there is now talk within the company itself that Ellis's involvement in that same project has left him bedridden, and possibly comatose, with only Strange monitoring his condition.

Ellis is not the first of World Corp.'s founders to disappear under mysterious circumstances. Thomas Walker left the company after only two years when his increasingly bizarre behavior made it apparent to his partners that he could no longer function in a responsible manner. A cheerful advocate of everything from hallucinogenic drugs to indoor cycling and table tennis, Walker granted a series of increasingly scurrilous interviews before vanishing completely. There have been reports of Walker popping up in remote parts of the world, whilst one eye witness claims to have spotted him eating ice cream at a gas station in Wales. Other stories have singled him out as, if not the instigator, then the inspiration for the aforementioned 'science punks.'

Meanwhile, the second member to be expelled from the company—although he himself maintains that his exit was self-determined—is Simon Grimshaw. Now living well outside the public eye at an undisclosed location widely believed to be somewhere within the Greek Isles, Grimshaw has emerged as a vocal critic of both the company he helped create and World Corp.'s de facto leader. Initially rumored to be the guiding light behind a venture that could have challenged World Corp's market dominance, Grimshaw has instead become involved in what he describes as "more personally fulfilling" pursuits, many of which have been discussed at length in an ongoing series of essays and books. Though he is reluctant to rule out a return to the world stage, Grimshaw has most recently stated that partnerships such as the one that led to the formation of World Corp. are simply not in line with his natural way of doing things, and he has described Strange's decision to continue promoting the World Corp. brand as "increasingly ill-advised."

Nevertheless, World Corp. remains the most well-known and highly regarded company in the world, responsible for a record-breaking list of patents and a growing number of inventions, many of which are taken for granted as necessary tools for making one's way through daily life. There is no doubting the long-term relevance of those innovations, but the way forward for the company behind them remains unclear. As numerous observers have pointed out, some of World Corp.'s greatest achievements were made not by Emerson Strange but by his now absent partners, and while he has distinguished himself again and again over the years, it simply is not possible for one man to do the work of four.

As it stands, World Corp. is at a crossroads. If the buzz surrounding Strange's interest in taking over the International Space Station proves true, it could well be the company is on the road to a new stage in its development. One of Thomas Walker's original goals was to see World Corp. lead the way in both interstellar and interdimensional research and exploration, and the acquisition of a fully operational space station would certainly be a means toward that end. Strange has tersely denied any interest in purchasing the ISS, though, and if his ongoing seclusion and growing detachment from the company's day-to-day operations are to be viewed as a sign of the company's long-term prospects, it could be that World Corp. is more likely on a road to nowhere. ∎ ***Paul Bradshaw***

> *As it stands, World Corp. is at a crossroads.*

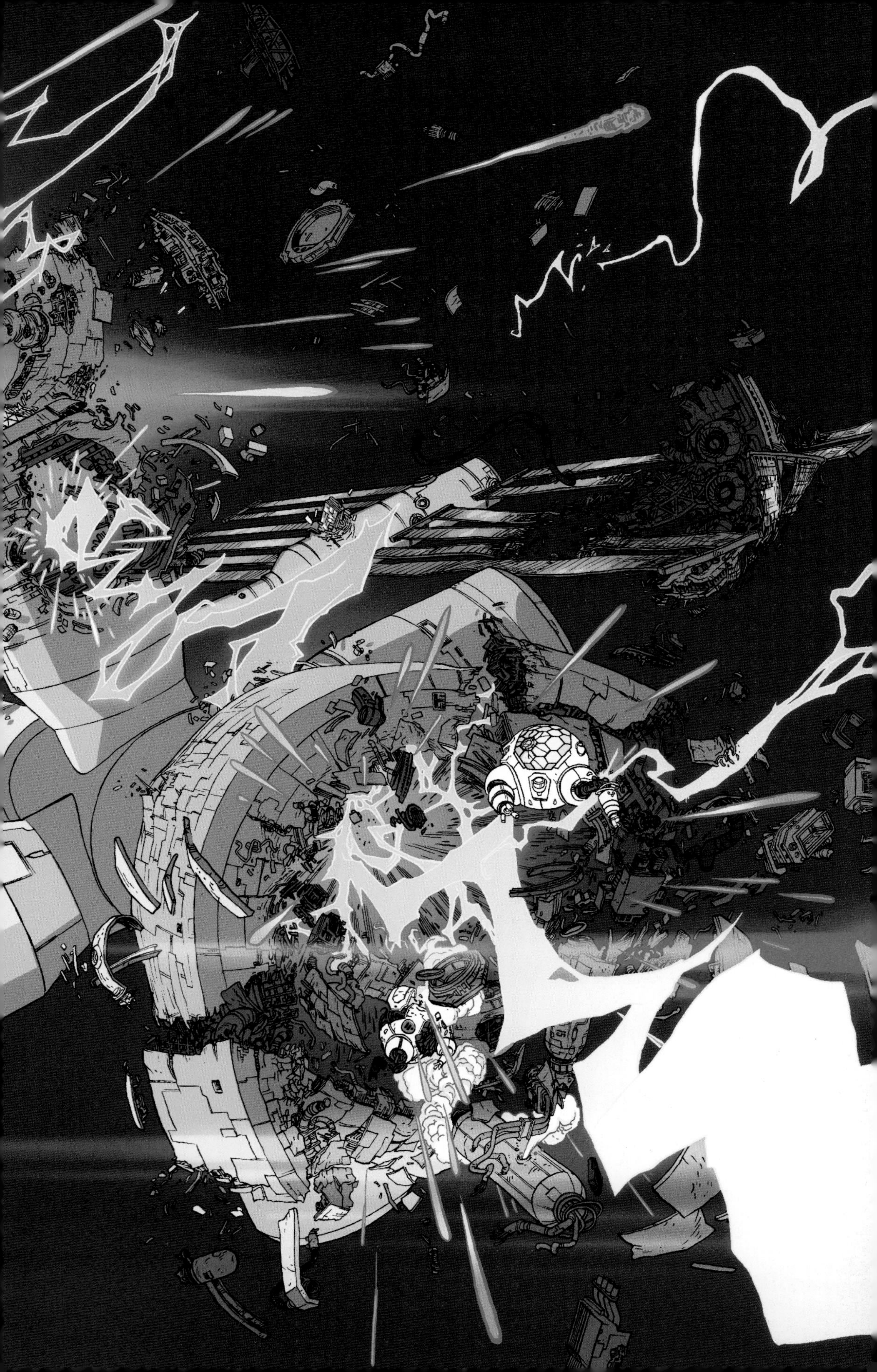

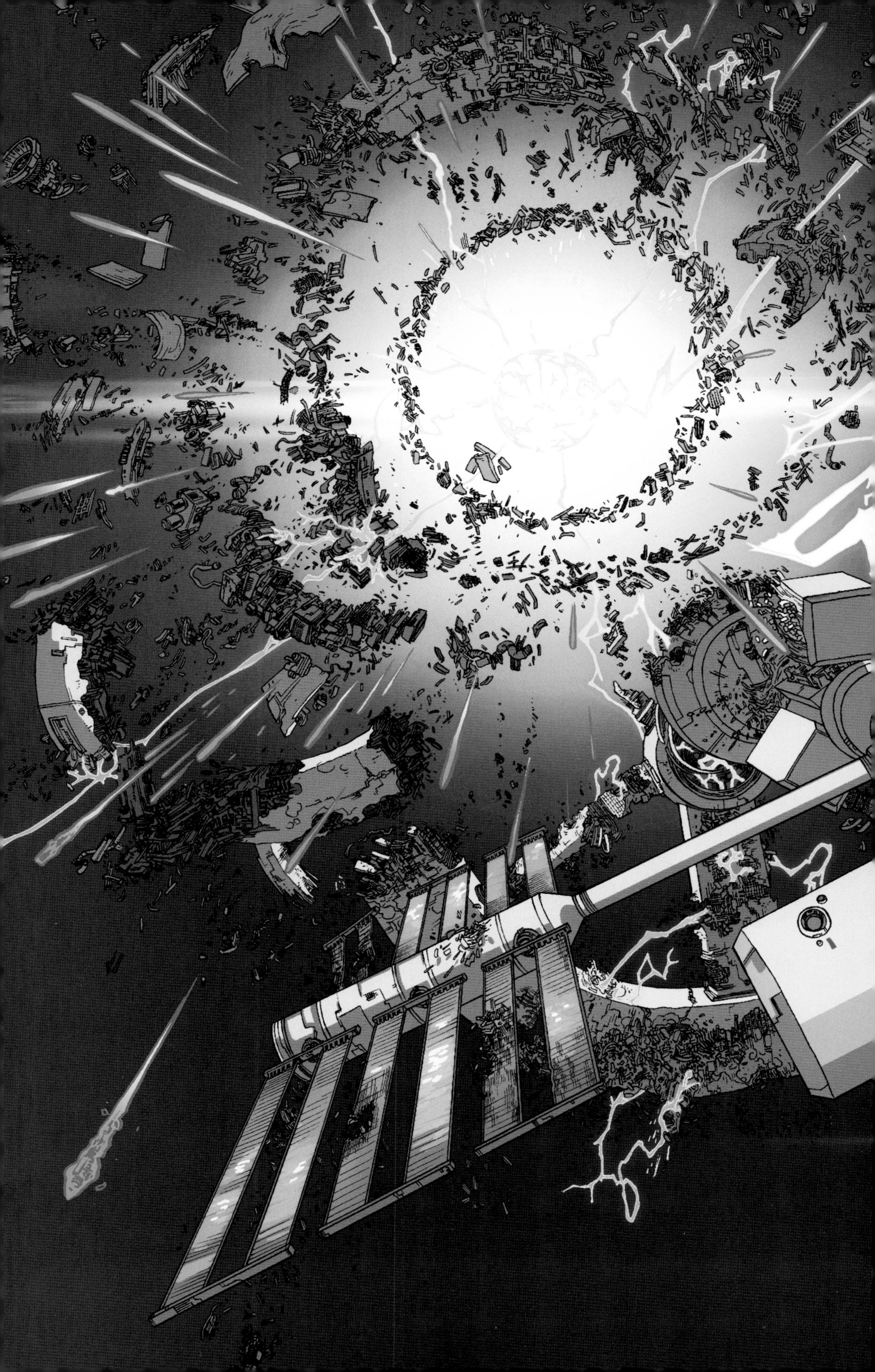

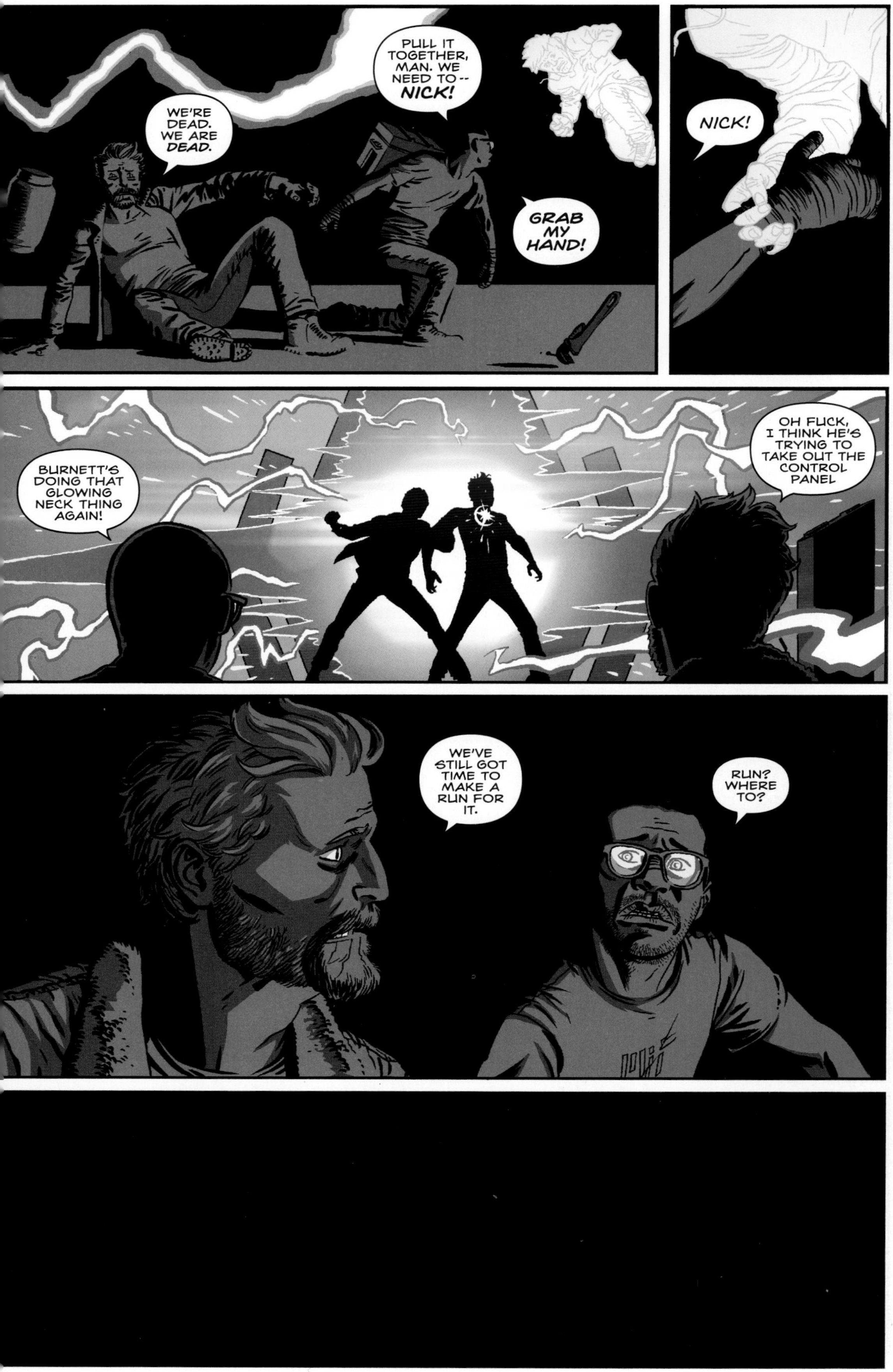
WE'RE DEAD. WE ARE DEAD.
PULL IT TOGETHER, MAN. WE NEED TO-- NICK!
GRAB MY HAND!
NICK!
BURNETT'S DOING THAT GLOWING NECK THING AGAIN!
OH FUCK, I THINK HE'S TRYING TO TAKE OUT THE CONTROL PANEL
WE'VE STILL GOT TIME TO MAKE A RUN FOR IT.
RUN? WHERE TO?

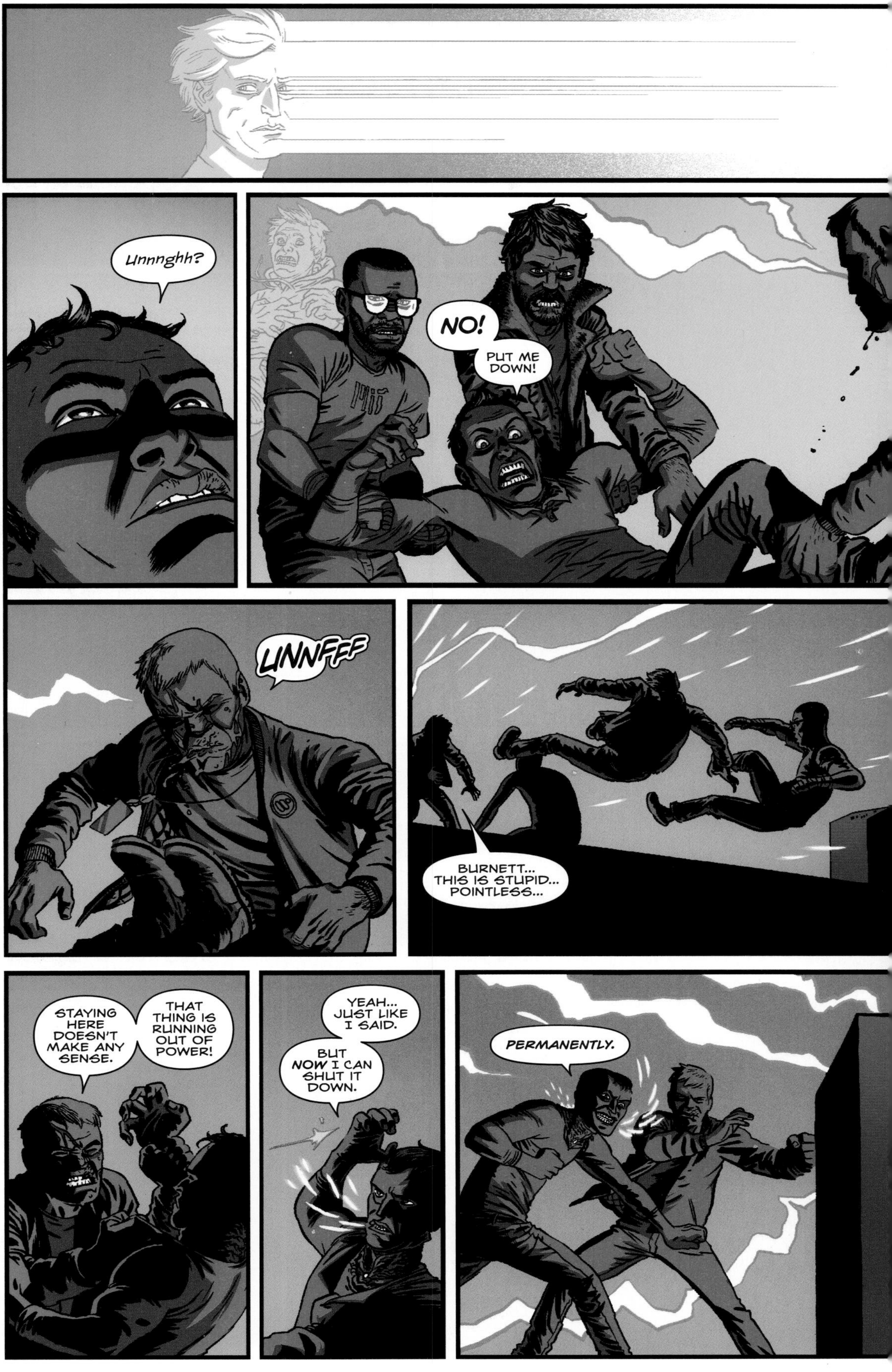
Unnnghh?
NO!
PUT ME DOWN!
UNNFFF
BURNETT... THIS IS STUPID... POINTLESS...
STAYING HERE DOESN'T MAKE ANY SENSE.
THAT THING IS RUNNING OUT OF POWER!
YEAH... JUST LIKE I SAID.
BUT NOW I CAN SHUT IT DOWN.
PERMANENTLY.

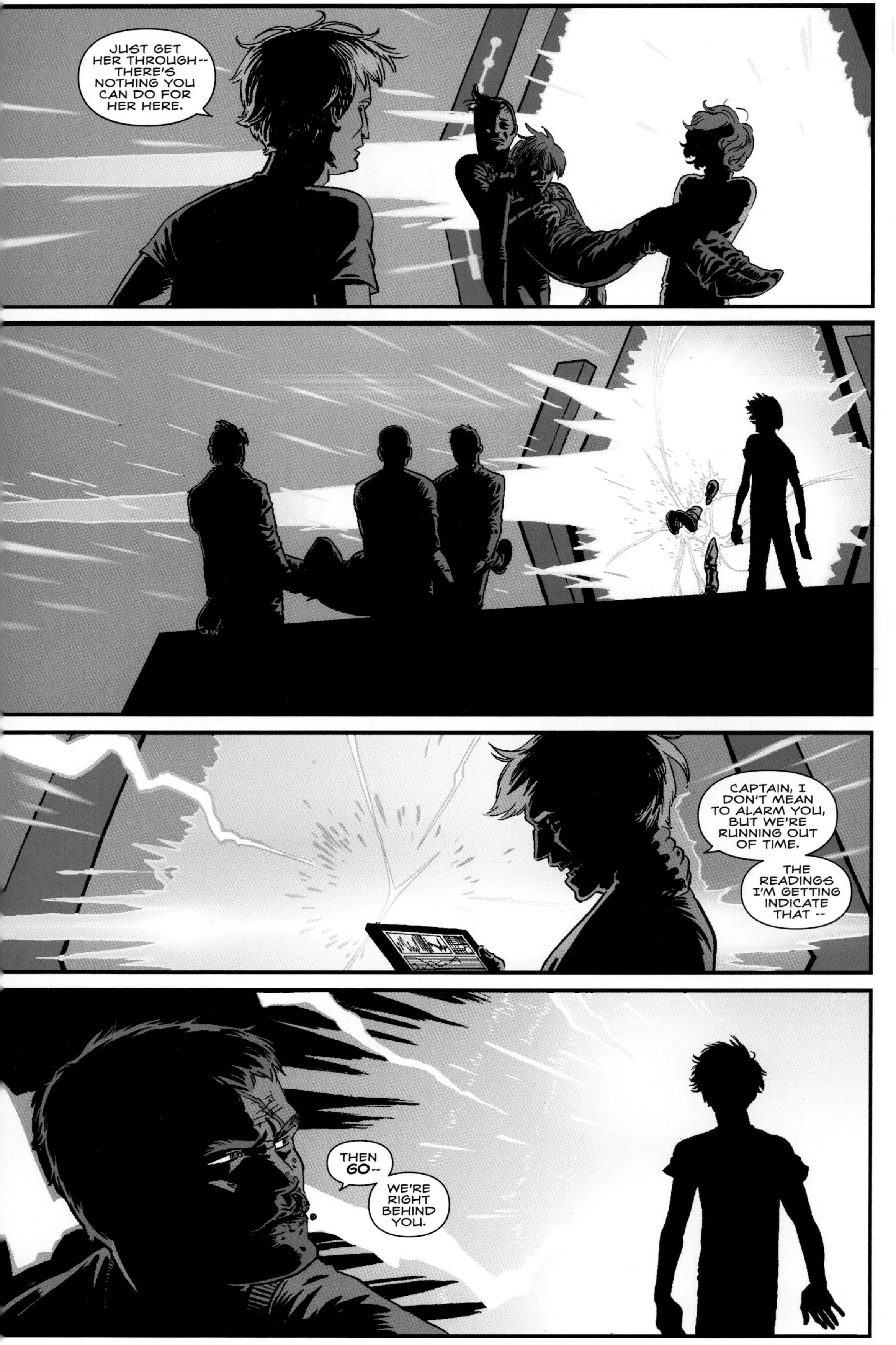
JUST GET HER THROUGH-- THERE'S NOTHING YOU CAN DO FOR HER HERE.
CAPTAIN, I DON'T MEAN TO ALARM YOU, BUT WE'RE RUNNING OUT OF TIME.
THE READINGS I'M GETTING INDICATE THAT --
THEN GO--
WE'RE RIGHT BEHIND YOU.

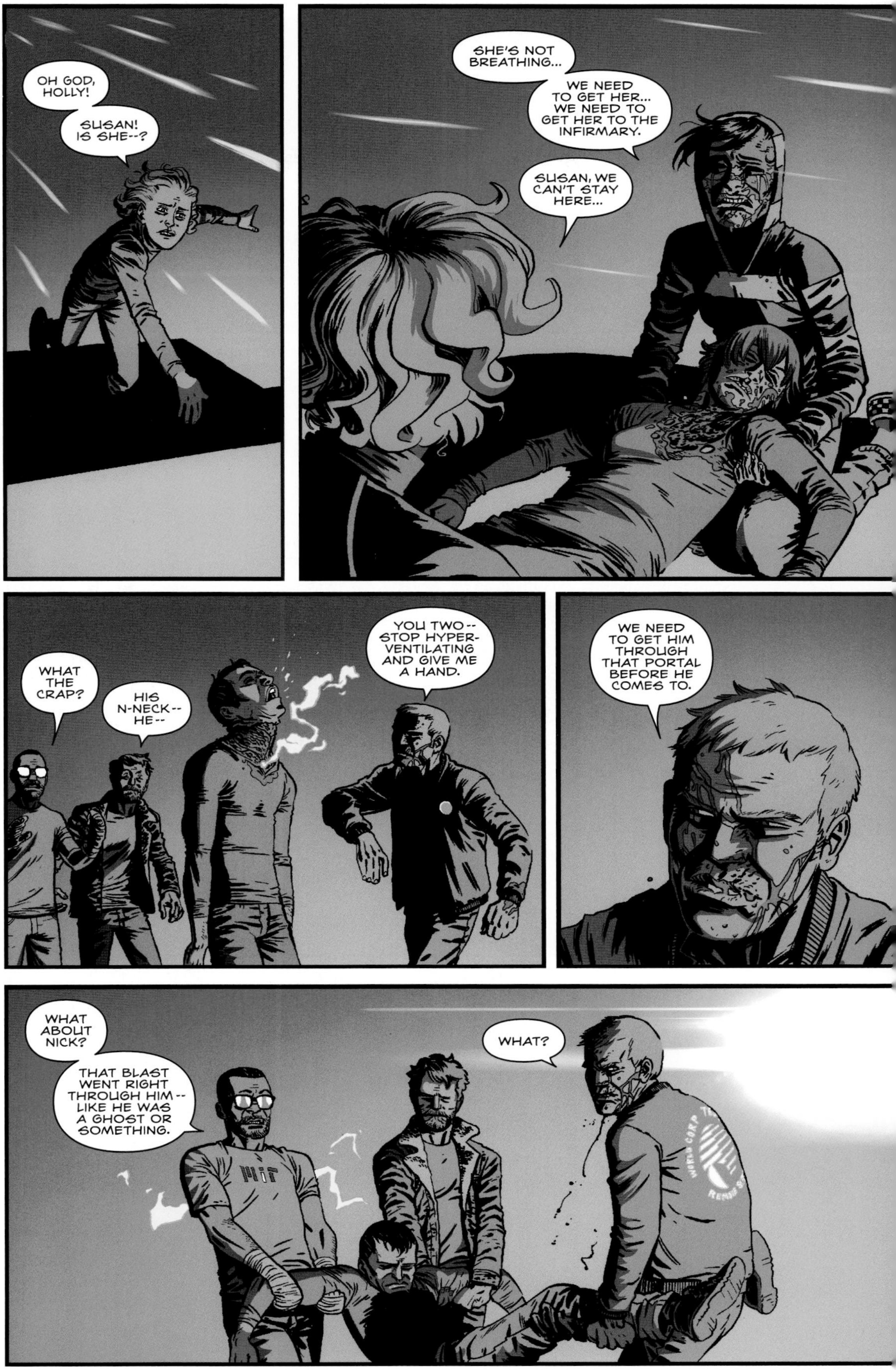
OH GOD, HOLLY!
SUSAN! IS SHE--?
SHE'S NOT BREATHING...
WE NEED TO GET HER... WE NEED TO GET HER TO THE INFIRMARY.
SUSAN, WE CAN'T STAY HERE...
WHAT THE CRAP?
HIS N-NECK-- HE--
YOU TWO-- STOP HYPER-VENTILATING AND GIVE ME A HAND.
WE NEED TO GET HIM THROUGH THAT PORTAL BEFORE HE COMES TO.
WHAT ABOUT NICK?
THAT BLAST WENT RIGHT THROUGH HIM-- LIKE HE WAS A GHOST OR SOMETHING.
WHAT?

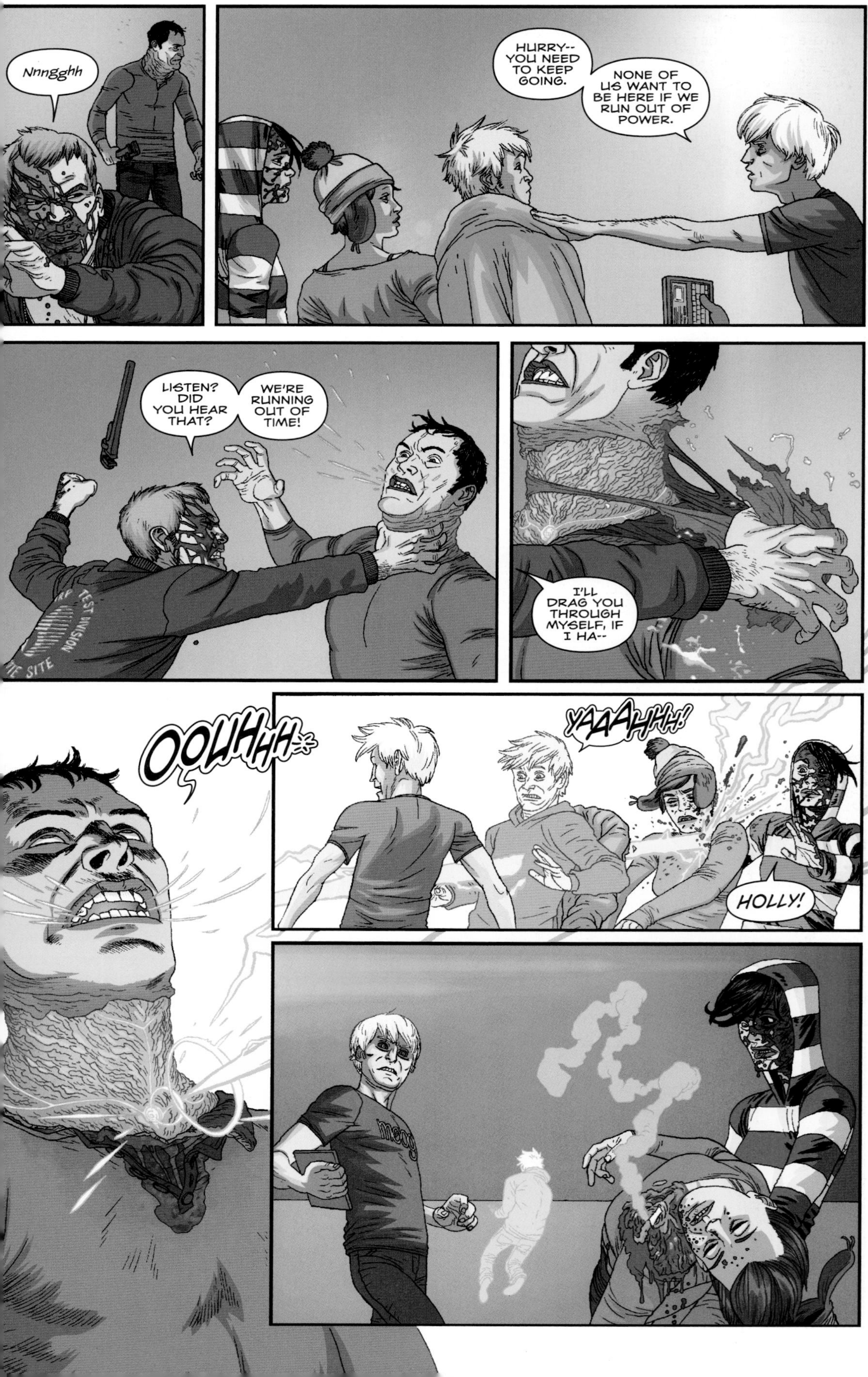
Nnngghh
HURRY--YOU NEED TO KEEP GOING.
NONE OF US WANT TO BE HERE IF WE RUN OUT OF POWER.
LISTEN? DID YOU HEAR THAT?
WE'RE RUNNING OUT OF TIME!
I'LL DRAG YOU THROUGH MYSELF, IF I HA--
OOUHHH
YAAAHHH!
HOLLY!

MAYBE IT'S JUST THE VIRUS TALKING, BUT YOU'RE WAY OUT OF LINE ON THIS, BURNETT!

EITHER GET ON THAT PLATFORM, OR GET OUT OF THE WAY -- BUT THIS NEEDS TO STOP *NOW*.

WITH ALL DUE RESPECT, CAPTAIN LANGLEY...

GO *FUCK* YOURSELF.

BRIAN -- HELP ME SHUT THIS THING DOWN.

Uh, DUDE...

WHAT?

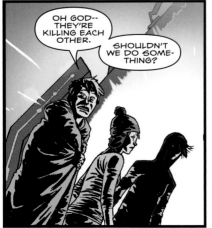

OH GOD-- THEY'RE KILLING EACH OTHER.

SHOULDN'T WE DO SOME-THING?

THE HELL?

MY NECK...

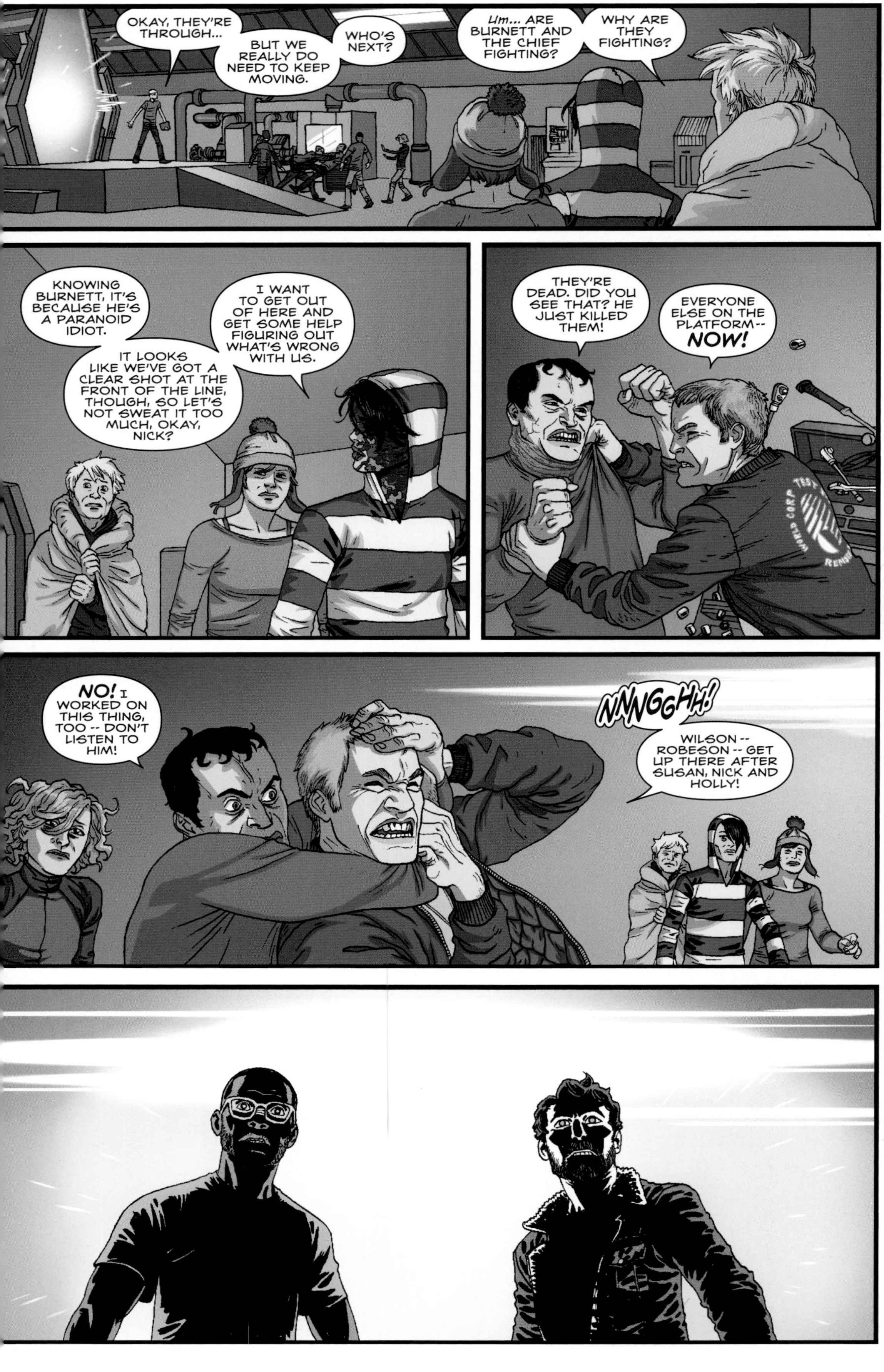
OKAY, THEY'RE THROUGH...
BUT WE REALLY DO NEED TO KEEP MOVING.
WHO'S NEXT?
Um... ARE BURNETT AND THE CHIEF FIGHTING?
WHY ARE THEY FIGHTING?
KNOWING BURNETT, IT'S BECAUSE HE'S A PARANOID IDIOT.
I WANT TO GET OUT OF HERE AND GET SOME HELP FIGURING OUT WHAT'S WRONG WITH US.
IT LOOKS LIKE WE'VE GOT A CLEAR SHOT AT THE FRONT OF THE LINE, THOUGH, SO LET'S NOT SWEAT IT TOO MUCH, OKAY, NICK?
THEY'RE DEAD. DID YOU SEE THAT? HE JUST KILLED THEM!
EVERYONE ELSE ON THE PLATFORM -- NOW!
WORLD CORP TEST
NO! I WORKED ON THIS THING, TOO -- DON'T LISTEN TO HIM!
NNNGGHH!
WILSON -- ROBESON -- GET UP THERE AFTER SUSAN, NICK AND HOLLY!

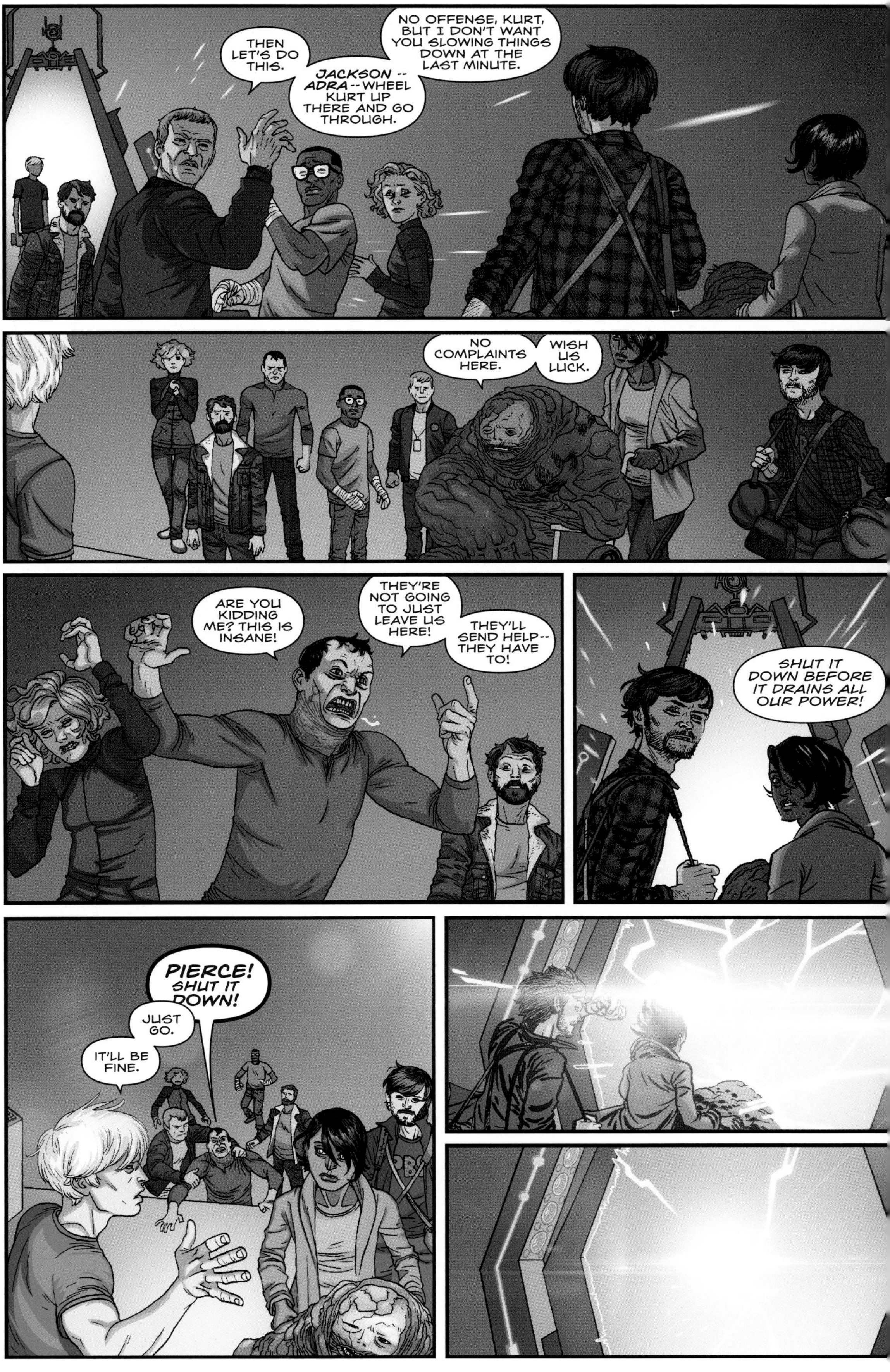
THEN LET'S DO THIS.
NO OFFENSE, KURT, BUT I DON'T WANT YOU SLOWING THINGS DOWN AT THE LAST MINUTE.
JACKSON -- ADRA -- WHEEL KURT UP THERE AND GO THROUGH.
NO COMPLAINTS HERE.
WISH US LUCK.
ARE YOU KIDDING ME? THIS IS INSANE!
THEY'RE NOT GOING TO JUST LEAVE US HERE!
THEY'LL SEND HELP-- THEY HAVE TO!
SHUT IT DOWN BEFORE IT DRAINS ALL OUR POWER!
PIERCE! SHUT IT DOWN!
JUST GO.
IT'LL BE FINE.

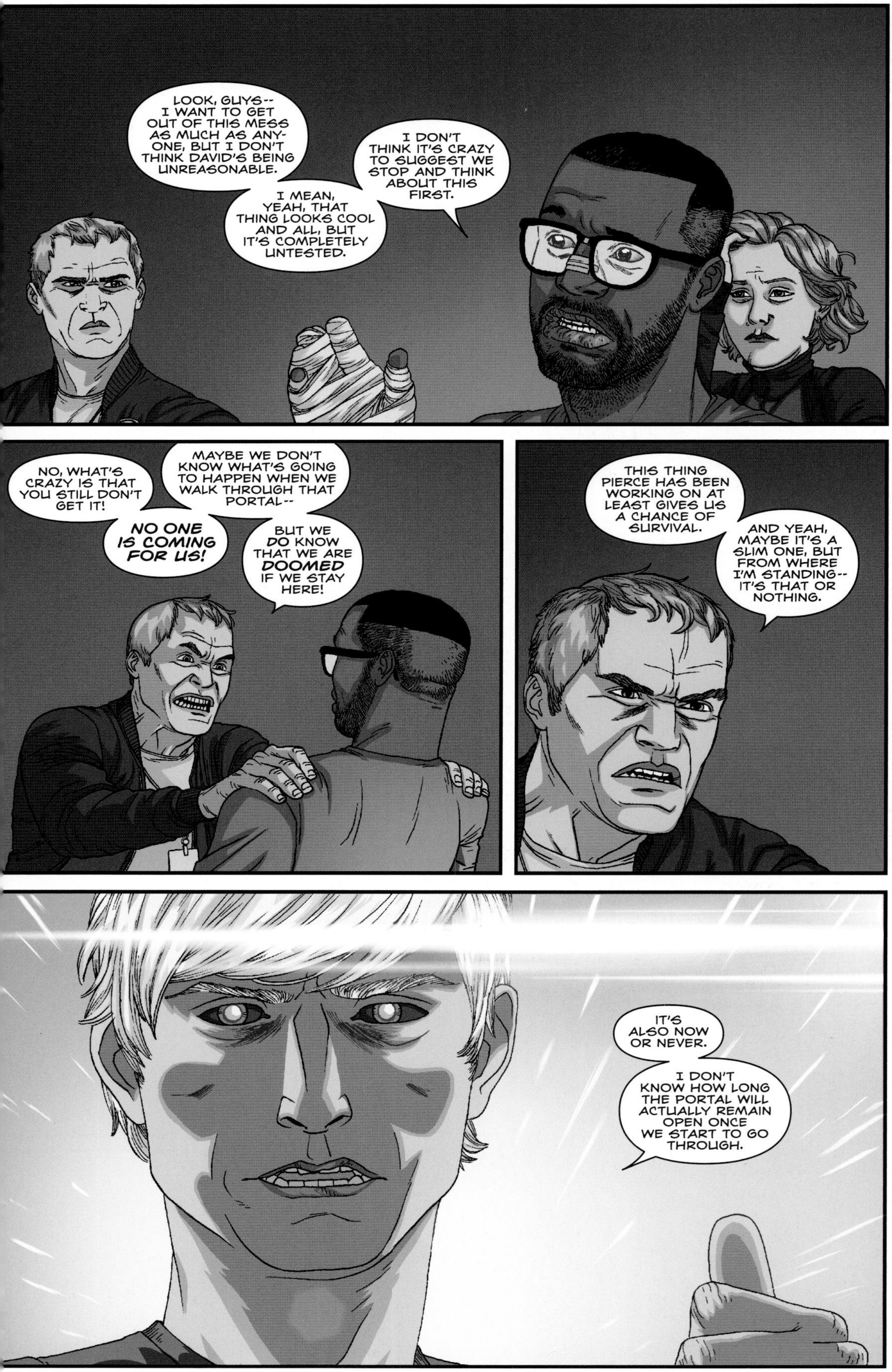
LOOK, GUYS-- I WANT TO GET OUT OF THIS MESS AS MUCH AS ANY-ONE, BUT I DON'T THINK DAVID'S BEING UNREASONABLE.
I MEAN, YEAH, THAT THING LOOKS COOL AND ALL, BUT IT'S COMPLETELY UNTESTED.
I DON'T THINK IT'S CRAZY TO SUGGEST WE STOP AND THINK ABOUT THIS FIRST.
NO, WHAT'S CRAZY IS THAT YOU STILL DON'T GET IT!
NO ONE IS COMING FOR US!
MAYBE WE DON'T KNOW WHAT'S GOING TO HAPPEN WHEN WE WALK THROUGH THAT PORTAL--
BUT WE DO KNOW THAT WE ARE DOOMED IF WE STAY HERE!
THIS THING PIERCE HAS BEEN WORKING ON AT LEAST GIVES US A CHANCE OF SURVIVAL.
AND YEAH, MAYBE IT'S A SLIM ONE, BUT FROM WHERE I'M STANDING-- IT'S THAT OR NOTHING.
IT'S ALSO NOW OR NEVER.
I DON'T KNOW HOW LONG THE PORTAL WILL ACTUALLY REMAIN OPEN ONCE WE START TO GO THROUGH.

OH, COME ON -- ISN'T IT OBVIOUS?

PIERCE'S BRILLIANT INVENTION IS SIPHONING ENERGY FROM THE REST OF THE STATION!

OF COURSE IT IS. THAT WAS THE WHOLE PLAN.

REALLY? AND THERE WASN'T SOME POINT WHILE WE WERE WORKING ON IT THAT YOU COULD HAVE MENTIONED THAT?

THERE'S NO WAY I COULD FULLY ENGAGE A DEVICE LIKE THIS WITH THE LIMITED POWER SUPPLY I WAS WORKING WITH DURING EXPERIMENTATION.

BESIDES, IT'S NOT LIKE IT WILL MATTER ONCE WE'RE GONE.

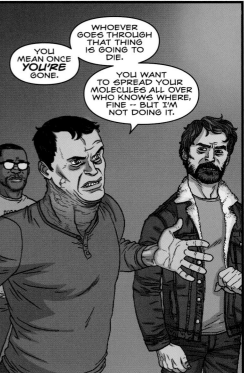

YOU MEAN ONCE *YOU'RE* GONE.

WHOEVER GOES THROUGH THAT THING IS GOING TO DIE.

YOU WANT TO SPREAD YOUR MOLECULES ALL OVER WHO KNOWS WHERE, FINE -- BUT I'M NOT DOING IT.

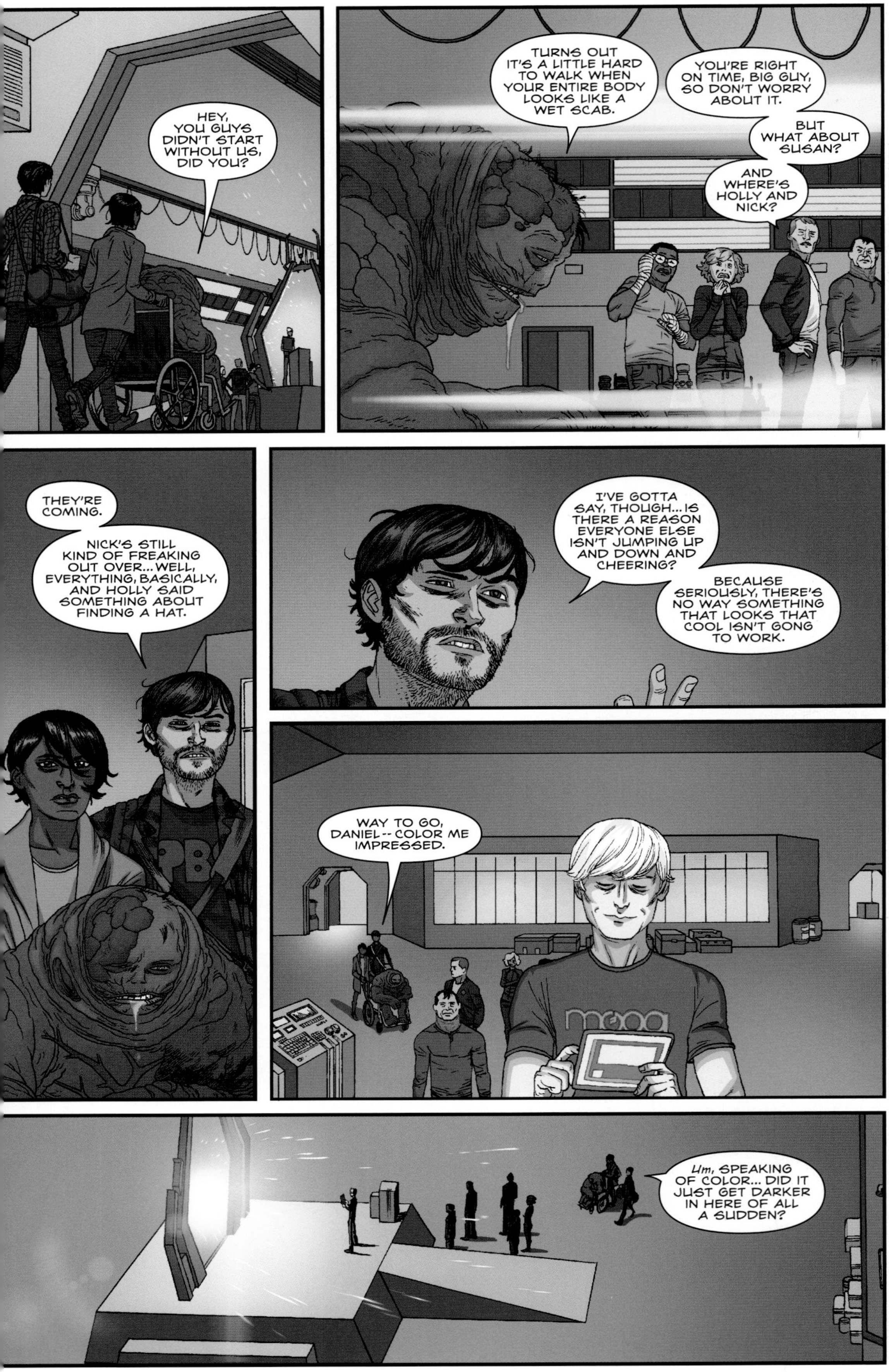
HEY, YOU GUYS DIDN'T START WITHOUT US, DID YOU?
TURNS OUT IT'S A LITTLE HARD TO WALK WHEN YOUR ENTIRE BODY LOOKS LIKE A WET SCAB.
YOU'RE RIGHT ON TIME, BIG GUY, SO DON'T WORRY ABOUT IT.
BUT WHAT ABOUT SUSAN?
AND WHERE'S HOLLY AND NICK?
THEY'RE COMING.
NICK'S STILL KIND OF FREAKING OUT OVER... WELL, EVERYTHING, BASICALLY, AND HOLLY SAID SOMETHING ABOUT FINDING A HAT.
I'VE GOTTA SAY, THOUGH... IS THERE A REASON EVERYONE ELSE ISN'T JUMPING UP AND DOWN AND CHEERING?
BECAUSE SERIOUSLY, THERE'S NO WAY SOMETHING THAT LOOKS THAT COOL ISN'T GONG TO WORK.
WAY TO GO, DANIEL-- COLOR ME IMPRESSED.
moog
Um, SPEAKING OF COLOR... DID IT JUST GET DARKER IN HERE OF ALL A SUDDEN?

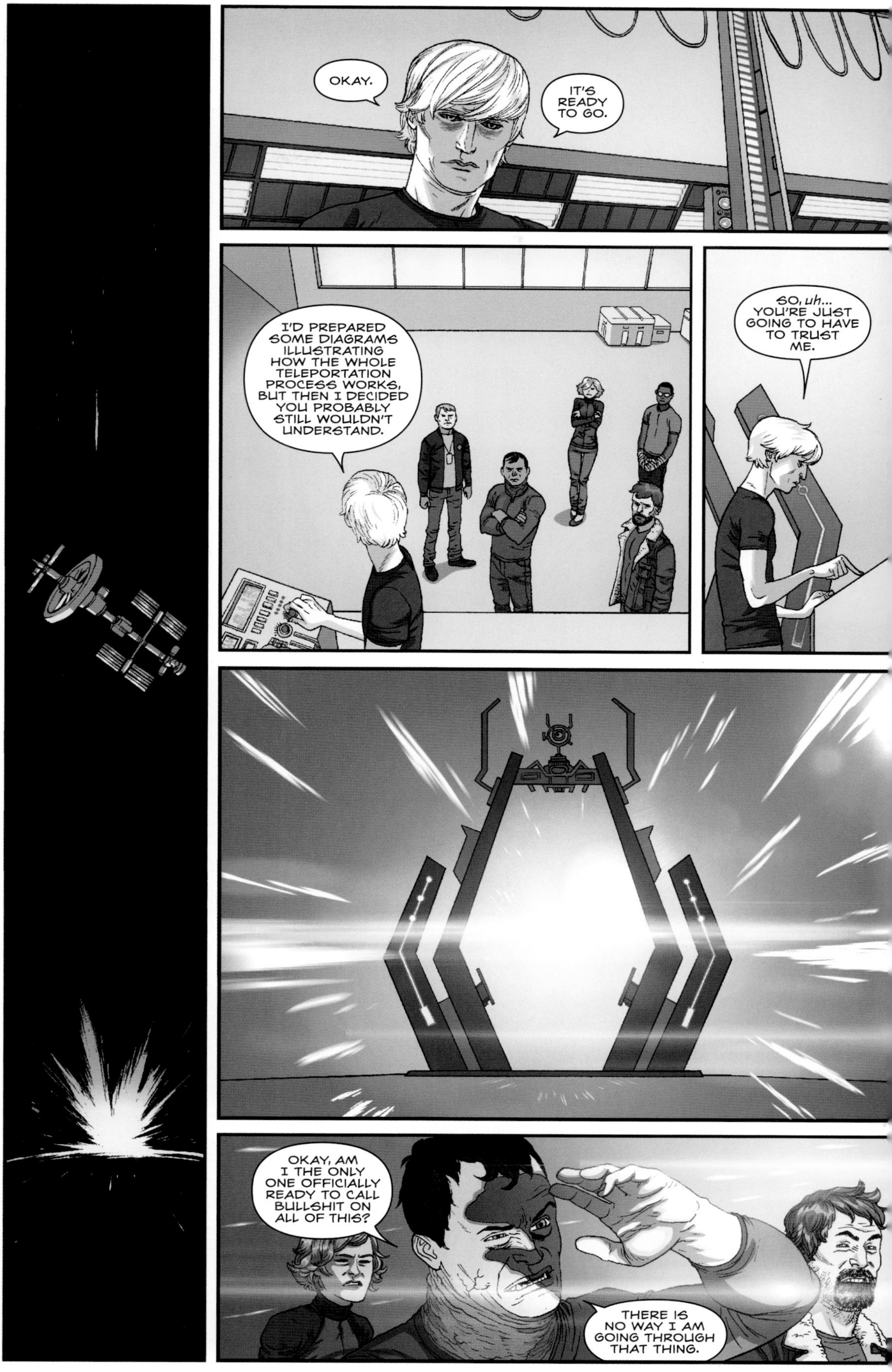
OKAY.
IT'S READY TO GO.
I'D PREPARED SOME DIAGRAMS ILLUSTRATING HOW THE WHOLE TELEPORTATION PROCESS WORKS, BUT THEN I DECIDED YOU PROBABLY STILL WOULDN'T UNDERSTAND.
SO, *uh*... YOU'RE JUST GOING TO HAVE TO TRUST ME.
OKAY, AM I THE ONLY ONE OFFICIALLY READY TO CALL BULLSHIT ON ALL OF THIS?
THERE IS NO WAY I AM GOING THROUGH THAT THING.

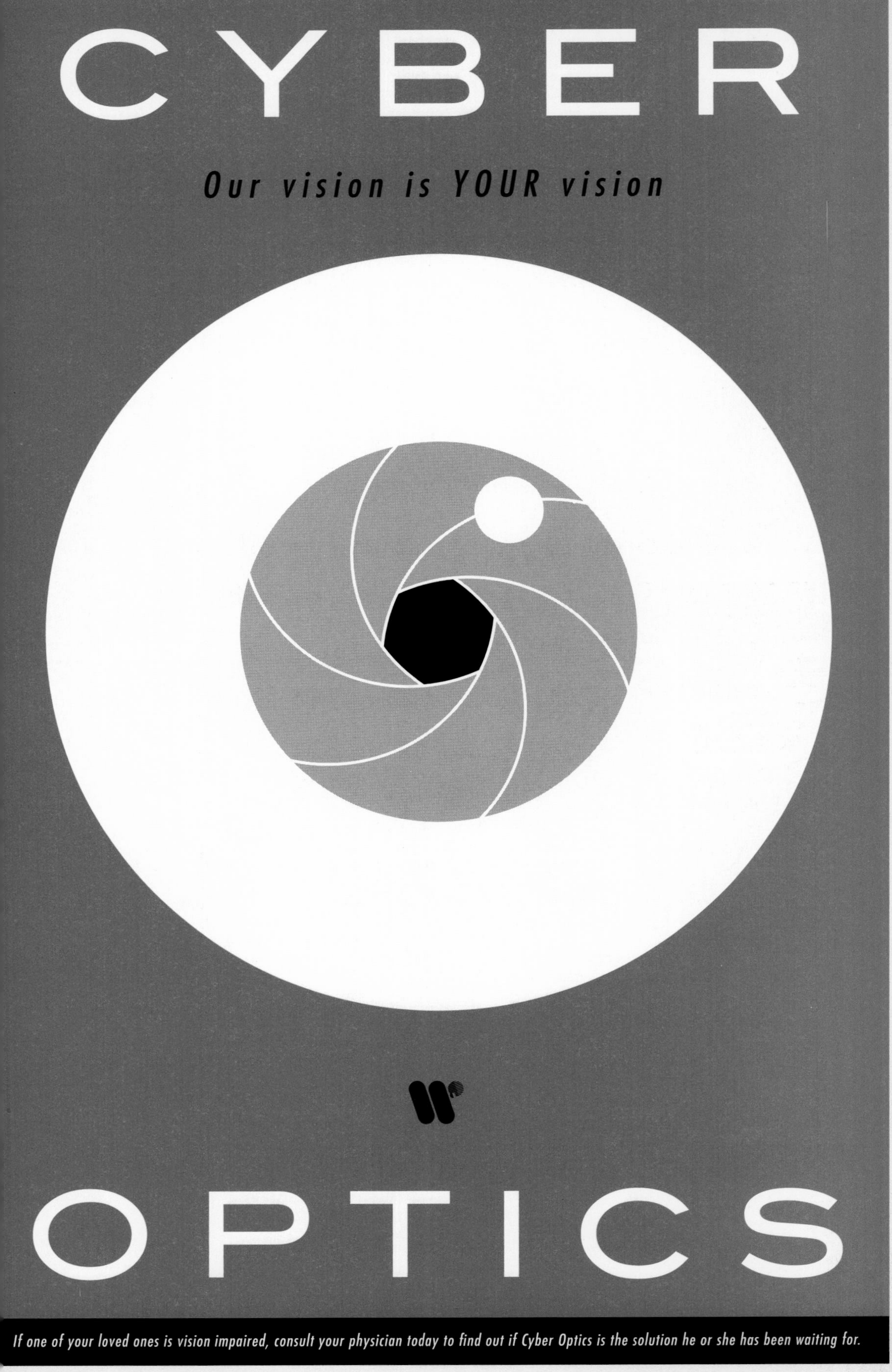
CYBER
Our vision is YOUR vision
OPTICS
If one of your loved ones is vision impaired, consult your physician today to find out if Cyber Optics is the solution he or she has been waiting for.

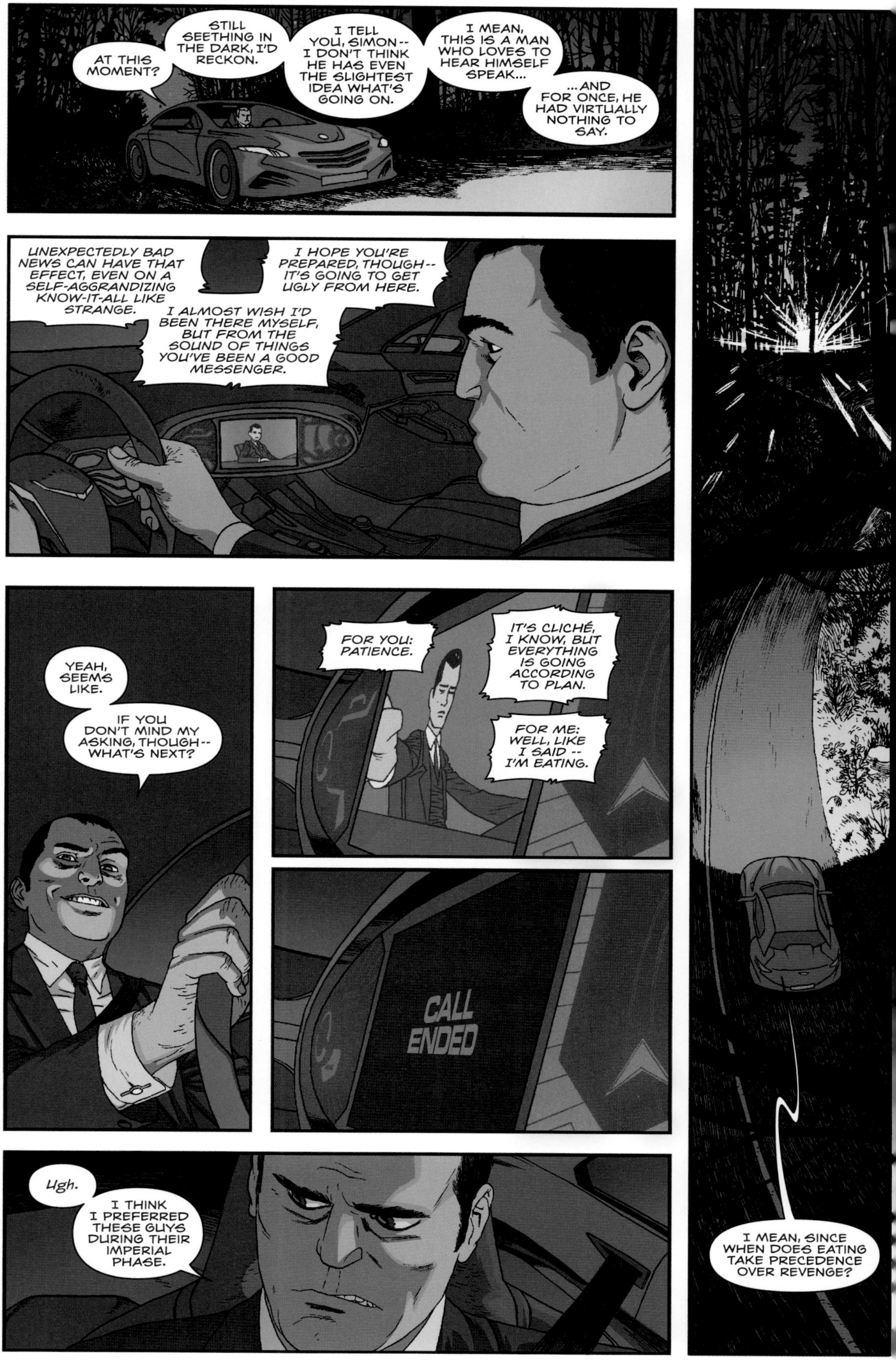
AT THIS MOMENT?
STILL SEETHING IN THE DARK, I'D RECKON.
I TELL YOU, SIMON-- I DON'T THINK HE HAS EVEN THE SLIGHTEST IDEA WHAT'S GOING ON.
I MEAN, THIS IS A MAN WHO LOVES TO HEAR HIMSELF SPEAK...
...AND FOR ONCE, HE HAD VIRTUALLY NOTHING TO SAY.
UNEXPECTEDLY BAD NEWS CAN HAVE THAT EFFECT, EVEN ON A SELF-AGGRANDIZING KNOW-IT-ALL LIKE STRANGE.
I ALMOST WISH I'D BEEN THERE MYSELF, BUT FROM THE SOUND OF THINGS YOU'VE BEEN A GOOD MESSENGER.
I HOPE YOU'RE PREPARED, THOUGH-- IT'S GOING TO GET UGLY FROM HERE.
YEAH, SEEMS LIKE.
IF YOU DON'T MIND MY ASKING, THOUGH-- WHAT'S NEXT?
FOR YOU: PATIENCE.
IT'S CLICHÉ, I KNOW, BUT EVERYTHING IS GOING ACCORDING TO PLAN.
FOR ME: WELL, LIKE I SAID -- I'M EATING.
CALL ENDED
Ugh.
I THINK I PREFERRED THESE GUYS DURING THEIR IMPERIAL PHASE.
I MEAN, SINCE WHEN DOES EATING TAKE PRECEDENCE OVER REVENGE?

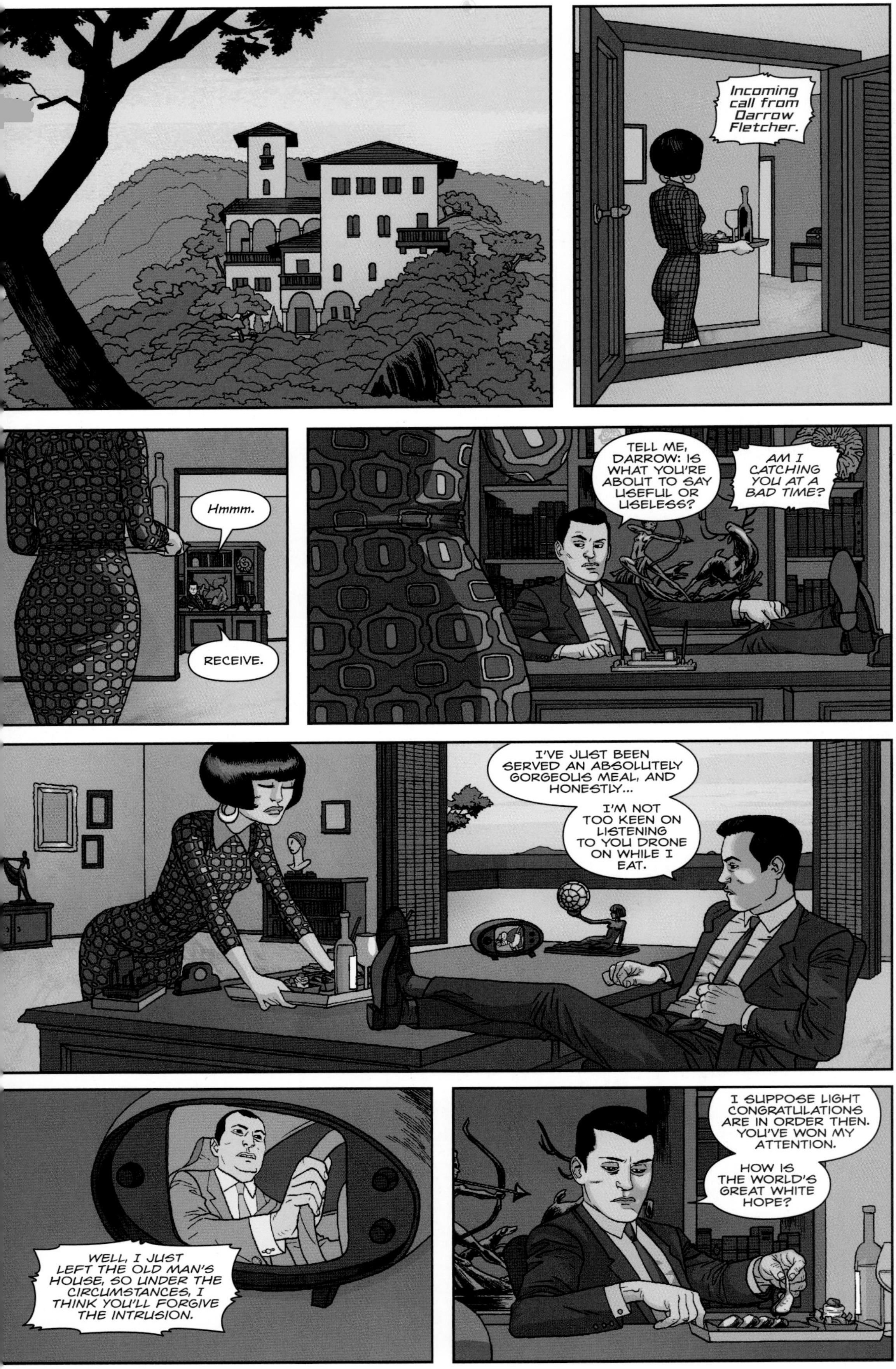
Incoming call from Darrow Fletcher.
Hmmm.
RECEIVE.
TELL ME, DARROW: IS WHAT YOU'RE ABOUT TO SAY USEFUL OR USELESS?
AM I CATCHING YOU AT A BAD TIME?
I'VE JUST BEEN SERVED AN ABSOLUTELY GORGEOUS MEAL, AND HONESTLY...
I'M NOT TOO KEEN ON LISTENING TO YOU DRONE ON WHILE I EAT.
WELL, I JUST LEFT THE OLD MAN'S HOUSE, SO UNDER THE CIRCUMSTANCES, I THINK YOU'LL FORGIVE THE INTRUSION.
I SUPPOSE LIGHT CONGRATULATIONS ARE IN ORDER THEN. YOU'VE WON MY ATTENTION.
HOW IS THE WORLD'S GREAT WHITE HOPE?

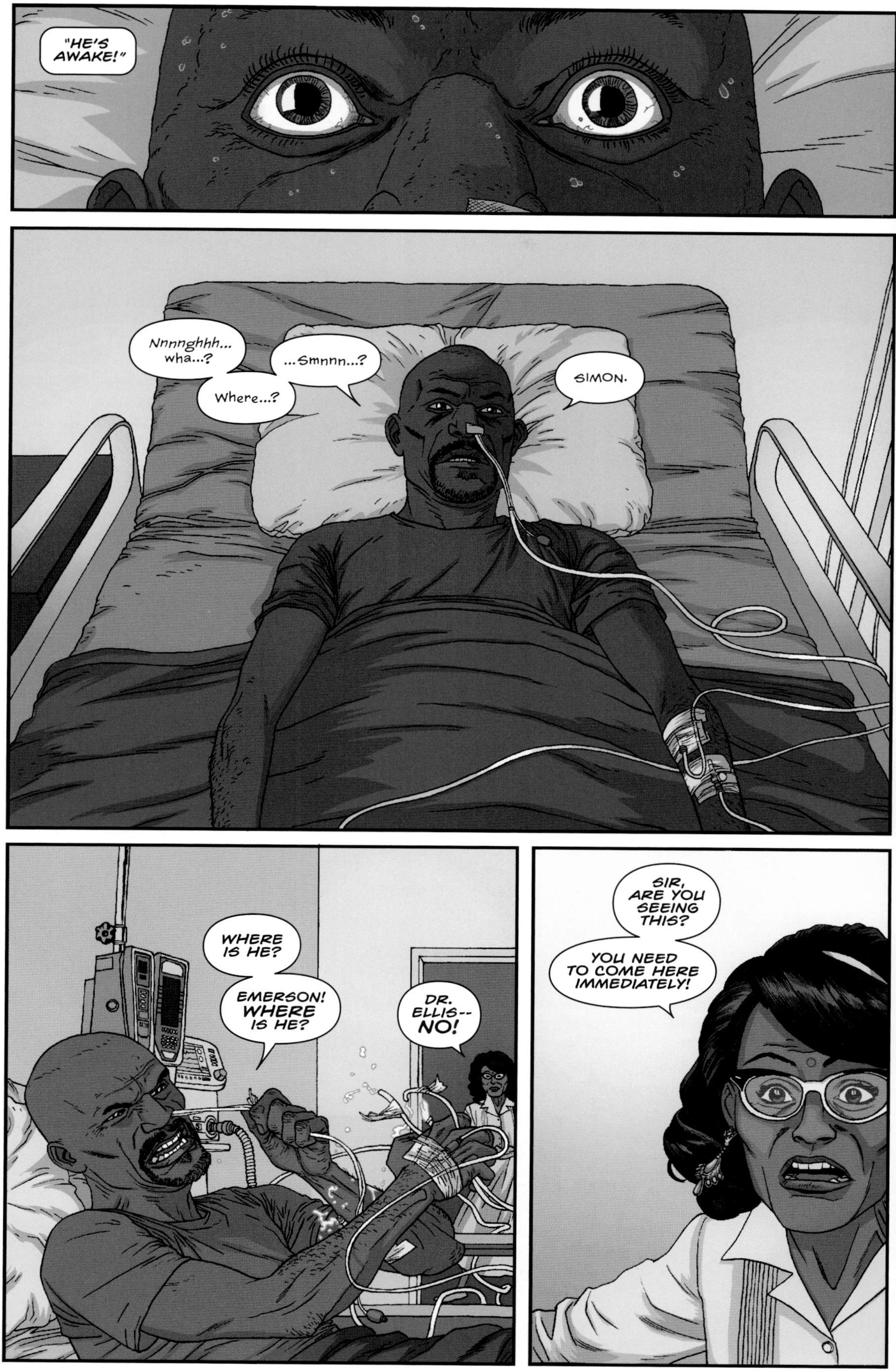
"HE'S AWAKE!"
Nnnnghhh... wha...?
Where...?
...Smnnn...?
SIMON.
WHERE IS HE?
EMERSON! WHERE IS HE?
DR. ELLIS-- NO!
SIR, ARE YOU SEEING THIS?
YOU NEED TO COME HERE IMMEDIATELY!

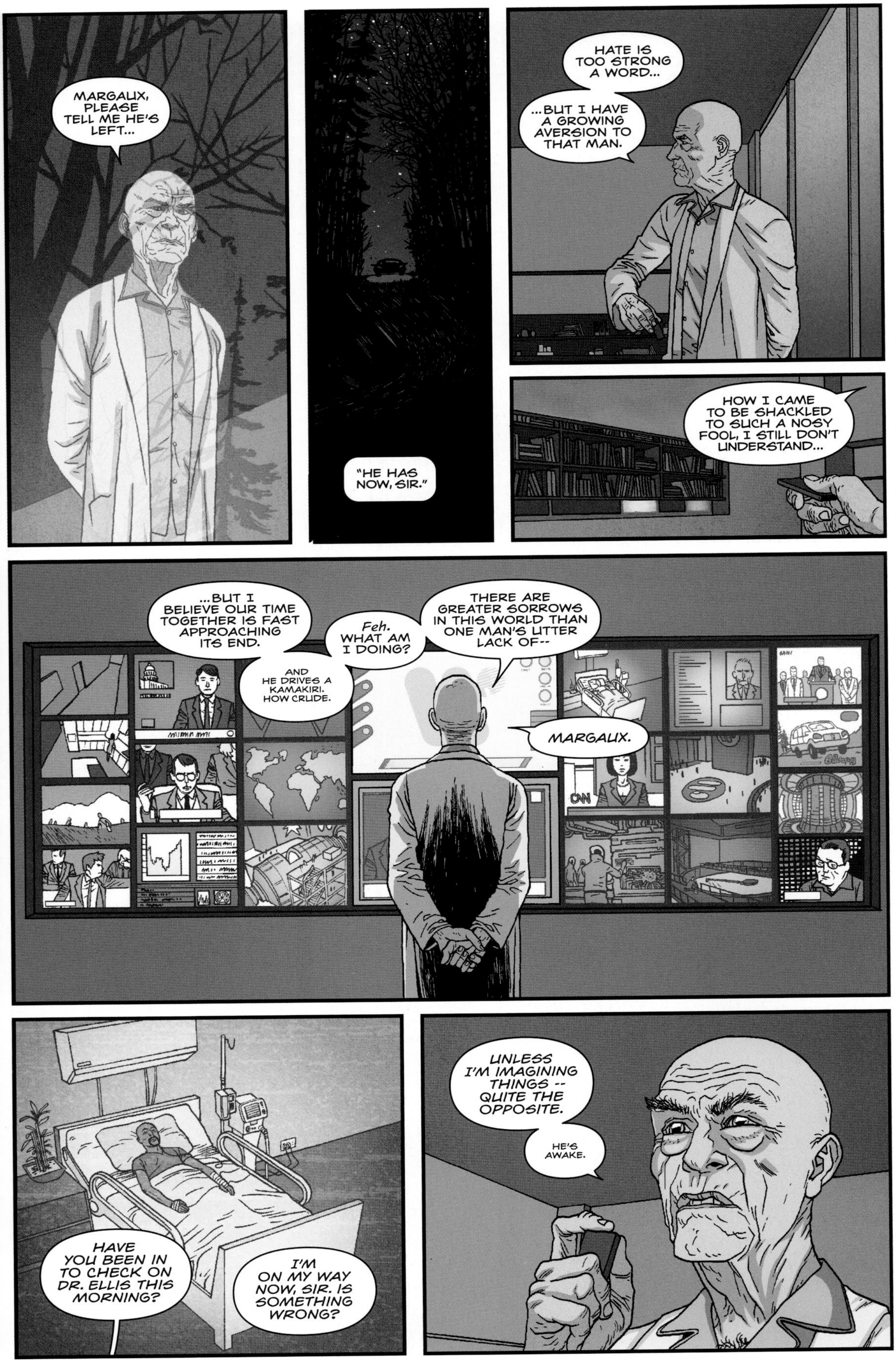

MARGAUX, PLEASE TELL ME HE'S LEFT...
"HE HAS NOW, SIR."
HATE IS TOO STRONG A WORD...
...BUT I HAVE A GROWING AVERSION TO THAT MAN.
HOW I CAME TO BE SHACKLED TO SUCH A NOSY FOOL, I STILL DON'T UNDERSTAND...
...BUT I BELIEVE OUR TIME TOGETHER IS FAST APPROACHING ITS END.
AND HE DRIVES A KAMAKIRI. HOW CRUDE.
Feh. WHAT AM I DOING?
THERE ARE GREATER SORROWS IN THIS WORLD THAN ONE MAN'S UTTER LACK OF--
MARGAUX.
CNN
HAVE YOU BEEN IN TO CHECK ON DR. ELLIS THIS MORNING?
I'M ON MY WAY NOW, SIR. IS SOMETHING WRONG?
UNLESS I'M IMAGINING THINGS -- QUITE THE OPPOSITE.
HE'S AWAKE.

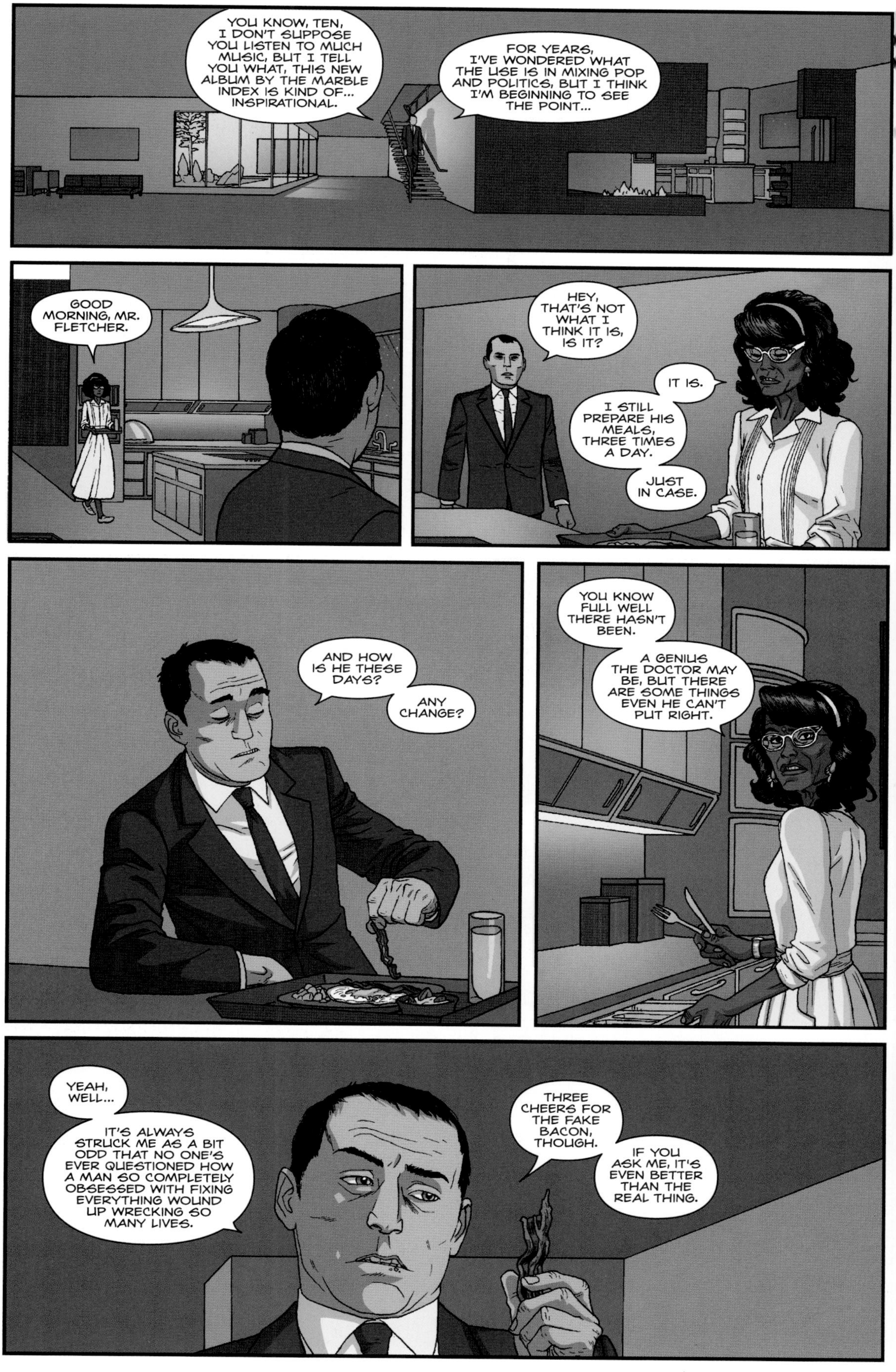
YOU KNOW, TEN, I DON'T SUPPOSE YOU LISTEN TO MUCH MUSIC, BUT I TELL YOU WHAT, THIS NEW ALBUM BY THE MARBLE INDEX IS KIND OF... INSPIRATIONAL.
FOR YEARS, I'VE WONDERED WHAT THE USE IS IN MIXING POP AND POLITICS, BUT I THINK I'M BEGINNING TO SEE THE POINT...
GOOD MORNING, MR. FLETCHER.
HEY, THAT'S NOT WHAT I THINK IT IS, IS IT?
IT IS.
I STILL PREPARE HIS MEALS, THREE TIMES A DAY.
JUST IN CASE.
AND HOW IS HE THESE DAYS?
ANY CHANGE?
YOU KNOW FULL WELL THERE HASN'T BEEN.
A GENIUS THE DOCTOR MAY BE, BUT THERE ARE SOME THINGS EVEN HE CAN'T PUT RIGHT.
YEAH, WELL...
IT'S ALWAYS STRUCK ME AS A BIT ODD THAT NO ONE'S EVER QUESTIONED HOW A MAN SO COMPLETELY OBSESSED WITH FIXING EVERYTHING WOUND UP WRECKING SO MANY LIVES.
THREE CHEERS FOR THE FAKE BACON, THOUGH.
IF YOU ASK ME, IT'S EVEN BETTER THAN THE REAL THING.

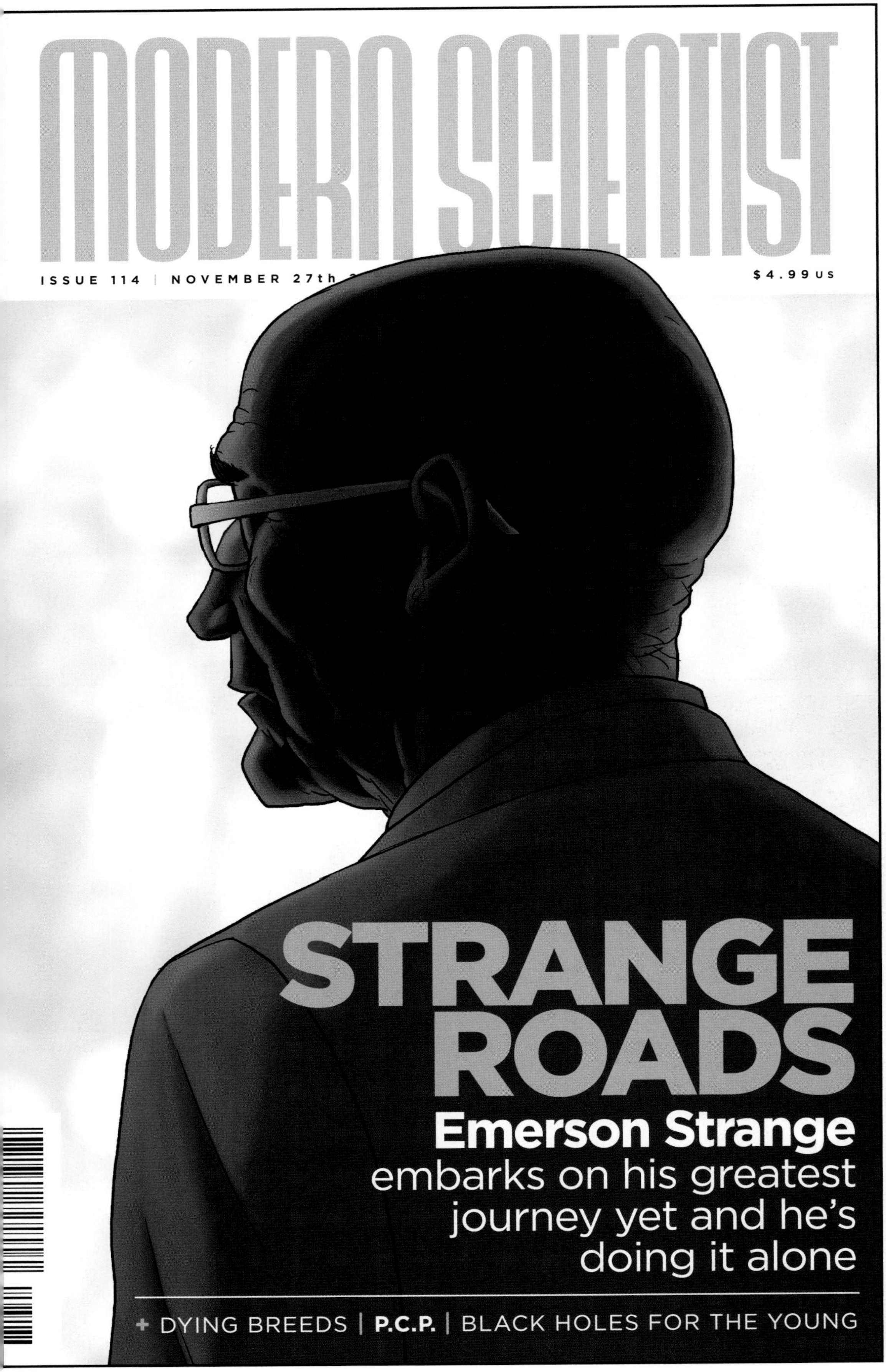
MODERN SCIENTIST
ISSUE 114 | NOVEMBER 27th
$4.99US
STRANGE ROADS
Emerson Strange
embarks on his greatest journey yet and he's doing it alone
+ DYING BREEDS | P.C.P. | BLACK HOLES FOR THE YOUNG

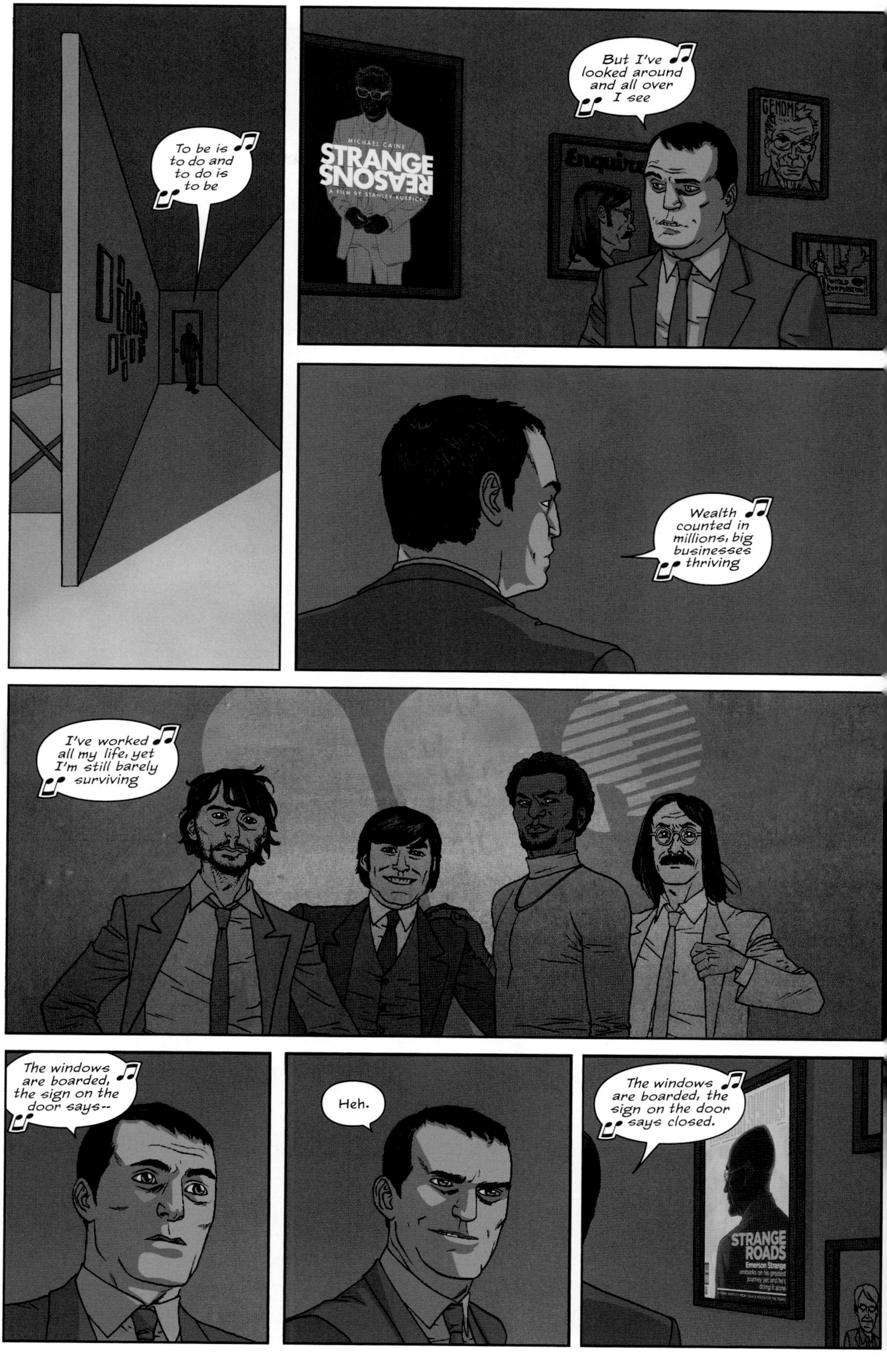
To be is to do and to do is to be
MICHAEL CAINE
STRANGE REASONS
A FILM BY STANLEY KUBRICK
But I've looked around and all over I see
GENOME
Enquirer
WORLD CORPORATION
Wealth counted in millions, big businesses thriving
I've worked all my life, yet I'm still barely surviving
The windows are boarded, the sign on the door says--
Heh.
The windows are boarded, the sign on the door says closed.
STRANGE ROADS
Emerson Strange

"WHAT DO I DO NOW?"

THIS VIRUS OR WHATEVER IT IS WE'RE CALLING IT-- PEOPLE ARE GOING TO BE ALARMED BY THAT.

IF YOU DECIDE TO BRING THE CREW HOME AND THEY SOMEHOW SPREAD THE INFECTION -- THERE'S GOING TO BE GENUINE PANIC.

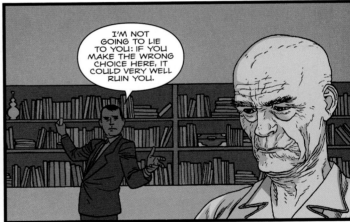

I'M NOT GOING TO LIE TO YOU: IF YOU MAKE THE WRONG CHOICE HERE, IT COULD VERY WELL RUIN YOU.

I'D ADOPT THOSE PERCEPTIONS AS MY OWN PRETTY DAMN QUICK.

I SEE.

THAT WILL BE ALL, DARROW.

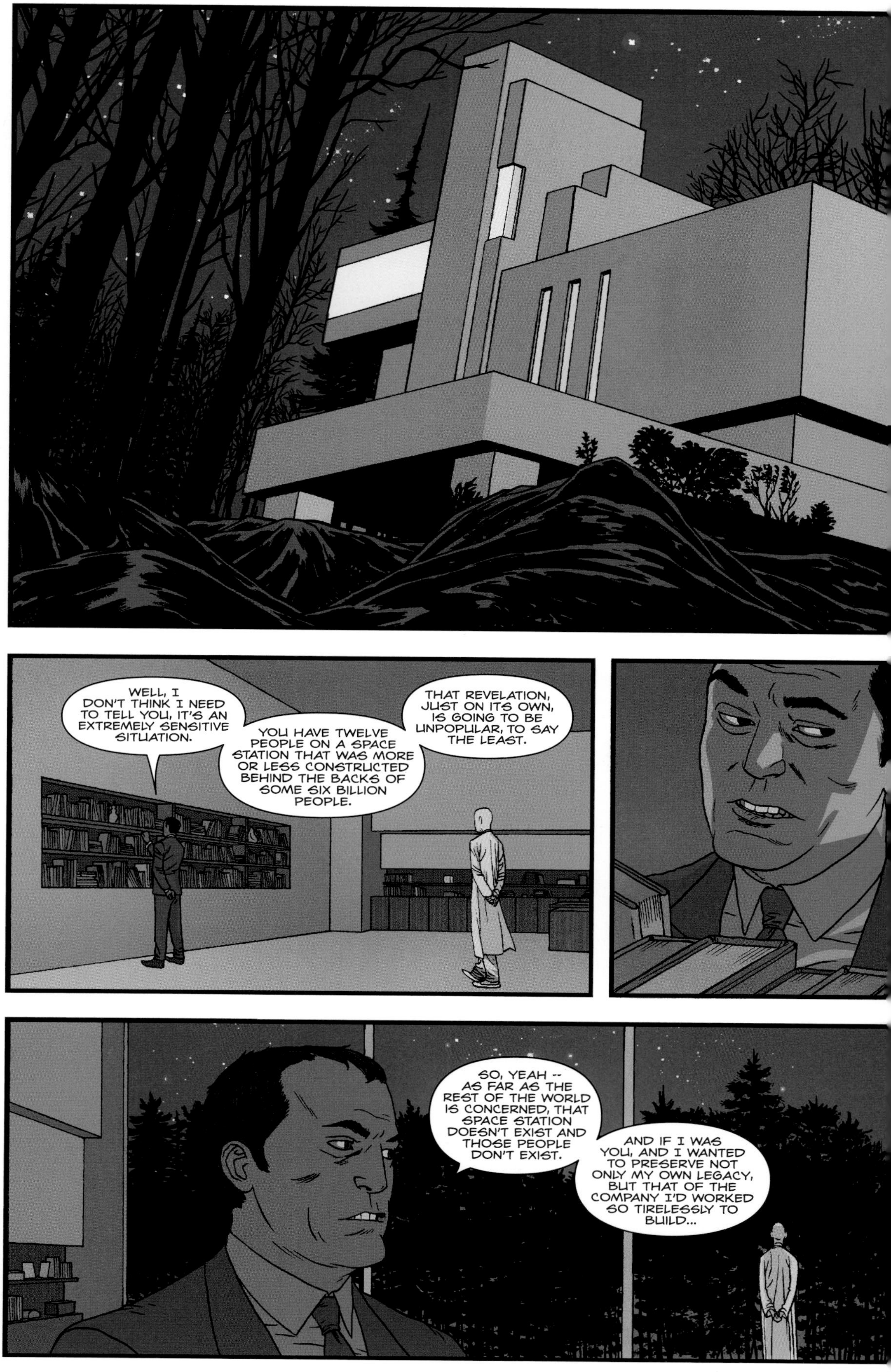
WELL, I DON'T THINK I NEED TO TELL YOU, IT'S AN EXTREMELY SENSITIVE SITUATION.
YOU HAVE TWELVE PEOPLE ON A SPACE STATION THAT WAS MORE OR LESS CONSTRUCTED BEHIND THE BACKS OF SOME SIX BILLION PEOPLE.
THAT REVELATION, JUST ON ITS OWN, IS GOING TO BE UNPOPULAR, TO SAY THE LEAST.
SO, YEAH -- AS FAR AS THE REST OF THE WORLD IS CONCERNED, THAT SPACE STATION DOESN'T EXIST AND THOSE PEOPLE DON'T EXIST.
AND IF I WAS YOU, AND I WANTED TO PRESERVE NOT ONLY MY OWN LEGACY, BUT THAT OF THE COMPANY I'D WORKED SO TIRELESSLY TO BUILD...

s other world. It was something I hadn't lored before. It's the longest I've ever com- tted myself to this kind of work.

:: *I want to talk a bit about the early ys of World Corp. Dade Ellis, one of your mer partners in the company, has said the past he wasn't sure the company uld survive more than a few years. Was at a feeling you shared?*

LKER: *My memory of that time shifts d changes depending on the moment. de is older than I am. He has a degree in chitecture. We met under challenging cir- mstances, but we shared common goals. u could say we were weaving similar webs. was maybe two or three years older and ready making an impact. It was an excit- g time, but he was the dowdy one. He gets t in his moods, one might say. I'm still uring that out.*

C: *Ellis has also said he finds you rather ange.*

LKER: *Strange is older still, but not in a d way. I have tremendous fun working th him. Smiling Simon has all the words d Dade can always find his way, but nerson Strange is the one I most admire.*

C: *Actually, what I meant is that Ellis gards you as something of an eccentric.*

LKER: *He just doesn't like my bicycle in e hallways.*

C: *You've said before that cycling is part your work.*

ALKER: *Yes, very much so.*

C: *Some of your colleagues have suggested 's more disruptive than productive.*

ALKER: *For them, perhaps. There's also a ying that goes "different spokes for differ- t folks." Some people need to be confron- tional. I'm not a troublemaker. I do my ork my own way. It's hard to tell why some ople react the way they do.*

C: *I think some might question how cling and astrophysics are related…*

WALKER: *Yeah, I suppose.*

TSC: *As a theoretical astrophysicist, your contributions to the study of everything from evolution to dark matter has provided some genuinely thrilling insight into the secrets of the universe. Can you understand how the notion of you riding your bike through the World Corp. offices might be confounding or off-putting to some?*

WALKER: *I can't explain away anyone's confusion. I can only tell you what works for me. I have my own process as far as my work goes. I find other methods rather unexciting. Uninteresting, at the very least. One thinks of the best way to approach a job and then does it as well as one can. I mount my bike and ask questions. When I finish riding, I have answers, and I find that rather wonderful. Juggling is an interesting technique, as well, and I can also get spectacular results for a good round of pinball.*

TSC: *Do you think your success went to your head?*

WALKER: *I think my success went to Simon's head. I don't view any of that as particularly necessary. Simon likes publicity, and once he got involved in my old group he used that to his advantage.*

TSC: *Wouldn't you say it was to everyone's advantage? World Corp. is one of the most successful companies of all time.*

WALKER: *I don't have a problem admitting that. I'm proud of the old group and what we have accomplished. We have done some very exciting things. We haven't been restricted by what others think. We did things our own way, we created our scene, and we have done very well as a result. You probably have some of our ideas in your home. Some people have our ideas in their bodies.*

TSC: *Do you like how ubiquitous World Corp. has become then? At one point, your critics regarded the company's popularity as a fad.*

WALKER: *Rock and roll had critics who said the same thing and what do they say now?*

TSC: *Well, you yourself have been quoted on a number of occasions as saying, "Science is the new rock and roll," so wouldn't that suggest the critics were right?*

WALKER: *I still like rock and roll music, though. I never said it would whither and die or that its influence would fade. I was making an observation about how exciting science can be. That's all, really.*

TSC: *A great many people took that observation to heart, though. You must be aware that it's become a slogan—a rallying cry, if you will, for a whole underground movement in science…*

WALKER: *That's very nice, but I don't have any control over slogans. One could just as easily say, "violence is the new black," and put that on a t-shirt, but it doesn't have much to do with anything. It might look terrific on a red shirt, but really, it says nothing about me or my work. I could see something like that coming to pass, but I wouldn't necessarily support that cause.*

TSC: *What about the people you've inspired through your work? Is that a cause you would support?*

WALKER: *I suppose so, yeah.*

TSC: *Have you thought of meeting with any of them, now that you're no longer associated with World Corp.?*

WALKER: *Well, I haven't given it any thought. You see, I'm very focused on my own work, and none of my visions have indicated that's a strand I should follow. I think they're still building that particular web, and I'm into different things right now, you know?*

TSC: *I have one last question for you: If science is the new rock and roll, then what's the new science?*

WALKER: *Oh, that's simple. Understanding.*

Dennis Blandon

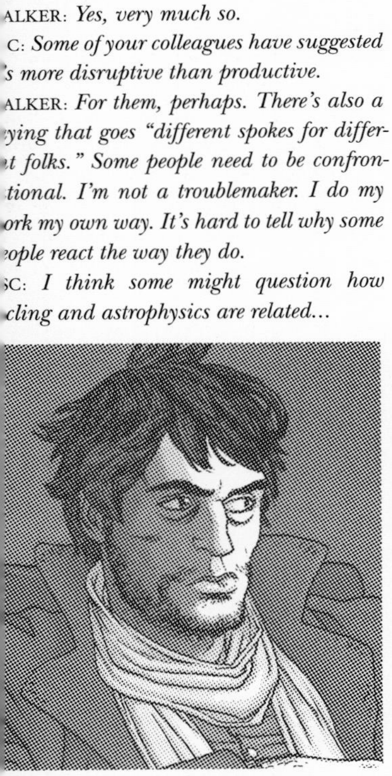

umors are simple to weave. There wasn't ally a battle of any kind. Just a matter of ebs getting all tangled."

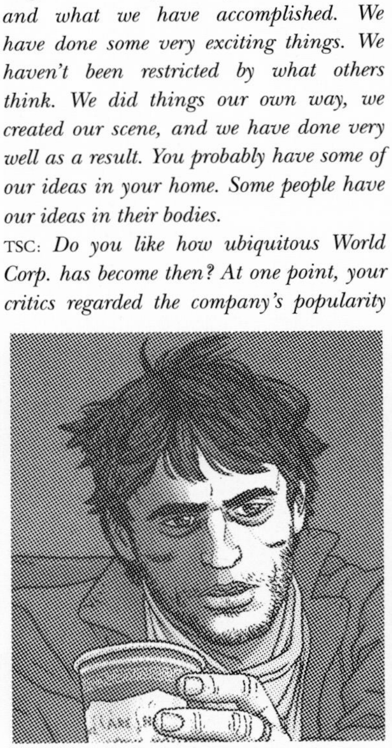

"My entire life is a web. All ours lives are a living tapestry of webworks that we weave, one delicate strand at a time."

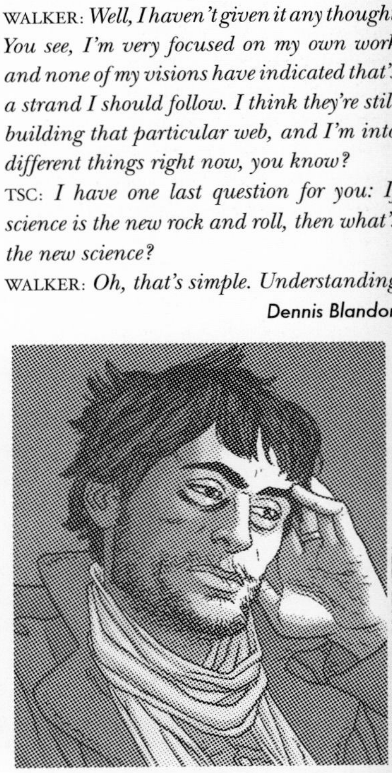

PHOTOGRAPHY BY ROGER KEITH

"There's a saying that goes 'different spokes for different folks.' Some people need to be confrontational. I'm not a troublemaker."

WALKING IN THE SPIDERWEBS

the science chronicle intervie
THOMAS WALKE

It has long been suggested that Thomas Walker has always been something of an enigma, even to those who know him best, and that the qualities that so befuddle those around him are in fact the very same qualities that have made him one of the leading lights in theoretical astrophysics. It's certainly an interesting—not to mention entertaining—notion, but on the basis of current evidence, it's difficult to fathom how that might work in practice.

Walker was in town last week and though notoriously press-shy, he agreed to his first interview since leaving World Corp. amid a flurry of speculation. There has been talk of a falling out with his famous partners, specifically of a rift between himself and Dade Ellis, the man many view as the company's heart and soul. It has been said he has suffered severe psychological damage as the result of his long-rumored drug use. There are stories, too, that his focus on theory and research put him distinctly at odds with World Corp.'s increasing cachet as a producer of life-changing consumer products.

His appearance is quite different at this point, his hair shorn closer to the head than in years past, perhaps symbolic of his break with the company he refers to time and again as his "old group." He is also somewhat haggard, the apparent result of lack of sleep in the service of an unwavering commitment to meditation, and his frequently non-linear conversation is at times difficult to follow. One moment he seems thoughtful and alert, the next it's hard to tell if he's there at all…

TSC: *Of all the World Corp. founders, you are notoriously difficult to pin down for interviews. Do you have a particular aversion to the press?*

WALKER: *Interviews are more Simon's thing. Simon diamond. Diamond geezer. Simon says. It's helpful to have that kind of outlook for that kind of work. I have… other work.*

TSC: *Of course. I imagine you're quite busy.*

WALKER: *My own work is quite involved. There are many wheels to turn, and I've got a gaping hole in my head that needs to be filled… You know, with knowledge, and there's only so much time in each waking day. It's a lot of pressure. This interview is a lot of pressure.*

TSC: *Then why did you agree to it?*

WALKER: *That's the question, isn't it?*

TSC: *At the moment, yes. Do you have an answer?*

WALKER: *I think answers become apparent when you open your mind and listen. Different moments tell you different things. You have to be ready for it.*

TSC: *Does it perhaps have anything to do with your recent decision to step down from the board of directors at World Corp.? You're obviously at somewhat of a crossroads in your career at this point.*

WALKER: *My entire life is a crossroads. I mean, really… my entire life is a web. All ours lives are a living tapestry of webworks that we weave, one delicate strand at a time. One day, we climb this strand. Tomorrow we shimmy down another. Sometimes the strands intersect. We're all working away on our different webs, but often when they overlap, magical things happen. That's how my old group got started, but then they decided the cut some of the strands and here we are.*

TSC: *Are you saying it wasn't your decision to resign from the board?*

WALKER: *Decisions are made at a much higher level. You would have to climb up through a lot of webs to get to the heart of it, I think.*

TSC: *World Corp. issued a statement that you'd resigned from the board and would no longer be a part of the company's day-to-day business, though.*

WALKER: *I am resigned, very much so.*

TSC: *There are rumors there was tension between you and the other founders…*

WALKER: *Rumors are simple to weave. There wasn't really a battle of any kind. Just a matter of webs getting all tangled. I don't think World Corp. had any real trouble, but I had a difficult time adjusting as the others spun their webs. Perhaps you could say I created some of that difficulty myself, having visions and doing my own work. I don't know.*

TSC: *Can you tell me about these visions?*

WALKER: *I've been expanding my experience through meditation. I have learned to open my third eye and I can see and feel things on a different level. There are things we can't see with our physical eyes.*

TSC: *Can you give me an example?*

WALKER: *Well, after meditating a bit, I found I would awake in the middle of the night and see things I wasn't aware of before. The most startling discovery was all the webs. There were webs everywhere, all above my bed, and the first time I saw them,*

it was an awful scene. There were spid everywhere, skittering back and forth, sp ning their webs, climbing their strand was so startled, I rolled out of bed and o the floor, desperate for the light switch was so shaken by the experience I had to out of my room and into the streets, beca I didn't realize the true nature of the w yet.

TSC: *Did you tell the others?*

WALKER: *I just dry-heaved in front o remarkably beautiful woman. We share moment. One hopes she understood.*

TSC: *I'm not entirely sure I understand…*

WALKER: *I can't explain then. This m tation thing is making me a genius a a little bit insane. I close my eyes to try sleep, but over time, I have developed ability to see like a bat! Every sound bou es off nearby objects and creates a vis impression in the shape of what it is! I c close my eyes and be very aware of wha around me. I know this sounds crazy, it makes it impossible to sleep since I c turn it off. There are times I think perh I should quit meditating for a bit, but changed everything for me.*

TSC: *Did that change make your partn feel trepidation around you?*

WALKER: *Not everybody is ready for t level of enlightenment.*

TSC: *Did it affect your role within the o all structure of the company?*

WALKER: *Some might say. I don't knou only know that from my point of view have always been the psychic equalizer.*

TSC: *There have been stories in the pr that some of your recent behavior is result of excessive drug use, that you ha been taking acid trips in the name experimentation.*

WALKER: *I'm sure some people are chat ing just to make themselves feel importan*

TSC: *Are you saying you haven't taken a then?*

WALKER: *Obviously, one does things th pertain to one's work. I won't deny I wa young person and as a member of a gene tion of switched-on young people, I thi I adopted a philosophy that allowed me expand my boundaries. Not everyone u so lucky, but I put my experiences to wor*

TSC: *You're a scientist. Your mind is yo greatest tool. Don't you think drug use any kind is risky?*

WALKER: *You see risk. I see opportunity. A I had to do was open my mind to the p sibilities. It seemed like great fun to en*

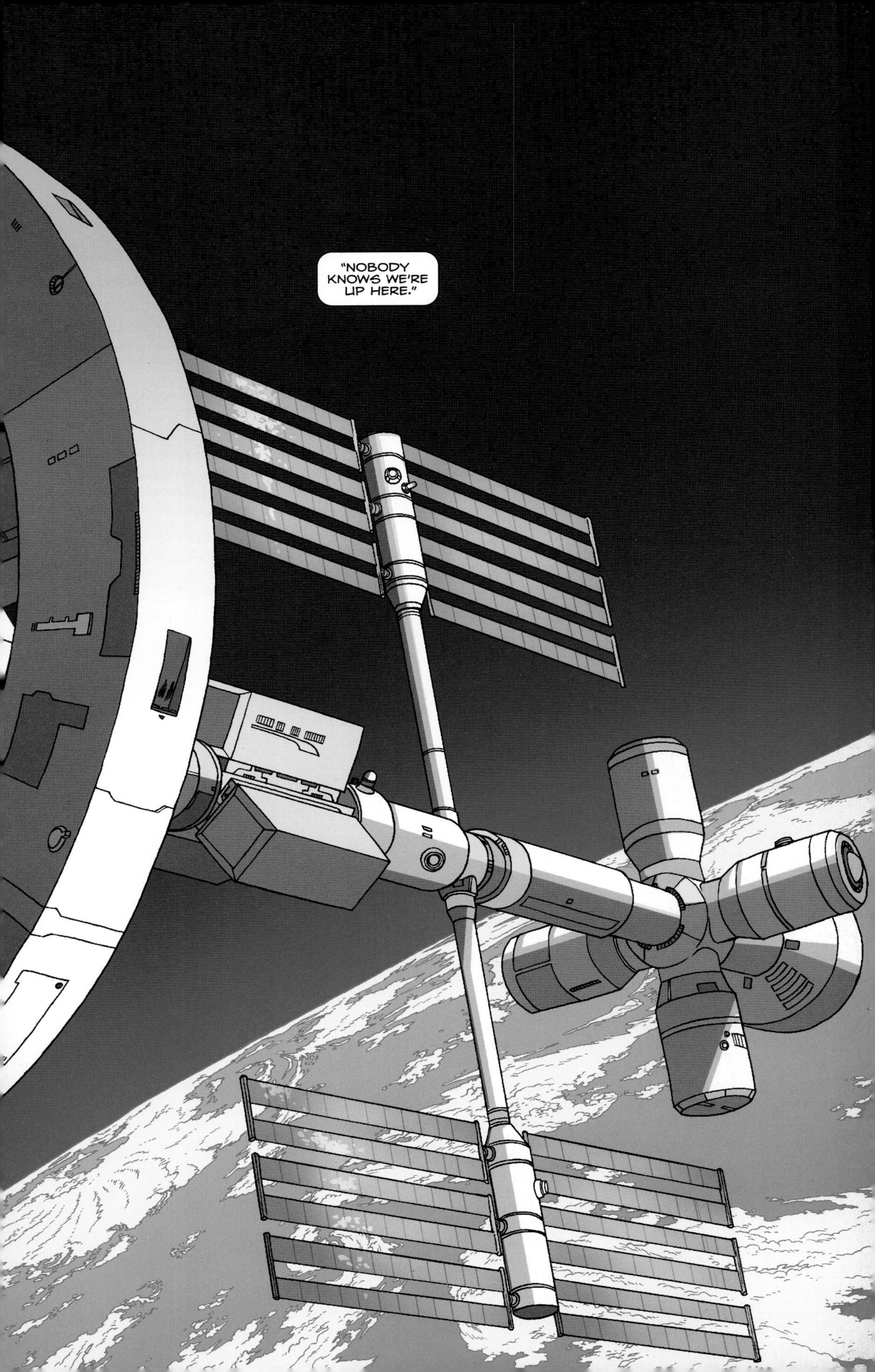
"NOBODY KNOWS WE'RE UP HERE."

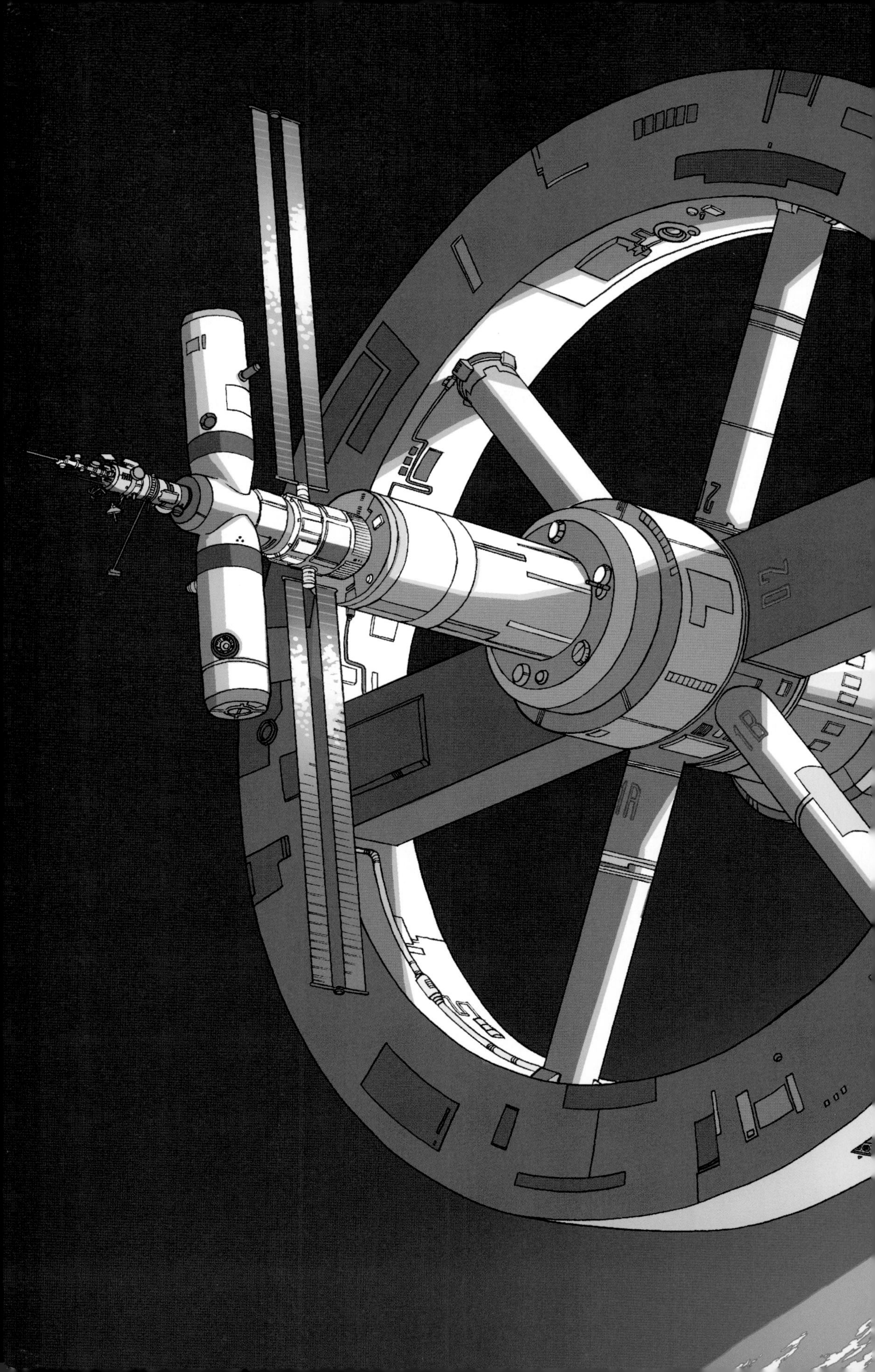

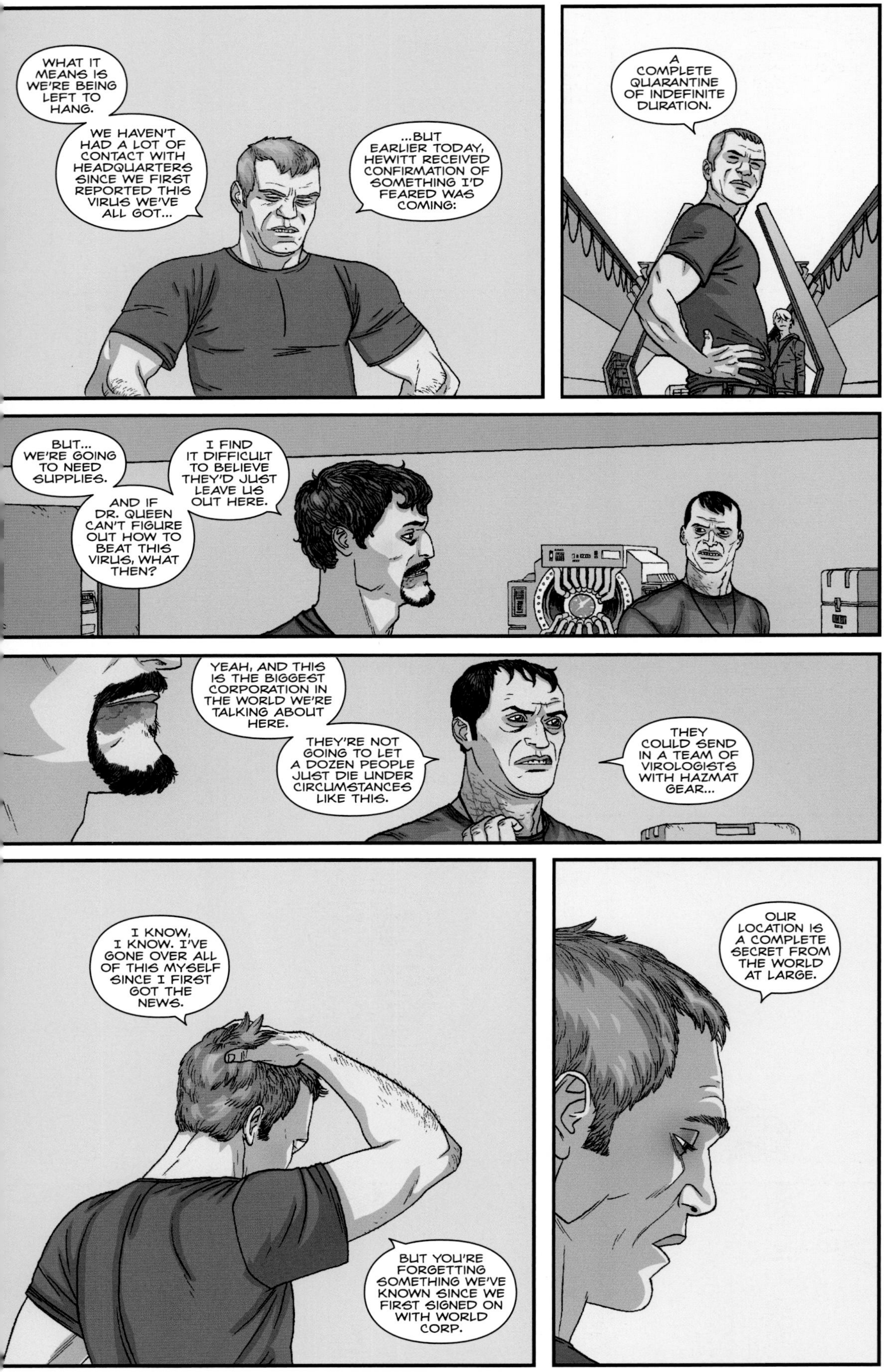
WHAT IT MEANS IS WE'RE BEING LEFT TO HANG.
WE HAVEN'T HAD A LOT OF CONTACT WITH HEADQUARTERS SINCE WE FIRST REPORTED THIS VIRUS WE'VE ALL GOT...
...BUT EARLIER TODAY, HEWITT RECEIVED CONFIRMATION OF SOMETHING I'D FEARED WAS COMING:
A COMPLETE QUARANTINE OF INDEFINITE DURATION.
BUT... WE'RE GOING TO NEED SUPPLIES.
AND IF DR. QUEEN CAN'T FIGURE OUT HOW TO BEAT THIS VIRUS, WHAT THEN?
I FIND IT DIFFICULT TO BELIEVE THEY'D JUST LEAVE US OUT HERE.
YEAH, AND THIS IS THE BIGGEST CORPORATION IN THE WORLD WE'RE TALKING ABOUT HERE.
THEY'RE NOT GOING TO LET A DOZEN PEOPLE JUST DIE UNDER CIRCUMSTANCES LIKE THIS.
THEY COULD SEND IN A TEAM OF VIROLOGISTS WITH HAZMAT GEAR...
I KNOW, I KNOW. I'VE GONE OVER ALL OF THIS MYSELF SINCE I FIRST GOT THE NEWS.
BUT YOU'RE FORGETTING SOMETHING WE'VE KNOWN SINCE WE FIRST SIGNED ON WITH WORLD CORP.
OUR LOCATION IS A COMPLETE SECRET FROM THE WORLD AT LARGE.

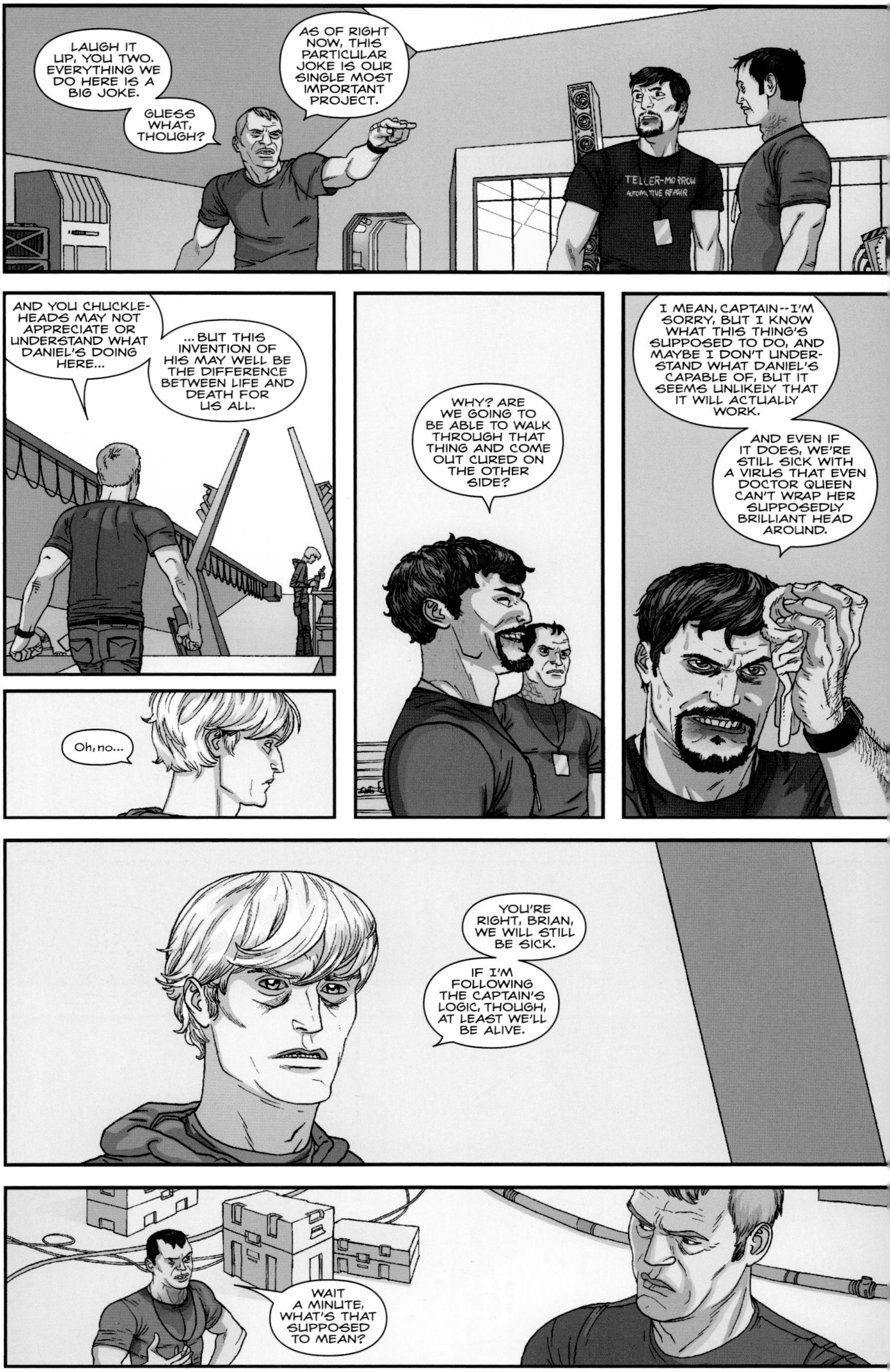
LAUGH IT UP, YOU TWO. EVERYTHING WE DO HERE IS A BIG JOKE.
GUESS WHAT, THOUGH?
AS OF RIGHT NOW, THIS PARTICULAR JOKE IS OUR SINGLE MOST IMPORTANT PROJECT.
TELLER-MORROW AUTOMOTIVE REPAIR
AND YOU CHUCKLE-HEADS MAY NOT APPRECIATE OR UNDERSTAND WHAT DANIEL'S DOING HERE...
...BUT THIS INVENTION OF HIS MAY WELL BE THE DIFFERENCE BETWEEN LIFE AND DEATH FOR US ALL.
Oh, no...
WHY? ARE WE GOING TO BE ABLE TO WALK THROUGH THAT THING AND COME OUT CURED ON THE OTHER SIDE?
I MEAN, CAPTAIN--I'M SORRY, BUT I KNOW WHAT THIS THING'S SUPPOSED TO DO, AND MAYBE I DON'T UNDER-STAND WHAT DANIEL'S CAPABLE OF, BUT IT SEEMS UNLIKELY THAT IT WILL ACTUALLY WORK.
AND EVEN IF IT DOES, WE'RE STILL SICK WITH A VIRUS THAT EVEN DOCTOR QUEEN CAN'T WRAP HER SUPPOSEDLY BRILLIANT HEAD AROUND.
YOU'RE RIGHT, BRIAN, WE WILL STILL BE SICK.
IF I'M FOLLOWING THE CAPTAIN'S LOGIC, THOUGH, AT LEAST WE'LL BE ALIVE.
WAIT A MINUTE, WHAT'S THAT SUPPOSED TO MEAN?

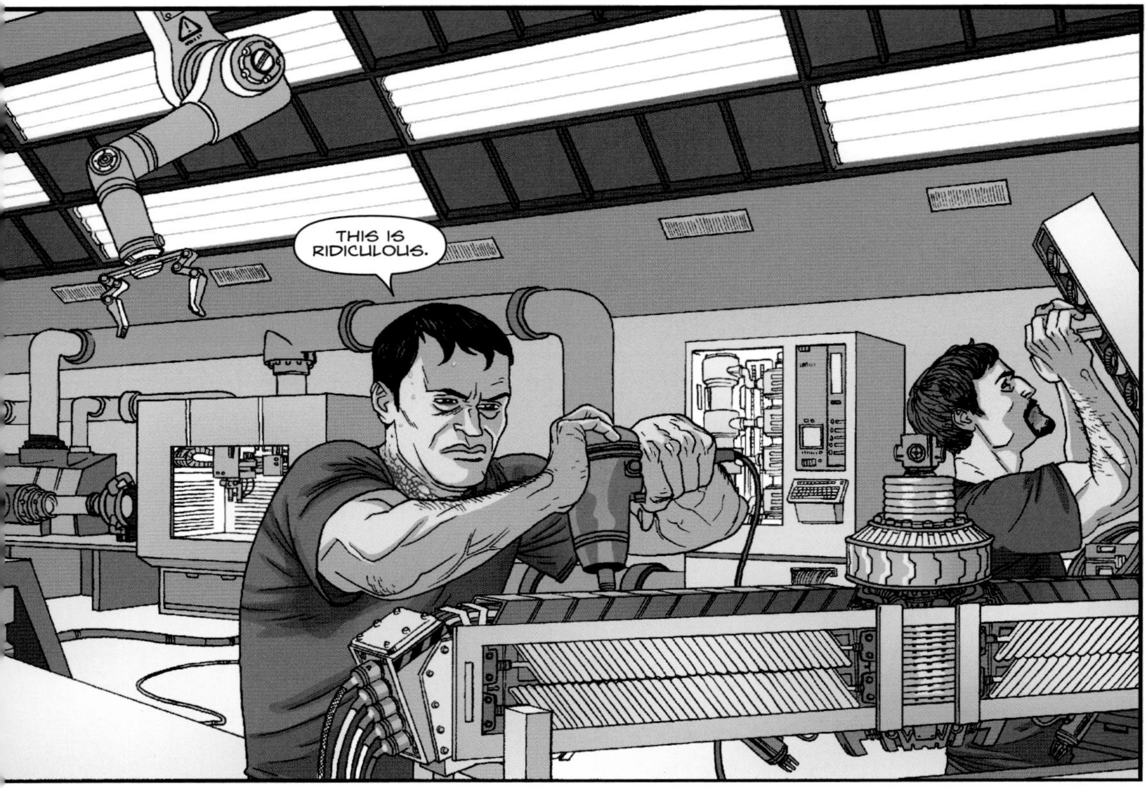
THIS IS RIDICULOUS.

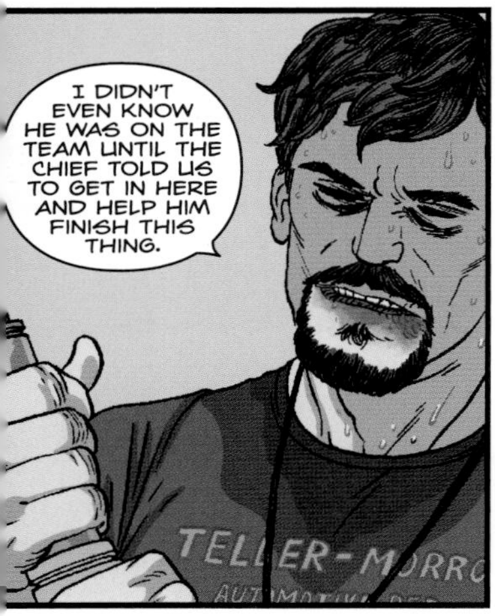
I DIDN'T EVEN KNOW HE WAS ON THE TEAM UNTIL THE CHIEF TOLD US TO GET IN HERE AND HELP HIM FINISH THIS THING.
TELLER-MORRO

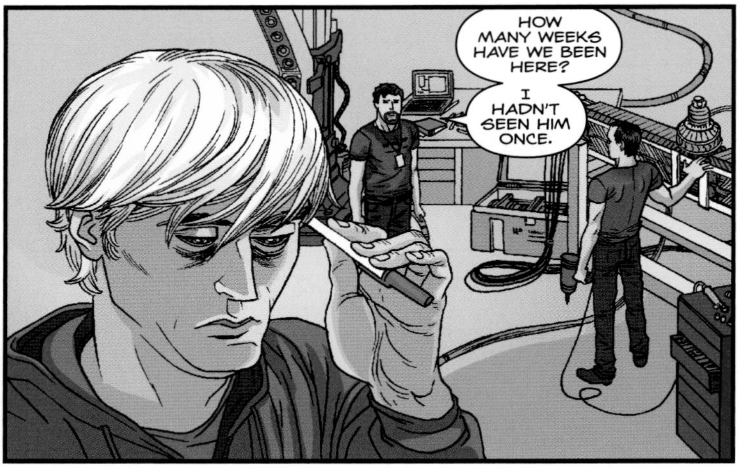
HOW MANY WEEKS HAVE WE BEEN HERE?
I HADN'T SEEN HIM ONCE.

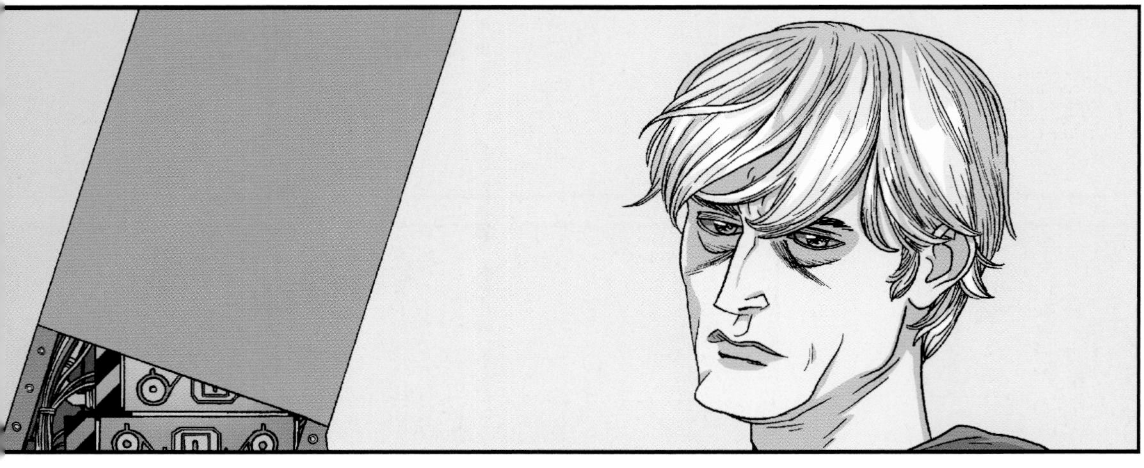

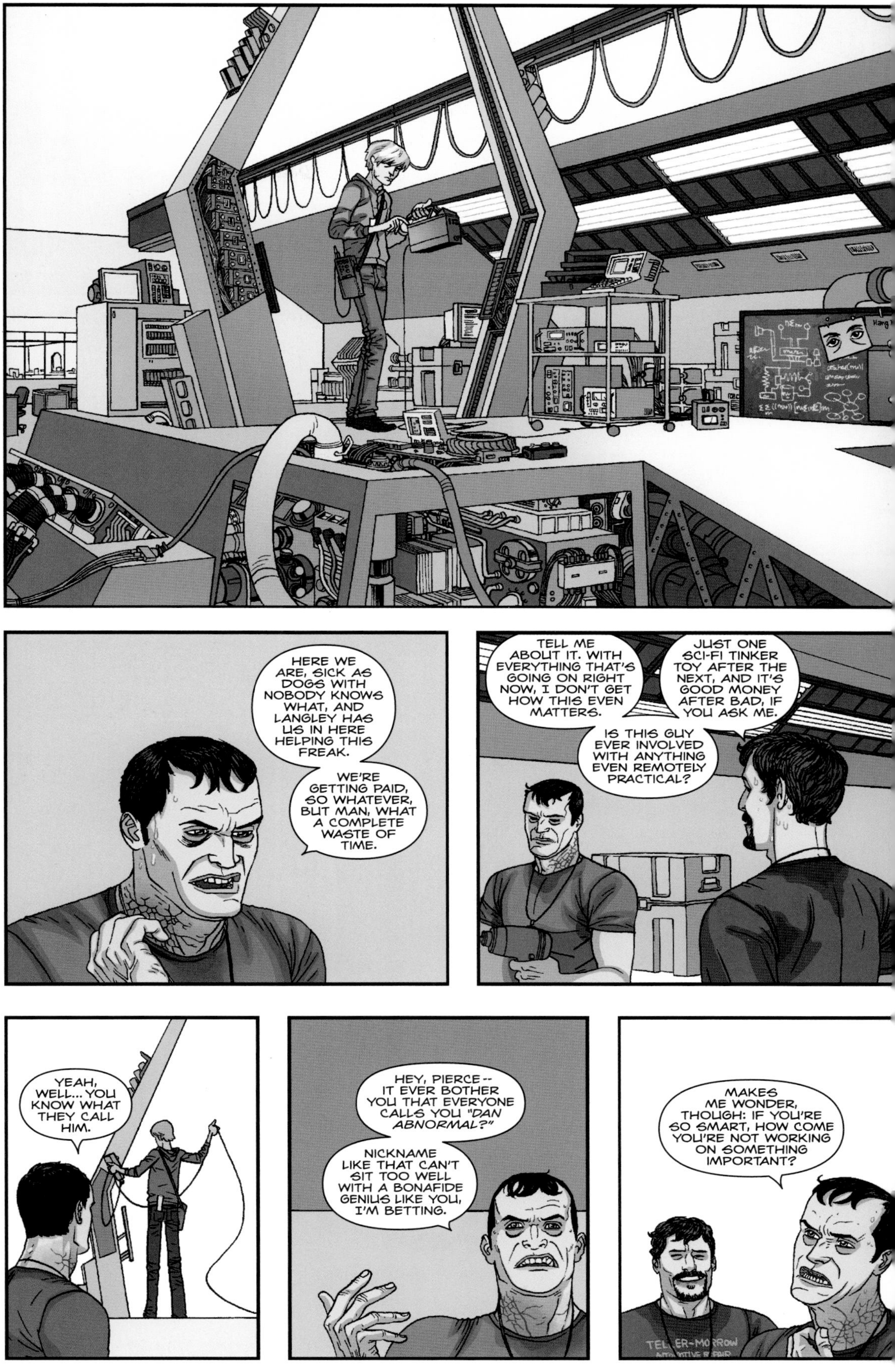

HERE WE ARE, SICK AS DOGS WITH NOBODY KNOWS WHAT, AND LANGLEY HAS US IN HERE HELPING THIS FREAK.
WE'RE GETTING PAID, SO WHATEVER, BUT MAN, WHAT A COMPLETE WASTE OF TIME.
TELL ME ABOUT IT. WITH EVERYTHING THAT'S GOING ON RIGHT NOW, I DON'T GET HOW THIS EVEN MATTERS.
JUST ONE SCI-FI TINKER TOY AFTER THE NEXT, AND IT'S GOOD MONEY AFTER BAD, IF YOU ASK ME.
IS THIS GUY EVER INVOLVED WITH ANYTHING EVEN REMOTELY PRACTICAL?
YEAH, WELL... YOU KNOW WHAT THEY CALL HIM.
HEY, PIERCE -- IT EVER BOTHER YOU THAT EVERYONE CALLS YOU *"DAN ABNORMAL?"*
NICKNAME LIKE THAT CAN'T SIT TOO WELL WITH A BONAFIDE GENIUS LIKE YOU, I'M BETTING.
MAKES ME WONDER, THOUGH: IF YOU'RE SO SMART, HOW COME YOU'RE NOT WORKING ON SOMETHING IMPORTANT?

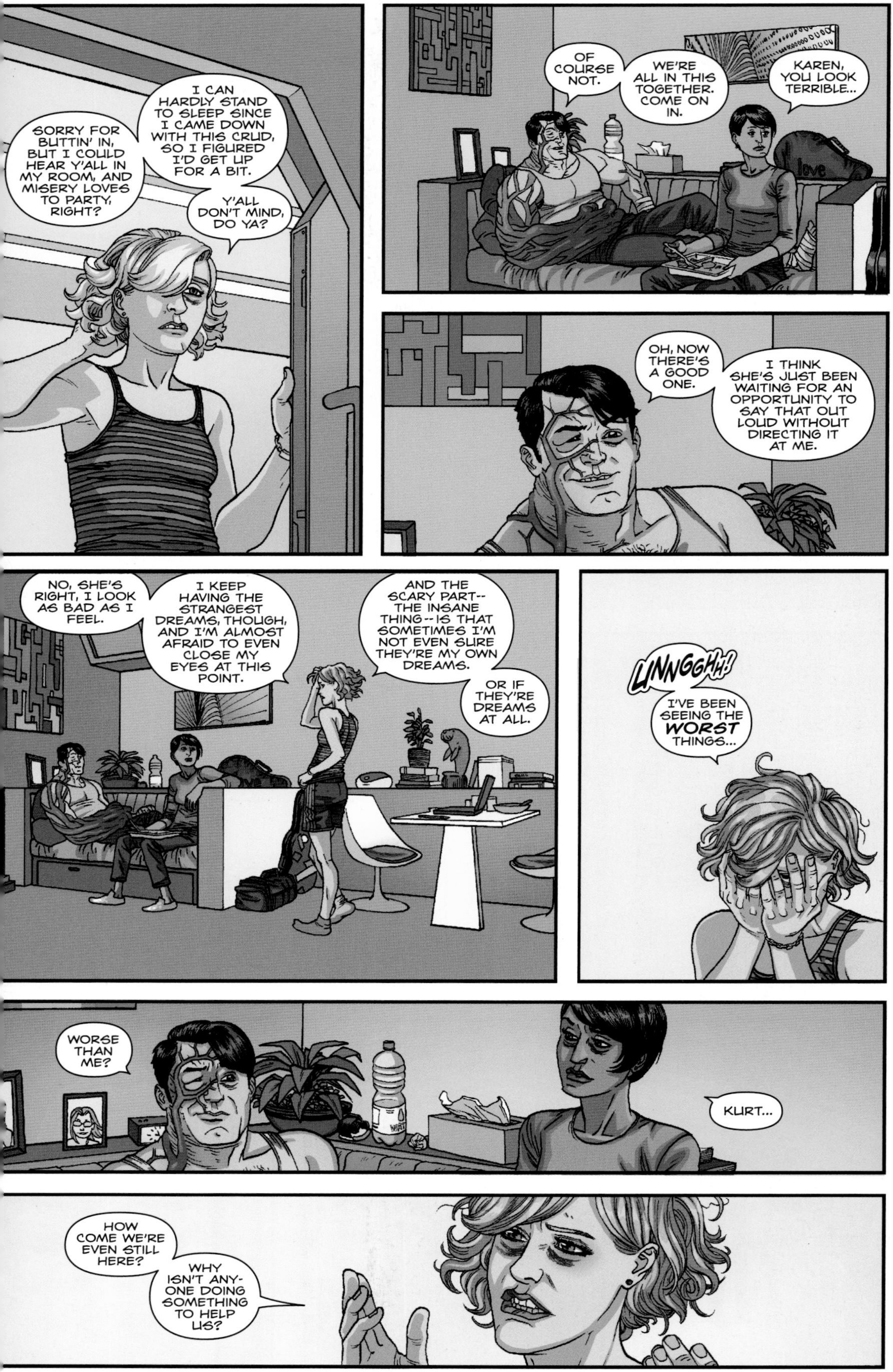
SORRY FOR BUTTIN' IN, BUT I COULD HEAR Y'ALL IN MY ROOM, AND MISERY LOVES TO PARTY, RIGHT?
I CAN HARDLY STAND TO SLEEP SINCE I CAME DOWN WITH THIS CRUD, SO I FIGURED I'D GET UP FOR A BIT.
Y'ALL DON'T MIND, DO YA?
OF COURSE NOT.
WE'RE ALL IN THIS TOGETHER. COME ON IN.
KAREN, YOU LOOK TERRIBLE...
love
OH, NOW THERE'S A GOOD ONE.
I THINK SHE'S JUST BEEN WAITING FOR AN OPPORTUNITY TO SAY THAT OUT LOUD WITHOUT DIRECTING IT AT ME.
NO, SHE'S RIGHT, I LOOK AS BAD AS I FEEL.
I KEEP HAVING THE STRANGEST DREAMS, THOUGH, AND I'M ALMOST AFRAID TO EVEN CLOSE MY EYES AT THIS POINT.
AND THE SCARY PART-- THE INSANE THING-- IS THAT SOMETIMES I'M NOT EVEN SURE THEY'RE MY OWN DREAMS.
OR IF THEY'RE DREAMS AT ALL.
UNNGGHH!
I'VE BEEN SEEING THE **WORST** THINGS...
WORSE THAN ME?
KURT...
HOW COME WE'RE EVEN STILL HERE?
WHY ISN'T ANYONE DOING SOMETHING TO HELP US?

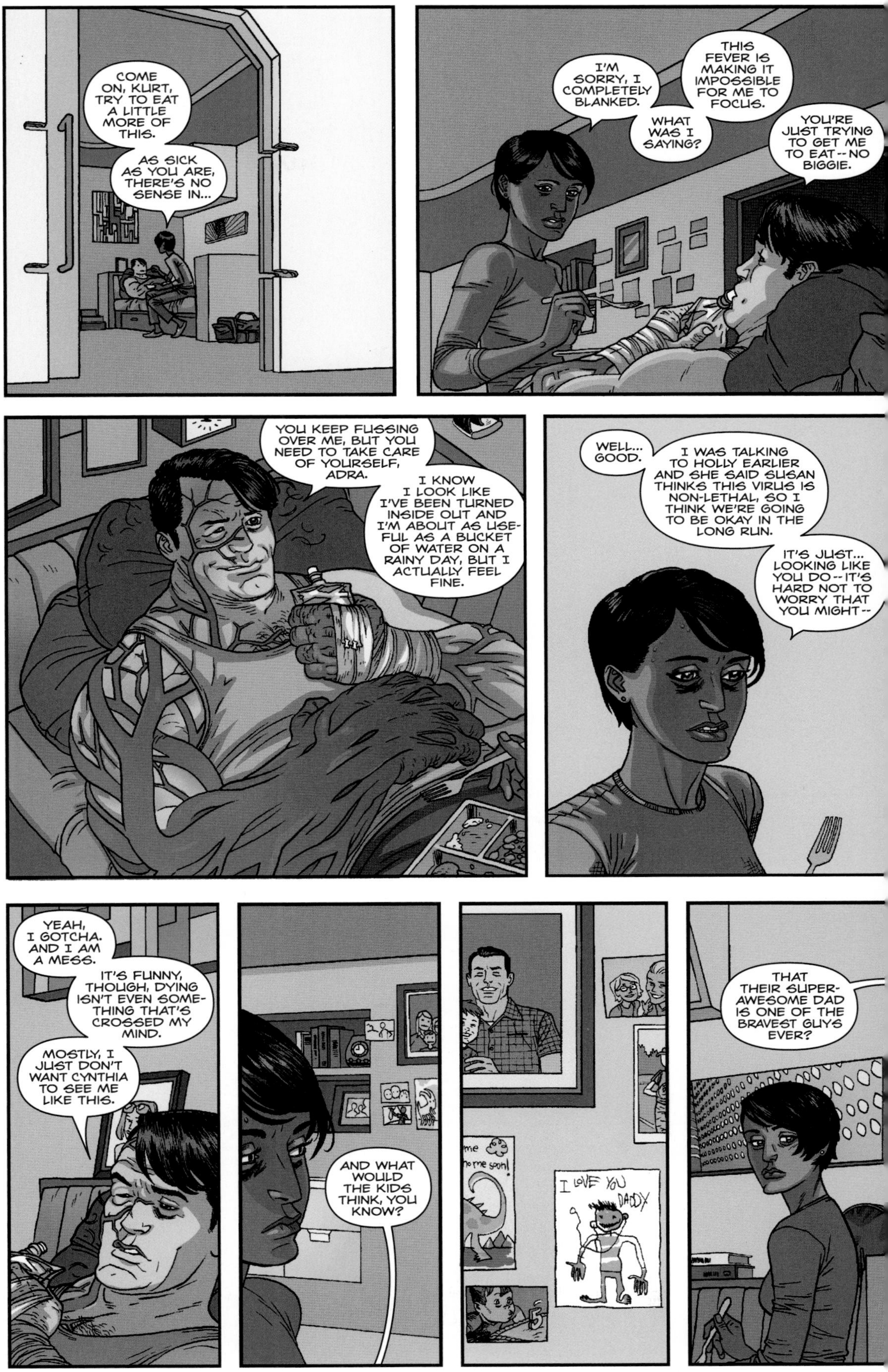
COME ON, KURT, TRY TO EAT A LITTLE MORE OF THIS.
AS SICK AS YOU ARE, THERE'S NO SENSE IN...
I'M SORRY, I COMPLETELY BLANKED.
THIS FEVER IS MAKING IT IMPOSSIBLE FOR ME TO FOCUS.
WHAT WAS I SAYING?
YOU'RE JUST TRYING TO GET ME TO EAT--NO BIGGIE.
YOU KEEP FUSSING OVER ME, BUT YOU NEED TO TAKE CARE OF YOURSELF, ADRA.
I KNOW I LOOK LIKE I'VE BEEN TURNED INSIDE OUT AND I'M ABOUT AS USE-FUL AS A BUCKET OF WATER ON A RAINY DAY, BUT I ACTUALLY FEEL FINE.
WELL... GOOD.
I WAS TALKING TO HOLLY EARLIER AND SHE SAID SUSAN THINKS THIS VIRUS IS NON-LETHAL, SO I THINK WE'RE GOING TO BE OKAY IN THE LONG RUN.
IT'S JUST... LOOKING LIKE YOU DO--IT'S HARD NOT TO WORRY THAT YOU MIGHT--
YEAH, I GOTCHA. AND I AM A MESS.
IT'S FUNNY, THOUGH, DYING ISN'T EVEN SOME-THING THAT'S CROSSED MY MIND.
MOSTLY, I JUST DON'T WANT CYNTHIA TO SEE ME LIKE THIS.
AND WHAT WOULD THE KIDS THINK, YOU KNOW?
I LOVE YOU DADDY
THAT THEIR SUPER-AWESOME DAD IS ONE OF THE BRAVEST GUYS EVER?

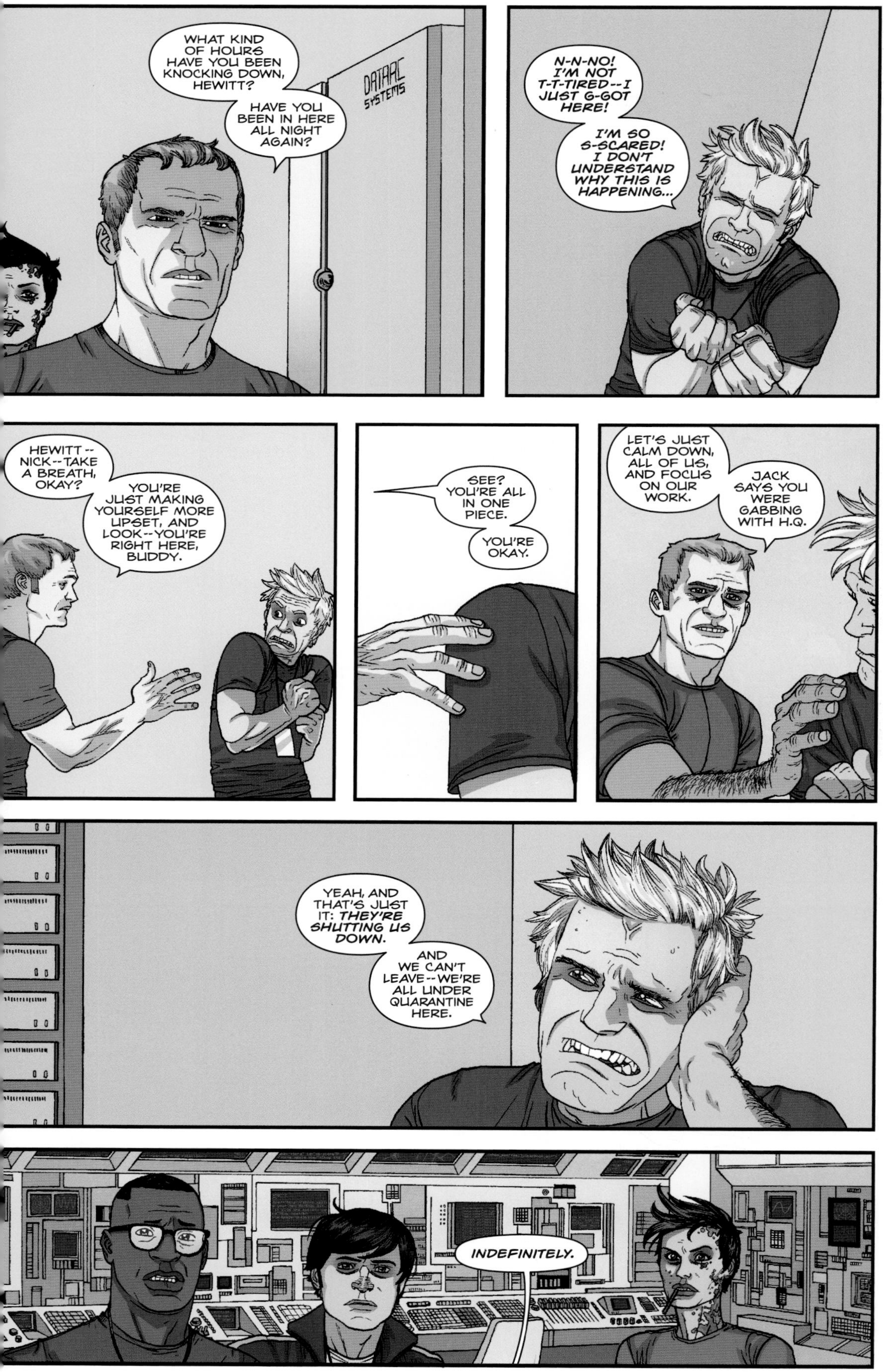

WHAT KIND OF HOURS HAVE YOU BEEN KNOCKING DOWN, HEWITT?
HAVE YOU BEEN IN HERE ALL NIGHT AGAIN?
DATARC SYSTEMS
N-N-NO! I'M NOT T-T-TIRED--I JUST G-GOT HERE!
I'M SO S-SCARED! I DON'T UNDERSTAND WHY THIS IS HAPPENING...
HEWITT--NICK--TAKE A BREATH, OKAY?
YOU'RE JUST MAKING YOURSELF MORE UPSET, AND LOOK--YOU'RE RIGHT HERE, BUDDY.
SEE? YOU'RE ALL IN ONE PIECE.
YOU'RE OKAY.
LET'S JUST CALM DOWN, ALL OF US, AND FOCUS ON OUR WORK.
JACK SAYS YOU WERE GABBING WITH H.Q.
YEAH, AND THAT'S JUST IT: THEY'RE SHUTTING US DOWN.
AND WE CAN'T LEAVE--WE'RE ALL UNDER QUARANTINE HERE.
INDEFINITELY.

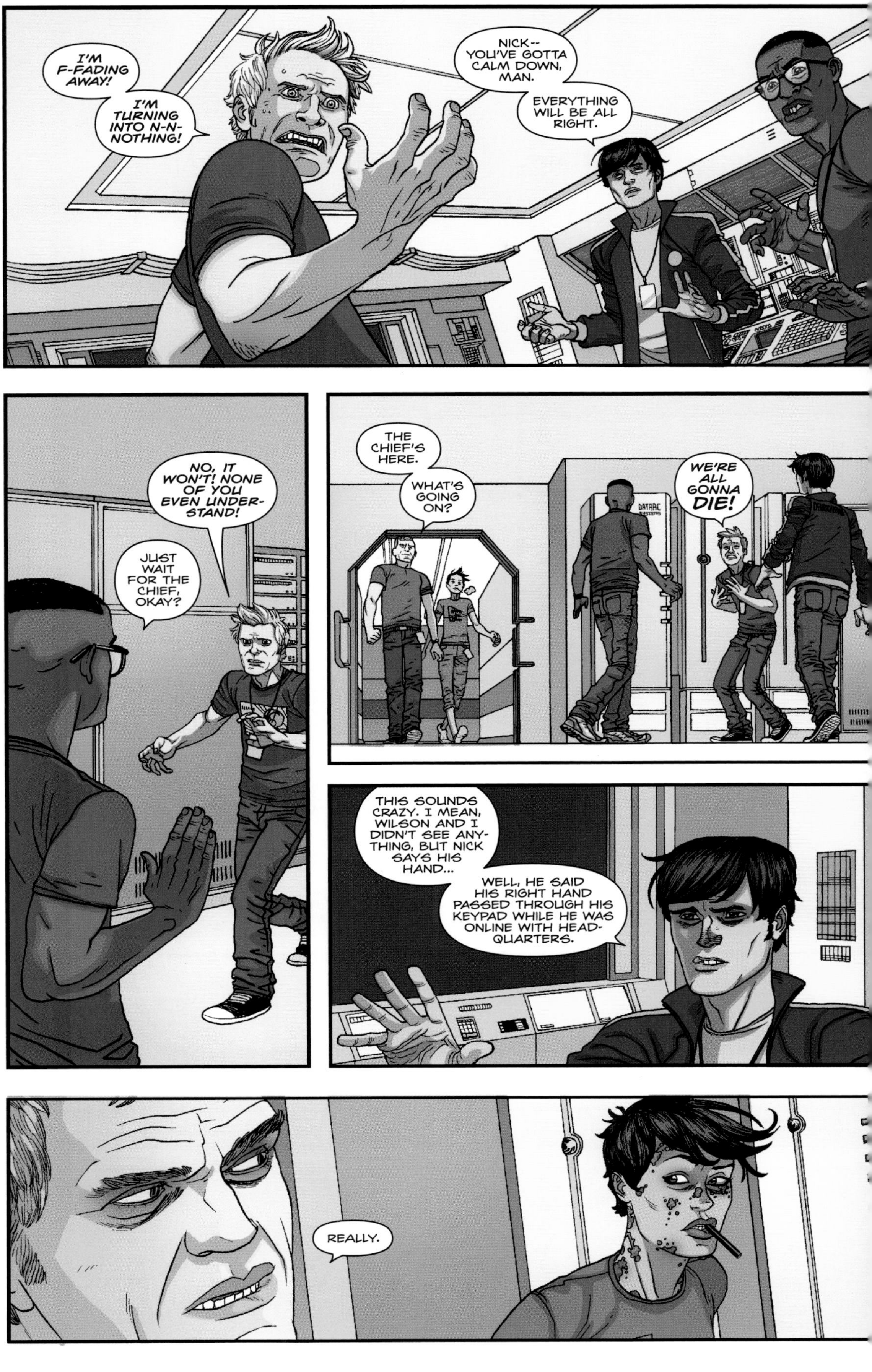
I'M F-FADING AWAY!
I'M TURNING INTO N-N-NOTHING!
NICK-- YOU'VE GOTTA CALM DOWN, MAN.
EVERYTHING WILL BE ALL RIGHT.
NO, IT WON'T! NONE OF YOU EVEN UNDER-STAND!
JUST WAIT FOR THE CHIEF, OKAY?
THE CHIEF'S HERE.
WHAT'S GOING ON?
WE'RE ALL GONNA DIE!
THIS SOUNDS CRAZY. I MEAN, WILSON AND I DIDN'T SEE ANY-THING, BUT NICK SAYS HIS HAND...
WELL, HE SAID HIS RIGHT HAND PASSED THROUGH HIS KEYPAD WHILE HE WAS ONLINE WITH HEAD-QUARTERS.
REALLY.

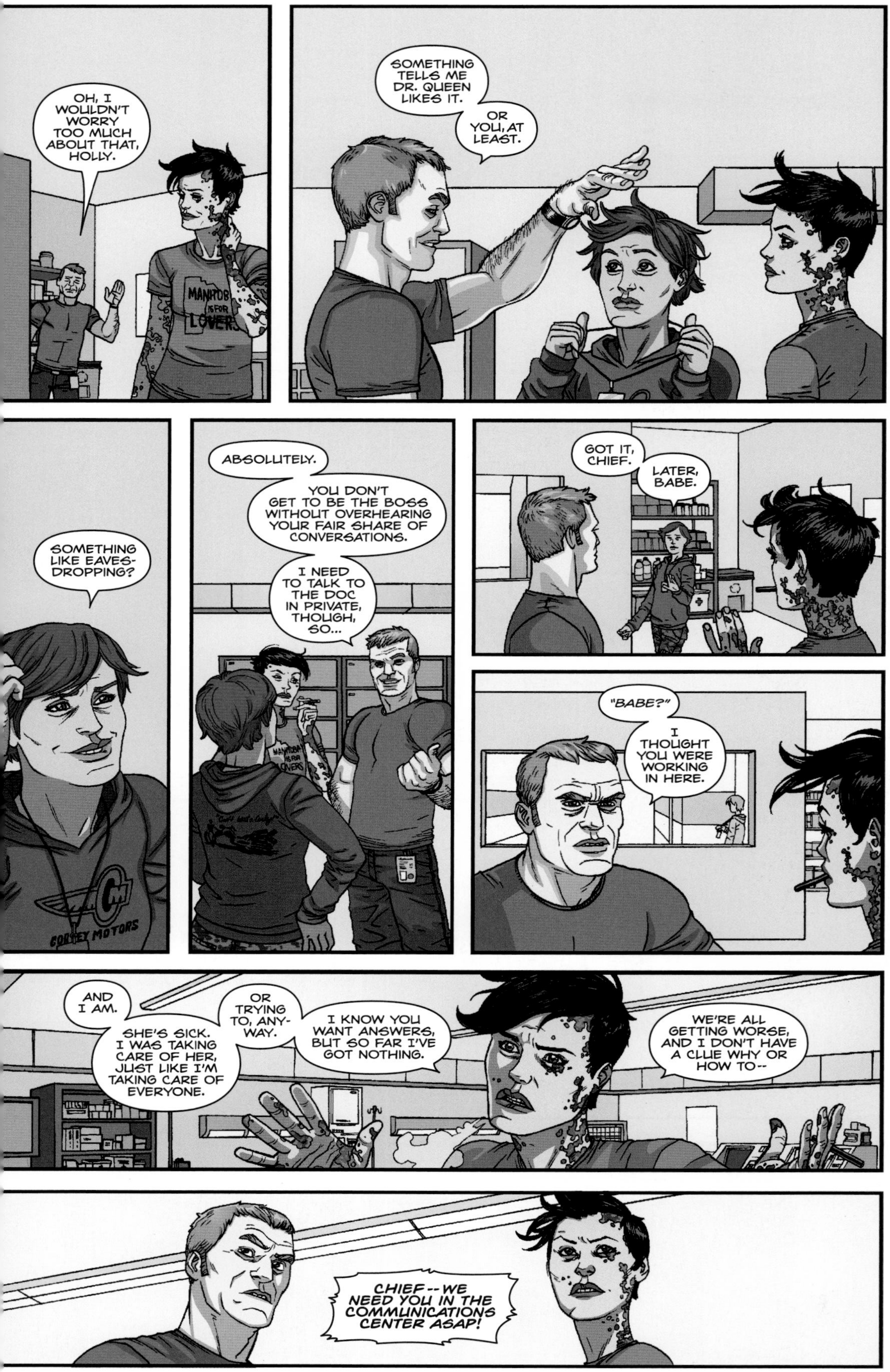

OH, I WOULDN'T WORRY TOO MUCH ABOUT THAT, HOLLY.
SOMETHING TELLS ME DR. QUEEN LIKES IT.
OR YOU, AT LEAST.
SOMETHING LIKE EAVES-DROPPING?
ABSOLUTELY.
YOU DON'T GET TO BE THE BOSS WITHOUT OVERHEARING YOUR FAIR SHARE OF CONVERSATIONS.
I NEED TO TALK TO THE DOC IN PRIVATE, THOUGH, SO...
GOT IT, CHIEF.
LATER, BABE.
"BABE?"
I THOUGHT YOU WERE WORKING IN HERE.
AND I AM.
SHE'S SICK. I WAS TAKING CARE OF HER, JUST LIKE I'M TAKING CARE OF EVERYONE.
OR TRYING TO, ANYWAY.
I KNOW YOU WANT ANSWERS, BUT SO FAR I'VE GOT NOTHING.
WE'RE ALL GETTING WORSE, AND I DON'T HAVE A CLUE WHY OR HOW TO--
CHIEF--WE NEED YOU IN THE COMMUNICATIONS CENTER ASAP!

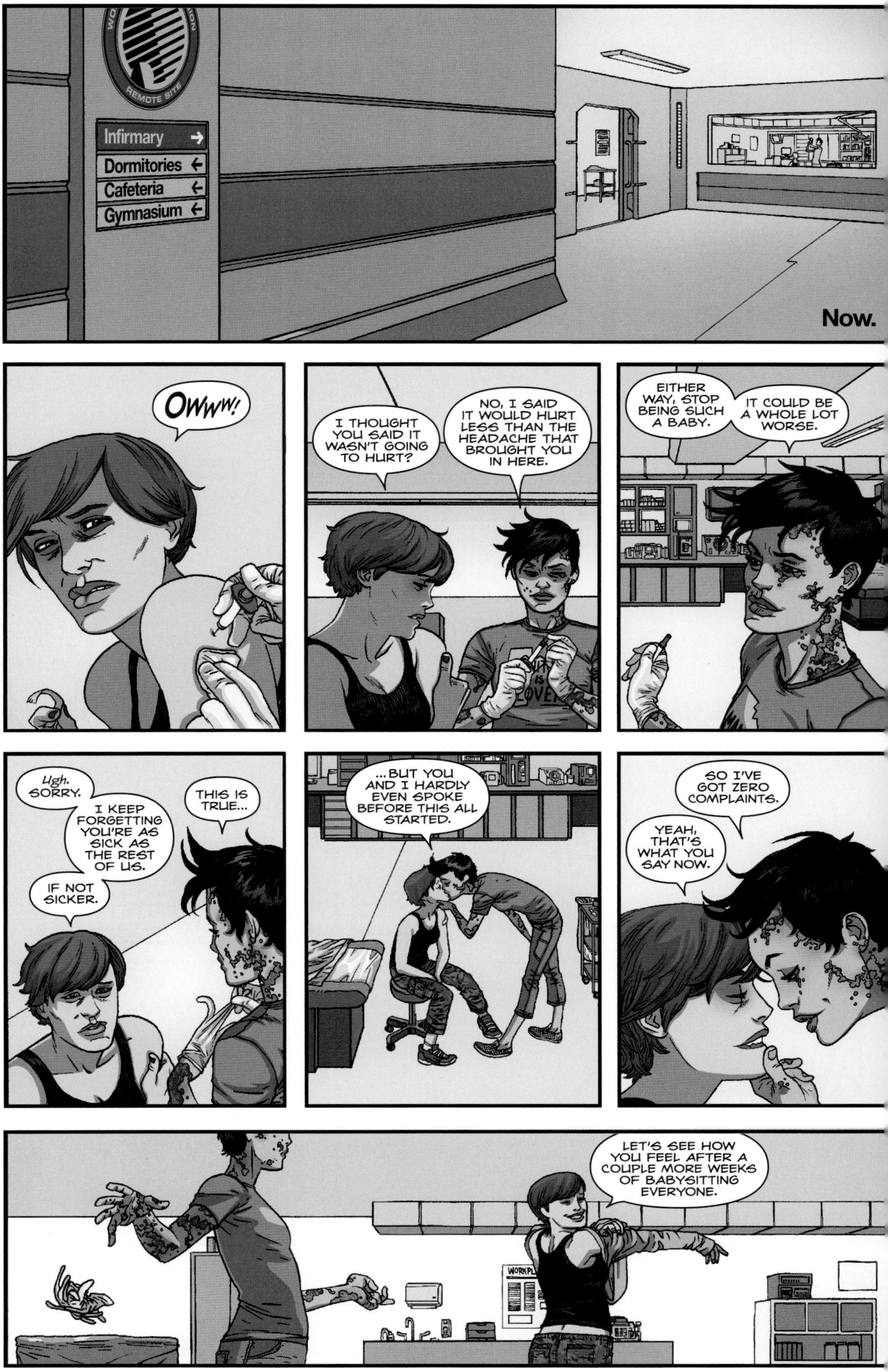
REMOTE SITE
Infirmary →
Dormitories ←
Cafeteria ←
Gymnasium ←
Now.
OWWW!
I THOUGHT YOU SAID IT WASN'T GOING TO HURT?
NO, I SAID IT WOULD HURT LESS THAN THE HEADACHE THAT BROUGHT YOU IN HERE.
EITHER WAY, STOP BEING SUCH A BABY.
IT COULD BE A WHOLE LOT WORSE.
Ugh. SORRY.
I KEEP FORGETTING YOU'RE AS SICK AS THE REST OF US.
IF NOT SICKER.
THIS IS TRUE...
...BUT YOU AND I HARDLY EVEN SPOKE BEFORE THIS ALL STARTED.
SO I'VE GOT ZERO COMPLAINTS.
YEAH, THAT'S WHAT YOU SAY NOW.
LET'S SEE HOW YOU FEEL AFTER A COUPLE MORE WEEKS OF BABYSITTING EVERYONE.

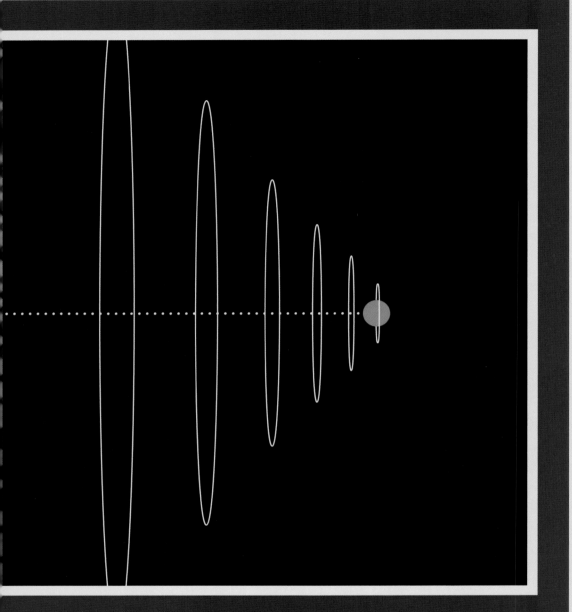

WORLD CORP.

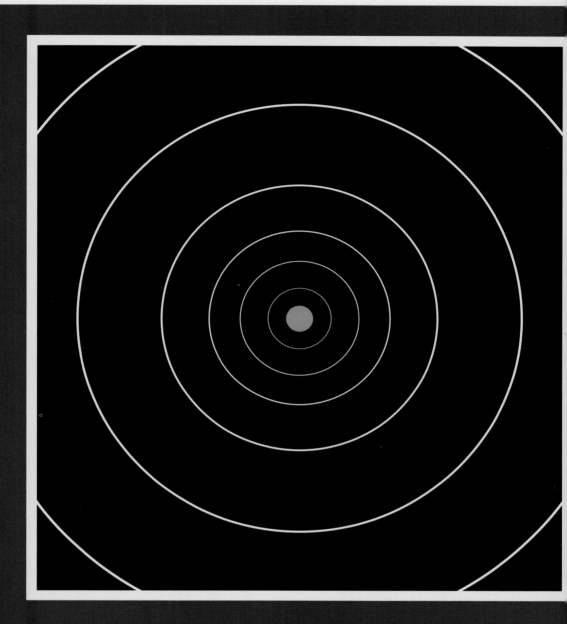

INTO
TOMORROW

WELL...THAT ACTUALLY WENT WORSE THAN I'D EXPECTED.

DID IT? WE ALL KNEW THIS DAY WOULD COME, EVENTUALLY...

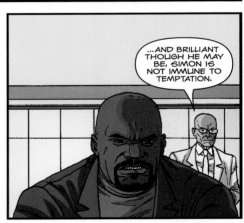

...AND BRILLIANT THOUGH HE MAY BE, SIMON IS NOT IMMUNE TO TEMPTATION.

MONEY--REAL MONEY--CHANGES EVERYTHING.

SOMETIMES IT REALLY IS AS SIMPLE AS THAT.

MAYBE.

OR MAYBE GRIMSHAW'S RIGHT AND WE'VE JUST BEEN FOOLING OURSELVES ALL THIS TIME.

MAYBE WE'VE DONE ALL WE CAN...

THAT'S NONSENSE, AND YOU KNOW IT.

THE WORK OF IMPROVING THE WORLD NEVER ENDS.

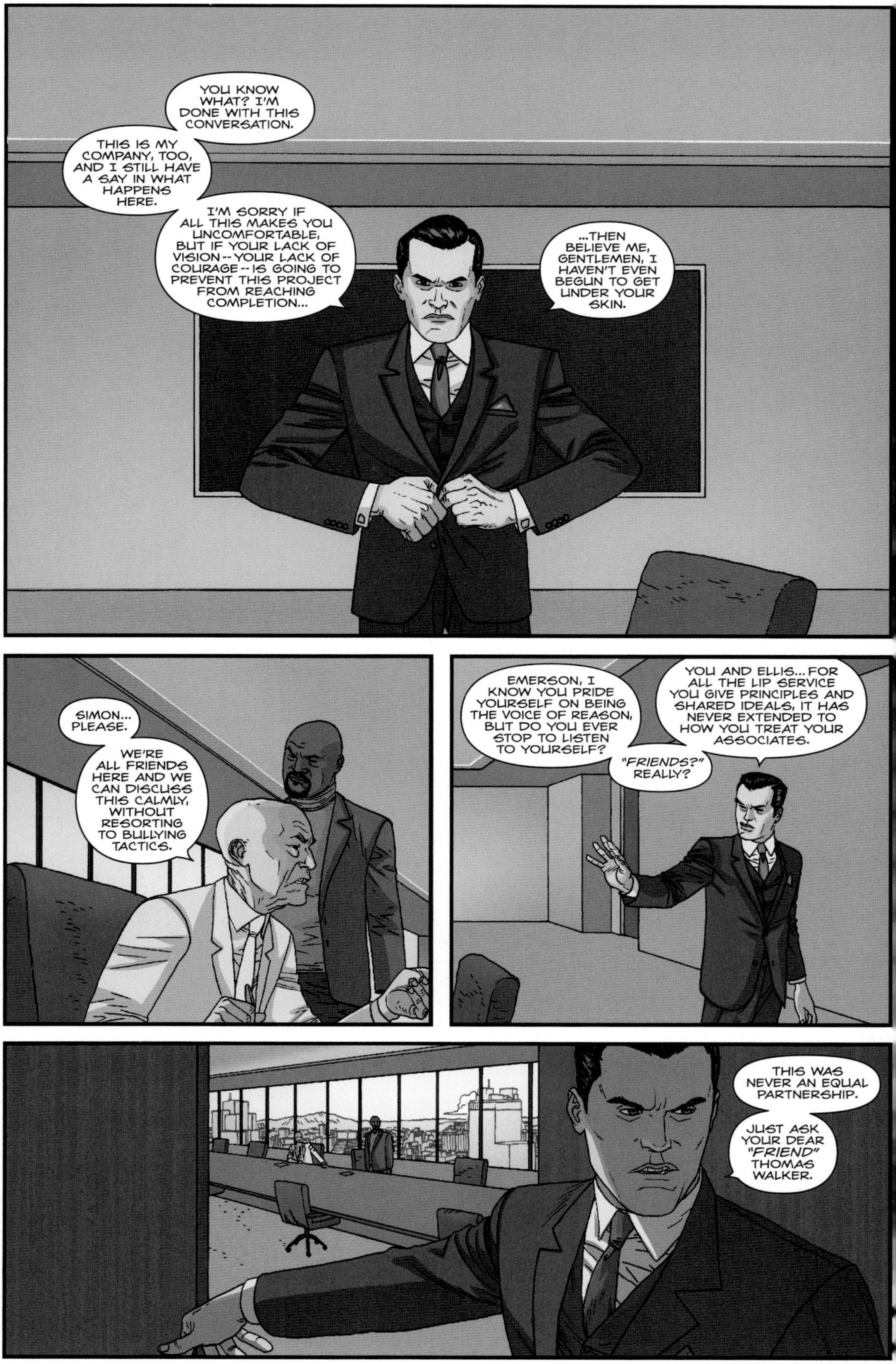
YOU KNOW WHAT? I'M DONE WITH THIS CONVERSATION.
THIS IS MY COMPANY, TOO, AND I STILL HAVE A SAY IN WHAT HAPPENS HERE.
I'M SORRY IF ALL THIS MAKES YOU UNCOMFORTABLE, BUT IF YOUR LACK OF VISION--YOUR LACK OF COURAGE--IS GOING TO PREVENT THIS PROJECT FROM REACHING COMPLETION...
...THEN BELIEVE ME, GENTLEMEN, I HAVEN'T EVEN BEGUN TO GET UNDER YOUR SKIN.
SIMON... PLEASE.
WE'RE ALL FRIENDS HERE AND WE CAN DISCUSS THIS CALMLY, WITHOUT RESORTING TO BULLYING TACTICS.
"FRIENDS?" REALLY?
EMERSON, I KNOW YOU PRIDE YOURSELF ON BEING THE VOICE OF REASON, BUT DO YOU EVER STOP TO LISTEN TO YOURSELF?
YOU AND ELLIS... FOR ALL THE LIP SERVICE YOU GIVE PRINCIPLES AND SHARED IDEALS, IT HAS NEVER EXTENDED TO HOW YOU TREAT YOUR ASSOCIATES.
THIS WAS NEVER AN EQUAL PARTNERSHIP.
JUST ASK YOUR DEAR "FRIEND" THOMAS WALKER.

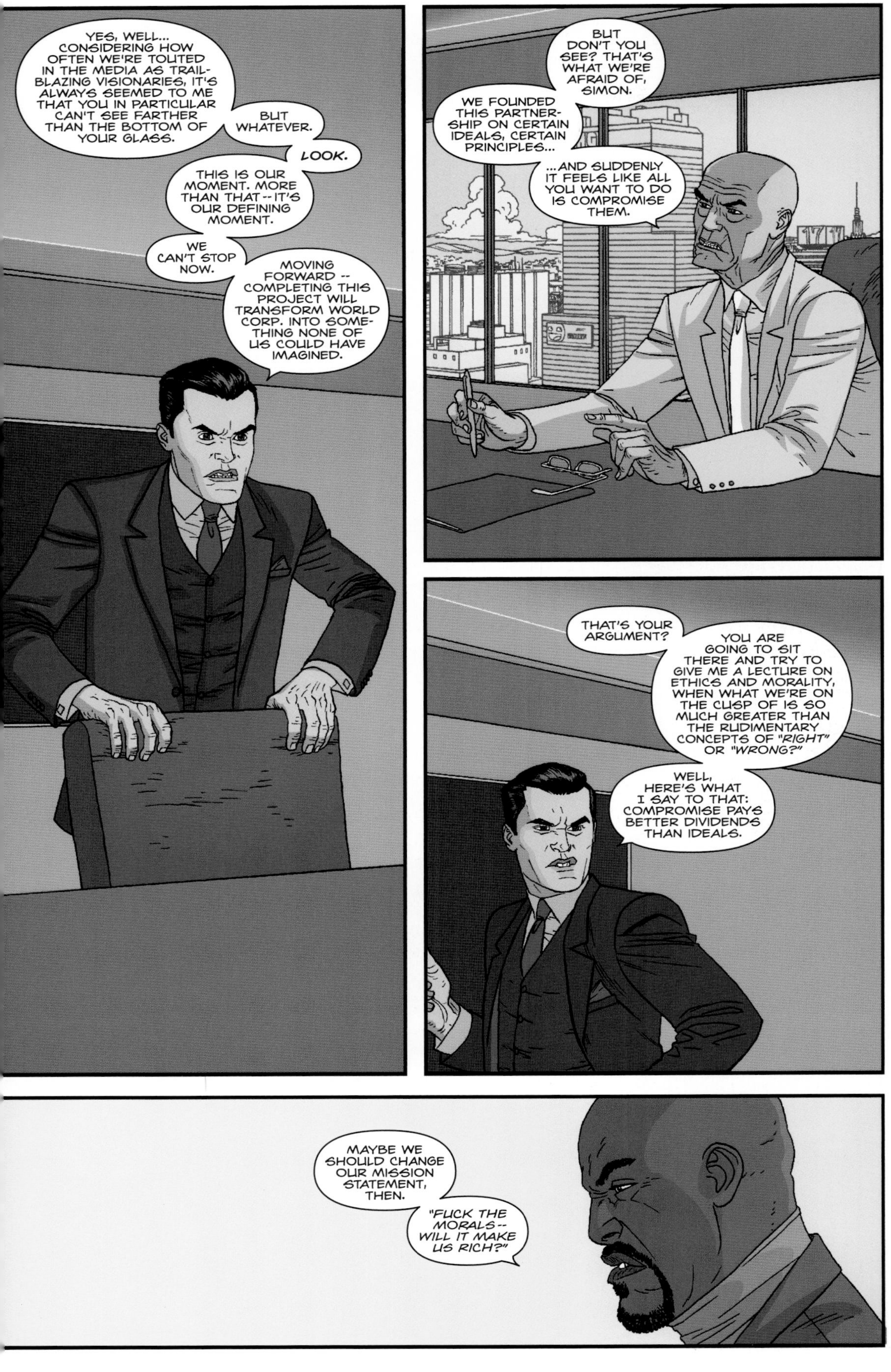
YES, WELL... CONSIDERING HOW OFTEN WE'RE TOUTED IN THE MEDIA AS TRAIL-BLAZING VISIONARIES, IT'S ALWAYS SEEMED TO ME THAT YOU IN PARTICULAR CAN'T SEE FARTHER THAN THE BOTTOM OF YOUR GLASS.
BUT WHATEVER.
LOOK.
THIS IS OUR MOMENT. MORE THAN THAT -- IT'S OUR DEFINING MOMENT.
WE CAN'T STOP NOW.
MOVING FORWARD -- COMPLETING THIS PROJECT WILL TRANSFORM WORLD CORP. INTO SOMETHING NONE OF US COULD HAVE IMAGINED.
BUT DON'T YOU SEE? THAT'S WHAT WE'RE AFRAID OF, SIMON.
WE FOUNDED THIS PARTNERSHIP ON CERTAIN IDEALS, CERTAIN PRINCIPLES...
...AND SUDDENLY IT FEELS LIKE ALL YOU WANT TO DO IS COMPROMISE THEM.
THAT'S YOUR ARGUMENT?
YOU ARE GOING TO SIT THERE AND TRY TO GIVE ME A LECTURE ON ETHICS AND MORALITY, WHEN WHAT WE'RE ON THE CUSP OF IS SO MUCH GREATER THAN THE RUDIMENTARY CONCEPTS OF "RIGHT" OR "WRONG?"
WELL, HERE'S WHAT I SAY TO THAT: COMPROMISE PAYS BETTER DIVIDENDS THAN IDEALS.
MAYBE WE SHOULD CHANGE OUR MISSION STATEMENT, THEN.
"FUCK THE MORALS -- WILL IT MAKE US RICH?"

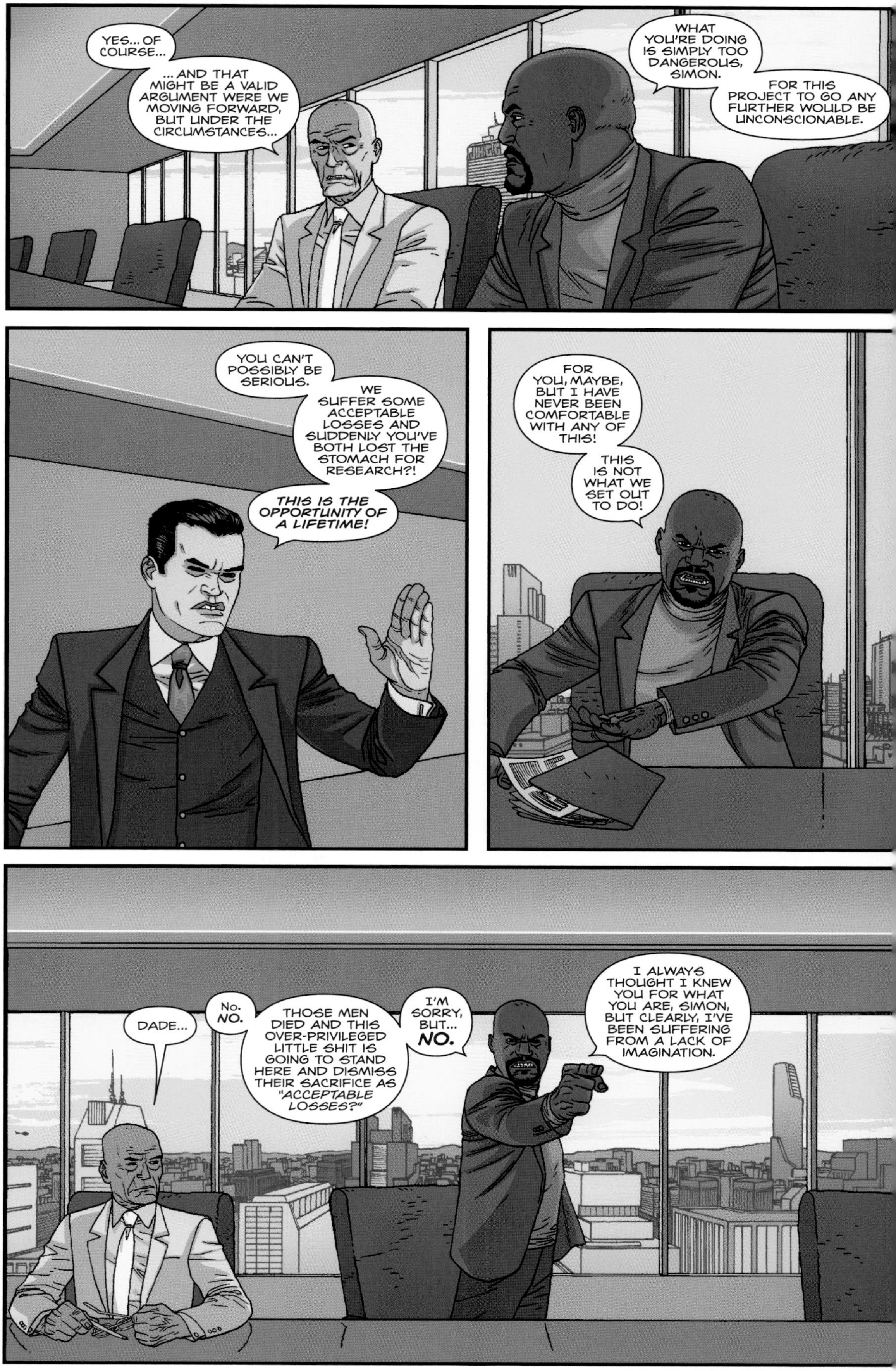
YES... OF COURSE...
... AND THAT MIGHT BE A VALID ARGUMENT WERE WE MOVING FORWARD, BUT UNDER THE CIRCUMSTANCES...
WHAT YOU'RE DOING IS SIMPLY TOO DANGEROUS, SIMON.
FOR THIS PROJECT TO GO ANY FURTHER WOULD BE UNCONSCIONABLE.
YOU CAN'T POSSIBLY BE SERIOUS.
WE SUFFER SOME ACCEPTABLE LOSSES AND SUDDENLY YOU'VE BOTH LOST THE STOMACH FOR RESEARCH?!
THIS IS THE OPPORTUNITY OF A LIFETIME!
FOR YOU, MAYBE, BUT I HAVE NEVER BEEN COMFORTABLE WITH ANY OF THIS!
THIS IS NOT WHAT WE SET OUT TO DO!
DADE...
No. NO.
THOSE MEN DIED AND THIS OVER-PRIVILEGED LITTLE SHIT IS GOING TO STAND HERE AND DISMISS THEIR SACRIFICE AS "ACCEPTABLE LOSSES?"
I'M SORRY, BUT... NO.
I ALWAYS THOUGHT I KNEW YOU FOR WHAT YOU ARE, SIMON, BUT CLEARLY, I'VE BEEN SUFFERING FROM A LACK OF IMAGINATION.

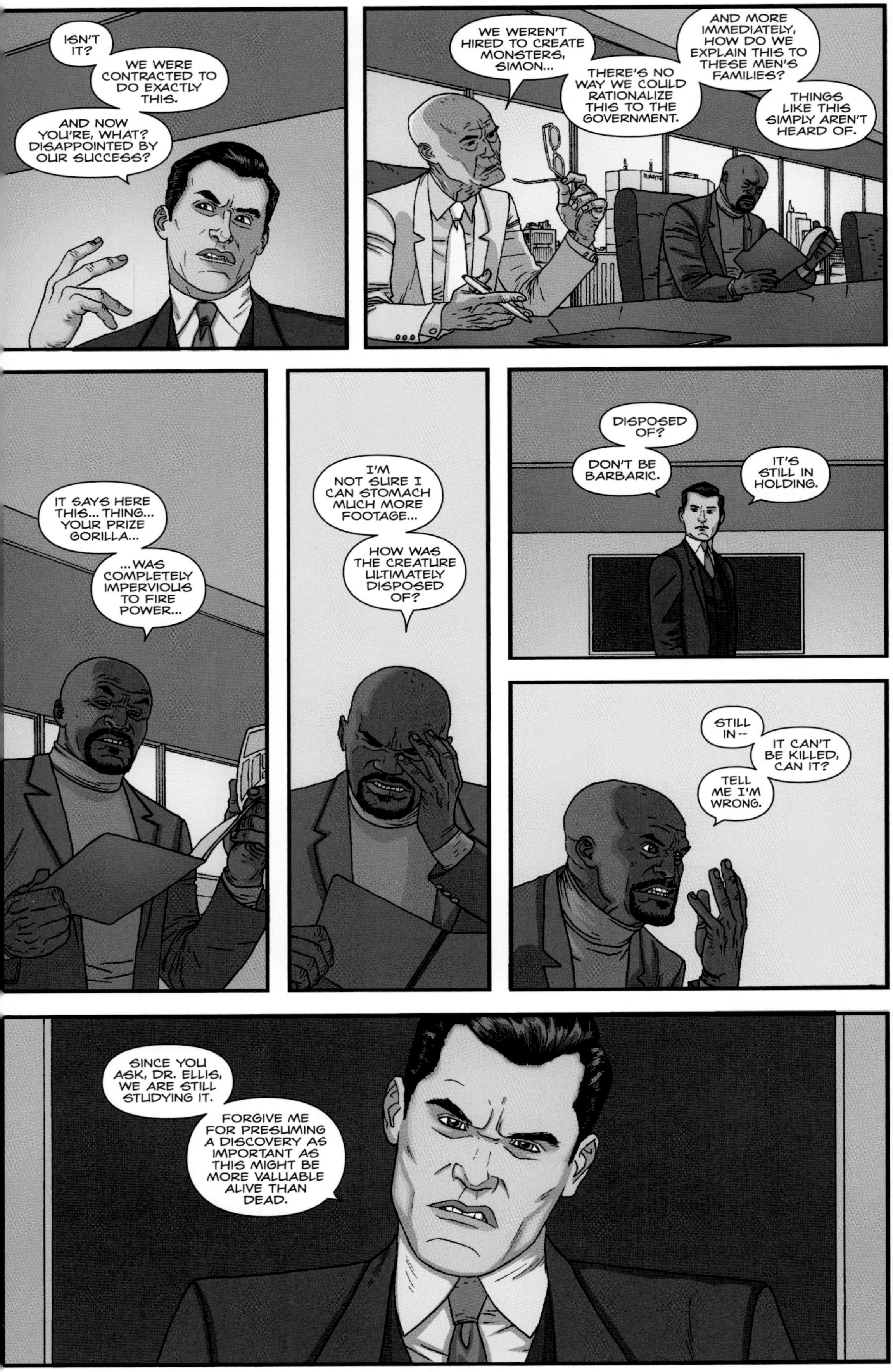
ISN'T IT?
WE WERE CONTRACTED TO DO EXACTLY THIS.
AND NOW YOU'RE, WHAT? DISAPPOINTED BY OUR SUCCESS?
WE WEREN'T HIRED TO CREATE MONSTERS, SIMON...
THERE'S NO WAY WE COULD RATIONALIZE THIS TO THE GOVERNMENT.
AND MORE IMMEDIATELY, HOW DO WE EXPLAIN THIS TO THESE MEN'S FAMILIES?
THINGS LIKE THIS SIMPLY AREN'T HEARD OF.
IT SAYS HERE THIS... THING... YOUR PRIZE GORILLA...
...WAS COMPLETELY IMPERVIOUS TO FIRE POWER...
I'M NOT SURE I CAN STOMACH MUCH MORE FOOTAGE...
HOW WAS THE CREATURE ULTIMATELY DISPOSED OF?
DISPOSED OF?
DON'T BE BARBARIC.
IT'S STILL IN HOLDING.
STILL IN--
IT CAN'T BE KILLED, CAN IT?
TELL ME I'M WRONG.
SINCE YOU ASK, DR. ELLIS, WE ARE STILL STUDYING IT.
FORGIVE ME FOR PRESUMING A DISCOVERY AS IMPORTANT AS THIS MIGHT BE MORE VALUABLE ALIVE THAN DEAD.

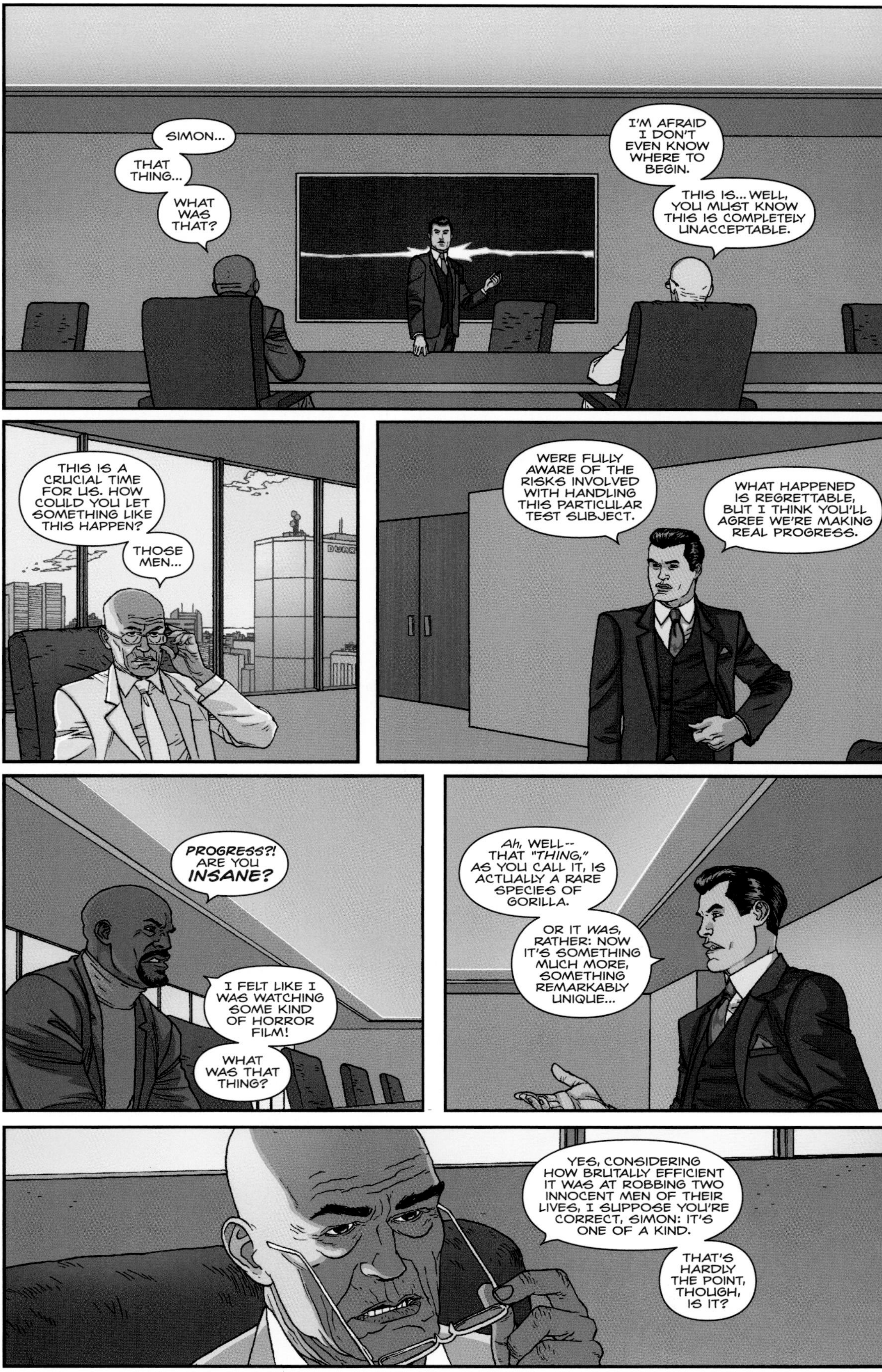
SIMON...
THAT THING...
WHAT WAS THAT?
I'M AFRAID I DON'T EVEN KNOW WHERE TO BEGIN.
THIS IS...WELL, YOU MUST KNOW THIS IS COMPLETELY UNACCEPTABLE.
THIS IS A CRUCIAL TIME FOR US. HOW COULD YOU LET SOMETHING LIKE THIS HAPPEN?
THOSE MEN...
WERE FULLY AWARE OF THE RISKS INVOLVED WITH HANDLING THIS PARTICULAR TEST SUBJECT.
WHAT HAPPENED IS REGRETTABLE, BUT I THINK YOU'LL AGREE WE'RE MAKING REAL PROGRESS.
PROGRESS?! ARE YOU INSANE?
I FELT LIKE I WAS WATCHING SOME KIND OF HORROR FILM!
WHAT WAS THAT THING?
Ah, WELL-- THAT "THING," AS YOU CALL IT, IS ACTUALLY A RARE SPECIES OF GORILLA.
OR IT WAS, RATHER: NOW IT'S SOMETHING MUCH MORE, SOMETHING REMARKABLY UNIQUE...
YES, CONSIDERING HOW BRUTALLY EFFICIENT IT WAS AT ROBBING TWO INNOCENT MEN OF THEIR LIVES, I SUPPOSE YOU'RE CORRECT, SIMON: IT'S ONE OF A KIND.
THAT'S HARDLY THE POINT, THOUGH, IS IT?

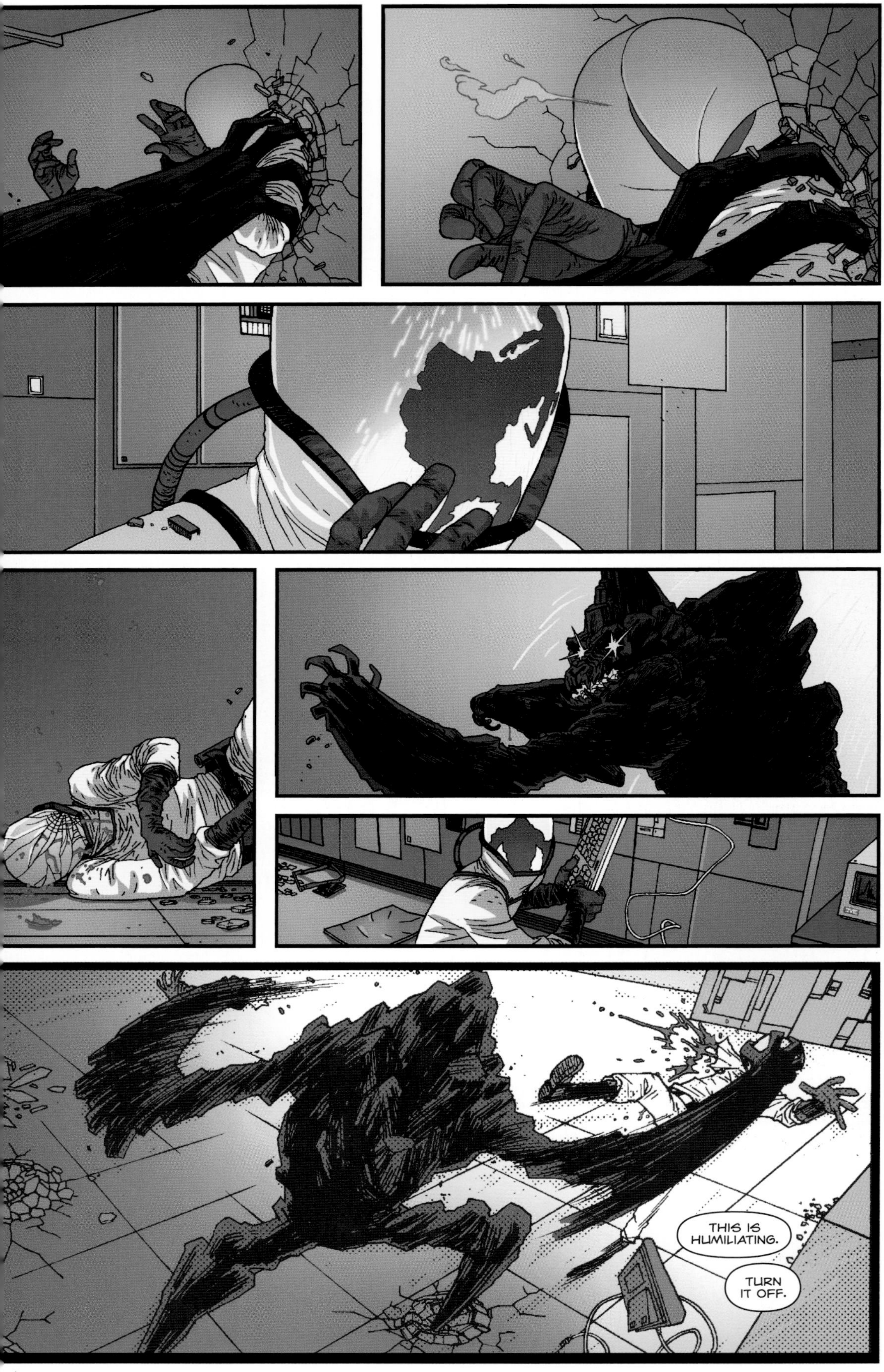
THIS IS HUMILIATING.
TURN IT OFF.

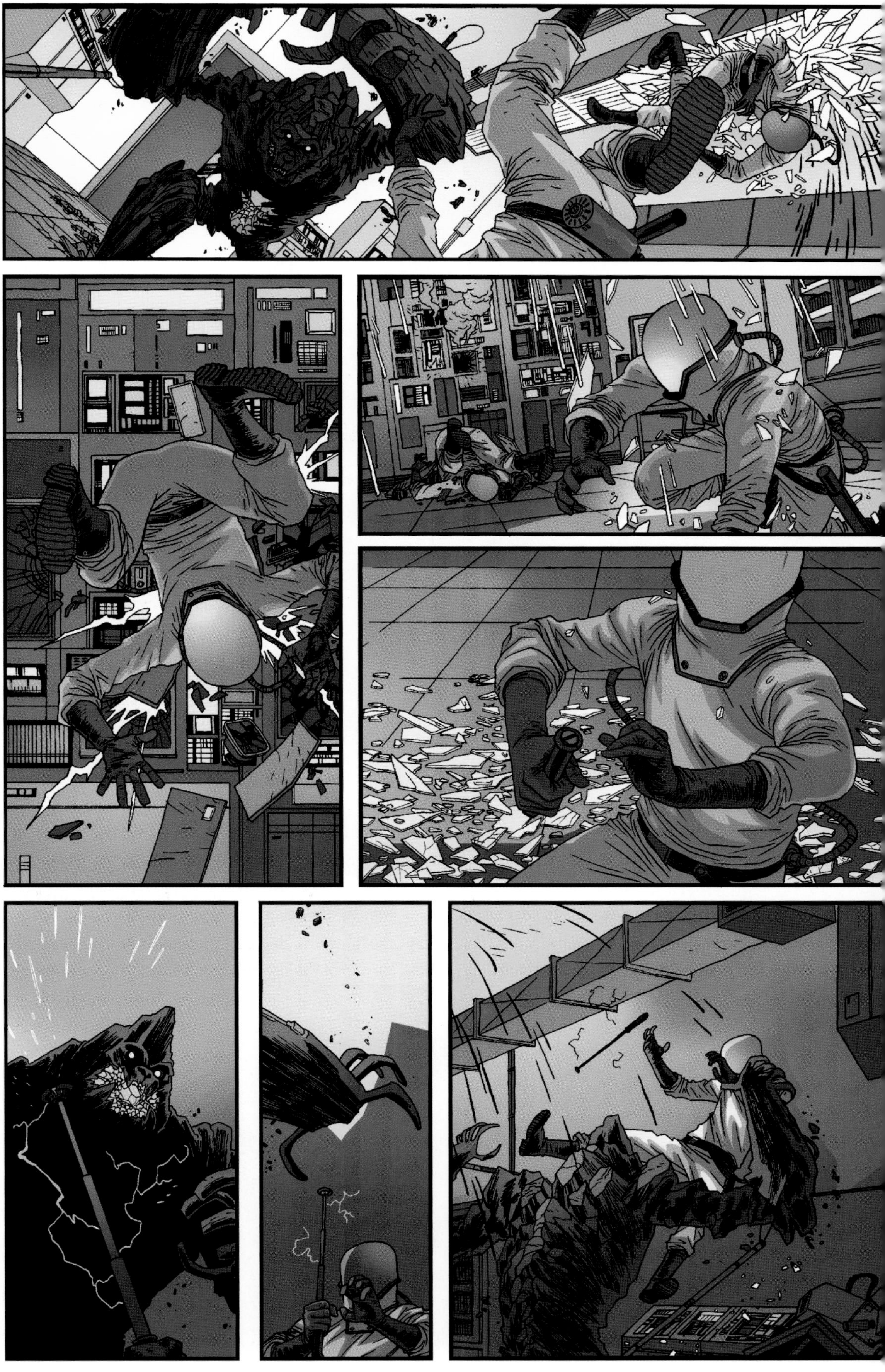

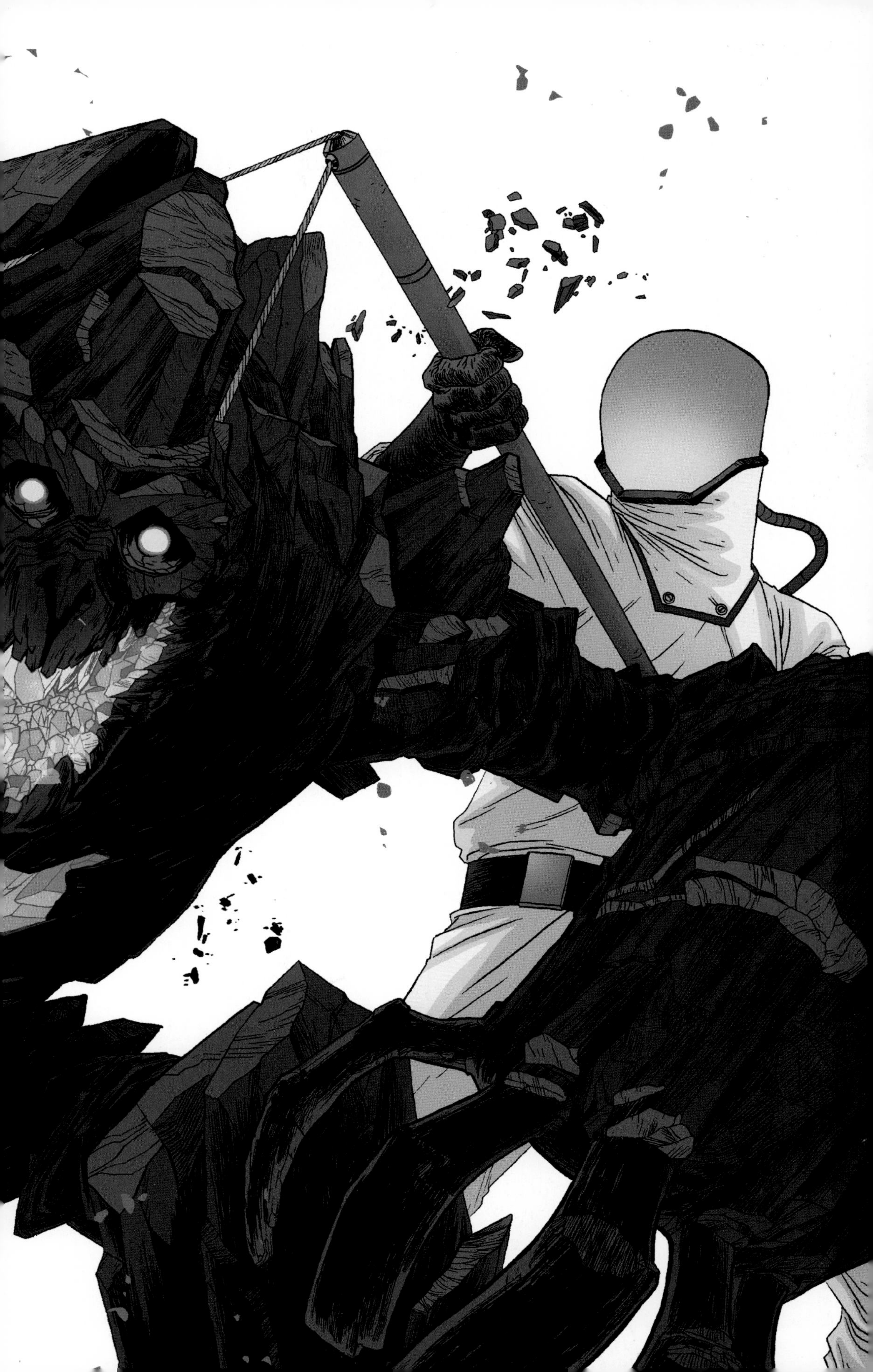

Years later.

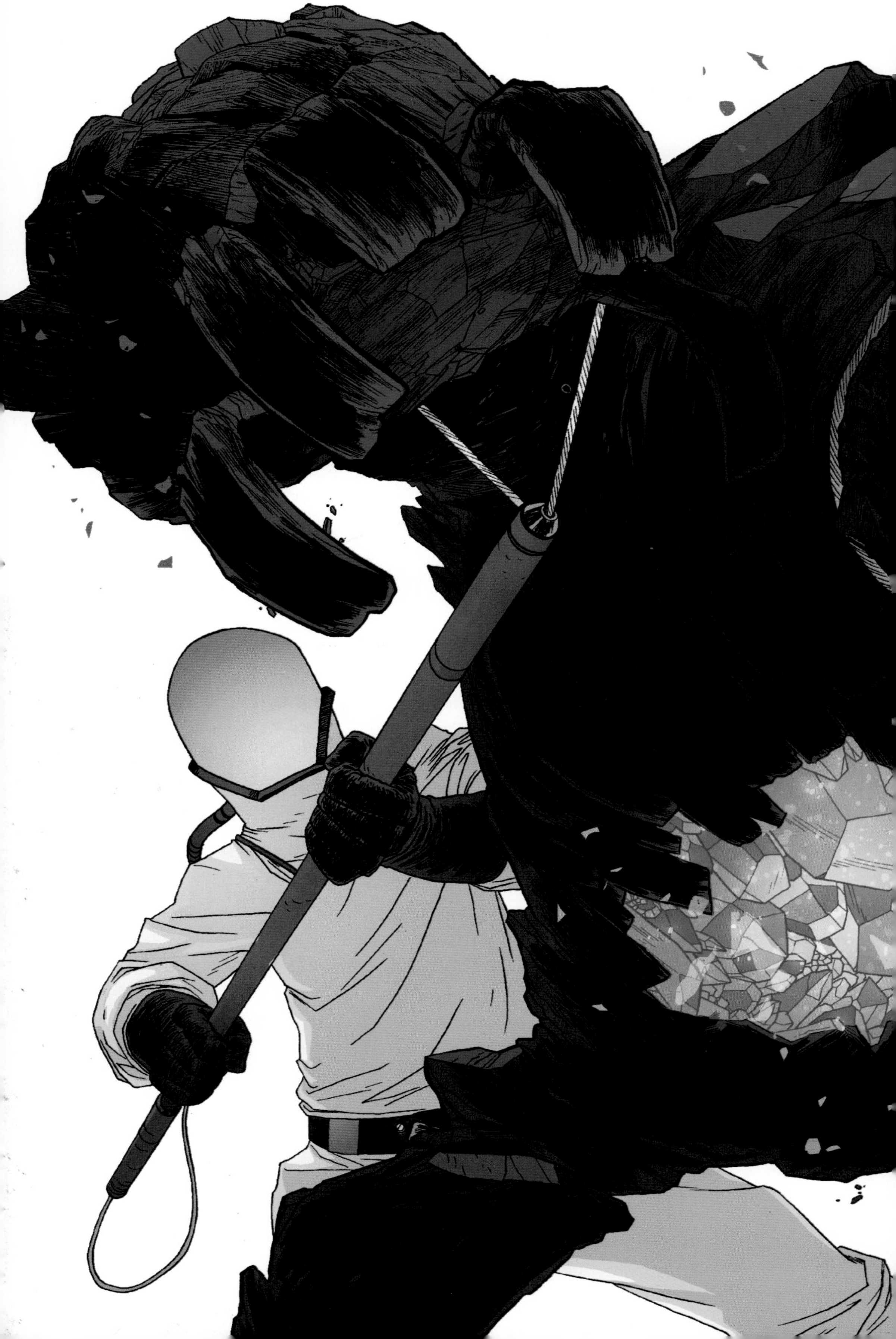

of the visionary group at the epicenter of a science revolution!

SIMON GRIMSHAW

BORN: April 16
HOMETOWN: Barrytown, NY
EDUCATED: New York University
FATHER: Randall
MOTHER: Susan
BROTHERS: None
SISTERS: None
DEGREE: Molecular Biology, Mathematics in Finance
CAREER: Geneticist
OTHER OCCUPATIONS: None
FAVORITE INVENTION: The pencil.
FAVORITE ARTICLE OF CLOTHING: Press does really good ties.
FAVORITE SONG: I don't have a favorite song.
FAVORITE FILM: I don't have a favorite film.
FAVORITE BOOK: *Atlas Shrugged* by Ayn Rand
FAVORITE PERSON: No one I care to name. Just because I've given up my own privacy doesn't mean that extends to everyone I know.
GREATEST INFLUENCE: The prospect of failure or poverty.
GREATEST ACHIEVEMENT: World Corp.
GREATEST AMBITION: Perfection.
STATUS: Single
HEIGHT: 5'10"
WEIGHT: 152 lbs
HAIR: Brown
EYES: Blue
WHAT'S YOUR TIPPLE? I don't drink.

EMERSON STRANGE

BORN: October 9
HOMETOWN: Mountain View, CA
EDUCATED: Stanford University
FATHER: Alfred
MOTHER: Julia
BROTHERS: None
SISTERS: Victoria
DEGREE: Mechanical Engineering, Computer Science
CAREER: Inventor, designer
OTHER OCCUPATIONS: Systems Analyst, Programmer, Lecturer
FAVORITE INVENTION: Whatever new thing I'm working on at the moment.
FAVORITE ARTICLE OF CLOTHING: White suits
FAVORITE SONG: At the moment, I'd have to say something by The Beach Boys, probably *Surf's Up*.
FAVORITE FILM: *Lawrence of Arabia*
FAVORITE BOOK: *The Magus* by John Fowles
FAVORITE PERSON: My daughter, Monica.
GREATEST INFLUENCE: Thomas Edison
GREATEST ACHIEVEMENT: The actual name is yet to be determined, but for now, I'm calling it 'The Everything Box'— more news as it develops!
GREATEST AMBITION: Ubiquity.
STATUS: Divorced
HEIGHT: 6'3"
WEIGHT: 159 lbs
HAIR: Black
EYES: Blue
WHAT'S YOUR TIPPLE? Gin and tonic.

THOMAS WALKER

BORN: January 6
HOMETOWN: Cambridge, England
EDUCATED: Cambridge University
FATHER: Arthur
MOTHER: Matilda
BROTHERS: Roger, Nicholas, Richard, David
SISTERS: None
DEGREE: Astrophysics
CAREER: Theoretical Physicist
OTHER OCCUPATIONS: Sweeping up
FAVORITE INVENTION: LSD
FAVORITE ARTICLE OF CLOTHING: Corduroy
FAVORITE SONG: *Carnival of Light* by The Beatles
FAVORITE FILM: *Fantasia*
FAVORITE BOOK: *A Clockwork Orange* by Anthony Burgess
FAVORITE PERSON: Mother
GREATEST INFLUENCE: Keeping my mind occupied.
GREATEST ACHIEVEMENT: I suppose the theories I've put forward on wormholes and dark matter, but I've also learned to juggle whilst riding my bike, which is terribly useful, I've found.
GREATEST AMBITION: Space
STATUS: Single
HEIGHT: 5'11"
WEIGHT: 155 lbs
HAIR: Brown
EYES: Grey
WHAT'S YOUR TIPPLE? Brandy Alexander.

TSC *FACT FINDER

WORLD CORP.

Discover the detail

Dade Ellis. Simon Grimshaw. Emerson Strange. Thomas Walker. Separately, they are among the greatest thinkers in the world, but together, they comprise the all-out scientific supergroup known as World Corp. Though they've only been together briefly, their incredible new venture is sending shockwaves through the science community, so we're giving you the lowdown on what makes these sensational young men tick in the latest edition of our exclusive Fact Finders series!

DADE ELLIS

BORN: January 8
HOMETOWN: St. Louis, IL
EDUCATED: Yale University
FATHER: Joseph
MOTHER: Edith
BROTHERS: None
SISTERS: Kimberly
DEGREE: Neurobiology, Geophysics, Architecture
CAREER: Neuroscience
OTHER OCCUPATIONS: Library clerk
FAVORITE INVENTION: Just for the pure enjoyment it's given me over the years, I think I'd have to say the record player.
FAVORITE ARTICLE OF CLOTHING: Well-made shoes are indispensable.
FAVORITE SONG: *Stolen Moments* by Oliver Nelson
FAVORITE FILM: *Strangers on a Train*
FAVORITE BOOK: *Dandelion Wine* by Ray Bradbury
FAVORITE PERSON: My partners.
GREATEST INFLUENCE: No one person in particular, but music always inspires me.
GREATEST ACHIEVEMENT: The near-eradication of blindness through cyber-optics.
GREATEST AMBITION: Sustainable peace.
STATUS: Single
HEIGHT: 6'3"
WEIGHT: 165 lbs
HAIR: Brown
EYES: Brown
WHAT'S YOUR TIPPLE? Rye whiskey

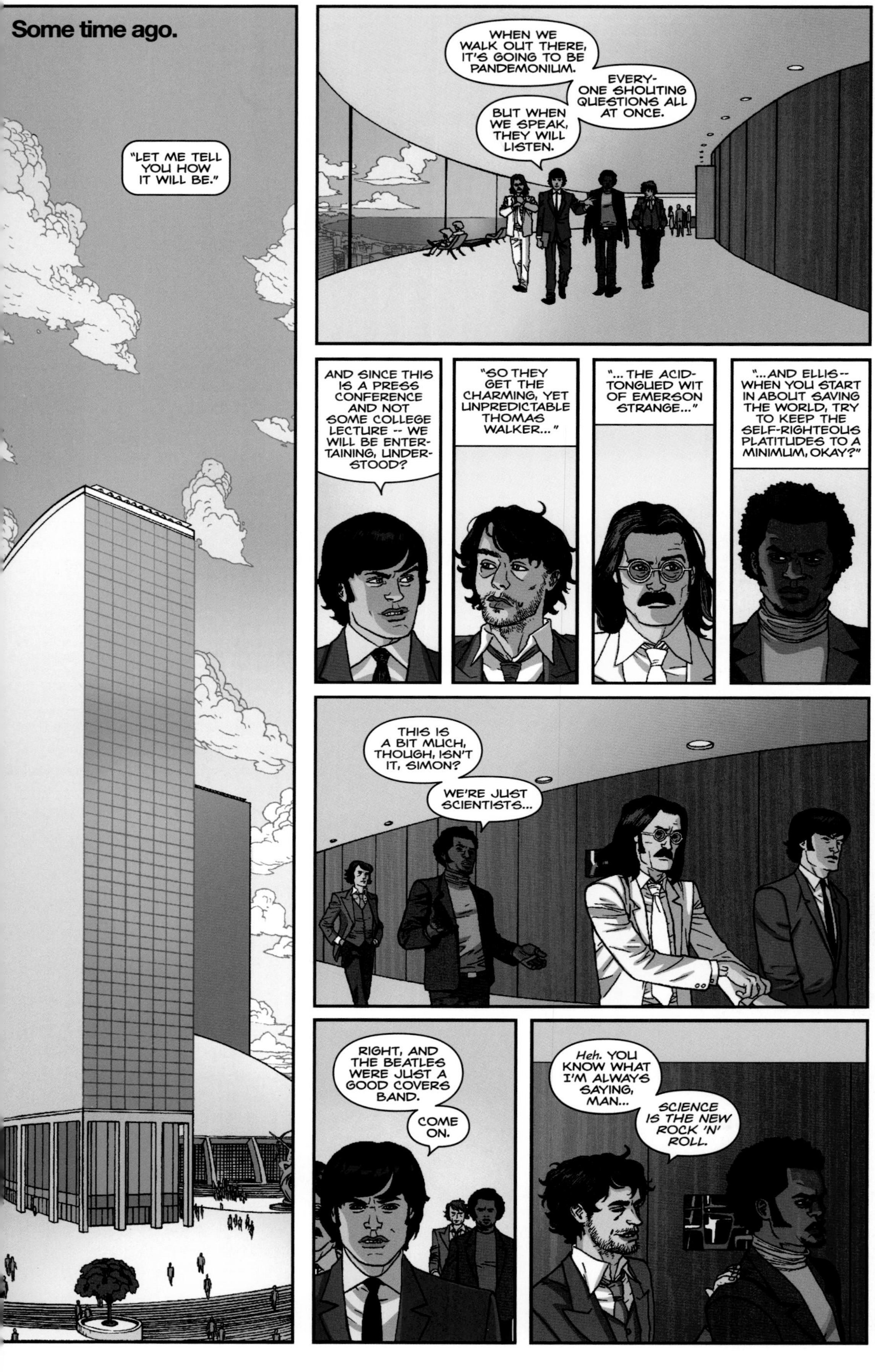
Some time ago.
"LET ME TELL YOU HOW IT WILL BE."
WHEN WE WALK OUT THERE, IT'S GOING TO BE PANDEMONIUM.
EVERY-ONE SHOUTING QUESTIONS ALL AT ONCE.
BUT WHEN WE SPEAK, THEY WILL LISTEN.
AND SINCE THIS IS A PRESS CONFERENCE AND NOT SOME COLLEGE LECTURE -- WE WILL BE ENTER-TAINING, UNDER-STOOD?
"SO THEY GET THE CHARMING, YET UNPREDICTABLE THOMAS WALKER..."
"...THE ACID-TONGUED WIT OF EMERSON STRANGE..."
"...AND ELLIS -- WHEN YOU START IN ABOUT SAVING THE WORLD, TRY TO KEEP THE SELF-RIGHTEOUS PLATITUDES TO A MINIMUM, OKAY?"
THIS IS A BIT MUCH, THOUGH, ISN'T IT, SIMON?
WE'RE JUST SCIENTISTS...
RIGHT, AND THE BEATLES WERE JUST A GOOD COVERS BAND.
COME ON.
Heh. YOU KNOW WHAT I'M ALWAYS SAYING, MAN...
SCIENCE IS THE NEW ROCK 'N' ROLL.